D0908268

GILBERT

of

GILBERT & SULLIVAN

GILBERT

of

GILBERT & SULLIVAN

His Life and Character

ANDREW CROWTHER

The History Press

For Suzanne.

… the English also contain pixies. They are enormously solemn, solid and venerable; suddenly there is a sort of rumbling within them, they make a grotesque remark, a fork of pixie-like humour flies out of them, and once more they have the solemn appearance of an old leather armchair.

Karel Čapek (trans. Paul Selver), Letters from England

First published 2011

The History Press
The Mill, Brimscombe Port
Stroud, Gloucestershire, GL5 2QG
www.thehistorypress.co.uk

British Library Cataloguing in Publication Data.
A catalogue record for this book is available from the British Library.

ISBN 978 0 7524 5589 1

Typesetting and origination by The History Press
Printed in Great Britain

CONTENTS

PREFACE

When I tell people that I am interested in W.S. Gilbert, the usual response is a polite, blank look. 'Of Gilbert and Sullivan,' I add, and the eyes fill with recognition. Gilbert tends to be remembered as one half of the indissoluble team: his name on its own means little or nothing. But in his long life he was much more than simply Gilbert-of-Gilbert-and-Sullivan – as I explain to people at great length, unless they are lucky.

I believe that there is no such thing as a 'definitive' biography. A writer always selects from the evidence the particular story that s/he wishes to tell, and sets to one side other stories, other equally valid interpretations of the evidence. This book is certainly not intended as 'definitive'. It is intended simply as a version of one part of the truth, going back to contemporary sources wherever possible and paying some attention to some of the things that other biographers may have neglected. I have tried to construct the book as a coherent narrative. This has meant having to leave out many little facts which, try as I might, I could not fit into the jigsaw puzzle. I have tried to eliminate the inaccuracies committed by previous biographers but am aware of the probability that I have introduced some of my own. I can only say that I have done my best.

I have benefited from the help of many people. Firstly, the previous biographers of Gilbert, on whose shoulders I have trodden and whose researches I have shamelessly used: Jane W. Stedman, Michael Ainger, David Eden, Hesketh Pearson, Sidney Dark and Rowland Grey, Edith Browne and others.

I am grateful for the help of many others, who have been generous with their time and expertise. My editor Simon Hamlet should top the list. I wish to thank Ralph MacPhail Jr for his invaluable comments on the manuscript; Brian and Kathleen Jones for hospitality, friendship and scholarship; Sam Silvers, who made us welcome in New York; Arthur Robinson, librarian extraordinary, for unearthing interviews, letters and news stories; Dr Esther Cohen-Tovee for kindly reading my theories about Gilbert's character and suggesting when I was going wrong; John van der Kiste for starting it all off; Stuart Box for saving the project at a crucial point; Jane Irisa for pointing out a vital internet resource at exactly the right time; also Vincent Daniels, Hal Kanthor, Simon Moss, Dr J. Donald Smith, David Stone, David Trutt and Marc Shepherd. All errors, misinterpretations of the evidence, ignoring of advice and examples of sheer forgetfulness are, of course, my fault.

I would like to give thanks to the staffs at the British Library, the Pierpont Morgan Library in New York, the Theatre Collection at the University of Bristol, the Archives at King's College, London, and Bradford Central Library, for their assistance.

Thanks are due to the Royal Theatrical Fund for their permission to quote from Gilbert's unpublished writings, and to Peter Joslin for providing many of the illustrations.

I wish to acknowledge the generous financial assistance of the Gilbert and Sullivan Society and of the Society for Theatre Research in the course of writing this book. Quite simply, I could not have completed the necessary research without their help.

The internet has of course revolutionised the whole business of research. In particular the British Library's nineteenth-century newspapers website, the University of Florida Collections' scans of *Fun*, and the scanned images of books available at Google Books and at openlibrary.org have been invaluable. Information available at the amazing Gilbert and Sullivan Archive has also been a great help.

Finally, the biggest thanks of all are due to Suzanne, for love and support, and for putting up with the whole business.

PROLOGUE: 1891

One day in the summer of 1891, two men took a tour of the grounds of Graeme's Dyke, a large house at Harrow Weald, north of London. One of the men was Harry How, the interviewer at *The Strand Magazine*. The other was W.S. Gilbert, who had bought Graeme's Dyke the previous year out of the profits of the Gilbert and Sullivan operas.

Gilbert — 54 years old, tall, grey-haired, moustached and muscular — guided Harry How through the walks of roses and sweetbriar, the banks of moss and ferns, the avenues of chestnut trees. He showed him the Dyke itself and the statue of King Charles II standing incongruously on its bank, which had originally stood in Soho Square. He showed him the farm which was also part of the property, with its Jersey cows, its horses, pigs and fowl, and its hayricks. He showed him the observatory, the pigeon house, which the pigeons had not yet been persuaded to use, and the green beehives with bees crowding round, looking, as Gilbert said, like small country theatres doing a 'tremendous booking'.

In the entrance hall there stood a model ship, 16ft in length, built around the mock-up set which Gilbert had had built for the original production of *H.M.S. Pinafore* in 1878. In another corner of the entrance hall perched two parrots. Gilbert pointed out one of them as being the finest talker in England. 'The other parrot, who is a novice,' he added, 'belongs to Dr Playfair. He is reading up with my bird, who takes pupils.'

Gilbert took Harry How on a guided tour of the building — a fine example of Victorian mock-Tudor designed by Norman Shaw. They passed up the oak staircase and into the billiard room, which was decorated with photographs of the Savoy actors in costume, photographs of old theatrical friends and statuettes of Thackeray and Tom Robertson. They visited the drawing room, with Frank Holl's dark, brooding portrait of Gilbert presiding over it; the dining room, with its massive Charles I sideboard; and finally the library, with seventy papier-mâché heads of Indian 'types' arranged on the bookcases, mingling with drawings by Watteau, Rubens and others. In all these rooms small *objets* of every sort were arranged on tables, placed on bookcases, hung from the walls. This was a house of 'things' in the Victorian style.

The two men sat in the library and talked. Gilbert talked of his life, his career as a barrister, his work as a man of the theatre:

> I consider the two best plays I ever wrote were 'Broken Hearts' and a version of the Faust legend called 'Gretchen.' I took immense pains over my 'Gretchen,' but it only ran a fortnight. I wrote it to please myself, and not the public. It seems to be the fate of a good piece to run a couple of weeks, and a bad one a couple of years – at least, it is so with me.[1]

Did he really think that *Broken Hearts* was a better piece than *The Mikado*? Few people today, if any, would agree with him. But he routinely disparaged the 'easy trivialities of the Savoy *libretti*',[2] apparently because he found them easy to write. He preferred his blank verse dramas because, as he said, 'in every line I am doing all I know … Blank verse always takes the best work out of me'.[3]

Harry How asked Gilbert if he would write some verses to be published with the interview. We can only imagine the tone of Gilbert's voice as he replied: 'Thank you, very much, but I'm afraid I must ask you to excuse me.' However, he did allow *The Strand* to publish a lyric which had not quite made it into *The Gondoliers* two years before. In it, a young woman pleads with the Grand Inquisitor, who is planning to separate her and her friend from their newly wedded husbands:

> Good sir, I wish to speak politely –
>   Forgive me if my words are crude –
> I find it hard to put it rightly
>   Without appearing to be rude.
> I mean to say, –you're old and wrinkled –
>   It's rather blunt, but it's the truth –
> With wintry snow your hair is sprinkled:
>   What *can* you know of Love and Youth?
>   Indeed, I wish to speak politely;
>   But, pray forgive me, truth is truth:
>   You're old and – pardon me – unsightly,
>   What can you know of Love and Youth!
>
> You are too aged to remember
>   That withered bosom's earliest glow;
> Dead is the old romantic ember

That warmed your life-blood years ago.
If from our sweethearts we are parted
   (Old men know nothing of such pain)
Two maidens will be broken-hearted
   And quite heart-broken lovers twain!
      Now pray, for goodness' sake, remember
      I've no desire to be uncouth;
     But we are June and you're December:
      What *can* you know of Love and Youth![4]

Something in this lyric may remind us of Gilbert himself: a man in his fifties who was also a great admirer of young women. The lyric inhabits the point of view of a young woman mocking an old man, but also, hidden between the words, another point of view is suggested, as if Gilbert were framing his own reply to the question: 'What can you know of Love and Youth?' The lyric expresses an attitude which reflects back and forth between truth and irony – as so often in Gilbert's works. He explained:

When I have just finished a piece I feel for a few days that I am absolutely incapable of further effort. I always feel that I am quite 'written out.' At first this impression used to distress me seriously – however I have learnt by experience to regard it as a 'bogie,' which will yield to exorcism.[5]

At one point during their talk Gilbert excused himself to make sure that a package containing the complete manuscript of his new comic opera went out in the post. He weighed the big blue envelope in his hand, and, after the servant had left with it, flung himself into a chair and said: 'There goes something that will either bring me twenty thousand pounds or twenty thousand pence!'[6] Later, he showed Harry How the model set of the new opera, with its little blocks of wood to represent the characters which Gilbert would use to work out the movements of the actors before starting rehearsals. Gilbert always directed his own pieces.

But Gilbert did not mention, or at any rate Harry How does not mention in his account of the interview, that this new comic opera was to be composed not by Sir Arthur Sullivan but Alfred Cellier. And it was not mentioned, though Harry How gives us the lightest of hints, that Gilbert had very recently had a highly public fall-out with Sullivan and with the impresario who had bound the two men together for so long, Richard D'Oyly Carte. The rift was being repaired and the three men would soon feel able to work together once more, but it was not something that Gilbert wished to discuss:

My operatic work has been singularly successful – largely, of course, to the invaluable co-operation of Sir Arthur Sullivan. When Sullivan and I first determined to work together, the burlesque stage was in a very unclean state. We made up our minds to do all in our power to wipe out the grosser element, never to let an offending word escape our characters, and never allow a man to appear as a woman or *vice versa*.[7]

These were words which Gilbert repeated with slight variations in interviews and speeches throughout his later career. They were true enough, in their way, but they tell us nothing of the operas' real quality. When Gilbert told Harry How at another point that he was a purveyor of 'rump steak and onions', a dish designed to appeal to all classes, and that the butcher boy in the gallery was the king of the theatre,[8] this tells us a little more but still not enough. What of the satire, the wit, the playfulness of the operas? Where did they come from? Who was this man, so proper and respectable in person, so curiously remote in his way of speaking of himself, so apparently unknowable?

Perhaps some of these questions occurred to Harry How of *The Strand Magazine*. When the interview was over, and Harry How sat at his desk and thought back over his day at Graeme's Dyke, at length he decided how to begin his article.

He wrote: 'Mr. Gilbert lives in a little land of his own.'

1

THE GILBERT FAMILY (1836–53)

'Harlequin, Columbine, Pantaloon, and Clown!' There is an agreeable magic in these words, although they carry us back to the most miserable period of our existence – early childhood. They stand out in our recollection vividly and distinctly, for they are associated with one of the very few real enjoyments permitted to us at that grim stage of our development.

'Getting Up a Pantomime', in *London Society* (January 1868)

William Gilbert, W.S. Gilbert's father, was the son of a successful grocer. He was born on 20 May 1804; he was an orphan before his eighth birthday, both his parents having died of consumption. He and his younger brother and sister (Joseph Mathers Gilbert and Jane Gilbert) then passed into the caring hands of their uncle and aunt, John Samuel Schwenck and Mary Schwenck.

William Gilbert's father, William Gilbert the grocer, had died a very wealthy man. He left enough money to make all three children financially independent (meaning that they did not need to work for a living). His will made the Schwencks trustees of a sum of money which was to be invested in stocks until the children came of age. Additionally, Mary Schwenck's father, Joseph Mathers, a wealthy soap-boiler, left a will ensuring that his money would go to the three Gilbert children after the deaths of his wife and daughter.[1] Thus William Gilbert lived from a very early age with the promise of being able to live on the proceeds of invested capital.

Many details of his early life lie shrouded in mystery.[2] However, it does appear that he spent some of his adolescent years in Italy (Milan or Ponte di Lombro), possibly in order to recover from an illness.[3] When he came of age and received his inheritance, in 1825, he was certainly back in London – lending money at extortionate rates, probably on the advice of his guardian John Samuel Schwenck.[4]

At about this time William Gilbert started to study to become a surgeon. It is not clear why he chose to study for this brutal, messy and exacting profession;

perhaps his guardians insisted on his having some useful skill to fall back upon in case of financial difficulty. He passed the examination of the Royal College of Surgeons in December 1830, but it seems he 'retired' after a couple of years at most, and it is unclear whether he ever had a professional practice at all. However, from 1828 onwards he was a Life Governor at the Westminster Hospital, and he regularly attended the hospital's committees right up to 1889, within a few months of his death.[5]

On 5 September 1832, he married Mary Ann Skelton at St James' church, Piccadilly. He was 28 years old; she was 19. We may safely assume that he did not marry her for her money: her father John Henry Skelton had been declared bankrupt the previous year. William Gilbert had distinct romantic tendencies in his youth – around this time he even committed the obligatory folly of his age in having a volume of his bad poetry printed privately – so it is even possible that he married her because he was in love with her.

She appears to have been consumptive. He seems to have tried to cure her illness in the clean air of Italy. She died in Milan on 15 October 1834. There were no children by this marriage.

On 12 February 1836 he married for a second time; his bride was Anne Mary Bye Morris. He was 31; she was 24. Her father was Thomas Morris, an elderly doctor whom William Gilbert had followed during his medical studies. Anne Mary Bye Morris will shortly become the mother of our hero, so it will be appropriate here to give some details about her life and personality. Appropriate, but not possible. There is little surviving evidence of her life – there are no photographs or portraits, and only a small handful of letters – so it would be easy to dismiss her as a cipher, were it not for the fact that her later actions suggest her to be anything but. Forty years later, in 1876, she separated from her dominating and bad-tempered husband in a storm of acrimony. Though we know very little about her, we can say one thing at least: she did not always fit the Victorian ideal of the obedient and submissive wife.

She was related, on her mother's side, to the Scottish Sutherland lords of Duffus and the earls of Sutherland. She was therefore somewhat higher born than William Gilbert the grocer's son, though not to an extent that would make their marriage a misalliance. If she was tangentially related to the Scottish aristocracy, he was lower born but wealthy enough to live without working, which was one of the great pre-twentieth-century criteria of 'respectability'. There is, again, no reason to suppose the alliance was based on anything except affection – no matter how the couple felt about each other forty long years later.

William Gilbert had not got round to finding a house suitable for a married couple during the two years of his first marriage. After this second wedding, he and his new wife resided temporarily at 17 Southampton Street, just off the Strand in central London, where Dr and Mrs Morris lived. It was in this house that W.S. Gilbert was born, on 18 November 1836, just nine months after his parents' marriage. On 11 January 1837 the baby was christened at the church of St Paul, Covent Garden. He was named William, like his father and his father's father before him, and Schwenck, in honour of his father's old guardians who now became his godparents. There is no evidence for the persistent rumour that Gilbert disliked his middle name. On the contrary, he was known within the family as Schwenck or Uncle Schwenck throughout his life, and when he began making his living as a writer and illustrator he gave his name as W. Schwenck Gilbert.

He was born at the very beginning of a great time of change. The year 1836 saw the publication of Charles Dickens' first book, *Sketches by Boz*, and the serialisation of the first instalments of *The Pickwick Papers*. King William IV was still alive but ill; the reign of Queen Victoria would begin in June the following year. English life was in the process of transformation from broadly rural and agricultural to mostly urban and industrial; London was on the brink of an uncontrolled expansion. Just over two years before, in October 1834, the old Houses of Parliament at Westminster had burned to the ground as the result of a semi-farcical accident; the new buildings which we know today were completed in 1870. In 1837 Euston Station, the first railway terminus, was built in London – the great railway boom of the 1840s would follow close at its heels. And all this change, expansion and transformation would take place during the years when W.S. Gilbert was growing up.

In the summer of 1838, when Gilbert was approaching his second birthday, the Gilberts were travelling on the Continent. William Gilbert had brought his first wife to Naples, and now he was bringing his second wife and their son to the same spot. The fact is intriguing, and suggests that the town had some deep private significance in his mind. On 5 October 1838, Anne Gilbert gave birth to her second child there. It was a girl, and the parents named her Jane Morris Gilbert.

Gilbert told his first biographer Edith Browne that he had been briefly kidnapped by brigands during this early visit to Naples: 'Gilbert distinctly remembers riding in front of a man on an animal through what seemed to be a cutting with steep banks on either side; in later days, when he was again in Naples, he recognised in the Via Posilippo the scene which had impressed itself on his infant memory.'[6] According to this account, he was ransomed for £25 and restored to his parents. Recent researchers[7] have scoured the records for evidence of such a kidnapping and found nothing: it seems that the event simply did not take place, at least in the manner described. However, we should not dismiss the basic memory out of hand, especially bearing in mind that he told Browne he remembered it 'distinctly'. We may doubt that he was kidnapped (while noting his fondness for romantic events – and for being the centre of attention), but that sharp image of the horse, the rider and the steep banks, held in his head for nearly seventy years, is another matter.

The Gilberts returned to England in 1839 and finally took a house of their own: 4 Portland Place, Hammersmith (this street is now called Addison Bridge

Place). Here they lived with two servants. There seems to have been a high rate of turnover of servants in the Gilbert household at this time, for in June 1841, when the census was taken, their names were Sarah Dobson and Ann Tucker, but when in November of the same year William Gilbert asked his servants to witness the codicil to the will of Joseph Mathers Gilbert, they were Mary Simpson and Dinah Searle.[8]

Almost nothing is known of these women, but, as they would have been among baby Gilbert's formative influences, let us give them a moment's attention. In the 1841 census, Sarah Dobson was described as being 30 years old and Ann Tucker 18, though it is important to note that all adult ages were rounded down to the nearest five years in this particular census. In Gilbert's 1876 short story *Little Mim*, the narrator looks back on his childhood and remembers being looked after by two servants: Nurse Starke, 'a tall, muscular, hardened woman of forty' who curled the children's hair into tight, painful coils, and a housemaid, the gentler Jane Cotter.[9] The story is, of course, fiction, but we may imagine Gilbert at least drawing upon his own childhood to create that little fictional world. When, in the last years of his life, he wrote a children's retelling of *The Mikado*, he included among those who 'never would be missed' another Nurse Starke: 'the nursemaid who each evening in curlpapers does your hair/With an aggravating twist.'[10]

According to Gilbert's own account made in 1867, at the age of 2 he:

> was clandestinely married … in a back garden somewhere in Hammersmith, to a very worthy young person in a quilted satin bonnet and knitted socks, which used to drop off in an inconvenient manner whenever she sneezed, or otherwise exerted herself. The marriage was afterwards set aside on the ground that the officiating priest, her nurse, was not a qualified functionary.[11]

As so often with Gilbert, the joke may also be something like the truth.

The Gilberts were now living conveniently close to some relatives on the mother's side, the Edwardses, and also to some more remote relatives, the à Becketts, with whom the Gilberts were friendly throughout this period.

Gilbert Abbott à Beckett (1811–56) was a prolific journalist, humorist and playwright, who had by this time founded and edited several short-lived journals, including *The Censor* (1828–29) and *Figaro in London* (1831–39). He had married in 1835, and his eldest son Gilbert Arthur à Beckett had been born on 7 April 1837. There is every reason to think that William Schwenck Gilbert and Gilbert Arthur à Beckett were close childhood friends.

The career of the elder Gilbert à Beckett was given an extra boost in 1841 by the creation of a new satirical journal: *Punch*. During its early years he was to be one of its most prolific contributors.

The year 1841 also saw the first scenes of a painful and grotesque drama in the Gilbert family.[12] The will of wealthy old William Gilbert the grocer had divided enough money and property between his three children to make them financially independent. Two of the three siblings were now on the verge of death.

Jane Gilbert died first, at Merton Lodge, Weybridge Common, on 5 October 1841. Her estate went to John Samuel Schwenck and to her brothers Joseph and William. Joseph died of consumption not long after, on 20 November, while staying with William. His main will directed that a fund should be created, the interest of which was to maintain his wife and two children. His wife was to be the children's guardian. A codicil made on 2 November, while staying with William, appointed William Gilbert as the children's second guardian.

In April 1842 William Gilbert persuaded Catherine Gilbert to sign a deed agreeing that, in the event of the death of Catherine's children, all their inherited wealth should go to William Gilbert. As the children were consumptive, their early death was a distinct possibility. William Gilbert argued that his brother Joseph would have wanted the money to stay in the Gilbert family rather than going to Catherine, as would happen if the children died intestate. The deed was signed on 27 April 1842.

They agreed that William Gilbert should sign a similar deed relating to his own children, but he later refused to do so, much to Catherine's disquiet.

This, then, was the situation: William Gilbert was guardian to two children, and their deaths would make him rich. To make the situation even more disturbing, there is every reason to believe that William Gilbert was running short of money – not surprising, given his taste for visits to Milan and his rapidly growing family. Little wonder that Catherine Gilbert wrote a couple of years later, when she realised the full situation: 'I … cannot feel much confidence in leaving my little children to his guardianship.'[13]

At this time William Gilbert started to make some first tentative steps towards professional writing. His English translation of the Donizetti opera *Lucia di Lammermoor* was performed at the Princess's Theatre on 19 January 1843,[14] though it earned devastating reviews which referred to his work as 'doggerel', a 'concoction of stupid trash'[15] and so on. Despite this, he continued to try writing for the stage, though even his son was caustic about these plays, telling us through Edith Browne that they tended to be 'of a model in which the heroine makes her *début* in the first act and does not appear again till the last scene, the interest in her being theoretically maintained during her lengthy absence by sundry references in the dialogue'.[16]

Young Gilbert was now 6 years old, with one younger sister and another on its way. And something was about to happen which would set the course of the rest of his life. He was about to fall in love – with the theatre.

The Christmas pantomime was a rather different animal in those days from what it is today. For one thing, it took place late at night. It was the last item in the long evening's entertainment, after a substantial drama and possibly a little curtain-raiser as well. It started at ten o'clock or possibly a little before. It consisted of an 'opening' – a little drama in rhyming couplets on some children's theme, but at this time not usually a fairy tale – followed by the harlequinade, which was what everyone was really waiting for. These late-night fantasies must have been, to a small child who would normally have been sound asleep at this hour, truly the stuff that dreams are made on. They burrowed deep and lifelong into the psyches of many Victorians, including that of W.S. Gilbert.

Despite its name, the harlequinade was not really about Harlequin. The central character, the beginning and end of its anarchic fun, was Clown. The first great clown, Joseph Grimaldi, stole the pranks and tricks of the old Harlequin and made them his own. Most of the jokes, catchphrases and songs of the Victorian clown were created by Grimaldi. It became a commonplace to say, after his retirement from the stage in 1828, that no other clown could hold a candle to him. But the harlequinade, with Clown as its presiding genius, somehow survived through the decades and only started to wither away round about the year 1880, when the music-hall artistes began to take over.

So the pantomime 'opening' would draw to a close, with a Fairy Queen arbitrarily transforming its characters into Harlequin, Columbine, Clown and Pantaloon, and an elaborate 'transformation scene' would take place with lots of sparkle and glitter, and the harlequinade would be inaugurated with Clown's exuberant cry: 'Here we are again!' Clown would play elaborate, cartoonish practical jokes on policemen, tradesmen and passers-by, with the assistance of his elderly accomplice Pantaloon. Harlequin and his sweetheart Columbine would dance through the scenes together, Harlequin sometimes varying the monotony by taking a 'Harlequin leap' through a window or door, or transforming household objects with his magic bat. But always it would be Clown – making butter-slides, tripping people up, crushing babies, flattening people by putting them through the mangle, stealing sausages, cheating Pantaloon and generally creating havoc – who stole the show.

Looking back on those early years, Gilbert exclaimed:

'Harlequin, Columbine, Clown, and Pantaloon!' Yes, they awaken, in *my* mind at all events, the only recollection of unmixed pleasure associated with early childhood. Those night expeditions to a mystic building, where incomprehensible beings of all descriptions held astounding revels, under circumstances which I never endeavoured to account for, were, to my infant mind, absolute realizations of a fairy mythology which I had almost incorporated with my religious faith ... To be a Harlequin or Columbine was the summit of earthly happiness to which a worthy man or woman could aspire; while the condition of Clown or Pantaloon was a fitting purgatory in which to expiate the guilty deeds of a life misspent.[17]

We do not know what Gilbert's first pantomime was. But the London-born humorist Francis Cowley Burnand tells us in his *Records and Reminiscences* (1904) that the first pantomime he ever saw was *Harlequin and William Tell; or, The Genius of the Ribstone Pippin* at the Theatre Royal, Drury Lane, on 26 December 1842. Burnand was just eleven days younger than Gilbert, so we will not go too far wrong if we imagine young Gilbert being taken to his first pantomime in the same year – perhaps, with a slight stretch of probabilities, even sharing the same auditorium with young Burnand.

The evening had started with a performance of *Jane Shore*, an eighteenth-century tragedy by Nicholas Rowe. The Burnands took their seats towards the end of the performance of *Jane Shore*. He remembered 'being considerably frightened by the awful noises, hootings, yellings, and shouting with which the last act, the only one we children arrived in time to see, was received',[18] and we may doubt whether the hoary old tragedy was heard or attended to by the audience at all. This kind of behaviour seems to have been typical of Boxing Night performances at this time: crush and riot; shouting, whistling and singing; much throwing of orange peel and fighting over seats, all through the attempted performance of the 'main piece' before the pantomime. It was as if the anticipated harlequinade were spilling out into the auditorium.

Whatever Gilbert's first pantomime may have been, we know it must have made a deep and abiding impression upon him. Those 'night expeditions to a mystic building', which in his description seem like the secret rites of a sect, stayed with him through his life and became, in his memory, 'the only recollection of unmixed pleasure associated with early childhood'. The mixture of spectacle, song, dance and sheer silliness that pantomime has always offered was at the heart of Gilbert's own idea of theatre, and was to be brilliantly re-invented in works such as *The Mikado*.

His pantomime allegiances changed with his development through the phases of boyhood. At first the innocent boy had admired the agile Harlequin and despised the mischievous Clown; but, he confessed in his maturity:

> as I grew older, I am afraid that I came to look upon the relative merits of these mystic personages in a different light. I came to regard the Clown as a good fellow, whom it would be an honour to claim as an intimate companion; while the Harlequin degenerated into a rather tiresome muff, who delayed the fun while he danced in a meaningless way with a plain, stoutish person of mature age.[19]

In short, he came to admire Clown and despise Harlequin as he went through boyhood's mischievous, anarchic phase.

Round about the beginning of 1843, the Gilberts went to live across the English Channel, in Boulogne.[20] William Gilbert asserted that this was done to provide 'for the education of his children, and by reason of no other cause whatever'.[21] All the available facts suggest that the Gilberts were in financial difficulties at this time. It seems likely that as things stood William Gilbert simply could not guarantee that he would be able to afford a decent education for his son and daughters. For this reason the Gilberts decided to retrench: to move to the Continent, where the cost of living was substantially reduced, for a number of years until they had saved enough money to provide for their children's education. Boulogne was a convenient location for them: as close to England as possible, but cheap. The place was, in fact, notorious as the haunt of Englishmen on the run from debt; this was probably why William Gilbert wished to emphasise there was 'no other cause' for their action.

The move to France took place after the fiasco of William Gilbert's *Lucia di Lammermoor* translation, and after the birth of his second daughter, Mary Florence. Little is known about their years in Boulogne, even where they lived. But it was here that Gilbert first went to school, and it was here, in 1845, that Gilbert's third and last sister was born, Anne Maude. We may imagine him picking up the rough grasp of the French language that was so useful to him in later years when translating farces, and perhaps also, in that French seaport, picking up that love of the sea that shows itself in so many of his works.

Though technically living in Boulogne, the Gilberts still seem to have spent substantial periods in London. Gilbert later remembered the time, around 1845, when the Theatre Royal, Haymarket was still lit with wax candles.[22] And it was in London that the last of the saga of William Gilbert's guardianship of his nephews took place.

It is not necessary to go into the full details of this final fight over the children. Catherine Gilbert was emotionally involved at this time with a Captain Harman Baillie Hopper, and she intended to marry him. At the beginning of January 1845 she left her children in the care of the Schwencks for a few days. One day, John Samuel Schwenck was talking with the children when they mentioned that Captain Hopper had rubbed ointment on to their mother's leg, and had lain on her bed afterwards because 'he was so tired'.[23] Schwenck was so disturbed by this revelation that he encouraged the children to renew the subject a few days later, in the presence of William Gilbert. The children repeated their previous story, adding that they had seen Captain Hopper and their mother lying on her bed and talking.

William Gilbert was now determined to remove the children from Catherine Gilbert's care. Having left the children with the Schwencks on 2 January, she now (16 January) returned to the house to collect them. Schwenck refused to hand them over. She returned the next day with her brother John Francis and a Bow Street officer. There was an angry and violent scene in which she tried to take the children, and the Schwencks prevented her. On 20 January she obtained a writ of habeas corpus against Schwenck and the next day an item in *The Times* ('In re Gilbert') gave a brief and inaccurate account of the situation.

The knowable details of the custody case that followed are recounted at length in David Eden's *A Tale of Two Kidnaps*. It is enough to say here that each side accused the other of neglecting the children; that William Gilbert does not come out of the case shining in glory; that during the course of the case he was accused of medical incompetence; and that when the case ended (in March 1846) Catherine Gilbert was given custody of her children, having substantiated most of her claims. William Gilbert technically remained a guardian to the children but his role was vastly reduced in proportion to the lack of trust in which he was now held. The children, in spite of their delicate health, both grew up to live long and (possibly) happy lives.

Young Gilbert, of course, was not immediately involved in any of this. Though he seems to have remained a frequent visitor to London, he was probably based in Boulogne, and his parents may have tried to keep him ignorant of the legal action which his aunt was bringing against his father and godfather. And yet these events must have had their impact on him. He must have been aware, at some level, of the bad feeling in the family.

The whole sordid story implies certain unpleasant things about his father, William Gilbert. There was a kind of hardness in the man's dealings, a pinched determination, which is easy to dislike. He may not have actually schemed to allow his nephews to die, but he does not look good in the light of the facts. Where is the warmth and affection which one would like to see in Gilbert's family background? Gilbert himself tells us precious little in the way of reminiscence about his family: a sketch of a grandfather, a few passing comments about his father, practically nothing about his mother or sisters. We are left only with a vague feeling of coldness, darkness and isolation. Little wonder, then, that Gilbert looked instead towards the fantasy world of theatre to provide light, warmth and joy.

This was the great era of popular drama. In the expanding metropolis there was an ever-growing audience of working-class and lower middle-class men and women, eager for entertainment. Melodrama, that much-derided product of the age, gained its strength from its combination of spectacle, rhetoric, action, excitement, humour, pathos and the final triumph of virtue. The best of the old melodramas (such as Douglas Jerrold's *Black-Ey'd Susan* of 1829) are superb. Farce, too, was a staple of the Victorian theatrical diet, usually a one-acter to round off the evening's entertainment. John Maddison Morton's *Box and Cox* (1847) is a classic of its type, with its recognisable lower middle-class characters and its everyday concerns (cooking a chop, paying the rent, avoiding marriage), all raised to a theatrical pitch and rendered absurd. Then, too, there was extravaganza, light parody of classical drama written in rhyming couplets with occasional songs, the master of the form being James Robinson Planché. Theatre did not really reflect real life, nor did it intend to do so: it transformed the realities of life into something bearable or turned its back on reality altogether in favour of a world of dream and fantasy.

The Gilberts returned to London in 1847, taking a house at 17 Brompton Square, in one of the rapidly expanding areas of the city, just south of Hyde Park and close to fashionable South Kensington. It was here that Gilbert's English education began, at the Western Grammar School, Brompton. Here he was taught Latin, Greek, French, English and mathematics.

Gilbert gave Edith Browne a brief list of his preoccupations as a boy: 'dreaming, drawing, desultory reading, and the hero-worship of everything and everybody connected with the stage.'[24] He also told her an anecdote of his youth which I will here quote in the version he wrote as part of a foreword to Rutland Barrington's autobiography:

> I remember that when I was a boy of thirteen I followed Mr. Tom Barry (the then well-known clown at Astley's Amphitheatre) all the way from Temple Bar to Westminster Bridge, trying to make up my mind to ask him the time. [In the version he told to Edith Browne, he trailed Barry from the Strand and across Waterloo Bridge – a much shorter journey.] Unfortunately, however, just as I had screwed up my courage to the sticking point, Mr. Barry baffled me by turning suddenly into a public house of refreshment, whither I had not the enterprise to follow him. I may state that I have long since given up the practice of shadowing clowns.[25]

It seems that young Gilbert was indeed absolutely obsessed with the theatre and its performers; everything else was a distraction or an anti-climax in comparison. He does not appear to have been particularly sociable either: the abiding impression is of a boy, alone.

In the autumn of 1850 Gilbert was sent, perhaps in the hope of drawing him out of his private world, as a boarder to Great Ealing School, about 10 miles west of Brompton. He later regarded this as his 'real' schooling. Whenever he recounted his life he hardly ever mentioned his education at Boulogne or Brompton; but Great Ealing School always took pride of place. It was a highly regarded private school and Gilbert clearly revelled in the prestige of having been there. Most of its pupils were day-boys; only about forty were boarders.

Here, for the first time, our image of Gilbert comes into focus. He told Edith Browne something of his character at Great Ealing School:

> [While there] he speedily won the reputation of being a clever, bright boy who was extremely lazy. It was soon discovered, however, that he could work so quickly that this natural tendency to idleness was no handicap to his abilities … He had an instinctive horror of being left behind, and spurred into activity by a healthy pride he would, by an easy effort generally made in the last moments of the term, catch up with the top boys of his class. But there was one lesson which he never neglected, one task into which he could throw himself wholeheartedly without being goaded on by character; this was the weekly translation into verse of a set portion of the classics, and he stead-

ily won fame and prizes for his English versification of Horace, Aristophanes, Homer, Virgil, and their like.[26]

Elsewhere, he mentioned other aspects of his early character. To Kate Field in 1879 he stated that he generally got into fights about three times a week.[27] To Rowland Brown he said: 'I was not a popular boy, I believe.'[28] And so the picture of the young Gilbert's character comes into focus. He was rather withdrawn and prone to 'dreaming', not good at making friends, quick to lash out, idle in the subjects that did not interest him, keen to prove himself in competition. No one is at his or her best in adolescence, when the elements of character are in place but appear as a series of masks and attitudes; still, it is useful to note these raw elements, some of which will develop further in the adult man and others of which will be combated or hidden. The aggression and the competitive streak were to come out clearly enough; the dreaminess and the withdrawn nature were to be disguised, but would show themselves in the unexpected elements that appear, as if from another world, in his plays and stories – the fantasy, for instance, and the strange streak of melancholy.

It was at Great Ealing that he began to write plays. These were performed by the other boys, with Gilbert directing them, designing the sets, and in the case of a melodrama called *Guy Fawkes*, playing the starring role.

In February 1852, Charles Kean starred in Dion Boucicault's new play, *The Corsican Brothers* at the Princess's Theatre, and was a sensational hit. Gilbert saw the play (probably during the Easter holidays) and, according to the account given to Edith Browne, 'packed up a few clothes in a handbag, and actually succeeded in interviewing Kean with a view to going on the stage'. The anecdote continues:

'So you would like to go on the stage?' said Kean.
'Yes,' murmured Master Gilbert, trembling in every limb.
'What's your name?'
The boy's imagination failed him at a critical moment in his life. 'Gilbert,' he replied, seeking refuge in the truth.
'Gilbert – Gilbert,' reiterated Kean, 'are you the son of my old friend William Gilbert?'
'Y-yes,' stammered the boy, and he was promptly sent home to his father.[29]

This must have been no small incident in Gilbert's youth, this running away from his home or school, followed by his humiliating return. In telling the tale to Edith Browne as an old man, he reduces it to a 'good story' and tells us nothing of its emotional background. Was it simply a matter of being stage-struck and adolescent disconnection from reality, or were there also shades of domestic unhappiness lurking behind this slight little anecdote? It is impossible to say.

Gilbert did not leave us much information about his early life: a broad outline garnished with a few oft-repeated stories, telling us a little but not quite enough.

However, during the ten years (1861–71) in which he wrote articles, stories and ballads for the comic paper *Fun*, he often fell back on the comic journalist's ever-reliable source of material: his own life. He wrote and illustrated several series of articles in which he called himself the Comic Physiognomist, and in which he pretended to analyse the people he saw round him in the streets, at parties, at social events, in fact everywhere. Some of these articles are clearly based on his own life, though of course distorted for comic effect. Throughout these pieces he always referred to himself, in the third person, as 'the C.P.' Now and in the next few chapters I will quote extensively from these columns, though always with the caveat that Gilbert was writing for the sake of comedy, not of literal truth.

'The C.P. has reason to believe that he was not at all a nice boy,' the Comic Physiognomist lamented at the start of one article.[30] Referring to himself and his schoolfellows, the C.P. also wrote that 'he has no hesitation in saying that a more miserable set of young tadpoles than he and they were, when he and they first met, don't exist out of a condemned cell'.[31]

In a column entitled 'His Schoolfellows, and What Has Become of Them', the C.P. made sketch drawings of some of the tadpoles in question. In the accompanying descriptions they appear as fairly standard public-school types: the 'sharp boy' who 'used to make a great deal of money by a variety of ingenious methods'; the 'very dashing lad' who was 'remarkable for a very tasty fancy in waistcoats'; the 'dreadfully intelligent' one who 'was always experimentalizing with little coloured bottles and small brass scales'; the boy who 'was always hopelessly in love with all the young ladies at every establishment in the neighbourhood' and 'Poor Old Fagg', who was '*the* heaviest, *the* stupidest, *the* dirtiest, *the* clumsiest, *the* most cowardly, and generally *the* most incompetent boy in the school'.[32]

He sketched the schoolmasters with equally broad strokes. The C.P.'s headmaster was an autocratic old man with a knobbly head. 'Mathematics and Writing' was a sallow young teacher in love with the headmaster's daughter, said to be 'the poet of the local newspaper – known to its readers as "The Passing Sad One"'.[33] Whilst:

> German and Moral Philosophy was a heavy, leaden, long-haired, sleepy Herr, with everything big about him except his intelligence … He, of course, was a smoker; but as the Doctor objected to smoking (as, indeed, he did to most things) on principle, the fat, sleepy, good-natured old muff used to conspire with us boys, and he and we enjoyed the stolen luxury in a gravel pit, together.[34]

And as for French and the Violin:

> Poor old MONSIEUR TELLECHOSE … He was a mild, long-suffering old gentleman, who was goaded about once every six months, by us young miscreants, into open rebellion against our despotic rule. He was very seedy, and used to take snuff out of a rag of paper. The C.P. must have been an unfeeling young

ruffian at that early age – he blushes to think of the indignities he heaped upon that uncomplaining old man.[35]

The C.P. was a mask, but not a fiction. Through these columns we see, as through a glass, something of life at Great Ealing School as Gilbert saw it. He looked back and summarised his experiences forthrightly: 'Somebody has remarked that our schooldays are the happiest periods of our lives. The C.P. has no hesitation in recording his conviction that Somebody is an ass. Probably Somebody never went to school at all.'[36]

He left Great Ealing School at the end of the autumn (Michaelmas) term, 1852. We do not know for a fact why this happened, when just one term of the academic year had passed; but there is good reason to suppose it was because Gilbert had contracted typhoid fever.[37]

In the 1950s a niece of Gilbert's called Mary Carter recalled an old family story, it went like this: young Gilbert, having contracted typhoid fever while a pupil at Great Ealing, became emaciated. Part of the treatment given to him involved his head being shaved. The family went to France to help him recuperate, and while there they saw Emperor Napoleon III and Empress Eugénie riding past in their carriage. (The emperor married Princess Eugénie on 30 January 1853, so the incident could not have taken place before this date.) Afterwards, Gilbert wrote the following verse, which was passed down through the family orally, until Mary Carter passed it on to posterity:

When the horses, white with foam,
Drew the Empress to her home
From the place whence she did roam,
The Empress she did see
The Gilbert Familee.
To the Emperor she said:
'How beautiful the head
Of that youth of gallant mien,
Cropped so neat and close and clean –
Though I own he's rather lean.'
Said the Emperor: 'It is!
And I never saw a phiz
More wonderful than 'is.'[38]

Gilbert's brush with death – for an attack of typhoid fever was just that – is usually glossed over, treated as an incidental fact leading to the really important event, the creation of his first extant work. But the episode is worth pausing over.

Londoners were at that time particularly vulnerable to diseases such as cholera and typhoid. This was because the rise of the flushing lavatory during the first half of the nineteenth century had led to drainage sewers being used for a purpose for which they were not intended – the removal of faeces and urine – and resulted in the flushing of huge quantities of untreated sewage into the River Thames. This disgusting situation was only addressed after the 'Great Stink' of 1858. The solution (the Thames embankment) would be completed long years in the future, in 1870. Back in the early 1850s, the nature of typhoid fever was not fully understood, but at least William Gilbert knew enough to take his son out of London and into healthier climes.

Typhoid fever was often confused with typhus at this time – even by doctors – but it will perhaps be best to assume that the diagnosis was, in this case, accurate. The *Salmonella typhi* bacterium is passed on through contact with infected urine or faeces, usually by flies or as a result of food having been prepared by someone with unclean hands. The fever would have taken one to two months to run its course. In the first few days Gilbert would have suffered a high temperature fever, accompanied by headaches and a sore throat, constipation, pain in the joints and abdomen, a loss of appetite and fatigue. The infection would have later led to intestinal sores. The course of his illness was no joke, and it may have taken him up to a year to recover fully.

But all this is conjecture. We may guess that Gilbert suffered typhoid fever in December 1852 and January 1853, and it fits very neatly with the disparate facts which we do know, but it cannot be taken as undisputed fact. The next thing we know is that in March 1853 he registered for the matriculation course at King's College, London, and that in September of the same year, at the age of 16, he entered the college's department of General Literature and Science.

2

DRIFTING (1853–61)

King's College, London, was not much older than Gilbert. It had been founded in 1828 on the basic principle that 'every system of general education for the youth of a Christian community ought to comprise instruction in the Christian religion as an indispensable part'.[1] The college buildings stood on the Strand in the heart of London, their rear looking over the stinking River Thames. Gilbert was registered as a student in the Department of General Literature and Science. According to the attendance list held at King's College, in his first year Gilbert attended classes on divinity, Greek and Latin classics, mathematics, French and, in the Easter term, German. The list records some comments on the pupils' progress; for instance, in the Lent term of 1854 Gilbert's divinity was noted as 'Indifferent', but his classics as 'much improved'. However, his French master commented in the Michaelmas term of 1853: 'more application required', and was even less impressed in Lent term 1854: 'Frequently abst. Inattentive.'[2] Possibly Gilbert, remembering the years he spent in Boulogne, felt that he already knew French and did not need to be told anything more about it.

The duties of the day began punctually at ten o'clock, Monday to Saturday, with prayers in the Chapel, all students being required to attend. Lectures began at 10.15am and the day's work continued, with only the briefest of breaks, until 4.45pm on weekdays and 12.30pm on Saturdays.

Gilbert walked to college every day from his parents' house in Brompton, a distance of about 1½ miles. (In 1854 the Gilberts moved from 17 Brompton Square to nearby 21 Thurloe Square; this would have increased Gilbert's daily walk by a couple of minutes.) He later recalled, in the guise of the Comic Physiognomist, some of the people he met on the journey. There was, for instance, the 'hairy stranger' who stood near the junction of Agar Street with the Strand 'stopped the C.P. morning and evening, called him "Captain," and wished to sell him cigars and pocket handkerchiefs'.[3]

He also recalled 'two lovely daily governesses whose sweet faces charmed his dreary trudge from Brompton to the Strand' when he was 17 years old:[4]

One was haughty, and treated the C.P. with the contempt which, at that early age, his immature charms deserved. The other, however, seemed to take pleasure in meeting the young philosopher, and in flashing her bright eyes at him as he blushingly passed. He knows not which of them he loved the most, but his self-pride was nettled by the pretty scorn of the former, and he made a solemn vow that one day she should be his. That vow is but one of many which he has failed to keep. But the space between Knightsbridge-green and the drapery establishment of MESSRS. HARVEY, NICHOL AND CO., is still a hallowed ground to him.[5]

The earliest portrait of Gilbert shows him at about this time, thick-necked and clean-shaven, with a squareish face, thick dark hair behind a broad brow; not an ill-looking young man but with the possibility of determination in his features.[6]

Throughout his life Gilbert was extremely susceptible to the charm of young women, taking great delight in flashing eyes, stolen glances and flirtatious conversation: 'To love and be loved by an exquisite female is a state of things which has always appeared to his susceptible mind to be the incarnation of earthly happiness.'[7] When we look at Gilbert in his maturity, so stiff and formal and seemingly so armoured against emotional vulnerability, it is in conversation with women that we see him relaxing, enjoying himself, engaging with others and even lowering his defences a little.

It is said that Gilbert contributed to *King's College Magazine*, though no copies from this period seem to survive.[8] Near the start of his second year he became involved with the King's College Scientific Society, as it was then called. This student society had been founded in 1847 as the King's College Engineering Society, its name being changed to the Scientific Society early in 1854. On Monday 23 October 1854, Gilbert was elected a member of this society. Two days later he was elected secretary, jointly with a Mr Thaine. On 8 November 1854 he read a paper to the society on 'The Theory of Apparitions'.[9] Possibly as a result of the discussion that followed, on 29 November he took Sir David Brewster's *Letters on Natural Magic* (1832) out of the society's library, a work which gives scientific explanations for supposedly 'supernatural' experiences.[10]

The new term, which began on 24 January 1855, brought new problems. From Monday 29 January onwards Gilbert was marked as absent from daily chapel and his course subjects. Two days later, on 31 January, Gilbert felt able to attend a meeting of the Scientific Society and to bring to their attention 'the fact that Mr Tolmé [the society's librarian] had not pasted the labels on the Society's books',[11] but the next note about him in the society's minutes, the announcement on 7 March that 'Mr Firby was elected as Secretary in place of Mr Gilbert', is a clear acknowledgement of Gilbert's continued absence from the college and the society. He is registered as sick in the chapel registers from 5 March onwards, and the attendance list simply notes that his attendance in the Lent term was 'Interrupted by illness'.[12] His name is completely absent from the registers for the Easter term; it seems he remained absent from college for the remainder of the academic year.

It is not known what Gilbert's illness may have been. For instance, it is just possible that he suffered his bout of typhoid fever not in December 1852, as I have surmised, but now in January 1855. The college's physical proximity to the Thames, which was in a horrible state of filth, is a point in favour of this idea. There are no family letters in existence which might shed light on what happened to Gilbert in these months of interrupted education, and in his autobiographical writings he made no mention of being ill during his college years at all.

Gilbert returned to the college at the start of his third year, on 3 October 1855, but he did not stay long; the register indicates that he took leave from 1 November onwards, and his name completely disappears from the registers for subsequent terms.[13] However, on Wednesday 31 October 1855, just before he left, he did attend a meeting of the Scientific Society, during which Henry Geary proposed its dissolution and the founding of a Shakespearian reading society: 'Mr Gilbert then moved that it be also called a Dramatic as well as Shakespearian reading society …'; the proposal seems to have been accepted by the meeting.[14] And with this last act Gilbert left the college.

Gilbert's education was an interrupted and troubled one. After some initial schooling in Boulogne, he had continued at Western Grammar School and then at Great Ealing, where he had apparently tried to run away and join the actors, finally leaving the school at Christmas 1852 for reasons we can only guess. He completed only one year and one term of education at King's College before being interrupted first by illness and then … by what?

The final break was clearly planned, since it is acknowledged in the register as official leave. King's College was at this time often used as a preliminary to study at the great universities, and Gilbert tells us in his autobiography that this had been his original intention: 'I was educated at Great Ealing and King's College, intending to finish up at Oxford.'[15] But now his intentions had changed.

Firstly, he had decided to make some first steps towards studying for the Bar. On 11 October 1855 (eight days after the start of college term) he registered as a student at Inner Temple. He was now required to 'keep terms' for three years; that is, to dine in hall a specific number of times for twelve terms, there being four terms in a year. A graduate student had to dine in hall three times per term and a non-graduate six times.

But more importantly, Gilbert now had a chance to gain a commission in the army, and he was determined to do so.

In February 1854 Britain had declared war on Russia. The field of battle was the Crimean Peninsula on the coast of the Black Sea. Gilbert wrote: 'At the age of seventeen, when I first saw, at the Chobham Camp, a field battery "unlimber and action front," I made up my mind to be a Horse Artilleryman.'[16] If this is correct (and Gilbert's memory for such details as dates and ages was extremely erratic),[17] he probably spent his day at the Chobham Camp sometime in the middle of 1854. At 17 years of age, and having just begun his course at King's College, he could do little in pursuit of his military ambitions during that first year, as the Crimean War descended into a hell of misery, suffering and incompetence.

His chance came now, in 1855, when some army commissions in the Royal Artillery and the Engineers were made available to competitive examination. The first examinations were held in August 1855, and were eligible to candidates between the ages of 19 and 21. Gilbert, aged 18, was unable to sit for these, but would have hoped to take the next set of exams after his birthday. This, surely, was his primary reason for wishing to take leave from college. However, when the second set of examinations was announced for January 1856, the rules were changed so that candidates would be considered only if they were aged between 20 and 22.[18] Gilbert would now have to wait until November 1856 in order to become eligible. In the meantime, according to Gilbert, 'I studied classics, mathematics, chemistry, engineering, and land surveying'.[19] This would have been private study with a tutor.

But when November 1856 came, the Crimean War had in fact come to an end. When Allied troops took Sebastopol in September 1855, the war-weary British government was quick to affirm that the war aims had been achieved, and the peace treaty was finally signed in March 1856.

It is not quite clear whether Gilbert ever took the examination. In his later accounts he seemed convinced that 20 had been the upper age limit for exam candidates, not the lower, and that he had secured a special dispensation from the Secretary of State for War, Lord Panmure, to sit the exam while several weeks overage. It is possible that he had in fact obtained permission to take the exam while underage. He may have taken the exam in June 1856 and failed it. His first flush of enthusiasm may have disappeared with the end of the war (there were no further exams for commissions after June 1856). None of this is known. Only one thing is certain: he did not, in the end, join the army.

His career plans, such as they may have been, were now in disarray. It seems he had sacrificed his last year at King's College in the pursuit of a commission which consistently fled from his step. Oxford was not a practical possibility in the face of his incomplete education. There only remained the distant prospect of the Bar. But in the meantime, he was a young man with no immediate prospects. He was probably undertaking a course of cramming to make up for the terms he had lost from King's College; on 5 December 1856 he applied for a reader's ticket at the British Museum, his sponsor being a Herman F. Lewis of University College, London.[20] At any rate, he took his BA exam at London University in

October 1857 and he passed it. (King's College was not able to award degrees at this time.)

The year 1857 seems to have been something of a crunch for Gilbert. On Tuesday 24 February he was appointed to the post of assistant clerk (third class) at the Committee of Council on Education, which was part of the Privy Council Office. He started work two days after his appointment.[21] It seems he also left the parental home about this time, though it is not known where his first lodgings may have been. His sister Jane also left that year, marrying Alfred Weigall, a painter of miniature portraits, on 7 September. The likelihood is that the Gilberts' finances were dwindling. At about this time William Gilbert's first books were published, *On the Present System of Rating for the Relief of the Poor in the Metropolis* (1857) and the novel *Dives and Lazarus* (1858), followed by many other works of fiction and fact published in magazines and in volume form. William Gilbert's sudden transformation, in his mid-fifties, into a prolific writer suggests that perhaps he found himself in need of a new source of income. It seems probable that Gilbert was put under some pressure from his parents to leave home and earn his own living. Whatever the reason, he now found himself an independent adult (he turned 21 in November 1857), and a very small fish indeed in the big pond of London.

The Education Office was, in Gilbert's words, 'ill-organized and ill-governed',[22] and he hated working there, later writing of it with barely disguised contempt. Apparently he did not hesitate to let his superiors know as much: in April 1858 he was 'reprimanded for disrespectful and insubordinate conduct'.[23] His later short story *The Key of the Strong Room* (1865) involves a government department called the Board for the Dissemination of Pauper Philosophy and an insubordinate young clerk, who features in an episode possibly drawn from Gilbert's own experience:

> [John] had a few days before, in resisting a piece of unnecessary petty tyranny on the part of a fellow clerk in temporary charge of his department, used stronger language than was absolutely necessary. This was reported to the Secretary … Fox (the complainant) was rebuked for having used unnecessary tyranny, but it was shown that young John was doubly culpable, for he not only resisted the order, which he should have obeyed and then complained of, but he had also sworn a bad oath, and otherwise misconducted himself (being a hot-headed young fellow) to the annihilation of all order and discipline.[24]

In 'The Comic Physiognomist in a Government Office' (*Fun*, 6 February 1864) Gilbert transformed the office into the Thread-Paper and Battle-Axe Department. This piece gives us a good idea of what Gilbert encountered in his place of work:

> The C.P. on entering the Thread-paper and Battle-axe Department in the capacity of junior clerk, made these important discoveries:

1. That it was expected of him that he should not wear light neck-ties or a beard.

2. That provided he blinded his official superiors by humiliating himself before them three times a day, he might consult his own tastes as to the amount of work he chose to do.

3. That a government office is a capital place in which to write copy on other people's paper.[25]

The C.P. also describes for us some of the types of people employed there, and we may suspect a little private vengeance creeping in:

1. A PIOUS CLERK, who is always 'feeling it to be his duty to report,' &c. He is a clerk to the back-bone, writes a hand like copper-plate, and has a poor opinion of all who don't. It is a treat to see him when he imagines that official injustice has been done to him. This is pretty frequently the case, for being a mere machine he is treated accordingly by his official superiors, and is often superseded …

3. THE LAW-STATIONER'S CLERK – This poor fellow is the drudge of the office generally, and of specimen No. 1 in particular. He is a quiet, inoffensive old gentleman (he *is* a gentleman), who has seen better days. He is not bright, but he is very patient, and has need for all the patience at his command.

4. THE OFFICIAL SNEAK – This is a repulsive creature, and there is a specimen of him in every Government office in England. He is a pale man, usually with red hair, and is always in a cold perspiration. He is a shambling, knock-kneed fellow, and generally drops his h's.[26]

When Gilbert started at the Education Office, he was paid £25 quarterly. The duties were not arduous, the working hours being 10 a.m. to 4 p.m., and he repeatedly complained in early contributions to *Fun* that government clerks had nothing to do.

Having failed in his attempts to obtain a commission in the army, Gilbert now turned to the civilian militia. In March 1859, he became an ensign in the Fifth West Yorkshire Militia. A photograph from about this time shows him in his ensign's uniform: over 6ft tall, slim and sporting a natty little moustache.[27] By January 1860 he had risen to the rank of lieutenant, when he was involved in an incident which came to court and was reported in *The Times*, among other papers. We learn from his witness statements that he was living at 25 Montpelier Square, Brompton.[28] At about half past midnight on the morning of Wednesday 18 January 1860 he was walking along Brompton Road towards the junction with Sloane Street. It is not known why he should have been there at that time. It has been suggested that he was on the way home after seeing a pantomime[29] but this does not explain why he should have been walking away from Montpelier

Square; perhaps he was in search of a drink. As he came towards Sloane Street he became aware of an incident which was drawing an interested crowd.

Two privates in the Coldstream Guards, George Hales and Charles Humphreys, had been drinking in the Clock House, Knightsbridge, and had become so drunk that the landlord asked them to leave. They refused, and the landlord brought in a policeman, George Stevens, to remove them. After an altercation another policeman, Henry Somerfield, joined him. The two soldiers continued to resist the policemen and, swearing horribly, took off their belts and swung them round their heads, 'expressing their intention of killing some one before the night was out'.[30] Hales ran among the crowd swinging his belt, cutting a man's chin open, wounding a woman's head and hitting Gilbert on the shoulder. Gilbert 'immediately pinioned him, and gave him into custody'.[31] With Gilbert's assistance the two policemen, though seriously injured by the soldiers' belts, were able to subdue and arrest the two guardsmen. They were brought before the magistrate's court in Westminster on 18 January, and the policemen and Lieutenant Gilbert all gave evidence:

Mr. PAYNTER [the magistrate] inquired of Lieutenant Gilbert whether the soldiers in his regiment wore such belts as those worn by the defendants?

The Lieutenant replied in the affirmative.

Mr. PAYNTER inquired whether they ever used them?

Lieutenant Gilbert replied that they sometimes became intoxicated and rowdy, as all soldiers would, but he had never heard of their using their belts. As far as his observation had gone that sort of thing seemed to be confined to the Guards.

A sergeant of the Coldstreams, who had been sitting at the solicitors' table, turned round and in a very angry tone said that Lieutenant Gilbert had no right to state what he knew was not correct; the use of the belt was common to every regiment all over the country.

The Lieutenant replied he had never heard so; the sergeant must bear in mind he had not stated it as a fact; he had only said as far as his own observation had gone.[32]

Later, the sergeant repeated his complaint that Lieutenant Gilbert should not have said what he did, 'as it might create ill feeling', but Mr Paynter said he thought 'the lieutenant was quite right', adding that the city's magistrates had been saying for some while that soldiers should not be allowed to wear their belts. It was a common form of assault at this time.

There was a second hearing on 21 January 1860 and then the case was brought before the Middlesex Sessions on Monday 6 February 1860. The judge, in the course of his summing-up of the case, said that 'the conduct of Lieutenant Gilbert deserved the utmost praise, and he was entitled to the thanks of the Court and of the public for what he had done'.[33] The two guardsmen were sentenced to a year's hard labour apiece.

Eight months later, on 3 October 1860, *The Times* published a letter from Gilbert, the content of which suggests that neither he nor the Coldstream Guards had forgotten or forgiven the previous episode. Gilbert wrote:

Sir,

Early on Sunday morning [I suspect he means late on Saturday night], as I was proceeding along the south side of the Knightsbridge-road, a little east of Sloane-street, I met three Guardsmen walking arm in arm with as many women. I gave them a wide berth, but one of the fellows deliberately came up to me and struck me violently on the chest with his elbow. The blow sent me staggering into the road in a most undignified manner. I seized the man, and informed him that I should detain him until I saw a policeman. After a short struggle he broke away from me, and one of the other two soldiers exclaimed, 'Let's give him a bit of belt.' They acted on the suggestion, and prepared to use their belts in true Guardsman style. I seized one of my assailants, and a passer-by seized another, just as the blow was about to descend on my head. The third soldier then occupied himself in endeavouring to release his comrade. After a short struggle the fellows broke from us, and finding that the odds were as much as two to three against them, the cowardly ruffians took to flight like so many startled sheep. I made my complaint at the barracks, and received the reply usually given in circumstances of a similar nature, 'that the matter should be inquired into;' but as my name and address were not requested, I presume that the investigation will not be particularly searching in its nature.

He gave details of his previous encounter with violent guardsmen and suggested a solution to the problem of belt assaults: 'If the authorities object to turn the men into the streets without their belts (and it must be allowed that a beltless soldier presents a very slovenly appearance), let the belt be stitched firmly to the tunic at the back.' He indicated at the end that he was a lieutenant in the Civil Service Rifles.

A few months later, when the census was taken on 31 March 1861, he had changed his lodgings and was living at 17 Victoria Grove in Kensington. It is tempting to wonder whether the change was caused by any continuing difficulties with the local guardsmen.

As his letter shows, Gilbert had moved from the Fifth West Yorkshire Militia to the newly formed Civil Service Rifle Volunteers regiment. This was presided over by a certain Captain Tom Taylor, who happened to be one of the most successful writers of drama in that era. On 18 July 1860 the Civil Service Volunteers gave an amateur performance at the Lyric Theatre of a new play by Tom Taylor, *A Lesson for Life*, with a cast including Lieutenant Gilbert, Captain Tom Taylor,

Captain Tom Hood (of whom more later) and two young girls called Kate and Ellen Terry. The performance was repeated at the Lyceum the following May.[34] At last Gilbert was starting to mingle with the people who mattered to him most: the dramatists, actors and journalists of bohemian London.

According to Gilbert's short autobiography, his first printed work was a translation of the 'Laughing Song' from Auber's *Manon Lescaut*, which the young singer Euphrosyne Parepa, 'whom I had known from babyhood',[35] asked him to make, to be printed in the playbill for Alfred Mellon's Promenade concerts. Gilbert thought this happened in 1858, but in fact the most likely date is August 1861.[36] Gilbert told William Archer in an interview:

> … I can perfectly remember standing in the 'promenade,' or pit, and seeing a man reading the verses as Parepa sang them. 'Ha!' I thought, 'if he knew that the person standing at his elbow was the writer of these lines, how thrilled he would be!' My subsequent experience teaches me that he would have received the information with fortitude. The thing was a laughing-song, and went like this:
>
> > 'An entertaining story,
> > A fiction amatory,
> > > About a legal star,
> > > Ha! ha! ha! ha! ha! ha!
> > A legal dignitary
> > Particularly wary,
> > > A member of the bar,
> > > Ha! ha! ha! ha! ha! ha!'
>
> and so on.[37]

Gilbert re-used this, in revised form, in his 1870 play *The Princess*.

Gilbert was also trying other means to break into literature as a career. He was sending plays to theatres, such as *All In the Wrong* which is now lost; only the covering letter survives, sent to W.H. Swanborough of the Strand Theatre, dated 17 October 1860, and written on Education Department notepaper.[38] He also wrote 'a long, quasi-humorous poem' called 'Satisfied Isaiah Jones' and sent it to the periodical *Once A Week*. The editor returned it because it was too long, but he added that it was 'clever and amusing'.[39] In the world of rejection in which the beginning writer lives, even such a scrap is encouraging, and it was enough to spur Gilbert on to write more pieces for other journals. Amongst these was a newly established comic paper, *Fun*.

3

BOHEMIAN NIGHTS (1861–64)

The first issue of *Fun* was published with the date 21 September 1861 (it was published every Wednesday, but dated the Saturday of that week). The editor was H.J. Byron, a young man of 26, who had already made a name for himself as a writer of pantomimes and burlesques. The paper was deliberately designed to look 'as like *Punch* as legally possible', as F.C. Burnand noted.[1] It was owned by Charles Maclean, a maker and seller of plate glass, and it had its office above Maclean's shop. This was at 80 Fleet Street, almost within spitting distance of *Punch* at number 85. It was a direct challenge to the older paper, selling for a penny while *Punch* sold for 3*d*.

H.J. Byron, E.L. Blanchard, William Brough and F.C. Burnand were among the contributors to the first issues of the paper.[2] They were all members of the same set, established or up-and-coming writers of burlesque and pantomime at the London theatres. *Fun* was a meagre affair in those early days, printed on cheap, coarse paper, and filled with stilted cartoons and uneasy attempts at jocularity. It was, as yet, a rough sketch of what it was to be. It needed time to discover itself: time and leisure and a healthy infusion of new blood.

Gilbert's first identifiable contribution to *Fun* appeared in the issue dated 26 October 1861: a half-page cartoon signed with a monogram of the letters 'W.S.G.' entwined. It shows a bearded gentleman playing the piano and a superior-looking servant addressing him. The bearded one's eyeglass is dropping from his eye in astonishment. The caption reads:

SOME MISTAKE HERE!

Morning Visitor, awaiting the Lady of the House, whileth away the time with sweet music. To him enters Chawles.

Chawles: – 'HO! IF YOU PLIZ, M'LADY SES, IS THERE A CANDLE, OR A DUSTER, OR ANY-THINK OF THE KIND YOU WOULD WISH BEFORE YOU BEGIN TO CHUNE THE INSTERMENT?'

It was not an auspicious start, but the quality of his work would soon improve. Gilbert later remembered:

> In 1861 *Fun* was started, under the editorship of Mr. H.J. Byron. With much labour I turned out an article three-quarters of a column long, and sent it to the editor, together with a half-page drawing on wood. A day or two later the printer of the paper called upon me, with Mr. Byron's compliments, and staggered me with a request to contribute a column of 'copy' and a half-page drawing every week for the term of my natural life.[3]

However, Clement Scott, who was to become a close colleague of Gilbert's on the paper, recalled things differently:

> W.S. Gilbert's plan of action was to go [not to the editor but] straight to the proprietor. Maclean, a shrewd Scotchman, saw he had got a prize in the young humourist and quaint artist. In those days there were weekly *Fun* dinners to settle cartoons and jokes … Gilbert, in virtue of his good work, soon found his way to the dining-table; and, I fear, at the outset, the 'young outsider' was unkindly chaffed by those who were very shortly to be his closest friends. It was not long before he was in power and position to turn the tables on those who had underrated his talents.[4]

A drawing for publication in *Punch* or *Fun* was made by the artist directly on to a block of boxwood, which was next 'cut' by the engraver. This process destroyed the artist's original work by replacing it with the engraver's precision copy. The printed product was as much the result of the skill and artistry of the engraver as of those of the artist; and there is reason to believe that an unskilled artist was to some extent dependent on the engraver to clarify the artist's intentions.[5] Gilbert's first cartoons for *Fun* are, unsurprisingly, derivative and have little in common with his later assured depictions of stylised homunculi. They are clear imitations of the almost realistic scenes of London life that appeared in *Punch*, and they have little intrinsic artistic interest. It would take Gilbert a year or two to find a style which would allow him, and the reader, to relax and have a little fun.

It is impossible to identify all Gilbert's contributions to these early issues. The written articles were unsigned and not all the cartoons were signed. However, no fewer than sixteen cartoons and 'initials' (vignettes incorporating the first letter of an article) that were published in the last months of 1861 can be attributed to Gilbert. These include five full-page political cartoons. Most bear the W.S.G. monogram, but there is one exception, which was signed 'Bab'.

This untitled cartoon appeared in the issue for 9 November 1861. In an austere schoolroom, a pompous looking school inspector addresses an old man, evidently the local schoolteacher, while a small child stands on a stool and weeps:

INSPECTOR:– 'I CANNOT RECOMMEND YOUR SCHOOL FOR A GRANT. THIS DIS-
GRACEFUL CHILD IS THREE YEARS OLD, AND IS UNFAMILIAR WITH THE FIRST FOUR
RULES OF ARITHMETIC!'

POOR VICAR:– 'THEN, SIR, AS I CANNOT DISCHARGE EVERY SCHOOL EXPENSE OUT
OF MY INCOME OF £150, I MUST CLOSE MY SCHOOL.'

The issue satirised in the cartoon is explained on the facing page under the heading 'Lisping in Numbers':

> In the new Education Code (which is certainly anything but a Code of Honour,
> for it systematically breaks faith with every certificated schoolmaster in the gov-
> ernment employ), we find that in order to entitle a school to a grant, a child of
> three years of age must not only be able to read a narrative in monosyllables,
> and to form on a black board from dictation capital and small letters, but also to
> form and name at sight figures up to twenty, and to add and subtract figures up
> to ten, orally. To take a baby of three years of age, and bid her play the part of a
> BIDDER, or to expect every specimen of mortality to display at such a babe-age
> the proficiency of a BABBAGE, appears to us unreasonable in the highest degree.

This little paragraph, so closely linked with Gilbert's cartoon, may also be by
Gilbert. Certainly Gilbert, employed by the Education Office, would have had
special knowledge of the subject. If we wonder why he should have chosen to
sign this particular drawing 'Bab', when all his other artwork from this period is
signed with his initials or not signed at all, two thoughts may occur to us. The
first is that he probably did not want his authorship of the cartoon to leak back
to his employers. The second is that, seeking a pseudonym, he seems to have been
struck by the pun on Babbage quoted above, his train of thought then leading
him to Bab, which had been his pet name as a baby.[6]

Fun returned to the subject of the Revised Education Code on 15 March
1862, in an article headed: 'The Education Office, Again' (which suggests it was a
direct sequel to 'Lisping in Numbers'). This too may be by Gilbert – the unsigned
'initial' suggests his style – and it is a fighting and somewhat sarcastic attack on
Robert Lowe, the politician in charge of the Education Office and the author of
the Revised Code:

> The Revised Code will assuredly prove the death of MR. LOWE, and MR. LOWE's
> evasions, excuses and explanations, would assuredly prove the death of us, if
> laughter could send us to our grave … [Lowe told Parliament:] 'We correspond
> with some 6,000 or 7,000 schools, *and it is impossible for me or for any other person
> to be responsible for every letter.*'
>
>   We have not the good fortune to occupy an arm-chair in a Government
> office … but we venture humbly to suggest that letters despatched from a

Government office are, as a rule, adorned with a signature of some kind, and experience has taught us that the person who signs a letter is usually held responsible for its contents …

Now, who is the audacious Education-office subordinate who has dared, on his own responsibility, to dictate to managers of schools terms which MR. LOWE publicly declares to be at variance with the principles and practice of the office? If we were in Parliament (which we are never likely to be), we would insist upon having the name of that subordinate, and we would move to have his official stool drawn from under him, and his official pen plucked from behind his ear, and we would have him drummed out of the service … One thing is very clear; although MR. LOWE may be the head of his own department, he is certainly not captain of his own ship.

It may be wondered whether Gilbert (if he was, as I believe, the author of this diatribe) wrote it on Education Office paper.

The 'Revised Code' was the department's main business at this time, and the clerks were largely employed in corresponding with the schools and the inspectors. A later article from *Fun*, entitled 'The Education Office Again and Again' (30 April 1864), was probably written by the same hand that wrote 'The Education Office, Again' and gives a bitter account of life in that department:

The Education Office is governed, nominally, by MR. LOWE, under LORD GRANVILLE; in point of fact, by some fifty or sixty underpaid clerks … Each clerk in the Education Office writes any letters he thinks fit to anybody whom he chooses to address on official business. No clerk is too junior or too inexperienced to be entrusted with the wigging of inspectors or the distribution of the public grant under an original Revised Code of his own designing. In short, the Education Office is, in this respect at least, a clerk's Paradise.

A cartoon appeared in *Fun* for 9 August 1862, signed by Gilbert and headed: 'Merchant's Clerks. – Hours, 9 a.m. to 9 p.m.' It shows two clerks in an office, one of them looking out through the window at some marching militiamen:

First Merchant's Clerk:– 'HULLO! WHAT CORPS IS THAT?'
Second ditto:– 'OH! CIVIL SERVICE.'
First ditto:– 'INDEED! MARCH WELL, DON'T THEY?'
Second ditto:– 'MARCH WELL? OF COURSE THEY MARCH WELL. WHY, THEY'VE NOTHING ELSE TO DO!'

Underworked and underpaid (his salary had increased since 1857, and by June 1862 he was being paid the heady sum of £31 5s quarterly),[7] Gilbert was in search of pastures new. On Friday 14 November 1862, he resigned from the

Education Office.[8] He had received some money as a gift, variously described as £300 and £400. It seems likely that it was an early birthday present from his great-aunt Mary Schwenck, now a rich widow. So, as he later wrote, 'I resolved to emancipate myself from the detestable thraldom of this baleful office; and on the happiest day of my life I sent in my resignation'.[9]

He decided to complete his law studies and become a barrister. He had registered at Inner Temple seven years previously, and had afterwards kept the necessary twelve terms. Peculiarly, there was no compulsory Bar examination at this time, though there was an optional examination which could be taken as an alternative to attending lectures at the Inns of Court.[10] Gilbert chose to attend lectures, if we may trust his humorous article 'Our Own Correspondent Called to the Bar' (*Fun*, 3 December 1864):

> [Your Own Correspondent] attended certain lectures of three-quarters of an hour's duration, and he did much copy in the course of his attendance. Many of the most soul-stirring articles in this publication were committed to writing in the course of a lecture on equity or on real property … [After a year of this,] your correspondent received a diploma, which addressed him in flattering terms, and informed him that he was Learned in the Law, which was a piece of information for which your correspondent was altogether unprepared.

In addition, Gilbert paid £100 to become a pupil of the barrister Charles James Watkin Williams for the term of one year.[11] In the first half of 1863 we find Gilbert providing *Fun* with a small handful of cartoons describing the behaviour of barristers in court. Serjeant Buz-Fuz makes 'an impassioned appeal on behalf of the unfortunate man at the bar' (a vicious-looking thug), unaware that his dramatic attitude casts a shadow suggesting that he is thumbing his nose at the court (28 February 1863). A rakish-looking barrister smiles quietly and murmurs to an unseen witness: 'You were sober, of course?' (16 May 1863). A third man of law addresses the court with unassailable rhetoric: 'And you are asked to convict on such evidence as this!' (23 May 1863). One can almost see young Gilbert as he sits long-legged behind Williams in court, sketching the absurdities he finds all around him.

At about this time Henry Sutherland Edwards, who was a cousin of Gilbert on his mother's side, handed over to Gilbert a regular job as London correspondent to a Russian newspaper, the *Invalide Russe*, which, Clement Scott confessed, 'caused rather envy or awe to many of us in those days'.[12]

By now, the *Fun* gang was taking shape. Burnand left them at the beginning of 1863 to join *Punch*; but the team took on many others, including Tom Hood (a young man from the War Office and son of the poet Thomas Hood), Clement Scott (another young War Office man), Tom Robertson (a struggling playwright), the artists William Brunton and Matt Morgan, and the poets and journalists

William Jeffrey Prowse, Arthur Sketchley and Henry S. Leigh. The paper contained topical jokes and sometimes biting satire, light verse, whimsical series such as 'Letters from a Young Married Lady' and 'The Comic Encyclopaedia', political cartoons and cartoons depicting the lives of Londoners in their hometown, in the country and at the seaside. (*Fun* was sold nationally, but like so many of its fellows, it was essentially a paper for London people.) Though based on *Punch* it developed a distinctive style of its own, less genteel and more forthright.

It reflected the changing face of London, which was in literal upheaval. The Metropolitan railway, the first underground railway in the world, was being hewn through the middle of London between 1859 and 1863, and a hygienic sewer system for London was being begun on the banks of the Thames in the same years – hence the temporary boardwalks and hoardings that characterised the city at that period.

Then there were the silent intellectual upheavals. There was a new sense of cynicism after the fiasco of the Crimean War, in which the government had proved itself so inadequate, and the publication of Darwin's *The Origin of Species* in 1859 started a deep though long-fused reaction in people's minds. There was an appetite for the startling and the disturbing which the new genre of 'sensation fiction' existed to satisfy. Novels such as *The Woman in White* by Wilkie Collins (1860), *East Lynne* by Mrs Henry Wood (1861) and *Lady Audley's Secret* by Mary Elizabeth Braddon (1862), with their stories of murder, madness and marital transgression in respectable English households, gave the Victorian public a message which they desperately wanted to hear. In the theatre the sensation effects (fires, earthquakes, cataclysms) became more spectacular and the comedy became broader. The actor E.A. (Ned) Sothern's wild caricature of the upper classes, Lord Dundreary, was the must-see sensation of the early 1860s. Rhymed burlesque, an established genre in Victorian theatre, reached new heights of popularity with the songs made slangier, the dances wilder and the puns faster and more outrageous. All this provides an essential background to the events of the 1860s.

Fun was, for its contributors, not simply a paper or an employer; it was also a social group, a part of the theatrical and journalistic Bohemian sub-world of 1860s London. They foregathered at the Arundel or the Savage Club, went to Tom Hood's convivial 'Friday nights' at his place in Brompton and most particularly convened at Evans's supper rooms in Covent Garden.

Evans's was a café and music hall, presided over at this time by an old Adelphi actor called 'Paddy' Green. In the café section, 'reserved for conversational parties', the *Fun* staff for several years had a regular table, just as the *Punch* people did. Here they ate devilled kidneys and potatoes in their jackets, drank whatever they pleased and caroused. A raised stage stood along the far wall where acrobats tumbled, a Herr Von Joel imitated birds, men sang comic songs, a choir of men and boys sang glees and madrigals and old English ballads. Here is a reminder, if one is needed, that the Gilbert and Sullivan operas draw strength from an old English tradition of ballads and madrigals which, in Gilbert's youth, still thrived in music halls and taverns.

Tom Hood's 'Friday nights' were more intimate affairs: the men would meet at Hood's home, enjoy a cold supper created by Mrs Hood, and afterwards discuss literature, tell stories and discuss projects through the night, finally wandering home as the new day dawned. They covered for each other in their various journalistic jobs, as Clement Scott explained: 'When Tom Robertson could not do his "Theatrical Lounger," in the dear old *Illustrated Times*, he handed it over to Gilbert; when Gilbert was too busy he passed it on to me; when I wanted a holiday, the *Sunday Times*, with all its attendant difficulties, was the perquisite of Gilbert.'[13] So they helped each other out in time of need. On another occasion Hood started a weekly paper called *Saturday Night*, and Gilbert, Burnand, Tom Archer, Tom Robertson, George Rose, Jeff Prowse and others contributed; but after a few issues it sank without trace.

'It was ever a great treat to hear Gilbert, H.J. Byron, Tom Robertson and Frank Burnand converse at the same dinner table,' Scott wrote:

> They were all brilliant talkers, all pronounced humourists, all as quick a lightning with quip, crank, or repartee; but the humour of each was of an absolutely distinct pattern. Gilbert was as sharp as a needle, but incisive, and got his teeth into the joke with a sudden snap. Byron twisted his moustache, and drawled out his puns and retorts … But what a contrast … was the sparkling style of Frank Burnand! He was as quick, if not quicker, than any of them. The jokes seemed to bubble up into his merry eyes.[14]

These were perhaps the closest friends that young Gilbert had ever known.

The actor John Coleman, who knew Tom Robertson, gives a rather unsympathetic account of the Arundel Club set, where Robertson was regarded as something of a leader:

> he led a new crusade against English art and English actors, more particularly poetic actors. His superior knowledge enabled him to detect blots, and to point out holes in the armour of the giants. His youthful colleagues followed suit, and amongst them they ran amuck at everything and everybody in their way … They modestly maintained that Shakespere was an antediluvian bore … The self-constituted mission of these airy youths was to deride, to ridicule, and to hold up to contempt everything noble and manly – everything which generations of educated men and women had been taught to esteem and admire.[15]

In short, they criticised what many held to be beyond criticism. Gilbert, for one, would retain this attitude to the end of his life.

On 31 October 1863, a little play called *Uncle Baby* was performed at the Lyceum, as a curtain-raiser to *Bel Demonio* by John Brougham. *Uncle Baby* was not a success and soon disappeared. The author was given as 'W. Gilbert', and part of the manuscript in the Lord Chamberlain's collection is in W.S. Gilbert's hand; Terence Rees has ascribed it to W.S. Gilbert, though others have suggested it to be the work of his father. The combination of anti-alcohol propaganda typical of William Gilbert and pithy dialogue certainly not typical of him, suggests a father-son collaboration, but its authorship remains a minor mystery. At any rate Gilbert never referred to the play in later years.

In the meantime, Gilbert's studies proceeded. He was finally 'called to the Bar' on 17 November 1863, the day before his twenty-seventh birthday, taking barrister's chambers at 11 Clement's Inn, Strand. It was not to prove a lucrative career move: in the next two years he was to earn only £75 from his bar work. A short story which he wrote about this time, entitled 'My Maiden Brief' and published anonymously in *Cornhill Magazine* in December 1863, gives a cheerful picture of the lifestyle of briefless young barristers, though it cannot always have been so cheery to live without an income.

Gilbert's contributions to *Fun* become much more frequently visible at this time. Several little articles under the heading 'Gossip of the Week' can be found, starting in the issue dated 24 October 1863, each with a closely related W.S.G. drawing. But the appearance in the 7 November 1863 issue of a new and ambitious series, under the heading of 'The Comic Physiognomist', signals the start of a new phase in Gilbert's career. The rate of pay was £1 for a column of text, with a separate payment for art work.[16] The profusely illustrated articles which Gilbert now started to produce week after week surely indicate a bargain struck between Gilbert and Byron in order to bring the newly called barrister some much needed extra money. The first article's opening paragraph (7 November 1863) hints at something of the sort: 'we decline to volunteer any statement of the motives that have induced us to turn all our subscribers into talented analytical physiognomists. It sufficeth to say that *we have our reasons*.'

The first few 'Comic Physiognomist' columns are fairly conventional examples of the humour of the day. They discuss, in succession, the various parts of the face and their characteristics – the forehead and eyes, the nose, the cheeks, the mouth and chin, and the whiskers and beard – all in a standard pseudo-pedagogical style replete with puns. The column in the issue for 19 December 1863, however, signals a change. Headed 'A Christmas Digression', the 'initial' features a Gilbert self-portrait (looking at us startled as a hand knocks at his door) and the text ditches the jocular style for a sarcastic outburst unmistakeably in Gilbert's own personal voice:

> Oh, the joys of merry, merry Christmas! Christmas, when all is happiness and mirth and unmitigated jollity! Christmas, when everybody makes up old differences with everybody else! Christmas, when all mankind kisses all

womankind under suspended vegetables! Christmas, when all the world give each other spontaneous and unregretted presents …

NOTE, ADDRESSED TO THE EDITOR OF 'FUN' BY HIS COMIC PHYSIOGNOMIST.– The C.P. has endeavoured to do the genial, jolly, open-hearted thing by Christmas, after the manner of the other illustrated papers, but on re-reading his M.S., he cannot close his eyes to the fact that what he has written does not seem to him to be altogether a success. It does not seem to come from the heart. Perhaps if the Editor would kindly contrive to embellish his C.P.'s article with a robin redbreast in oily colours that come off on the hands, or a 'Chryesttmasse in ye oldenne tyme,' it would have the effect of making his sentiments appear more genuine. The C.P. puts it to his Editor, whether he can be reasonably expected to go mad with joy (to order) at the approach of Christmas, when every knock at his chamber door brings his heart (so to speak) into his mouth?

A week later he returned to the theme, writing of 'the preposterous frivolities of a season sarcastically called festive' and sketching the six people, including a boot-maker and a washerwoman who stood crowding outside the C.P.'s chamber in the vain hope of him settling his bills. Through his work at this time a picture emerges of Gilbert in cheap lodgings, living from hand to mouth and in fear of dunning tradesmen.

There is also the occasional whiff of late nights and drunken revels. In one W.S.G. cartoon (16 January 1864) two men, very much the worse for drink, stagger through the night in the vicinity of the Palace of Westminster. In the background we can see the clock tower of Westminster, with two illuminated clock faces, alongside a full moon. One of the men, who looks like Gilbert, turns to the other and complains that he can see six moons.

The C.P. turns his attention to barristers, to clergymen, to the audience at a pantomime, to actors, to the army. The columns are patchy in quality, Gilbert's attractive thumbnail illustrations sitting alongside some not very inspired descriptions of character types; but they remain interesting because of their autobiographical elements and because of the sometimes outrageous comedy he gets from the character of the C.P. himself – a false-modest egomaniac who assures his readers, for instance, that he is 'a gentleman of a singularly modest and retiring disposition; indeed it has been said that in his moral characteristics he strongly resembles the violet'.[17] He portrays himself as a philosopher graced with a 'gushing love for the millions who have worshipped at his poor feet',[18] living a Sybaritic life appropriate to his high estate:

… as the Comic Physiognomist was quietly supping a cup of frothed chocolate on the luxurious couch upon which he usually passes the night … ALPHONZO, his favourite valet, entered the room and communicated to the C.P. the startling piece of news that several hundred gentlemen and ladies were in attendance below … So the Great Observer, who is as urbane as he is beautiful, leaped out of bed, and in a quarter of an hour had performed a simple but tasty toilet – such a one as befitted a man of his philosophic tastes.[19]

In the last column of the first series (5 March 1864) the urbanity turns vicious:

> The C.P. has often in the course of his novel-reading experiences, been much moved at the author's confession, at the end of the third volume, of his unfeigned regret at parting for a while from his beloved public … But the C.P. (who, with all his faults, is not a humbug) is free to confess that, as far as regards himself, no such feeling of regret exists. To tell the truth, he has a very poor opinion of the public as a mass. They are but a flock of sheep who go whither they are driven, who applaud that which they are told to applaud, and who hiss that which they are advised to hiss … The public are the people who go to executions in jewellery, who buy HOLLOWAY's pills, who send stamps to fortune-tellers, who are always being run over, assaulted, insulted, overcharged, and generally taken in and done for. The C.P., in short, has the supremest contempt for the British public, and as he is a man who is safely shrouded under an impenetrable *incognito* he doesn't hesitate to tell them so. It is true that they buy their FUN eagerly, but they wouldn't do so unless people, who perhaps know no better than they themselves do, hadn't told them it was a good penn'orth; and above all, if the proprietors didn't advertise largely. The public do things because they are told to do them, and the C.P. tells them to go home and go to bed, and be ashamed of themselves, and he hasn't the slightest doubt but that they will do it.

Gilbert discovered, in the process of writing these columns, that they gave him an opportunity to flex his writing muscles, which had until now been cramped in short single articles where there had been no space for him to do anything except commit a few conventional gags and take his leave. Gilbert created, in the Comic Physiognomist, an alter ego who could voice opinions that could not be expressed in normal society. Some of these techniques would inform his later work. The matter-of-fact conceitedness, for instance, returns in the character of Archibald Grosvenor in *Patience* ('Yes, Patience, I am very beautiful!'), while the telling of rude truths is integral to Gilbert's 'Palace of Truth' style. The C.P.'s assumption that the world revolves around him reprises the joke in his early poem about Napoleon and Eugénie. Part of the humour derives from the shock of saying that which should not be said (a kind of humour which persists very strongly today, in other forms), and it is almost of secondary importance whether what is said is true. The C.P.'s attitudes suggest in Gilbert an awareness of his own appearance and attitudes that hovers between conceit and a repudiation of that conceit.

By now Gilbert was a very visible presence in *Fun*, week upon week, not only with his Comic Physiognomist columns but also with other illustrated articles: an account of the opening of Parliament; lampoons of Royal Academy pictures; illustrations for an anti-Napoleon satire called 'The Lie of a Lifetime' which had been written by another hand;[20] illustrations and apparently also the words of 'The Baron Klopfzetterheim' in five instalments; several other illustrated poems; two articles 'On Pantomimic Unities'; a couple of personal attacks on Gilbert's fellow barristers and a judge; the occasional stand-alone cartoon; a full-page cartoon strip of 'Our Own Correspondent at the Guildford Fight', and so on. One poem, 'Mr. Morell and the Privy Council Office', which is probably by Gilbert, consists of a rather clumsy attack on Ralph Lingen, who as secretary of the Education Department had been the civil servant in charge throughout Gilbert's time there. The poem's 'initial' is signed 'W.S.G.' and contains a caricature of Lingen with ass's ears. Scarcely a week passed without some identifiable contribution by 'W.S.G.' – and on occasion he could be found drawing the majority of the artwork in an issue (2 April 1864, for instance). The likelihood is that he was also contributing other items which cannot now be identified as his.

The Comic Physiognomist returned in May and continued sporadically until October, but Gilbert was clearly beginning to find the persona too restrictive and wrote more and more as 'Our Own Correspondent' (liberally illustrated by W.S.G.), a persona that gave him greater flexibility of subject and style. The C.P. and Our Own Correspondent tell us much about what Gilbert was doing and seeing, where he went and how he reacted.

So we follow the C.P. on a steamboat from London to Gravesend as he conducts a mild flirtation in glances with an 'exquisite fairy' (4 June 1864). He goes to Epsom for the Derby, where he knocks down 'an insolent livery-stable groom' and encounters a 'swell-mobsman' con artist (9 July 1864/23 July 1864). He visits 'those abominations of desolation, the London Music-halls' and spends his time despising the clientele and the performers (16 July 1864). He admits that he 'abhors the very sight of a man-servant, for he is afraid of him, and whatever the C.P. is afraid of he hates', and after describing the kinds of servants that he most fears he concludes with a humorous but sincere-seeming hymn of praise to his clerk and his laundress: 'clerk, because you write nothing; laundress, because you wash nothing.' The C.P. 'prefers the humble and unromantic squalor of economical Temple chambers to the gilded glitter of marble halls with vassals and slaves by his side' (6 August 1864). In such moments Gilbert takes off the fantastical disguise of the C.P. and speaks more or less in his own voice.

Between 13 August and 1 October, Gilbert contributed seven columns entitled 'Our Own Correspondent Out for a Holiday', which seem to be based fairly closely on his own experiences over the summer. Travelling by train from London to Folkestone, Our Own Correspondent sits opposite a 'lovely being' called Gazella, who is travelling to Switzerland with her father. They strike up a conversation, and Our Own Correspondent accompanies Gazella and her father as they journey by steamer to Boulogne, resolving to follow them all the way to Lake Geneva.

Firstly, however, they spend some time in Gilbert's beloved Boulogne. He draws a caricature of the Boulogne customs man; he contrasts the town's fish-women as portrayed in watercolour sketches with their appearance in real life; he ridicules the behaviour of the British tourist abroad. At the start of the second column in the series (20 August 1864) he describes the experience of sea-bathing in what is for Gilbert surprisingly sensual terms:

> go into eighteen inches of water, lie on your back, and let the wavelets break their little necks on your smooth, glistening body. To lie so ... to feel that frothi-ness running all over you, under your arms, between your legs, behind your ears, rolling you over and over to shore, and then carrying you out again with that graceful curtsey that precedes a second attack ... is to have lived for something.

By the third column (27 August 1864) Our Own Correspondent has relaxed into the holiday mood to an offensive extent:

> Fun, my boy, what a delightful difference there is in our respective situations. You are working away in that hot, uncomfortable portmanteau of a place which you are pleased to dignify by conferring upon it the style and title of editor's room. You are arranging a heap of badly written slips; you are swearing at the calligraphy of your correspondents, and you vow that a butcher's bill is copper-plate to it. You are perspiring freely; you are dusty; you are using much bad language; your boots pinch you, and your collar rucks up behind. For this is August, and in a London August boots always pinch, and collars always ruck up behind. I, on the other hand, am writing amusing copy at a window which commands the greater part of the Lake of Geneva, together with the Jura range. Cool breezes fan my heated brow. They come from the mountains behind Gingulph, and they breathe of vines ... What do you think of that?

He tells us of his adventures on the journey from Boulogne into Switzerland (still in pursuit of the delightful Gazella), with all the usual problems of dealing with baggage, and also gives his readers some accurate sounding but devious advice about how to cheat your way into a first-class sleeping carriage.

The next column (3 September 1864), entitled 'Mountains and Alpenstocks', sees Our Own Correspondent in excellent form, both as a writer and as an illustrator. He description of how to practise for the experience of descending a mountain – 'The intending tourist selects a tall house, and places a vindictive creditor on each landing. He scatters small tables, large chairs, expensive crock-ery, and large pieces of glass chandelier on various portions of the flight, and he smears all critical turnings with guava jelly' – shows the beginnings of Gilbert's gift for extraordinary flights of fancy, while the illustration of Gazella descending a mountain with the aid of an alpenstock is drawn with obvious affection.

He has a close encounter with a riot in Geneva (17 September 1864), and crosses a glacier at Chamonix with the doubtful assistance of a guide (24 September 1864), informing us wisely that 'getting over a *moraine* is very like climbing up the side of a house in a pair of imperfectly adjusted skates'.

The last column of the series, entitled 'Coming Home' (1 October 1864), brings Our Own Correspondent from Chamounix to Martigny on 'a maniac mule'; from Geneva to Paris by overnight train, during which he spends the entire night in pleasant conversation with Gazella, chaperoned only by her sleeping father; from Boulogne to Folkestone on a rough sea that leaves Our Own Correspondent desperately pretending good health in Gazella's presence; and finally to the station at Charing Cross, where to his great heartbreak he finds Gazella met by a martial young gentleman. So the romance ends with Our Own Correspondent stabbing himself in grief. There is enough observation amongst the fantasy to make us feel we have eavesdropped on a genuine holiday flirtation.

Our Own Correspondent reappeared in the columns of *Fun* during the closing months of the year, and among other things attended a *bal masqué* where he encountered 'human idiocy in its most aggravating form' and, returning home in a state of depression, 'cried himself to sleep' (29 October 1864); went to a *séance* conducted by the Davenport brothers and remained profoundly unimpressed (26 November 1864); visited a pantomime rehearsal (10 December 1864); and saw a not very good performance of *Orphée aux Enfers* at the Oxford music hall (24 December 1864). 'Our Own Correspondent Out of Sorts' (17 December 1864), suffering from delirium after eating too much pork, was haunted with disturbing apparitions such as an 'amiable and uncomplaining' being with a hat too small for him, who 'confines his remarks to exclaiming "BELINDA! BELINDA!"' which, notwithstanding that Y.O.C. always sympathizes with an honourable attachment, becomes monotonous'. The crude and hallucinated drawings accompanying this column suggest that Gilbert was probably indeed in the grip of some feverish illness.

Despite his increasing success as a comic journalist, Gilbert was clearly in a state of discontent with both himself and other people; his visit to the *bal masqué*, for instance, left him trying to argue himself into believing he was not of the same species as the 'drivelling revellers', but something more amiable, such as 'a pig or a dog'. At about the same time, he was busy illustrating a little pamphlet called *An Algerian Monkey versus British Apes: A Satirical, Political, Poetical Squib* which was published by Chapman & Hall in December 1864. This rather heavy-handed satire was written by 'The Spectre', and Gilbert's name as illustrator was given as W. Schwenck Gilbert. The drawings were by far the best thing about the pamphlet, which was an over-extended comparison between a monkey and corrupt British society. As *The London Review* noted: 'The comparison is foolish *per se*, and proves nothing' (10 December 1864). But The Spectre's theme matched Gilbert's depressed state of mind.

4

THE ROAD TO RECOGNITION
(1865–66)

There was a mood of change in the offices of *Fun* in the first months of 1865. In May, the paper was taken over by a new proprietor and a new editor. But even in January, something seemed to be afoot; the Comic Physiognomist and Our Own Correspondent had disappeared, and W.S.G. contributed no signed drawings to the paper after a cartoon on 28 January (though an unsigned 'initial' on 1 April may be by him). He may have written small items for *Fun* between January and May, but only two or three can even be guessed at without the aid of his distinctive drawings. Was there some dispute between Gilbert and the editor? We do not know, but it is not unlikely. The clearest indication of a dispute lies in the fact that Gilbert was considering the possibility of defecting to *Fun*'s great rival, *Punch*.

Four items by Gilbert appear in *Punch* for 22 April 1865:[1] three small topical jokes and one longer article called 'Ballad Minstrelsy'. After a one-liner in the issue for 29 April, he returned on 17 June with a substantial illustrated article entitled: 'The Royal Academy Exhibition (By a Critic Who Couldn't Get In).' The significance of this article (which is not very funny in itself) lies in the fact that it includes six stylish illustrations, five of them signed 'Bab'. This was only the second time Gilbert had used the pseudonym in his published work. After having previously used it to sign a cartoon criticising the policy of his employers at the Education Office, he resurrected it now, seemingly because he wished to conceal his work for *Punch* from his colleagues on *Fun*.

Edward Wylam took over the ownership of *Fun* in May 1865, Tom Hood becoming the new editor, and Hood insisted as a condition of his accepting the post that the great Victorian engravers the Dalziel brothers should take over the engraving of all the drawings.[2] (This suggests another possible source of discontent under the old regime.) Hood was to remain editor through the paper's best years, until his early death in 1874, and was to prove a valuable supporter of Gilbert's work. But perhaps the most significant aspect of the change of regime from our point of view is the fact that from the second issue in the 'New Series' of *Fun* there exists an almost complete 'Proprietor's Copy' with markings to indicate who wrote what.[3] It is therefore possible to state Gilbert's contributions with certainty from this point on. This fact is especially useful because during the first twelve months of the new series of *Fun*, Gilbert did not illustrate any of his contributions at all.

He was providing a wide variety of material for the paper: among other things, short pieces ridiculing the prose style of newspaper adverts, scathing attacks on the latest legal abuses, theatrical reviews, excruciating riddles (in the guise of letters signed 'A Trembling Widow'), theatrical parodies and a series of 'Out-of-Town Talk' signed 'Snarler'. In view of his later career, it is interesting to note a couple of items which attempt to place the normal situations of Victorian life in an 'operatic' setting: 'The Derby Day Operatized' (3 June 1865) and 'Piccadilly: An Opera' (1 July 1865). The actual content, however, is rather disappointing:

> *Chorus of deserted wives to remorseless husbands.*
> AIR. – 'Doodah, doodah, da.'
> London ladies sing dis song – Darby! Darby!
> Darby race-course very long – Darby, Darby Day!
> Darby, Darby Day,
> Oh, take us with you, pray,
> HUSBANDS (expostulating):   No; owing to the scrummage
> It's not considered *frummage*
> For a lady on a Darby Day!

His 'Out-of-Town Talk' columns, running from 29 July through to 28 October, are similar in content to the previous year's 'Our Own Correspondent Out on a Holiday': touristy and slightly jaundiced accounts of his travels through the 'out of season' months. He begins with a diatribe (29 July 1865):

> An editor can be dear to no one ... As a man, I respect you – as an editor, you are the mark for my foulest scorn. It is you who garble my 'copy'; it is you who reject (now and then) my manuscripts; it is you who take upon yourself to tell me that this is too personal, and that that is not personal enough; it is you who tell me that such and such a publication must not be scarified because BROWN is on it, and BROWN is a good fellow; it is you who tell me that I must not hold up to scorn that article of SMITH's, because (forsooth) SMITH and you Saunter in Society together. What is BROWN to me, and in what respect can the goings on of SMITH and *you* be supposed to affect me? Bah!

He continues with the information that he is 'on the French coast at – Biarritz, Brest, Boulogne – anywhere' – Gilbert's impenetrable disguise for his beloved

Boulogne. By the time of the third column (12 August 1865) 'Snarler' has begun to justify his name in earnest. He suddenly chooses to rage against 'those drunken blackguards whom railway authorities term excursionists, dressed in nothing at all worth mentioning, and all of them with a bottle of two-franc brandy inside their fat and filthy bodies,' and adds, 'The drunken ruffians were all killed, no doubt, by some excursion accident or other before they reached home, but why, *why*, WHY, do not these things happen to them on their way *to* a respectable watering place, and not, invariably, on their way back *from* it?'

These savage tendencies return the following week, while describing (of all things) the street paving:

> It is rare to find any smooth flagging on the *trottoir*, and the greater part of it is laid down with big irregular stones of a generally spherical shape, and about as big as your head ... many of them are much worn, and so take the semblance of the friends and enemies it has left at home. I have found W.J.P. and T.W.R. [*Fun* colleagues W.J. Prowse and T.W. Robertson], and my tailor (on whom I stamp whensoever I pass in his direction). I have not been able to find you, Editor, yet, but I am looking for you, and may yet succeed in finding you. If I do I shall let out upon you all that bile which prudential considerations induce me to keep to myself in London. I will kick you (in effigy), and stamp upon you, and spit upon you, and otherwise maltreat you when I find you. I am obliged to be so disgustingly civil to you when I have to do with you in Fleet-street, and I have come here for a little change. [19 August 1865]

This was clearly intended by Gilbert, and received by Hood, as banter between friends. At the same time there is an obvious sense of aggression seeking an outlet. The writings of Snarler, like the writings of his predecessor Our Own Correspondent, are not those of a contented man.

As a barrister Gilbert was not a success. He later admitted that 'I was always a clumsy and inefficient speaker, and, moreover, an unconquerable nervousness prevented me from doing justice to myself or my half-dozen unfortunate clients'.[4] As a journalist on the staff of *Fun* he was achieving greater success, but, since his contributions were anonymous, it was not the kind of success that brings fame nor, at the rate of a pound a column, the kind that brings wealth.

What is more, while certain of his contemporaries (H.J. Byron and F.C. Burnand spring to mind) had gained solid success as burlesque writers in their early twenties, he had not yet achieved his first big break into the theatre (though he may have contributed anonymously to the occasional pantomime at about this time). A letter dated 5 February 1865 finds him writing to Ben Webster of the Adelphi Theatre about his unproduced farce *A Colossal Idea*: 'I shall feel obliged if you will leave it at the stage door – as I have every prospect of getting it played at another metropolitan theatre.'[5] The air of self-confidence was artificial;

no other theatre showed any interest in the play, and it remained unproduced in Gilbert's lifetime.

Little wonder, then, that his writings should demonstrate a tendency to lash out. He was discontented with everything, not least himself. Thus on the 26 August issue he addresses his editor again:

> I well remember how kindly you said to me before I started: 'Go, my boy, to somewhere, some distance off, that you may not be tempted to run up to the office every other day, and let us know how you get on; and mind, *mind*, that the longer you stop away the better we shall be pleased.' I remember how affectionately W.J.P. and T.W.R. and others congratulated me on being sent on an out-of-town mission, and how unanimously they expressed their pleasure at the idea of my enjoying myself all alone for a very long while in a foreign clime, and how they all hoped that many months would elapse before I returned to the slavish monotony of your muddy metropolis.

A month later (23 September) Snarler starts off on his journeys again, this time to Antwerp, Brussels and Spa. An anecdote related in the 7 October issue is illuminating:

> Now these porters [at Continental railway stations] should not be tipped, [but] the universality of the practice has caused them to demand the *pour boire*, and when they don't get it they swear openly at you. On one occasion (it was in Paris), a fellow actually seized me by the collar and refused to let me go until I had given him some sous. The departure bell was ringing at the time, and I struck him such a mighty blow beneath the chin that I heard his teeth dance about in his mouth like peas in a drum. So far my conduct was BAYARD-like, but I am bound to admit that my subsequent behaviour was cowardly, for in a mortal fright I bolted into the train and was whirled off to Geneva by an express which wouldn't hear of stopping until it reached the Swiss frontier, where I felt myself comparatively safe. I believe that, in France, to expostulate with a fraudulent railway clerk is galleys for life, and to strike a porter is murder without extenuating circumstances.

Throughout his life, from schooldays to old age, Gilbert was always eager to solve disputes with his fists. More interesting, perhaps, is the fact that he should have been in such fear for the consequences – and also that he should have the honesty to tell us so. Indeed, one of the characteristics of Snarler's columns is his determination to tell the brutal truth about himself and his attitudes – the more brutally the better.

It is difficult to know what reliance, if any, should be put upon the opinions in these columns. Writers, especially humorous writers, have an unfortunate habit of writing things that they do not completely believe; they exaggerate, they make-believe, they assume an attitude like a garment. But many of these early columns in *Fun* contain passages which tell us something of Gilbert's concerns, the attitudes that interested him and the opinions he wished to voice in order to scandalise his readers. These include the expression of absolute selfishness of attitude and conduct in clear reaction against conventional Victorian morality, and a suggestion, possibly borrowed from a work such as Bernard Mandeville's *Fable of the Bees*, that such selfishness is the basis of all human behaviour. Gilbert would be concerned with these ideas throughout his life: people's social pretensions as opposed to their real desires; the fantasies promoted in plays and stories as opposed to the reality of how life works.

Thus in *Fun* for 11 November 1865 Gilbert contributed an outrageous parody of melodrama under the title 'Vice Triumphant', with a prefatory note stating: 'Sensation dramas should mirror Society as it is, not as it ought to be.' The melodrama itself, which looks forward to *H.M.S. Pinafore* and *Ruddigore*, ends with the evil Sir Rockheart the Revengeful killing all his enemies and, according to the stage direction, 'after a long and happy life, [dying] at a good old age, surrounded by hosts of faithful and attached dependants'.

It is unfortunate that because Gilbert deliberately, and for satirical effect, shows us some of the worst aspects of his character, the result is that we are left to discover the better aspects for ourselves. As *Fun* assured 'A Fluttering Querist' in its 'Answers to Correspondents' column in the 4 November 1865 issue, 'There is not the slightest foundation for your belief that our esteemed correspondent "Snarler" is deeply attached to MISS ANN THROPY'.

Meanwhile, in May 1865 Gilbert's rich great-aunt Mary Schwenck died, and in July her will was proved, leaving him a legacy of £500, two houses in the Edgware Road and some shares. This did not, of course, make him a rich man, but it would have made his life immeasurably easier by erasing any outstanding debts and making possible a generosity of outlook that was previously beyond him.

In June he took up an appointment as lieutenant in the Royal Aberdeenshire Highlanders (he rose to the rank of captain in 1868), which involved as its most onerous duty an annual outbreak of militia training.

He was also engaged in illustrating his father's book, *The Magic Mirror*, described as 'A Round of Tales for Young and Old'. This series of linked folk-like tales relating to a mirror that grants wishes is probably William Gilbert's most attractive work. Gilbert contributed eighty-four small woodblock illustrations. The book was published at the end of the year, with *Fun* commenting: 'The cuts are very grotesque and full of character, the demons in particular being so original that we hope the artist, with an eye to appropriative property men, has patented them.'[6]

The fortunes of one of the *Fun* gang, Tom Robertson, underwent a fortunate reversal at this time. He had been living in genteel poverty for some years, trying to scratch a living first by writing and acting for the theatre and then by journalism, without any great success; but his new play *Society* was taken up by the Bancrofts at the Prince of Wales Theatre in November 1865, after a successful try-out in Liverpool that summer. Squire Bancroft and his wife Marie Bancroft (Miss Marie Wilton) had created the Prince of Wales Theatre out of the squalor of the old Queen's Theatre earlier that same year, and since then had been surviving on programmes based around burlesques by H.J. Byron. Robertson's play was a notable success, set largely in London's journalistic and theatrical bohemia, and written in a colloquial style that came as a breath of fresh air after the bombast and staginess of much of the drama of that age. Robertson's career seemed at last to be taking an upward turn; in this play and its successors at the Prince of Wales, which he directed himself, he gained a reputation as a theatre reformer, with his gift for easy, natural-seeming dialogue and his appreciation of what we would now call subtext – the idea that apparently trivial conversations can hide deep emotions. It is typical of the fates that this triumph should have taken place immediately after the death of his wife.

Tom Hood's Friday night gatherings continued, and the *Fun* stalwarts who attended there decided to collaborate on a Christmas annual. The book they created, *A Bunch of Keys*, appeared for Christmas 1865 and consisted of a series of related short stories by Tom Robertson, Thomas Archer, Gilbert, Tom Hood, William J. Prowse and Clement Scott. It was, as Hood wrote in the book's preface, 'the growth of friendly communion, of pleasant chats of an evening, of fellowship of taste and feeling'. Gilbert's contribution, 'The Key of the Strong Room', bears little of his distinctive style apart from the occasional tart turn of phrase, but is interesting because of its processing of Gilbert's experience of life in a government office and of the feelings abroad in London at the time of the Crimean War.

His last contribution to *Punch* also appeared at this time: a 'Bab' illustration in the 16 December 1865 issue, accompanying an article by Frank Burnand. Gilbert finally severed his connection with the paper in circumstances which he later related to M.H. Spielmann:

> I was told by Mark Lemon [the editor of *Punch*], or rather a message reached me from him, that he would insert nothing more of mine unless I left 'Fun,' with which I was connected. This I declined to do unless he would take me on the regular staff of *Punch*. This *he* declined to do, and so the matter ended.[7]

Perhaps in an attempt to consolidate his position at *Fun*, Gilbert established a 'coterie of young dramatists, critics and journalists',[8] which he called 'The Serious Family' in allusion to a play by Morris Barnett which satirised puritanical religiosity. Gilbert's Serious Family consisted mostly of members of the *Fun* gang: Tom Hood, Clement Scott, George Rose ('Arthur Sketchley'), Henry S. Leigh, Paul Gray, Jeff Prowse, Tom Robertson and others. They met every Saturday from

23 December 1865 through to 19 May the following year, at Gilbert's chambers on the second floor of 3 South Square, Gray's Inn, to which he had moved earlier that year. Gilbert recalled:

> Tom Hood was the head of the family, and I was known as the 'enfant terrible.' They met weekly at my chambers at Gray's Inn, and I was absolved from the necessity of paying a two-guinea subscription in consideration of my under-taking to supply a rump-steak pie, a joint of cold boiled beef, a Stilton cheese, whisky-and-soda, and bottled ale every Saturday night for the term of my natural life. Financially speaking, it was one of the worst bargains I ever made, but I have never regretted it.[9]

Amongst Gilbert's miscellaneous contributions to *Fun* at this time may be found some of the poems that he was later to collect as *The Bab Ballads*. The earliest of these, 'Tempora Mutantur' (15 July 1865), was a fairly serious semi-romantic offering; 'To The Terrestrial Globe' (30 September 1865) suggested a mood of self-pity and depression:

> Roll on, thou ball, roll on!
> Through seas of inky air
>   Roll on!
> It's true I've got no shirts to wear;
> It's true my butcher's bill is due;
> It's true my prospects all look blue–
> But don't let that unsettle you!
>   Never *you* mind!
>   Roll on!
>
> [It rolls on.

'Ferdinando and Elvira' (17 February 1866), a whimsical little tale of the quest that Ferdinando undertakes to win the love of Elvira by discovering the man who writes the mottoes in crackers, has the distinction of being the first of Gilbert's works to achieve a real vogue. As soon as it appeared its lines were quoted:

> At a pleasant evening party I had taken down to supper
> One whom I will call ELVIRA, and we talked of love and TUPPER …
>
> There were noblemen in coronets, and military cousins,
> There were captains by the hundred, there were baronets by dozens …
>
> And I said, 'Oh, gentle pieman, why so very, very merry?
> Is it purity of conscience, or your one-and-seven sherry?'

Shortly after this he scored a second hit with 'The Yarn of the "Nancy Bell"' (3 March 1866), an *Ancient Mariner*-like tale of murder on the high seas which had been previously rejected by *Punch* on the grounds that it was 'too cannibalistic for [*Punch's*] readers' tastes'.[10] The readers of *Fun* clearly had other views, and it became popular enough to be set to music by Alfred Plumpton the same year (his brother Joseph performed it at Wilton's Music Hall in December 1866).

Another more serious poem, 'Haunted: By Our Depressed Contributor' (24 March 1866), seems autobiographical in parts, a self-lacerating description of the bad memories that haunt him: 'Mine are horrible social ghosts,/Speeches and women and guests and hosts,/Weddings and morning calls and toasts'; dismal memories of school, of 'Black Monday – black as its school-room ink'; of '"Caesar" unprepared'; of seeing his first love married to another man; of 'my first cigar –/Of the thence-arising family jar –/Of my maiden brief (I was at the bar),/When I called the judge "Your worship!"/Of reckless days and reckless nights,/When I wrenched off knockers, extinguished lights/And finished it up with unholy fights,/Which I strove in vain to hush up!'[11]

On 15 March 1866 his career at the Bar was given a boost when he was elected to the Northern Circuit, his proposer being the Circuit's leader John Holker. He attended the Manchester and Liverpool Assizes, also the Liverpool Sessions and Passage Court. In the summer of 1866 the Bancrofts and the Prince of Wales company went to Liverpool for six weeks, and Marie Bancroft recalled seeing Gilbert's maiden speech at the assizes, prosecuting an old Irishwoman for stealing a coat:

> He was very anxious about his first essay, and we all assembled [at St. George's Hall] to hear it. Mr. Gilbert tried for a long time to speak, but the old woman interrupted him so persistently that he could not get a word in edgeways, with such polite remarks as, 'Hold your tongue!' 'Shut up, yer spalpeen!' 'Ah, if ye love me, sit down!' 'It's a lie, yer honour!' 'Hooroo for ould Ireland!' etc. She jumped about and made such a noise every time Mr. Gilbert attempted to speak, that the Judge ordered her to be taken down until the next day; and as she left the dock, the prisoner made a grimace at Mr. Gilbert, which I will not attempt to describe! So, after all, the maiden speech never came off, and I fear we were all immensely amused at Mr. Gilbert's discomfiture.[12]

She also recalled more informal events which foreshadow *Trial by Jury* and *The Sorcerer* a few short years later:

> Our legal friends came down to Waterloo [where the Bancrofts were staying] once every week, and the evenings were dedicated to entertainments improvised by ourselves. We had several mock trials in which Mr. Hare was always condemned to the ignominious position of representing the criminal in the dock. It was interesting to hear the clever speeches, all about nothing, delivered

by these rising young barristers. I was sometimes the Judge, and gave imitations of the various gentlemen I had seen on the Bench … On one occasion, for variety, we got up a mock opera, in which I was the *prima donna*, Mr. Gilbert the lover, Mr. Hare his rival, with large cloak, broad-brimmed hat, and knives and daggers all over him; Mr. McConnell was the *prima donna's* father, whom he made a deaf old man, so that we were obliged to shout all our recitatives at him through an improvised ear-trumpet. The opera was sung throughout in Italian gibberish, and was a most amusing bit of foolery.[13]

In the meantime, his work for *Fun* continued apace. He began contributing illustrations to the paper again, now signing his drawings with the soon-to-be-familiar name 'Bab'. The first of these accompanied his poem 'The Story of Gentle Archibald' (19 May 1866), an attractive item about a little boy who dreams of being transformed into a pantomime clown and causing mayhem. (A reminiscence of Gilbert's own clown-worshipping boyhood, perhaps?) From July through to October Snarler returned with his 'Out-of-Town Talk', travelling through Scotland (presumably at the same time that Gilbert was training with the Royal Aberdeenshire Highlanders), and then spending several idyllic weeks at a village in Essex which he called 'Blackbury'. His now customary taunt to the editor of *Fun* at the start of the series tells us a little about his position on the paper:

I am beyond your reach. You can't be down upon me *now* for two more columns of biting satire at five minutes' notice, neither can you insist upon my 'throwing off' forty or fifty lines of verse on some such a promising subject as 'EVE's astonishment at beholding the First Shoestring,' or 'BOADICEA to her umbrella.' [14 July 1866]

A sizeable proportion of Gilbert's work for the paper was, it seems, written literally as space-filler.

One of Gilbert's closest female friends at this time was Annie Thomas, a young novelist described by the publisher William Tinsley as 'a bright, merry, and light-hearted girl, and a writer of bright, easy-reading fiction',[14] though this sells her talents much too short. She is almost completely unknown today, but her novels are witty, perceptive and intelligent, and written in an enviably fluid and natural style. Unfortunately, she seems to have found writing altogether too easy; according to Tinsley she boasted that she could write a three-volume novel in about six weeks.[15] Much of her output reads like a brilliant but slapdash first draft, chatty and somewhat diffuse. Born in 1838, she had taken up writing as a way of earning money after her father's death. Her first published piece dated from 1862, and by 1866 she was already the author of several accomplished novels. Intelligent and spirited, she and Gilbert were more than a match for each other. There was even talk that they might marry.

Something of their relationship seems to be portrayed in her novel *Played Out*, published in December 1866. The novel's hero, Roydon Fleming, is certainly based closely on Gilbert, and the flirtatious heroine, Kate Lethbridge, may have more than a little of Annie Thomas in her make-up. Roydon Fleming, the discontented young government clerk with the taste for humorous writing, is introduced to the reader in these terms:

> As he stands with his back to his writing table, leaning against it, his hands in his pockets, and his legs crossed, he looks uncommonly like the majority of well-grown, well-bred young Englishmen. That his brains were a trifle brighter than those apportioned to the masses was a fact that dawned upon you soon, but not immediately, for though Roydon Fleming had a vein of humour, and a tolerable command of brilliant language in which to clothe it, he was apt to be reserved, almost brusque, to strangers and to those whom he did not like …
>
> 'Rather German-looking,' was the very usual verdict passed upon him by young ladies who had done the Spas; for he had a fair face, close shaven, save for the long, drooping, tawny moustache; the close-cropped hair that covered his small head was tawny too, and his eyes were as blue as eyes with anything besides feeling in them can be. But the delicate aquiline line of the nose and the perfect oval of his face were not German.[16]

There is admiration and affection in this portrait, but there is a typical Annie Thomas barb in the description of his eyes. Roydon chafes against his thraldom at the office, until (in three-volume-novel fashion) the death of a brother makes him heir-apparent to the estate of Helston. As he reflects after hearing of his brother's death: 'It was queer altogether! One of the highest of his ambitions but this very morning had been to get a burlesque (which, if once read, would put him on the same platform as the "busy bees," he felt sure, and his friends felt surer) accepted.'[17]

The sitting-room in Roydon's lodgings is described as containing:

> Boards with studies for sketches on them – slips covered with writing that was meant to aid in the propagation of certain weekly papers – editorial reminders, uncorrected proofs, copy marked 'returned – unsuited to the character of the magazine' – confirmation strong, in fact, on every side, of the young Somerset House clerk being a soldier in that noble army which fights the hard fight of the weekly journals and the daily press.[18]

Roydon has a surprisingly passive role in the novel; it is not really he who is the central character in the plot, but Kate Lethbridge. Still, his tart wit runs throughout, to the evident delight of Kate and others.

On first acquaintance, Kate sets him down as a man of unusual talent:

> he was, unquestionably, the cleverest man who had crossed her path as yet. Not a profound scholar … but a man who had the art of wording nonsense epigrammatically … It was the quality of managing his words with a due regard to both metre and meaning together, with a certain half-expressed carelessness as to whether people were pleased with him or not, which first attracted the girl's attention to Roy Fleming … [But] He knew – none better – that his best had not yet come upon the surface.[19]

All this shows a startling insight into the character of the young Gilbert, who at the time of his thirtieth birthday had barely even begun to write to his full potential.

Annie Thomas understood his character well, and she displays its aspects superbly: his tendency to witty insult; the directness to the point of rudeness of his expression; his sardonic and sometimes fantastic humour; his inability to yield to any other power ('I have been my own master for some years now; it's the only rule I can stand');[20] his occasional social awkwardness; the self-consciousness that made him sensitive to all supposed slights; his determination to act according to his own standards of honour; his inflexibility; and, through all this, his ability to charm and entertain. When Roydon, referring to an amateur violinist who has just bored a social gathering with half an hour of variations on a theme, mutters 'A man who does that ought to be destroyed',[21] the comment contains a genuine touch of Snarler. There is even, in one scene, a clear allusion to the success of 'Ferdinando and Elvira', when Roydon jokingly tells Mrs Darrock that he has been exploiting his 'gift for verse' by writing 'the sweetest thing in couplets for this year's bon-bon wrappers'.[22]

Annie Thomas' novels are fairly unblinkered accounts of the games of flirtation and misunderstanding that, for well-born Victorian women, decided their futures by settling their husbands. There are no perfect happy endings in her world; there can only be, perhaps, a final resolution to make the best of a bad job. In *Played Out* Roydon hesitates too long before deciding to marry Kate and so loses her; it seems he will marry his cousin Georgie instead. Kate becomes a governess and, meeting Roydon for one last time, is shocked to find that his love for her has disappeared, leaving only friendship. He asks: 'But we are friends?' and she replies absently: 'Oh! yes, I suppose so … it matters very little what we are called, or what we call ourselves; it's over now.'[23]

It is difficult to say how much in *Played Out* is fiction and how much is fact. However, like Roydon and Kate, Gilbert and Annie Thomas were seen together so much that it was taken for granted they would marry; and as in the case of Roydon and Kate, the marriage did not, in the end, take place. Gilbert remained on good terms with Annie Thomas, even after the novel's publication and the discovery that she had made him a three-volume hero; he responded by giving her a mildly joshing but good-humoured sketch parodying the Millais picture 'Trust Me'. The original painting shows a young woman with a letter concealed behind her back, and her hunting-pink-attired father holding out a hand commandingly. In Gilbert's version Annie Thomas is trying to hide the novel from Gilbert.[24] Gilbert would not have drawn such a sketch if he had been seriously offended by his transformation into Roydon Fleming.

When, on 18 November 1866, Gilbert turned 30, he was indeed, like Roydon Fleming, a soldier in the noble army of London journalism; he was also, like Roydon, frustrated at being nothing more. Tom Hood was still giving him publishing opportunities: he contributed to Warne's Christmas annual, *The Five Alls*, and to a collection of linked short stories called *Rates and Taxes*, both edited by Hood. But his ambitions lay primarily in another direction.

He had long wished to gain a name for himself a name as a burlesque writer like his contemporaries Burnand and Byron. He had been lurking on the fringes of the London theatre scene for some years. The unsuccessful short play *Uncle Baby* may have been written or co-written by him; and it is also possible that he was providing additional material, uncredited, for the occasional Christmas pantomime. But he remained an unknown name and he wished to be given a chance to shine openly.

And now, at long last, he was to be given that chance. The success of Tom Robertson's *Caste* had been followed by that of his Crimean War play *Ours*, performed at the Prince of Wales in September 1866; and Robertson was beset by theatre managers who persisted in asking him to write pieces for them. One of these was Miss Ruth Herbert, the lessee of St James' Theatre, who wanted a Christmas piece. Robertson was forced to turn her down but recommended Gilbert as a promising young writer who could fulfil the commission instead.

Gilbert wrote his piece, a burlesque of Donizetti's *L'Elisir d'Amore* entitled *Dulcamara; or, The Little Duck and the Great Quack*, in great haste (he later estimated that it took him ten days),[25] and it was first performed at St James' on 29 December, having been 'stage-managed' (that is, directed) by a new member of the theatre's company, a young actor named Henry Irving. Gilbert and Irving discussed the play together during the rehearsal period, Gilbert often inviting him back to his chambers to work out improvements.[26]

The play was a resounding success. It was a burlesque in the approved mid-Victorian style, written in rhymed couplets interrupted by songs and dances set to the well-known tunes of the day, and sprinkled throughout with ingenious but excruciating plays on words. The script makes very little sense outside this context, and is no way a literary work in its own right. But its importance to Gilbert as a herald to his career in the theatre was enormous. The review which appeared in *The Daily News* on 31 December 1866, for instance, exclaimed:

Mr. W. S. Gilbert, a young author and artist of sound and rising reputation, made his first bow to a theatrical audience on Saturday night, at [St James' Theatre], as the writer of a new and highly successful burlesque … It is rare to find the first work of an author new to dramatic literature, well constructed, free from redundancy, short, sharp, and to the point, clearly telling what little story it has to tell, and giving fair opportunities for the display of varied comic acting. Mr. Gilbert's burlesque, or 'eccentricity,' as he prefers to call it, possesses all these merits, and is remarkable for the wit and brilliance of its dialogue.

A dramatist could scarcely hope for a better first review. Though Gilbert's 'eccentricity' was placed last on the bill, after Boucicault's play *Hunted Down* (in which Irving acted) and a one-act farce by John Maddison Morton called *Newington Butts!*, this does not seem to have worked to his disadvantage. The auditorium was packed, the audience was appreciative, almost every song was encored, and a duet sung to the tune of 'Champagne Charlie' was encored at least twice:

> Our lovers all desert us for these military swells,
> And all alike they've gone on strike, these fickle village belles;
> We'll lay it on as thick as mud before we go to bed,
> And 'beautiful for ever' in the morning be instead.
>> For sham complexion is our aim,
>> Sham complexion is our aim;
> We'll put it on the latest thing at night, boys;
> Tomorrow we'll be fascinating quite, boys![27]

The author was called on stage at the end, and so Gilbert for the first time took his bow before an enthusiastic audience.

5

ENFANT TERRIBLE

This seems a good point at which to pause and take a more detailed look at Gilbert's character.

The golfer and writer Horace G. Hutchinson, who first got to know Gilbert some years later in the 1880s, listened with care as Gilbert reminisced about the days of his youth. Hutchinson summed up Gilbert's early years succinctly:

> Life, just at first, does not seem to have used him very kindly. He was disappointed in an ambition to enter the regular army and to become a gunner, in the Royal Artillery; as barrister he had to go through all the embittering processes of hopes deferred; I believe that he found the career which a Government office promised dull to the point of suicide. And in each of these attempts at making good he had found men, whom he must have known to have brains of not half the agility or subtlety of his, making better than he, for some reason or other, was able to. It is not the kind of youthful experience which sets a man at peace with his world.[1]

Throughout most of his life, Gilbert gave the impression of being a fundamentally angry man. Though he did not exist in a perpetual state of active rage, as almost invariably portrayed in caricature, and we may imagine him amiable in good company and courteous in most social situations, still the accounts of those who met him in later years generally describe some underlying aggression or tension: from P.G. Wodehouse who noted that 'even when in repose his face was inclined to be formidable and his eye not the sort of eye you would willingly catch',[2] to Seymour Hicks who wrote that Gilbert 'always gave me the impression that he got up in the morning to see with whom he could have a quarrel'.[3] Hutchinson, again, suggested this aspect of his character when he wrote: 'I do not know what his family motto was, but I do know very well what motto I should have handed out to him personally ... *Nemo me impune lacessit* [No one attacks me with impunity].[4] This aggressive tendency was fundamental to Gilbert's character even in these early days of the 1860s, when he was happy to call himself Snarler and Enfant Terrible.

He wrote in 1867 (as part of a series called 'Men We Meet', in which he returned to his guise as the Comic Physiognomist):

There is a growing tendency on the part of mankind to pay honour only to those qualities which tend to the advantage of mankind at large; and either to ignore, or to utterly condemn every exercise of intelligence which has for its only beneficial object the person who employs it. Now this is manifestly unjust. Man was sent into the world to contend with man, and to get the advantage of him in every possible way. Whenever the C.P. happens to see a human being in the act of assisting, directly or indirectly, another human being, he pictures to himself a foot-race in which the candidates are constantly giving place to each other from motives of sheer politeness. The great object of life is to be first at the winning-post, and so that a man attains that end, and yet goes conscientiously over the whole course, it matters nothing how many of his fellow candidates he hustles on the way. The C.P. cannot find it in his heart to be seriously angry with a mere amiable weakness, so he contents himself with describing those who prefer to lose rather than hustle, as donkeys. The C.P. has always hustled, and the C.P. always will hustle to the end of the chapter.[5]

Here, as elsewhere, Gilbert takes advantage of humorous licence to state baldly a fact which is usually concealed. It is important to realise that Gilbert was, keenly and fiercely, an ambitious man. Believing life to be a foot-race, he must have felt frustrated and humiliated to be squashed for so long at the back, amongst his fellow assistant clerks (third class). He was determined to demonstrate his intellectual superiority by making a name for himself in the world, as he felt to be his due.

He was ambitious, hustling, caustic, brutal, selfish and insensitive to the feelings of others. All this may be said of Gilbert, and with justice. And yet it is grossly inadequate to leave the matter here. The picture is not entirely consistent. He was generous as well as grasping; good company as well as bad; kind as well as caustic. We may think of the Education Office clerk who was reprimanded for disrespectful and insubordinate conduct and wonder how that fitted into his plan to win the foot-race of life. We may visualise Lieutenant Gilbert as he pinioned a drunken and violent guardsman, and ask whether he was thinking only of his own material interests when he did so.

The man that is so often sketched in reminiscences and biographies, the 'hard cynical man of the world' described by George Grove[6] for instance, must have had more to him, much more, if he could be capable of writing the words of the Gilbert and Sullivan operas, which are not only brilliantly witty but also understanding and forgiving, melancholic, clear and truthful. Where, in the head of this man of narrow ambition, is to be found the fantasies and fairies of the historical Gilbert's imagination?

No one becomes so deeply angry with life for so long simply because he has suffered a temporary frustration in his ambitions. There are worse fates than working for the Privy Council in Downing Street. If we seek a cause for Gilbert's basic unhappiness (and I assume that an angry man is also unhappy) then we must go further back.

Gilbert called early childhood 'the most miserable period of our existence', and added that his only recollection of unmixed pleasure from that time was of going to see the pantomime. His evident unhappiness at school, his practice of getting into fights three times a week, his attempt to run away to join Charles Kean's troupe of actors, and the other interruptions to his education, all add to our sense of the boy's real and lasting unhappiness. He found his only escape in the romance and fantasy of the theatre.

Very little is known about his relationship with his parents, but this is, in itself, significant. There survive no family letters in which love or affection are expressed, nor is there any surviving trace of his grief at his parents' deaths, though it must have been there. In fact, Gilbert always found it extremely difficult to express affection or warmth. As Hutchinson noted, 'it seemed to be very hard for him to say a kindness. And it never seemed at all difficult for him to say an unkindness, if only he might point it with a glint of wit.'[7] This quirk of his contributed to the many arguments and misunderstandings which characterised his life. He certainly felt the emotions that it was such agony for him to express. To quote Hutchinson one last time:

> I believe Gilbert to have been essentially, and at heart, an exceedingly kind man. He would do any friend, and very likely a foe too, if he did not happen to have a quarrel with him at the moment, a kindness ... A kind man in deed, not a kind man in word, is a summing up that we might make of him, and at least that is better than its opposite.[8]

If the question is asked why Gilbert should have grown up with an inability to express his emotions that was noticeable even to his fellow Victorians, there is an obvious hint towards an answer in the character of his parents, and especially in the strange gap in the evidence where parental affection ought to be.

The publisher William Tinsley wrote that Gilbert's father always had 'a craze of some kind, or something or some one to dispute about or with ... He was one of those curious people who over-love or over-hate; there was no father medium about him.'[9] In 1872 William Gilbert went into a branch of W.H. Smith's booksellers and, having asked to see all the copies of his novel *Clara Levesque*, tore them up in front of the manager because the book's proofs had not been properly corrected.[10] These memories relate to William Gilbert in the 1860s and 1870s, when he was an old man; but it is reasonable to suppose that something of this temper was also present in him when he was younger. He seems to have resembled his son in being hot-headed and intolerant of imperfection in other people.

It is difficult to imagine William Gilbert as a tender and loving father, and indeed the evidence suggests he was nothing of the sort. It is easier to imagine him sour, ill-tempered and impossible to please. He almost certainly considered young Gilbert a great disappointment. William Gilbert's stories in such books as *Shirley Hall Asylum* (1863), *The Magic Mirror* (1865) and *The Wizard of the Mountain* (1867) repeatedly follow a few well-worn narrative paths and reveal much about his moral beliefs. For instance, they contain the persistent idea that the worst evil that can befall a person or a family is poverty, particularly when it is brought about by a deliberate wasting of money (on gambling, drink or investments, etc.). Vices of character – pride, gluttony or simply weakness of purpose – are punished harshly by fate. Weakness and profligacy are considered to be great evils. Alcoholism is viewed with the exaggerated abhorrence of the temperance preacher; in William Gilbert's stories, a glass of wine leads inevitably to collapse and shame.

It is easy to see that a child could respond to such a parental character with a mixture of acceptance and rebellion. Gilbert certainly drank to excess as a young man – though no more than a young man usually does, and not to his lasting harm – there was perhaps a touch of defiance in this. But some of William Gilbert's deeper lessons caught hold. W.S. Gilbert always felt the supreme importance of money: in every deal he negotiated ruthlessly to his own advantage and while he was often generous and charitable with his wealth, he never lost sight of its primacy. And most importantly, behind everything he did the figure of father William may be sensed, judging him by a standard of perfection which could hardly be attained. When in close succession Gilbert dropped out of college, failed to get to Oxford, failed to get a commission in the army and scraped a lowly job as a government clerk, he was apparently setting the seal on his own failure, and we may be sure that his father understood all this to be the consequence of young Gilbert's inherent weaknesses. Poverty and failure are the vices to be avoided; it is in success and in wealth that a man's character is proved worthy. So when Gilbert joined the staff of *Fun* he had a point to prove, to his father and to himself: he wished to prove that he could succeed.

Another passage from the series 'Men We Meet' describes a more tender side to Gilbert's character:

> The C.P. has no recollection of any period of his career which is not identified in his mind with a romantic association with the name of a beautiful young lady. To love and be loved by an exquisite female is a state of things which has always appeared to his susceptible mind to be the incarnation of human happiness …

the C.P. may congratulate himself on being a singularly fortunate philosopher, for he who can boast that he has attained but one half of human felicity may be said to be a truly happy man. He has always loved an exquisite female – and this is the half upon which he takes the liberty of congratulating himself.[11]

Notoriously, a man in middle- and upper-class Victorian society was expected to enjoy the company of his fellow men only; women were things apart, companions for an idle hour or for the unavoidable time when one returned home from the club. Though Gilbert was a persistent clubman for many years, he was never completely at ease in the gentlemen-only atmosphere in which his contemporaries revelled, much preferring the company of women, and some found this bewildering. Men were his rivals in the foot-race of life. But with rare exceptions he did not view women in the same way, and it was to them that he felt able to show his kinder, more emotional side.

This, then, was our man: trained up with a ruthless determination to succeed, but held back by a hot temper and a tendency to impulsiveness; underneath this forbidding carapace, dreamy and prone to fantasy; antagonistic to his fellow men and romantically attracted to women. He was, by material standards, a failure for some years, or at least a desperate underachiever. He lived frustrated, angry at himself and the superiors who held him back, discontented and unhappy and inclined to rage against his surroundings. Some people effortlessly swim with the currents that lead to success; for them the establishment and those who run it are their natural allies. But for others success, if it comes at all, is the result of a desperate fight against the current. Gilbert, let it be said plainly, did not fit in. His abrasive personality was not of the sort that wins friends easily. His one touch with the ruling powers, at the Education Office, did not make him fond of politics, and indeed it may have been this experience that left him with his lasting distrust of the party system. While working here he was officially reprimanded for disrespectful and insubordinate conduct. Three years later he felt angry enough, and rash enough, to draw a cartoon in *Fun* mocking the policy of his employers; and it seems probable that he also wrote two scathing attacks on the Education Office around the same time. As Annie Thomas perceptively wrote of Gilbert's alter ego in *Played Out*: 'Against the lightest attempt to regulate his line of life; against the smallest effort at coercing him, Roy Fleming had always rebelled.'[12] Gilbert always seemed to take care to attack anyone who stood in a position of power over him: aggressively in the case of the Education Office, teasingly in the case of *Fun* editor Tom Hood. It was, perhaps, his way of redressing the balance of power.

In some lights Gilbert seems a very typical product of his age: emotionally repressed, 'proper' to the point of prudishness, a hard man convinced of his own virtue. But should we change the light by even the slightest degree, he suddenly appears to be at odds with the same age. He was not a happy or contented inhabitant of his society. He mocked it; he insisted again and again that it was selfish, mean and worthless. His was not a political vision, an intellectually derived appreciation of the basis of English society, but a revelation based on personal antagonism. This was the society that opposed him and held him back. Enraged, he was determined to have his revenge. He cruelly held up a mirror to show society what it really was. And society laughed and called it Topsyturvydom.

6

MARRIAGE (1867)

On 6 August 1867, William Schwenck Gilbert married Lucy Agnes Blois Turner, at the church of St Mary Abbots, Kensington. Their marriage lasted until Gilbert's death nearly forty-four years later.

Lucy was born on 14 November 1847, so she was 19 years old when they married. She was the daughter of Captain Thomas Metcalfe Blois Turner of the Bombay Engineers in the East India Company, and Herbertina Turner (*née* Compton), who was the daughter of the Lord Chief Justice of Bombay. Lucy's father died before she was born; she and her brother and sister were brought up by her mother with assistance from the extended family. She had met Gilbert in about 1864, and by the end of 1866 they were intimate friends, possibly engaged; late in life she still remembered the delight she and Gilbert both felt when a critic compared Gilbert's *Dulcamara* favourably to the work of Planché.[1] From her point of view, it was a risky match: she was marrying a failed barrister whose income effectively relied upon writing burlesques and anonymous columns for a cheap comic paper. He was an ambitious young man and he evidently had brains, but it was still a matter of speculation whether he would make good. However, his prospects must have been good enough to persuade Lucy – and, more importantly, her family.

To Gilbert, Lucy was Kitten, later Kitty or Kits. He drew several sketches of her about the time of their marriage, in which he emphasised her large doe-like eyes and small nose and chin, conforming to the child-like pattern of beauty that Victorians preferred. Photographs, however, show a directness and poise in her stance, and a firm line to her mouth, which are absent from the drawings. She had more self-will than her prospective husband perhaps wanted to notice.

'Men We Meet', a series of columns that constituted the Comic Physiognomist's final outing, appeared in *Fun* between February and May 1867. These columns are slightly mellower than their predecessors, and a significant number of them relate obliquely to his emotional circumstances: notably 'The C.P. in Love' (2 March

1867), 'Some Engaged Men' (16 March 1867), 'Some Old Bachelors' (20 April 1867) and 'The C.P. at a Wedding' (27 April 1867). The last column in the series (18 May 1867) marked the end of Gilbert's use of autobiographical personae at *Fun*; as his wedding approached, coincidentally or not, he moved away from his previous practice of writing comic journalism based on his own life and experiences, and towards the writing of ballads, stories and plays set in a world of grotesque fantasy. The first of the Bab ballads had already appeared, and after Gilbert's marriage they would become a regular and stylistically assured fixture in *Fun*.

In April 1867, Annie Thomas and her mother moved out of their London home at 28 Eldon Road, Kensington, and moved to Yealmpton in Devon. Gilbert, in need of a marital home, took over the tenancy; he clearly remained on amicable terms with the Thomases. On 11 July he wrote to Annie from this address, enclosing a letter for her mother which had been addressed to Eldon Street. His letter, friendly in tone and full of private jokes, congratulates Annie on her impending marriage to 'the Rev Pen (I can't read the rest)' – actually the Reverend Pender Cudlip, an absurd name worthy of Gilbert himself. He insists that he is 'heartily glad [at the news] – after a little qualm of irritation and unreasonable jealousy', and with a concluding barb that he was clearly unable to resist adds: 'I trust you had no difficulty in getting [your mother's] consent – she was always obdurate.'[2] So this, it seems, was the reason why Gilbert did not marry Annie: her mother did not approve the match. Annie's marriage to Cudlip must have surprised many, not least the churchgoers of Yealmpton, who were startled to find their curate suddenly married to a lively young horsewoman who rode with the hunt.

Gilbert's letter concludes with a P.S.: 'I die the first week in August' – an allusion to his own approaching marriage. This association of marriage with death can be found in several of the Gilbert and Sullivan operas. For instance, it is a recurring motif in *The Yeomen of the Guard*, where the characters sing of a young woman who 'must marry,/Though the altar be a tomb'. In *The Gondoliers*, however, marriage is associated with birth, as when the central characters, newly wed, insist that it is their birthday and that they are only ten minutes old.

So, on 6 August 1867 Gilbert the bohemian bachelor died and Gilbert the sober husband was born. Responsible for Lucy as well as himself, he settled down in real earnest to the serious task of creating a name for himself and making money.

But first, of course, came the honeymoon. The happy pair travelled to the Continent, beginning and ending their holiday in Gilbert's beloved Boulogne. A descriptive article called 'Britons at Boulogne', which Gilbert contributed to *London Society* a year later, talks of the brides and bridegrooms who come to Boulogne 'in the season' and of 'the harmless transparent dodges' they indulge in to prevent people from realising they are newly married:

> Girls, who in their ordinary relations are remarkable for a timid, shrinking, bashful nervousness, often develop into brides of astounding *sang-froid* … whereas

men who have acquired a sort of celebrity for cool nonchalance … tremble at the publicity of a wedding … I know a very cunning fellow who changed his wedding garments for a tourist suit of the coarsest make, and compelled his bride to 'go off' in last-year-but-one's alpaca, and a winter bonnet, and who, on getting into the railway carriage that was to take him and his bride to Folkestone, disarmed suspicion among his fellow-travellers by requesting them to allow his niece to sit near the window. But Fate is not to be so easily baulked, and Nemesis, in the shape of the Newman's postilion who drove them to the station, came up to the carriage window with a favour as big as a cheese plate in his button-hole, and covered them with confusion by wishing his honour and his honour's good lady all health and happiness, a long life, and a numerous progeny. The harmless fib about their supposed relationship crumbled to atoms on the spot – the uncle sank into his boots, and his niece … smiled in triumph at the first of probably a long succession of matrimonial victories.[3]

We may suspect this little comedy of bride and groom to derive from personal experience; but it must remain only a suspicion.

The relationship between Gilbert and Lucy is a little shadowy. We have the evidence of a handful of letters and the passing comments of memoirists, and the occasional hint from other sources. Lucy was a keen follower of her husband's work, usually attending the first nights and reporting back to him when, as in later years, he did not attend himself. Indeed, her memory of his plays was sometimes better than his own. She could play the society hostess when required. She tended to let her husband dominate on social occasions; in private, she was apparently a more controlling force in the household.[4] One may be reminded of the character of Minnie Symperson in Gilbert's 1877 comedy *Engaged*, who says of her fiancé Cheviot Hill: 'it is my duty … to fall in with Cheviot's views in everything *before* marriage, and Cheviot's duty to fall into my views in everything *after* marriage. I think that is only fair, don't you?'[5]

The Gilberts, it seems, intended to have children but they were unable to do so. A family Bible in the possession of Brian Jones is inscribed with their names and leaves blank spaces for the children they never had. There is no reason to suppose either Gilbert or Lucy was less interested in sex than their contemporaries.

Gilbert later told his friend Rowland-Brown that he wrote one of the Bab ballads while travelling to Folkestone on his honeymoon.[6] For the four weeks following the wedding, Gilbert's contributions to *Fun* consisted of ballads and nothing else, and these may have been written on the honeymoon or stockpiled for *Fun*'s use before he departed. (One of these, 'Babette's Love', concerns the affection that a Boulogne shrimp girl called Babette feels for a British tar called Bill.) However, Gilbert was certainly back in London by the end of September, when he started writing parody reviews of the current plays once more. He and his wife settled in at 28 Eldon Street, and he resumed his daily task of writing, and writing, and writing.

7

BAB, BALLADS AND BURLESQUES (1867–69)

Dulcamara had been written and produced at St James' Theatre with such haste that it was only after the first night – at the very end of December 1866 or the beginning of January 1867 – that Gilbert was able to arrange financial terms. He discussed the matter with W.S. Emden, the acting manager at the theatre, and suggested 30 guineas. 'Oh, we don't deal in guineas – say pounds,' said Emden, and Gilbert agreed. Emden wrote the cheque and Gilbert signed a receipt. Then, the deal completed, Emden told Gilbert: 'Take my advice as an old stager. Never sell as good a piece as this for thirty pounds again.'[1]

This piece of advice stayed with Gilbert through his professional life: he was still quoting it forty years later when Edith Browne wrote his biography.[2] The time would come, not so many years down the line, when his profits from a single play could be reckoned in thousands of pounds.[3] And the most successful of the Gilbert and Sullivan operas brought him more money than could have been dreamt of by the young man who thought £30 was a fair price for a play.

He was soon at work on a second burlesque, and *La Vivandière; or, True to the Corps!* was first performed at St James' Hall in Liverpool on 15 June 1867, where it was received favourably and ran for about a month. However, he intended the piece ultimately for London, and he set about almost immediately trying to place it and at least one other burlesque. He managed to secure *La Vivandière*'s London production for January 1868, and that of another burlesque, *The Merry Zingara*, in March. He was suddenly in demand as a burlesque writer, and he was determined to make the most of his opportunities.

Burlesque, in the sense that the Victorians understood it, is virtually unknown today. Technically, it is an artistic form in which subject and style are mismatched to comic effect. In 'High Burlesque' a vulgar or trivial story is told in an inappropriately serious style, while in 'Low Burlesque' a serious or classical story is told in a trivial style. In Gilbert's time theatrical burlesques usually took stories from classical mythology or some other branch of high culture and subjected them to a process of complete trivialisation, filling them with cheap puns and parodies set to popular tunes. From the audience's point of view, one of the main attractions of the genre was the convention that many of the men's roles were taken by attractive young women dressed in tightly cut men's clothes and tights.

Gilbert preferred to take his stories from Italian and French opera. The results were slightly more tasteful than many of their rivals, but otherwise virtually indistinguishable. The Gilbert and Sullivan operas have a very strong burlesque element: for example 'A Nice Dilemma' in *Trial by Jury*, in which ridiculous words are given a full-blown operatic setting, is a magnificent example of High Burlesque. The influence of burlesque on the operas should not be exaggerated, however; the operas go far beyond anything that is achievable in a purely burlesque mode. Gilbert soon outgrew the form; but when he was starting out, the writing of burlesque was the thing he thought he could do well, and he did it to the best of his ability.

A couple of one-act farces which he had written were performed towards the end of 1867. For instance, *Allow Me to Explain*, adapted from the French, shared the bill with Tom Robertson's *Caste* at the Prince of Wales for a time. He was also commissioned by E.T. Smith of the Lyceum to write the theatre's Christmas pantomime, for which he was paid £60 – 'eventually', as Gilbert noted sourly.[4] Entitled *Harlequin Cock Robin and Jenny Wren; or, Fortunatus, the Three Bears, The Three Gifts, the Three Wishes, and the Little Man who Wooed the Little Maid*, it wove together several different nursery tales and was perhaps over-elaborate considering the haste with which it had to be produced. Sensibly, pantomimes were now performed much earlier in the evening than they had been in Gilbert's youth; Gilbert's *Harlequin Cock Robin* began at about eight o'clock, after a brief farce called *Cabman No 93*. The first night was a memorable fiasco. Gilbert later described the episode:

> The piece was written in four days and produced in about three weeks after it was commenced … Mr. E.T. Smith had bought a vast crystal fountain, and this property was to be the principal scenic effect of the pantomime. Four scenes had to be introduced to give time to 'set' this absurdity and three scenes to strike it.

The rehearsals were brief and chaotic. One of the performers wanted to introduce a dance of his own, and took Gilbert down into a dark cellar to demonstrate it. The man:

> placed the lantern on the ground and solemnly began to dance at me. The lantern lighted his legs and nothing else, and the terrific spectacle of those weird and wizened limbs dancing a cellar-flap by themselves haunted my dreams for many a night after … They were striped red and white like a stick of peppermint.[5]

E.T. Smith was also the lessee of Cremorne Pleasure Gardens in Chelsea, and he had decided that the pantomime's scenery should be painted at Cremorne and then transported to the theatre. Unfortunately, the scenery did not start arriving at the theatre until about four o'clock on Boxing Day, so the pantomime had to be performed with only a small proportion of the scenery actually in the building, and as a result: 'the performance on Thursday night cannot be fairly treated as more than a dress rehearsal', as *The Examiner* noted (28 December 1867).

The Daily News went into more detail (27 December):

> there were more disasters attending last night's performance than are commonly looked for in the first representation of a Christmas piece. Trap doors refused to act, to the discomfiture of demons, who were at last compelled to enter at the wings like any ordinary person; stage machinery obstinately kept in view scenes which were done with, and fairy aquarium, mystic fountain, wood and castle got in each other's places to such a confusing degree that the dialogue was not always appropriate to the locality in which it was delivered.

The performance became more desperate as the evening wore on, and at last came to an absolute standstill, the essential 'transformation scene' not being ready to unfold. Gilbert, who seems to have been in the audience throughout this disastrous event, recalled that there was a painful interval during which Smith encouraged various members of the cast to go on stage and fill in time – 'a plum pudding on two legs hopped to the centre of the stage, turned to the audience, bowed politely, turned towards the opposite wing, and hopped off' – followed by a fish ballet performed in the middle of the forest scene:

> [They] entered (very shiny and scaly, but otherwise not like any fish I have ever met), and danced a long ballet, which they themselves thoughtfully encored. Then came the clever and hardworking lady with another song (from last year's pantomime). Then a can-can by the Finette troupe. Then a party of acrobats. Then the spotted monarch's mystic dance. Altogether a chain of events calculated to arrest the attention of a wayfarer through that wood and set him pondering.[6]

After which, the so-called transformation scene attempted to unfold, only for it to become painfully obvious that half of it was still at Cremorne. The patience of the audience was by now wearing very thin. According to Gilbert, the evening was saved, in a fitting climax of absurdity, by E.T. Smith himself:

> Mr. Smith (he was a bold man) rushed on to the stage amid a storm of execrations. The noise was awful. I don't know what he said; *he* didn't know what he said. He told me afterwards that he merely opened his mouth as if he were speaking, but that he said nothing. At last he concluded with a pleasant smile

and a polite bow, and backed off. Suddenly the humour of the house changed, and a round of applause greeted his exit. He had not uttered an audible word, but he had convinced the house nevertheless.[7]

It was, perhaps, this valuable lesson in the dangers of putting an under-rehearsed and under-prepared play upon the stage that settled Gilbert's decision to try and stage-manage his own pieces, starting with the London production of *La Vivandière*, which opened at the Queen's Theatre on 22 January 1868. He was determined to ensure he had artistic control over his material. Few dramatists of the day had such control over the staging of their plays, Dion Boucicault and Tom Robertson being shining exceptions to the rule; although, as Gilbert observed in 1872, it was 'the common custom in France'.[8] He learned much from Robertson, having attended rehearsals of his friend's plays, as he told William Archer much later in his life: 'Robertson showed how to give life and variety and nature to the scene, by breaking it up with all sorts of little incidents and delicate by-play.'[9]

At the same time that Gilbert was learning to master the theatre rather than letting it master him; he was also continuing with his work at *Fun* and elsewhere. He wrote humorous articles for *London Society* and *Belgravia* and occasional short stories for anthologies and annuals. Most of his early stories are semi-sentimental tales of 'real life', but 'The Triumph of Vice' for *The Savage-Club Papers* (1867) takes us into a hermetic world of the impossible and the absurd, and here the true Gilbert note is struck, concluding with a typically provocative 'moral': 'Thus, notwithstanding all that has been said to the contrary, vice is sometimes triumphant. Cunning, malice, and imposture may not flourish immediately they are practised, but depend upon it, my dear children, that they will assert their own in the end.'[10]

Gilbert was becoming slightly less prolific with his contributions to *Fun*, and this reflected his altered circumstances: he had burlesques to write and a wife to go home to. The Comic Physiognomist and Snarler were no more, but Gilbert remained active at the paper, and indeed, it was in these years from 1867 to 1871 that he was to write and illustrate the bulk of his Bab ballads, that first flowering of his distinctive personal imagination. With life's usual irony, Gilbert's first glimpse of immortality is to be found not in his first plays, into which he invested so much time and effort, but in his throwaway ballads for a penny paper.

Many of these ballads experiment with reversing the natural order of things, an idea which was to become one of Gilbert's stocks-in-trade. In 'The Precocious Baby' (*Fun*, 23 November 1867), the child of an elderly man is born old; he is described as 'A dear little lad/Who drove 'em half mad,/For he turned out a horribly fast little cad.' Another ballad, 'The Rival Curates' (*Fun*, 19 October 1867), relates the story of a curate, famed for his mildness, who finds his fame threatened by the arrival of another very mild curate, and so orders his sexton and his beadle to pay the man a visit and threaten to kill him unless he changes his ways. Religious mildness and gangsterism are, the narrator blandly assumes, natural allies. But Gilbert's humour did not begin or end with Topsyturvydom. He focused on absurdity however he found it: whether through taking an accepted idea and pursuing it to its insane conclusion ('Etiquette'); taking a standard romantic plot and giving it a harsh, non-standard ending ('Joe Golightly'); presenting to us the behaviour of people without moral filters ('Ellen McJones Aberdeen'); or simply relating a story completely devoid of logic or meaning ('Pasha Bailey Ben'). Gilbert's is not so much a topsy-turvy universe as a disorientated one: a universe where the accepted rules do not apply and the apparently familiar may at any moment be disrupted by the anarchic.

Much of the ballads' impact springs from their 'Bab' illustrations, in which Gilbert can be seen trying out a grotesque style which is in fact specific to these few years from 1867 to about 1871: the stretched expressions, the bodies stylised to the far extreme, the angular postures, each figure as rigid and fixed as a wood carving. These illustrations, like the ballads, express Gilbert's vision of an arbitrary and senseless world.

But the ballads were not Gilbert's only contributions to *Fun* at this time. He was also writing caustic parodies of the current plays:

LUCY.–   'Tis now some seventeen years since Clara Vernon first met Lieutenant Crayford. It's a long story – I will tell you all about it.
MRS. S.–   No – don't – some other time. *I*, also, have a long story to tell. It takes twenty minutes; but, nevertheless, I will give it to you.
LUCY.–   Spare me!
MRS. S.–   Never!

[*Tells her a long story that lasts twenty minutes. Any jumble about the Arctic regions, polar bears, and second sight will do.*]

LUCY (*awaking*) – You astound me! Now let *me* tell you the story of the loves of somebody in the Arctic regions – say Lieutenant Frank Aldersly?
MRS. S.–   Well, it's certainly your turn. (*Sighing*) Do get on with it!¹¹

Between 1865 and 1871 he wrote about seventy of these parodies, which dissected stage absurdities to devastating effect. He reduced plot and dialogue to their essence, exposing any weaknesses of plot or probability – as in this from his parody review of *East Lynne* (17 February 1866):

MR. C.–   ... I will not run after her, for I might catch her as she has only been gone a few minutes, and that would spoil the plot. I will simply tear my hair.
[*Simply tears his hair.*]

Gilbert would mock any aspect of the play or the performance that struck him as ridiculous:

ALDARIM.—   Stay! A death by stabbing were far too easy and merciful. Tie her to yon tree with a handkerchief, while we retire and ponder on our vengeance. [*They tie her to a tree with a cotton handkerchief, and exeunt.*]
FIREFLY.—   How to break the irresistible bond that holds me prisoner. Ha! my trained Etna, with his wonderful Horse Effects!
Enter ETNA, *the pink-eyed horse. He unties the slip-knot and* FIREFLY *is free.*
FIREFLY.—   Free! Free! Away to other climes! But first, my Etna, ring the belfry bell, that the Arabs may know that I am going.[12]

He took particular relish in the melodramatic extremes, cheap scenery and shambolic supernumeraries of productions at the Adelphi. The so-called 'Adelphi guests' who were called upon to appear during crowd scenes were the object of his special scorn. Thirty years later, Clement Scott's memory of these parody reviews remained vivid:

Even before he made a great mark with the 'Bab Ballads' ... young Gilbert was talked about as the author of the burlesque criticisms of plays and players in duologue form that appeared in *Fun* every week, and made people roar with laughter. The thing had been done before, but never so well done as by Gilbert ... Week after week he chaffed the Adelphi guests, the Adelphi moon, the eccentric scenery, the old clothes rag-bag dresses, and the ludicrous stage management of those deplorable days.[13]

So, side by side, Gilbert's contributions to *Fun* developed different aspects of his creativity, which were to burst out together in his plays and operas, the extravagance and absurdity of the ballads appearing in alternation with the gleeful demolition of melodrama and all its assumptions that characterised the parody reviews. It was here and now that his distinctive voice as a writer – poised, critical, coolly presenting us with a vision of life in a nonsensical universe – started to be heard. His plays, especially the burlesques, seem negligible in comparison, though it was the success of the burlesques that first put him on the map as a popular writer. For instance it was the success of *La Vivandière* in the first months of 1868 that emboldened him to give up his practice at the Bar (such as it was) and devote his professional life entirely to writing.

Towards the end of 1868 he was preparing a selection of his ballads for volume publication. He sounded the idea out with the proprietor of *Fun*, Edward Wylam, and Wylam decided on John Camden Hotten as a suitable publisher. Hotten was an adventurous and sometimes disreputable character, who had published Swinburne's poems when others had turned him down; he had also published unauthorised editions of American writers, and pornographic and semi-porno-graphic works such as *A History of the Rod* (1870). Gilbert's dealings with Hotten were far from smooth. Hotten printed 300 copies more than the 2,000 speci-fied for the first edition, apparently hoping to pocket the full profits of the extra copies without informing Gilbert, but Gilbert found out and angrily demanded an extra £50 in payment.[14]

The book which eventually came out in November 1868, slightly later than scheduled, was a significant marker in Gilbert's career. Here, for the first time, the poems were given the name *The 'Bab' Ballads*. The cover of the handsome green-bound volume bore the title and Gilbert's signature gilt-written in a fac-simile of his handwriting, as if pointedly laying claim to these verses of previously disguised authorship. The book gave permanence to little masterpieces which would otherwise have disappeared with the back numbers of *Fun*. Gilbert wrote in the book's preface:

> I have some reason to believe that the Ballads, which now appear for the first time in a collected form, have achieved a certain whimsical popularity among a special class of readers … With respect to the Ballads themselves, I do not know that I have anything very definite to say about them, except that they are not, as a rule, founded upon fact.

He added: 'I have ventured to publish the illustrations with them because, while they are certainly quite as bad as the Ballads, I suppose they are not much worse.'[15]

The self-deprecating tone may not be entirely insincere. In later years he insisted that the verses were too hastily written and the drawings were too grotesque. But he must have seen some virtue in them; he certainly thought them good enough to form the basis of his first book, and they were to prove a treasure-trove of ideas for him in years to come. The soldiers and sailors, peers and policemen, babies and bishops who dance through the book's pages are the first inhabitants of his recog-nisably Gilbertian universe. A critic writing in *The Contemporary Review* in 1869 marvelled at the poems' strange tone, which consisted of a 'contrast between the mechanical and apparently causeless insanity of the conception, and the ordered, luminous, and musical sanity of Mr. Gilbert's manner'.[16]

He was now earning a very decent living as a writer of burlesques, farces, ballads, reviews and miscellaneous humour. The Gilberts felt able, in April 1869, to move house to 8 Essex Villas in Kensington, which was larger and more com-fortable than their Eldon Road residence. He was starting to make a name for himself, and they were reaping some of the benefits.

The Pretty Druidess, the last of Gilbert's conventional burlesques, opened at the Charing Cross Theatre on 19 June 1869. He had started out as a dramatist with the writing of burlesque as his main ambition and goal; now, two and a half years later, he found his horizons were much broader than he had previously imagined. There were new lands to discover and conquer. The epilogue of *The Pretty Druidess* is a frank and affectionate farewell to the genre:

> So ends our play. I come to speak the tag,
> With downcast eyes and faltering steps, that lag,
> I'm cowed and conscience-stricken – for tonight
> We have, no doubt, contributed our mite
> To justify that topic of the age,
> The degradation of the English stage.
> … The piece is common-place, grotesque,
> A solemn folly – a proscribed burlesque!
> So for burlesque I plead. Forgive our rhymes;
> Forgive the jokes you've heard five thousand times;
> Forgive each breakdown, cellar-flap, and clog,
> Our low-bred songs – our slangy dialogue;
> And, above all – oh, ye with double-barrel –
> Forgive the scantiness of our apparel![17]

8

IN DEMAND (1869–72)

Gilbert had written a play, not a burlesque, feeding off an existing plot and mocking it, nor a farce, adapted from the French, but an original comedy of modern life, full of racy prose dialogue, wit and unconventionality. Entitled *Quits*, it concerned what today we would call a dysfunctional family: a pious rogue called Colonel Calthorpe who sponges off everyone he can, and his son Harold, who runs up enormous debts and drinks too much. Harold has a blazing row with the father and storms out of the house, accompanied by Mary Waters, a nursery governess whom he loves. He takes chambers in Gray's Inn and starts a scurrilous journal called *The Weekly Tormentor* which becomes a roaring success by abusing everything. He falls ill but Mary Waters nurses him back to health. The Colonel (now promoted to Lord Ovington as the result of a yachting accident) gets his comeuppance at the hands of a rough-spoken but good-hearted man called Casby, and all ends (precariously) happily. The play is based partly on a short story called 'Diamonds' which Gilbert had written for *Routledge's Christmas Annual for 1867*, and also owes something to Tom Taylor's 1855 play *Still Waters Run Deep* and Tom Robertson's *Society*. However, it has a tone distinctive to itself, harsher and more uncompromising than anything that Robertson, for instance, ever wrote.

It was written not as the result of a commission, like most of Gilbert's performed plays, but simply because it was something he wanted to write. He had the play set up in type and printed before he sent it out to the theatrical managers (in those pre-typewriter days most manuscripts were written out in a semi-legible scrawl). John Hollingshead, manager of the new Gaiety Theatre, accepted the play as soon as he read it.

The Gaiety had opened in December 1868 with a programme that included a Gilbert burlesque, *Robert the Devil*. So Gilbert and Hollingshead already knew each other and were happy to work together. 'He was somewhat of a martinet in his stage management,' Hollingshead wrote, 'but he generally knew what he wanted, was more often right than wrong, and was consequently an able director of his own pieces. He was always ready to accept a suggestion if he thought it was good and reasonable.'[1] They went into rehearsal immediately, and the play (retitled *An Old Score*) opened on 26 July 1869.

The critics were generally positive. *The Era*, for instance, noted: 'There is a freshness in the design and a cleverness in the writing that will commend it to the favour of a playgoing public' (1 August 1869). However, audiences did not take to the play. The *Sunday Times*, in the course of a generally positive review (1 August 1869), suggested the reason:

> We own to being a little sick of characters of the goody-goody type, and would rather have full blooded men and women such as Mr. Gilbert presents us with than the amiable nonentities or the impersonations of abstract virtues to which we are accustomed. But an atmosphere of something rather worse than wickedness hangs around the *dramatis personae* of the play … throughout the piece, we could show there is no person we thoroughly respect or like … On the whole, then, we admire Mr. Gilbert's comedy a great deal and do not like it much.

Hollingshead agreed: 'It was too like real life, and too unconventional. The leading characters were a rascally father, and a son who did not hesitate to tell him of his rascality. The dialogue was not playhouse pap.'[2]

The mid-Victorian play-going audience was, in general, conventional in outlook and intolerant of anything that disturbed that outlook. Social and moral attitudes were there to be confirmed, not challenged; and a new idea was looked upon as a threat. This was perhaps the major obstacle that Gilbert now faced in his ambitions. As a writer he was intellectual rather than emotional: he could not believe in the artificial happy ending of a story, or in the easy emotional satisfaction of such a happy ending, and his works reflect this fact almost in spite of themselves. *An Old Score* lasted just four weeks before it was replaced by a revival of Tom Robertson's play *Dreams* (with *Robert the Devil* as an afterpiece).

Before this happened, however, the play provoked two unusual responses in the comic papers. *Fun* contributed a parody review in its 7 August 1869 issue, written by Gilbert himself, in which he makes Harold say: 'I will do anything for money. Indeed, every one in the piece (as far as I can judge) would do anything for money.' A brief criticism written in Gilbert's own voice at the end also called attention to the play's poor construction, the ridiculous innocence of the heroine and the resemblance of one of the characters to John Mildmay in *Still Waters Run Deep*.

More outrageous, and perhaps more interesting, is the parody review which appeared in *The Tomahawk* (7 August 1869), a satirical weekly edited by Gilbert's childhood friend Arthur William à Beckett. The review was written by à Beckett, who clearly thought Harold Calthorpe was a satirical portrait of himself, and *The*

Weekly Tormentor a parody of *The Tomahawk*. Enraged, he let fly in wild toma-hawking style, telling us what he thought of Gilbert as he did so:

> Harold caught the scarlet fever, edited a satirical paper, and prospered. But he was sad, he said.
>
> 'My old friend, Mr. W.S. Gilbert, is having a row with me. I am awfully sorry. He declares that I sell my friends at a guinea a piece. Too bad. I know it's a crime in the literary world for a young man to succeed, but then it's really too bad!... His 'Bab Ballads' in *Fun* were not bad; I mean some of them. The *Spectator* said they were coarse; well, *I* like coarseness. However, my friend W.S.G. has been too severe; he shall see that he has wronged me. *If ever I write a comedy I will never be such* AN UNUTTERABLE CAD *as to put a man I have regarded from childhood as my friend, and with whom I have never had a quarrel, into it for all the town to stare at.* NO, NO – THAT WOULD BE TOO COWARDLY AND BLACKGUARD! Yes, W.S.G., you shall see that you have wronged me – wronged me deeply!'
>
> And Harold wept. He felt that his friend had been too hard upon him.

Elsewhere in the parody à Beckett uses the character of Harold as a vehicle for a personal attack on Gilbert: 'His enemies said that he was coarse, and deserved a good thrashing for his impudence; his friends, on the other hand, declared him to be blunt if cynical, with an honest heart, but an unpleasant vocabulary.' The piece concludes with what seems like an intentionally hurtful attack on Gilbert person-ally, when Harold says: 'I will give you a glimpse of the future. I shall marry Mary, and perhaps leave her a good deal to herself (women like it), and perhaps write a burlesque, or something equally intellectual – and oh! I shall be *such* a lady's man!'

À Beckett was a hot-tempered young journalist – maybe even more so than Gilbert himself – and these words contain an obvious intention to wound. But there was perhaps a kernel of truth in them. Gilbert was busy writing and direct-ing his plays, writing his weekly contributions to *Fun*, attending his clubs and keeping in with his friends in the bohemian set. His weakness for female beauty was well known, and while it appears to have expressed itself as innocent flirta-tion, it may not have seemed an appealing trait in a newly married man.

Gilbert approached à Beckett after the appearance of the attack, and *The Tomahawk* for 21 August 1869 contains a retraction: 'Mr. W.S. Gilbert having … assured us that in writing [*An Old* Score], neither ourselves, nor the TOMAHAWK, nor anyone connected with it, entered his mind … we gladly declare that we withdraw [our] strictures, with an expression of sincere regret that we should have misunderstood him.'

Between 1869 and 1875 Gilbert wrote no fewer than thirty plays, only a small handful of these being adaptations or translations, and most of them displaying some aspect of Gilbert's suddenly fecund imagination in a more or less concen-trated form. He was also, at the same time, writing stories and other imaginative works for various publications such as *Tom Hood's Comic Annual* and a new weekly paper called *The Graphic*. In fact these periodicals became, for a time, a kind of testing ground for his work; a substantial proportion of these stories were later reworked into plays or libretti.

The first issue of *The Graphic* appeared on 4 December 1869, edited by Gilbert's cousin Henry Sutherland Edwards, and Gilbert contributed to it almost immediately. One of his best works appeared in that year's Christmas number: the Bab ballad 'Etiquette' which told the story of two Englishmen who were shipwrecked on a desert island but 'couldn't chat together – they had not been introduced'.

It will not be possible to go into detail about all Gilbert's plays and other writings from this period: he was simply writing too much. But this was the time in which he developed his mature style and gave full expression to his philosophy of life, and certain key works deserve at least a degree of attention.

The year 1869 saw, among other things, the start of Gilbert's involvement with the Royal Gallery of Illustration on Regent Street, run by Mr and Mrs German Reed. They specialised in intimate, small-cast entertainments with music. These entertainments were never referred to as plays, nor was the Gallery of Illustration called a theatre. The Reeds ingeniously avoided all such terminology. Throughout the 1850s and 1860s theatres were still regarded as 'not respectable' by many decent middle-class people, particularly churchgoers. Many who would gladly attend a concert, a lecture or an exhibition at a gallery would not think of setting foot in a theatre. These were the people that the Reeds particularly wished to attract. The plays, or rather 'illustrations', that they performed were of the most innocent kind, dependent on wit, humour and performance. So the pretence was kept up that the Gallery was not a 'real' theatre and that the Reeds' performances were in the nature of private entertainments.

Gilbert's first piece for the Gallery, *No Cards*, was first performed on 29 March 1869, with music apparently by German Reed. This amusing though slight comedy was performed in a double-bill with another short comic opera, *Cox and Box*, with words by F.C. Burnand adapted from J.M. Morton and music by Arthur Sullivan. This was the first time that the names of Gilbert and Sullivan were united on the same programme.

The two pieces formed the evening's entertainment at the Gallery through to August, at which point the company left London but continued to perform the pieces in the provinces. On 22 November *Cox and Box* found a new partner in the double-bill: *Ages Ago*, written by Gilbert and the composer Frederic Clay. It became Gilbert's first real popular success. This whimsical piece, in which portraits step from their frames and converse and quarrel and flirt, was full of wit and invention, and was the Gallery's greatest success, remaining in the German Reed repertory for several years.

It was at the Gallery that Gilbert found the freedom to develop his ironic and fantastic style in the direction that would bring him his reward in the Gilbert and

Sullivan operas. Here the impossible is accepted as normal and reality crumbles in the face of chop-logic. Paintings step from their frames and talk like prosaic citizens of 1860s London, commiserating with one another for having been badly restored by Royal Academicians and so on. As in Gilbert's burlesques, the scripts are dotted with songs, but here for the first time the songs are integral to the whole and Gilbert's gifts as a lyricist are given their chance to develop. His lyrics for *Ages Ago* seem undeveloped, even meagre, but he was still feeling his way.

The Princess, first performed at the Olympic on 8 January 1870, looks back to the burlesques of the 1860s but also tries to suggest a path for Gilbert's future development as a writer. It could be described as a fairly standard burlesque of Tennyson's poem *The Princess*, but it is written in blank verse rather than rhyming couplets, the new lyrics to existing tunes are more substantial than previously, there are no 'breakdown' dances, the puns are less forced and the tone, though frivolous, is less objectionably vulgar than in a standard Victorian burlesque. Gilbert looked back upon the play with pride, though with a lasting regret that it was necessary, burlesque-like, to cast three women in the three main male roles.

It was immediately after the opening of *The Princess* that J.B. Buckstone, manager of the Haymarket, commissioned Gilbert to write a blank verse comedy for his theatre. Buckstone, born in 1802, was a much-loved actor and comedian of the old school, the original Box in Morton's 1847 farce *Box and Cox*; and the Haymarket, of which Buckstone had become the manager back in 1853, was a much-loved theatre with an illustrious history. The Haymarket company included several greatly admired actors, such as W.H. Kendal and his wife Madge Robertson (Tom Robertson's sister). To be commissioned to write for Buckstone at the Haymarket was an undoubted honour. The dramatist and critic Palgrave Simpson had suggested the subject of a play to Gilbert: *Le Palais de la Vérité*, one of the *Contes Moraux* written for children by the Comtesse de Genlis (1746–1830). This moral tale of a palace in which everyone is magically compelled to speak the truth and so is stripped of polite dissimulation it may have reminded Simpson of Gilbert because of Gilbert's own blunt social manner.

The writing of the play seems to have taken Gilbert several months, rather than the more usual matter of weeks. He took great care over it, restructuring the story and writing it in blank verse to give it a 'classical' feel. In the middle of this process – probably in July 1870[3] – a small, insignificant incident occurred. Gilbert met Sullivan.

Ages Ago had finished its initial run at the Gallery of Illustration on 18 June and was replaced by another Gilbert piece, the inventive and hilarious *Our Island Home*. In this piece the performers play distorted versions of themselves, cast away on a desert island during an Asiatic tour of *Ages Ago* and squabbling about their territorial rights (in an extension of Gilbert's recent poem 'Etiquette'). The improvisatory plot ends with an extended scene involving a pirate called Captain Bang or Byng, mistakenly apprenticed in infancy to a pirate instead of a pilot – an idea that Gilbert would return to nine years later when writing *The Pirates of Penzance*. However, in spite of the brilliance of the script, *Our Island Home* was not particularly successful with audiences and after a few weeks it became necessary to help it along by presenting it in a double-bill with an abridged version of *Ages Ago*.

At a rehearsal for this shortened *Ages Ago*, Frederic Clay, who was there to supervise his music for the piece, introduced Gilbert to Arthur Sullivan, who was a close friend of his. Gilbert, according to his later account, took the opportunity to ask a question:

> I am very pleased to meet you, Mr. Sullivan, because you will be able to settle a question which has just arisen between Mr. Clay and myself. My contention is that when a musician who is master of many instruments has a musical theme to express, he can express it as perfectly upon the simple tetrachord of Mercury (in which there are, as we all know, no diatonic intervals whatever) as upon the more elaborate disdiapason (with the familiar four tetrachords and the redundant note) which (I need not remind you) embraces in its simple consonance all the single, double, and inverted chords.[4]

This was a piece of musicological gobbledegook which Gilbert had just written into his dramatisation of *Le Palais de la Vérité*, and as he explained in an interview in 1891, he was curious 'to know whether this would pass muster with a musician'.[5] Sullivan asked for Gilbert's question to be repeated, then said he would like to think it over before giving a definite reply. Gilbert said in 1891, 'I believe he is still engaged in hammering it out.'[6]

While all this was happening, strange events had been taking place in the larger world. France had declared war with Prussia on 19 July, and the conflict had culminated in a battle at Sedan on 1 September, during which the Prussians captured the French Emperor Napoleon III. France's Second Empire fell and a new republic was declared in Paris, led by a Government of National Defence. The Prussians, essentially unopposed, began to march on Paris, and the French capital prepared to resist the enemy. The British papers dispatched representatives to Paris to report on events, including the Sunday newspaper *The Observer*, who decided to send Gilbert as a 'special correspondent', presumably because of his knowledge of French.

He left at very short notice on 6 September, travelling via Dover and Calais. He spent some time in the early hours of the next day in a waiting room at Amiens station, which was crammed with fugitives displaced by the threat of the approaching Prussians, before catching the night mail train to Paris. He shared his carriage with 'four very noisy Frenchmen of the small *bourgeois* type'[7] who grew suspicious of the stranger in their midst who had his full name written on a bag, including the very German middle name 'Schwenck'. Gilbert, in an attempt to defuse the situation, handed them a card on which he had written the word

Observer. However, this made the matter worse, as one of the Frenchmen wondered if 'observer' might be another word for 'spy'. Gilbert managed to convince them otherwise, but it was a narrow escape; those suspected of being Prussian spies were not treated gently.

Arriving in Paris at eight o'clock on the morning of 7 September, he lost no time before venturing out into the damp, rainy city to report on conditions. He found the streets all but deserted, except for a small crowd outside the Hotel de Ville where the Government of National Defence was stationed. He tried to insinuate himself into the seat of government, but was stopped by a 'stout and spectacled' National Guardsman.[8] At the cafés he heard nothing but denunciations of their ex-emperor and he wondered what had happened to all the people who had been shouting '*Vive l'Empereur!*' in the streets six weeks before. Reading that many of the theatres were still open, he visited them that evening, curious to know who would want to see a play at such a time; but he found them all closed. He was unimpressed by the soldiers that he saw, ill-disciplined and apparently unfamiliar with the right way of treating their firearms. He heard nothing but outrageous boasts, preposterous rumours and wholesale denunciations of their ex-emperor. 'Frenchmen are children,' he concluded.[9] The sudden political reversal from empire to republic baffled him:

> Frenchmen with Imperialist sympathies have become rabid Red Republicans because Louis Napoleon is an unskilful general … to renounce an Imperial *régime* and go to the other extreme because their Emperor has disappointed them is about as reasonable as it would be to renounce money for ever, because you had been swindled into taking a bad shilling. So, indeed, it appears to me, who am in truth but a poor politician.[10]

The Observer printed two of his dispatches in their issue for 11 September, alongside a report from another correspondent. But the lines of communication from Paris were closing down as the Prussians approached, and *The Observer* recalled Gilbert to London. He left on Monday 12 September, his train passing over the bridge at Creil only a few minutes before it was blown up by French engineers. Within days Paris closed up completely against the Prussian army, and the city was locked in a state of siege for the next four months.

Back in London, Gilbert was able to concentrate on the production of his new play, *The Palace of Truth*. It opened at the Haymarket on 19 November 1870, to mixed reviews. *Reynolds's Newspaper*, for instance, called it 'a genuine, a triumphant, and a most merited success' (27 November 1870), while the *Pall Mall Gazette* complained that the plot was weak, the characters unsympathetic and the verse unpoetic, adding rather spitefully that the play 'may prove to be one of those productions which an author's friends admire enthusiastically, but which the general public avoid with almost equal eagerness' (24 November 1870). But in spite of this the play enjoyed 140 performances before being taken off at the end of the following April, which in those days of ephemeral drama was considered a long run.

Gilbert called the play a 'fairy comedy', presumably because of its fairy-tale atmosphere. It is set at the court of King Phanor (played by Buckstone), and concerns the visit of the king and his well-mannered courtiers to an enchanted palace which compels everyone to speak the exact truth. Manners, courtesy and hypocrisy are stripped rudely from everyone who enters its portals. The flatterer speaks rudely, the ardent wooer reveals his philandering nature and even the blunt-spoken cynic reveals that his rough manners are a pose.

Eleven years later, the young theatrical critic William Archer wrote in his first book, *English Dramatists of To-Day* (1882), that in *The Palace of Truth* 'the keynote of Mr. Gilbert's peculiar talent is struck, his style of satire is epitomized'.[11] Characters speak the truth of their hearts in spite of themselves, no matter how rude or brutal the truth may be. The idea does indeed recur in many of his later plays and operas. But in fact the truth-telling aspect of Gilbert's 'peculiar talent' had been evident years before *The Palace of Truth*, in his Snarler columns and in *An Old Score*, for instance; this play merely refined the idea and turned it into a point of style.

Gilbert's star was in the ascendant. Five years before, no theatre would look at his plays but now the theatrical managers clamoured for his work. The year 1871 saw no fewer than seven new stage works by Gilbert on the stages of the London theatres: three full-length plays, three libretti and a dramatisation of *Great Expectations*. When the new Royal Court Theatre opened on 25 January, it was Gilbert's new comedy *Randall's Thumb* that formed the main attraction of the evening. This theatre, managed by the young actress Marie Litton, was to provide a regular source of commissions for Gilbert over the next three or four years; indeed, she was to ask him for, and receive and perform, three more pieces for the Court that same year.

Gilbert's account of how to write a play, written in 1872, is probably a fairly accurate description of his own practice as a jobbing playwright at this time:

> We will assume that the author, Mr. Horace Facile, has such a recognized position in his profession as to justify a manager in saying to him, 'Facile, I want a three-act comedy-drama from you with parts for Jones and Brown and Robinson. Name your own terms, and get it ready, if you can, by this day two months.'[12]

Facile selects a 'general idea' to form the basis of the play, a thesis to be discussed or proved, and tailors his plot to suit the actors who will perform it. He sketches the construction of the three acts then starts to write the dialogue: 'As a rule, this is not written straight off. He first tries his hand upon bits of dialogue that arise from suggestive situations ... After he has "settled" half a dozen little scenes of this description, he feels that it is time to arrange how the piece is to begin.'[13] So he frets his way through the actual writing of the script, composing separate scenes and piecing them together, bringing the whole to a swift and snappy conclusion. 'Facile … has a theory that no piece has ever yet been written which deserves to arrest the attention of an audience for more than two hours at a time.'[14]

He reads the play to the cast in the theatre's green room: 'This is an ordeal that Facile particularly dreads. He reads abominably – all authors do – and he knows it.'[15] He supervises the play through rehearsals:

> Facile knows something of stage management, and invariably stage-manages his own pieces – an exceptional thing in England, but the common custom in France. He is nothing of an actor, and when he endeavours to show what he wants his actors to do, he makes himself rather ridiculous, and there is a good deal of tittering at the wings; but he contrives, nevertheless, to make himself understood, and takes particularly good care that whatever his wishes are, they shall be carried out to the letter, unless good cause is shown to the contrary … At the same time, if Facile is not a self-sufficient donkey, he is only too glad to avail himself of valuable suggestions offered by persons who have ten times his experience in the details of stage management.[16]

And at last, 'the piece is ready for representation – three weeks' preparation is supposed to be a liberal allowance – and with one imperfect scene rehearsal, and no dress rehearsal at all, the piece is presented to the public'.[17] Though Gilbert was far from satisfied with such a meagre allowance for rehearsal time, he was not powerful enough to insist upon longer – yet. He had no leisure to sit back and reflect. He was writing play upon play, taking each one from conception through writing and rehearsal to the first night, and then starting again.

Only five days after the first night of *Randall's Thumb*, the Gallery of Illustration premiered *A Sensation Novel* with music by German Reed, the most inventive and brilliantly written piece Gilbert had yet authored. A writer of sensation novels of the Mrs Henry Wood/Mary Elizabeth Braddon type enlists the aid of a demon to fulfil his obligations and learns that his characters are allowed three periods in which they can come to life and express their own hopes and desires, which are the opposite of the hopes and desires they express within the novel. The characters come to life as promised and express their scorn for the Author, who has been manipulating their behaviour and pressing them towards a 'happy ending' they detest. ('Marry and live happily ever after!' the hero, Herbert, exclaims scornfully. 'And this is a novel that pretends to give a picture of life as it is.')[18] Finally, after an outrageous succession of events including the villain's suicide by beheading (offstage), the characters rebel against the Author and insist upon their own version of a happy ending, in which the hero marries the villainess and the villain (hastily revived) marries the heroine. The whole piece revels in its own invention and wit, and the song lyrics have a new sense of assurance. It was a distinct success, lasting for 186 performances.

Just as Gilbert's star was rising, however, the theatrical world and Gilbert in particular suffered a cruel blow with the death of Tom Robertson. It was not, in the end, unexpected: Robertson had been seriously ill with heart disease for the past year. He died on 3 February 1871, at the age of 42. He had lived a life of bitter struggle up until his first taste of success, which he experienced only six years before his death. He was buried alongside his first wife at Abney Park Cemetery, Stoke Newington, on 9 February, in a ceremony attended by his family and his old friends from London's journalistic and theatrical worlds: W.H. Kendal, Tom Hood, Tom Archer, Dion Boucicault, Squire Bancroft, John Hare, Andrew Halliday, Gilbert and many others.

'As we stood round the open grave on that bitter cold February day,' Gilbert remembered, 'my attention wandered from the words of the burial service (it was mumbled almost inaudibly by the reverend gentleman who officiated), and I began to think of other things.'[19] At this moment he saw in the crowd, to his astonishment, what appeared to be the face of Tom Robertson himself. After the ceremony he tried to find the man who had such a close resemblance to his old friend: 'I was unsuccessful in my quest, and the almost ghostly nature of his disappearance increased the eeriness of the incident. I went home feeling rather uncomfortable.'[20]

This strange episode led to his writing the short story 'Tom Poulton's Joke', which was published in the first issue of a new periodical called *The Dark Blue* in March 1871. Tom Poulton, the president of an informal club called the Serious Family, plays a joke on the other members by creating a fund for the loaning of money and then faking his death before the members can gain any advantage from the scheme. When the club members attend his funeral, Tom is also to be found among the mourners, much to their confusion. The Serious Family discover that they are made rich by Tom's death, after which he finds it impossible to persuade them he is really alive. This coolly ironic story is an odd thing for Gilbert to have written so soon after his dear friend's death; but one feels that Robertson himself, who had a sardonic turn of mind, would have appreciated it.

Gilbert was concentrating now on his theatrical work. He had given up his sideline as a reviewer at the *Illustrated Times* and *The Observer*, and was contributing less and less to his old mainstay *Fun*. He had still been writing the occasional Bab ballad or parody review (including a parody of his own *Randall's Thumb*), and there had even been some talk of his being given a regular salary on the paper, but this came to nothing. His last regular contribution appeared in May 1871.

The second half of 1871 was occupied in part by the writing of a second 'fairy comedy' for the Haymarket to succeed *The Palace of Truth*. Turning to classical mythology, he reinvented the Pygmalion myth for his own times, and in the process seemed to reveal something of himself. Pygmalion the sculptor creates fine statues of women, with the one fault that they all have the features of his wife, Cynisca, as she was when they met ten years before. Pygmalion has one great regret: that his statues, though imitating life, do not live:

Cyn.	It all but breathes!
Pyg. (*bitterly*)	It all but breathes – therefore it talks aloud!
	It all but moves – therefore it walks and runs!
	It all but lives, and therefore it is life![21]

Cynisca goes to Athens for a day, and while she is away Pygmalion's new statue of Galatea miraculously comes alive. This beautiful and innocent young woman immediately loves Pygmalion as her creator, and Pygmalion, seeing in her the perfect image of what he loves in his wife, responds. Much of the play gains its comedy from Galatea's innocent responses to social conventions: the love that must not be expressed or the appreciation of one's own beauty that must not be shown. But the plot reaches its crisis when Cynisca returns and, seeing her husband involved with a very affectionate young woman, calls forth a curse that strikes him blind for his infidelity. The curse can only be revoked in forgiveness, and this takes place when Galatea, finding that Pygmalion loves his wife only, returns to her pedestal and becomes the marble that she originally was.

We know that Gilbert, married four years, continued to find young women attractive, and throughout his life found great pleasure in more or less innocent flirtation. We also know that he was, and would remain, childless. In the coming years he would act as a mentor to several young actresses, guiding their early steps in the theatre, often using *Pygmalion and Galatea* as a showcase for their talents. Knowing all this, we may be tempted to see in Pygmalion an image of Gilbert himself, seeking in younger women a combination of lover, daughter and creation. Fanciful, perhaps, but not necessarily untrue.

Gilbert's writing schedule was somewhat overcrowded during these months. His comedy *On Guard* was rehearsed and produced at the Court Theatre in October, by which time Gilbert had already committed to writing a Christmas piece for Hollingshead at the Gaiety – a comic opera to be set to music by Arthur Sullivan. His work on *Pygmalion and Galatea* must have been disrupted severely by these competing projects. Conversely, his work on the opera must also have been disrupted by rehearsals for *Pygmalion and Galatea*, which opened at the Haymarket on 9 December, just seventeen days before the premiere of the Gaiety piece, now entitled *Thespis; or, The Gods Grown Old*.

Pygmalion and Galatea was well received on the first night. The second act climax, a furious speech by Cynisca (played by Caroline Hill), resulted in enthusiastic applause as the curtain fell. Gilbert came behind the curtain and joined the actors, beaming with delight. 'My play is a great success,' he told them rather tactlessly. Madge Robertson (Galatea) reminded him, 'It's not over yet, Mr. Gilbert.

There's another act to be played.' But Gilbert assured her: 'Oh, but the gist of the play is over.' It seems this did not go down well with the actors. Essential or not, the third act still had to be performed. However, Madge got her applause after the final curtain, 'the greatest ovation ... that I ever had in my life', so all ended well.[22]

The critics were enthusiastic on the whole, though the *Pall Mall Gazette* reviewer was distinctly lukewarm in his praise: 'That the story of Pygmalion gains much from the dramatist's treatment of it can hardly be said; but a pleasant and acceptable work has nevertheless resulted from his labours' (11 December 1871). There was some comment on the play's use of the supposed Aristotelian unities: there was only one scene and the action took place over a period of twenty-four hours. It was a notable success, running until the following July at the Haymarket and being frequently revived thereafter. The fate of *Thespis*, the first Gilbert and Sullivan opera, was quite different.

Arthur Seymour Sullivan's character and work were to have a profound effect on Gilbert's own life. In many ways the two men were polar opposites. Born on 13 May 1842, Sullivan was five years younger than Gilbert. He was the son of Thomas Sullivan, a sergeant bandmaster at the Royal Military College, Sandhurst, and Mary Clementina Sullivan (*née* Coghlan). They were a close-knit family: Sullivan was to remain on deeply affectionate terms with his parents and his brother throughout their lives. It was clear from an early age that Sullivan's life would be dedicated to music and his parents fully supported him in this. He wrote an anthem, 'By the Waters of Babylon', at the age of 8; in 1854, shortly before his twelfth birthday, he became a chorister at the Chapel Royal; the following year his sacred song 'O Israel' was published by Novello; in 1856 he became the principal soloist in the choir and in the same year he was awarded the first Mendelssohn scholarship at the Royal Academy of Music. He was awarded this scholarship every year for four years, the latter two of which were spent at the Leipzig Conservatory. He was able to spend a third year at Leipzig partly through money sent by his father and partly because the Conservatory waived his tuition fees. In this final year he wrote a suite of concert music for *The Tempest*. He returned to London, and his *Tempest* music was performed at the Crystal Palace in April 1862 and received with acclaim: the *Athenaeum*, for instance, suggested that 'it may mark an epoch in English music' (12 April 1862). Sullivan was not yet 20 years old.

The contrast with Gilbert's curtailed education, frustrated ambitions and years of misery as assistant clerk (third class) is complete. By 1862 the younger man had become immeasurably the more famous of the two. To take one small but cruel detail, Gilbert greatly admired Dickens but it was to Sullivan that the great man offered the hand of admiration, when, having just heard the *Tempest* suite, he exclaimed: 'I don't pretend to know much about music, but I do know that I have been listening to a very great work.'[23] Sullivan's innate talent combined with his immense personal charm smoothed the way before him in these early years as if he were protected by the attentions of some benevolent fairy.

He wrote songs and anthems, ballet music, overtures, a symphony and a cello concerto – all the expected products of a respected composer. The first inkling of another, puckish side to the man was his composition for a private gathering called the Moray Minstrels, of the one-act operetta *Cox and Box* (1866), an adaptation by Frank Burnand of J.M. Morton's brilliant little farce *Box and Cox*. Sullivan relished the chance to write mock-operatic scenas for a landlord and his lodgers, not to mention a comic song about going on holiday and a most beautiful lullaby sung to a slice of bacon. The piece was a great success, and Sullivan and Burnand collaborated on a full-length comic opera the following year, *The Contrabandista*. It lasted for only seventy-two performances and so came close to being a failure, largely because of Burnand's mediocre libretto. Burnand was good at small-scale humour but had very little instinct for what was interesting or well-constructed dramatically. Sullivan needed a different collaborator if he wished to succeed as a composer of comic opera – a writer with a sure sense of metre, rhythm and sense, with theatre in his blood and an attitude to life. His decision to work with Gilbert was perhaps the most fortunate moment of a fortunate life, though there would be times when Sullivan himself would certainly have disagreed.

Thespis was written in great haste. A current theory suggests that a proportion of the music may not have been original to Sullivan, but adapted from Offenbach.[24] As the score of the opera is for the most part lost, this must remain speculation; but it would make a great deal of sense bearing in mind the nature of the piece. *Thespis* was, in essence, a burlesque of a classical subject, in the Offenbachian mode; Gilbert's first and only experiment in the genre. Where Offenbach (or rather, his librettists Halévy and Crémieux) had made a burlesque version of the legend of Orpheus the archetypal musician, Gilbert (with Sullivan's aid) created his burlesque using the character of the archetypal man of the theatre. It was a deliberate reply to Offenbach and the French school of comic opera. Thespis and his troupe of actors are picnicking on Mount Olympus when they stumble upon the Greek and Roman gods, now grown old and creaky. The gods and the actors agree to change places for one year; the result is chaos, and the piece concludes with the gods returning to their positions and banishing the actors back to earth.

The rehearsals for *Thespis* took place after *Pygmalion and Galatea* had opened, over a period of about ten days. There was scarcely time to do anything except drill the cast on the basics of the material, but Gilbert clearly had some idea of the new things he wanted to accomplish with comic opera. The ineffective 'Adelphi supers' were fresh in his memory when he turned his attention to the Gaiety chorus. As Sullivan recalled: 'Until Gilbert took the matter in hand choruses were dummy concerns, and were practically nothing more than a part of the stage setting. It was in "Thespis" that Gilbert began to carry out his expressed determination to get the chorus to play its proper part in the performance.'[25] Sullivan also remembered from the *Thespis* rehearsals an early example of Gilbert's caustic way with obstinate actors: 'one of the principals became quite indignant and said,

"Really, Mr. Gilbert, why should I stand here? I am not a chorus-girl!" to which Gilbert replied curtly, "No, madam, your voice is not strong enough, or no doubt you would be."[26]

The first night of *Thespis* was not a complete success. Some of the performers sang badly, not all the words could be heard distinctly and the performances were in general rough and ready. Clearly, the ten days of rehearsal were not enough. What was perhaps worst of all, the opera (which started at about 9.15 p.m.) finished after midnight. This was too much for even a boisterous Boxing Night audience, expecting to finish at about 11 p.m., and hisses could be heard amongst the applause as the final curtain fell. The critics were mostly sympathetic, acknowledging the quality of the material and commiserating that the standard of performance should have let it down.[27] But within a few days the opera was in good shape (also a good deal shorter) and the *Penny Illustrated Paper* was able to assert that 'Mr. Gilbert's Gaiety extravaganza grows in public favour and deservedly so' (6 January 1872). The critic for the *Pall Mall Gazette* wrote: 'In almost all conjunctions of music and words there is a sacrifice of one to the other; but in "Thespis," Mr. W.S. Gilbert, the author, and Mr. Arthur Sullivan, the composer, have worked harmoniously together' (3 January 1872). It was a good sign.

Thespis lasted for only sixty-three performances before being taken off, though this was a fair run for an ephemeral Christmas entertainment. It was performed once more in April 1872, as a benefit for one of the Gaiety performers, and has never been heard again with Sullivan's original score. *Pygmalion and Galatea*, on the other hand, was revived many times during Gilbert's lifetime and was perhaps his most popular non-Sullivan piece.

On 28 January the theatrical paper *The Era* contained a lengthy article in praise of Gilbert. It was barely five years since *Dulcamara* had first brought his name forward as a writer of plays. His career had scarcely begun. As the article noted: 'Few authors have become famous in so short a space of time.' Already he was being hailed as a pioneer and one of the foremost writers for the English stage. The article is worth quoting at some length, in spite of its gushing tone and long-winded rhetoric.

'It is … the fashion to cry down everything connected with the modern stage,' the article began, adding that English theatre was indeed in a desperate state, largely because of its 'fatal want of system'. However, 'in spite of overwhelming difficulty … it is possible to point at this very moment to artists and authors concerning whose talent there is no question':

Amongst these pioneers, surely Mr. W.S. Gilbert deserves a conspicuous position … We select Mr. Gilbert because he possesses in a more striking degree than his fellow labourers the rare gift of originality; because, unaided, he has triumphed; because, belonging to no school, and following the teachings of no school, he has forced his way to the front; because, more than all others in our day, he had given us plays which possess rarer merit than the pleasure of the passing moment; plays which we keep by us and read; plays which add to our wealth of dramatic literature; plays which must live; and because, as far as we know, Mr. Gilbert has given us nothing of which either he or we have cause to be ashamed.

'A master of rhythm and most accurate rhymester, a song-writer of unusual excellence, a comic ballad writer, who has really no rivals', Gilbert could easily have been content to write 'burlesque according to the accepted pattern' – but, the article insists, 'From the first he had higher aims'. His burlesques were 'conscientiously composed', but Mr Gilbert:

> deserted the operatic burlesque for a novel kind of extravaganza designed with the laudable object of bringing poetical fancy and taste to the front without cutting away the humour. But it was no revival of the extravaganza of the old days. Just as Mr. Gilbert had parted company with Mr. Byron and Mr. Burnand, so did he refuse to imitate Mr. Planché … His *Princess* was the first conspicuous sign of talent which borders closely on genius, while the two Haymarket comedies are … entirely things of themselves and by themselves.

After all this effusive praise, the article's later section becomes more critical and interesting. The reference to Gilbert's proficiency in 'the peculiar art of topsy-turvy' is especially acute:

> It will be urged, and no doubt truthfully, that as a comedy writer, he has not succeeded so well as in those daring flights which have astonished while they succeeded. This is quite true. There are certain rules in comedy writing which must be followed, and the indisposition Mr. Gilbert has ever felt to follow any lead is the main cause of his present want of success as a comedy writer. He refuses to be fettered. He persists in telling his story in his own way, and strains where it is least wanted the conspicuous talent he possesses in the peculiar art of topsy-turvy. He delights in involvement, and is never so happy as when he is looking at life upside-down. In this art he is unrivalled … A warm love for the unnatural, for the quaint, for freaks of fancy, for fairydom and romance, for perpetual upsetting of tradition, and for the cultivation of the trick of topsy-turviness, could hardly co-exist with those special gifts which belong to the best comedy writers. Mr. Gilbert is perpetually living in a kingdom of his own, and taking us into it. When he writes comedy he must live with us, and sketch the characters of every day life. Be this as it may, there have been many worse comedies (and highly praised) than either *The Old Score, Randall's Thumb,* or *On Guard*. Merit they all contained, traces of anxious thought, and frequent signs of care and polish, but they broke down because their author's tastes and

inclination do not fascinate him with the serious business of the world, with studies of the human heart, or mankind in general.

It was a complaint that would be levelled at Gilbert's work many times through-out his life and beyond; and yet, strangely, exactly the opposite complaint would also be levelled at some of his plays, such as *An Old Score*. His work seemed, to some, far removed from the realities of this world, and to others, all too brutally realistic. His plays took their audiences into realms of fantasy or rubbed their noses in the basest aspects of real life. There was something wrong with these plays, they felt, something that made them uncomfortable; but what it was exactly, the puzzled critics could not say.

9

THE LORD HIGH DISINFECTANT (1873)

Sometime in the middle of the year 1870,[1] Gilbert sat down at his desk to compose a story for *Tom Hood's Comic Annual for 1871*. He wrote:

> Here is a blank sheet of paper – several blank sheets of paper. What shall I put upon them? I declare I don't know. Shall it be a fashionable story of modern life? I know nothing of fashionable life. A mediæval romance? It would take too much cramming. A sea story? I know nothing about the sea, except that it makes me sick. A fairy tale, then? Well, a fairy tale be it.

The illustrated story that resulted, which he called 'The Wicked World', reads like an improvisation, evolving and developing as he wrote. He set his story in Fairyland, where there are no men – because 'I know so much about men' – and his fairies are all 'supremely lovely' women with 'large soft downy wings – six feet high, like the wings of angels'.[2] These fairies discuss the nature of life amongst the mortals, and are shocked and intrigued by the ways of the wicked world, and decide to summon a mortal man to Fairy Land (so spelt in this play). The story is a strange mixture of melodrama and lampoon. The Fairy Queen becomes the object of a love rivalry and the victim of a consuming love, and the other fairies become overwhelmed with mutual jealousy. The Queen concludes: 'Let us forgive one another, and endeavour to think more charitably of the errors of those who are subjected to temptations from which we are happily removed.'[3]

Only one new Gilbert play was premiered in 1872: his one-act musical piece for the Gallery of Illustration, *Happy Arcadia*, which plays with the idea that all human beings are discontented with their lot – even in Arcadia. This typically witty and caustic little libretto, which looks forward to *Iolanthe*, was first performed in October 1872. But he was concentrating his creative energy on a third fairy comedy. Casting about for a subject, he returned to his 'Wicked

World' story. He reworked it completely, confining the action to Fairy Land and compressing the action to the space of twenty-four hours. The fairies, curious about the ways of the Wicked World below, summon three mortal men to their kingdom – two medieval knights and a comic manservant. These men (Ethais, Phyllon and Lutin) bring with them the gift of mortal love, which, as the Fairy Queen Selene says, 'nerves the wearied mortal with hot life,/And bathes his soul in hazy happiness.'[4]

They destroy the smooth calm of life in Fairy Land, inspiring love, jealousy and hatred. The play ends with the three mortals returning to earth with much relief, an act which causes the fairies to 'seem to wake as from a dream'. At this moment, fairy messengers arrive bearing the promise of 'a priceless gift … that we may love as mortals love!' and Selene refuses immediately:

> Such love is for mankind, and not for us;
> It is the very essence of the earth,
> A mortal emblem … [5]

She is, it seems, talking about sexual love; not the act itself, but the emotions that surround it. This was a very dangerous topic for a Victorian writer even to hint at, especially in the theatre. Gilbert was anxious about the new play and wrote to his old hero Planché: 'It is rather a risky affair & will either be a big hit or a big failure.'[6]

It premiered on 4 January 1873. The cast included many of the usual Haymarket stalwarts: Buckstone, Kendal, Madge Robertson and, in a small role, Marie Litton. Buckstone spoke a prologue before the curtain dressed as a fairy. On the first night, the audience greeted his absurd appearance with shouts of laughter, but the old man's memory failed him in the middle and he came to a stop. 'He was so deaf that the prompter could do little or nothing to help him,' T. Edgar Pemberton wrote a quarter of a century later, 'and, after a painful struggle, he had to leave the remainder of the introductory verse unspoken'.[7] This was fortunate or unfortunate according to one's point of view, for Gilbert's witty introductory verse took pains to stress that the moral of the play was that 'Love is not a blessing, but a curse', though a necessary one:

> It's easy to affect this cynic tone,
> But, let me ask you, had the world ne'er known
> Such Love as you, and I, and he [the author], must mean –
> Pray where would you, or I, or he, have been?[8]

Otherwise, the play went well. The Fairy Queen Selene's powerful speech to the mortal men at the end of Act 2, ending 'Behold! I am a devil, like yourselves!' was received with special enthusiasm. Gilbert came before the curtain at the end to 'loud and prolonged cheering' (*Era*, 12 January 1873). The reviews were mixed, however, and *Lloyd's Weekly Newspaper* was not alone in thinking that the play was 'not equal in dramatic worth to *The Palace of Truth* and *Pygmalion and Galatea*' (12 January 1873).

The review which appeared in *The Figaro*, a somewhat scurrilous weekly paper, on 11 January 1873 was particularly hostile. The critic, after a paragraph praising 'the height to which [Gilbert] has soared above most rival playwrights', added that 'in his latest work, Mr. W.S. Gilbert has carried the defect, which only peeped out in "The Palace of Truth" and in "Pygmalion and Galatea," to an almost disastrous extent'. This defect was that of artistic vulgarity. The harshest passage in the review occurs in the middle of a dissection of the play itself:

> With a cynicism which artistic feeling, if nothing better, should have forbidden, [Gilbert] suddenly imbues his fairies with a love that can only be purely animal: he allows no medium between sisterly affection and brutish desire; for it is to utter brutes that he makes his dainty fairies forthwith offer their devotion.

All this provoked Gilbert to write a characteristic pair of letters to fellow author James Albery. In the first, dated 19 January and beginning with a stiff 'My dear Sir', he wrote, in terms combining apparent politeness with suppressed fury, that he had been told that Albery had written the *Figaro* review, and that 'I only wait your denial to silence the malicious propagators of a report which is likely to do you so much injury'.[9]

The second letter was written later the same day and shows a complete reversal. It begins with a friendly 'Dear Albery', and continues, 'I feel that I have done you an injustice and I must at once apologise for it':

> I was told by three people – all of whom were likely to know – that the 'Figaro' article was written by you. I had only glanced at it (for I make a rule of never reading a 'slate') and, in a moment of irritation (I am liable to such moments, as you are perhaps aware) wrote the note that you will receive with this. This evening I came across a copy of the 'Figaro' and I read the article *through*, and I had only to do so to feel convinced that it never proceeded from you. I want no denial from you as the thing speaks for itself. It is weak, foolish and vulgar – epithets which your work never has and never can deserve.[10]

Gilbert was an extremely hot-tempered man. When he felt that a person was not according him his due respect, he could become disproportionately enraged, responding with violent abuse. When he cooled down, he sometimes apologised if he felt he had been wrong; often an appeal to his sense of humour did the trick. But if he continued to feel he was in the right, he was capable of continuing a quarrel over years and even decades. He viewed life as a constant battle waged between himself and the rest of the world. He was always catching the world in the act of showing disrespect towards him, and he was always finding it necessary to teach the world a lesson. This extreme sensitivity to insult suggests that, though seeking the world's respect, he did not really think he deserved it. Certainly he was capable of disparaging his own work to an extent that he would never have forgiven in anyone else.

The *Pall Mall Gazette* had already reviewed the play unfavourably on 6 January ('it wears the air of laborious trifling, and its lack of action and interest becomes oppressively manifest'), but on 23 January it also published a long letter signed 'Amuetos' which went much further:

> It is time to protest against the exaggerated praise bestowed by some of the newspaper critics on the new 'fairy comedy' at the Haymarket. One special offender spoke in terms that could only have been warranted by another 'As You Like It' or 'Midsummer Night's Dream,' calling it 'one of the sweetest of stage-poems,' &c. I venture to think that a little examination of the piece will show that it fails as an imaginative conception, that a halting imagination is allied to coarseness of workmanship, and that this general coarseness occasionally hardens into actual offensiveness.

Amuetos then proceeded to criticise the play's 'want of poetry, [and] want of consistency', and – most seriously of all, in Victorian terms – its 'coarseness both of general idea and detail'. A scene of flirtation between the fairies and the mortal men is described as 'vulgar through the air of barmaidish sentiment running through it, and coarse by the exhibition of endearments lavished on creatures in whom manner and bearing are doubtfully attractive'. Moreover, 'The scene where the sisters taunt Selene for her vigil seems to me simply indecent'. (In this scene, the fairies profess themselves outraged that Selene should have spent six hours alone with the wounded knight Ethais.) Describing the climax of the play, in which the men, disgusted at being chased after by the fairies, throw themselves off the cloud of Fairy Land and back to earth, Amuetos thundered: 'one line … is unfit to be spoken in a theatre at all.' This was Ethais' parting speech in which he declares: 'I go to that good world/Where women are not devils till they die!'[11]

The Wicked World is, to modern eyes, a strange, antiquated thing; but to read Amuetos' letter is to be reminded that mainstream Victorian attitudes were stranger still. Gilbert, reading the letter, was outraged that he should be accused of indecency and decided to sue the paper for libel. His moment as the critics' favourite dramatist was passing, and he would resist.

One night during the run of *The Wicked World* Madge Robertson, performing Selene, was astonished to find that when her husband made his usual entrance in Act 1 as the knight Ethais he was accompanied, not by Mr A.R. Arnott as expected, but by Gilbert himself, taking over Arnott's role. In her autobiography she explained that 'Mr. Arnott and another gentleman had been playing at boxing and his opponent had made Mr. Arnott's face rather terrible to look upon, so he could not be seen in public'.[12] However, she had previously told Gilbert's biographers that the incident was the result of Gilbert himself having 'quarrelled with the actor and ... come to blows with him'.[13] This second version of the story is certainly the more colourful of the two, and one would hope it was true. Gilbert, though becoming more well-fed and broader in the frame as he grew older, retained his zest for the fight, but Madge Robertson's memory was not always reliable. At any rate, the conclusion she drew from performing with Gilbert that night was that 'brilliant genius that he was, [he] was the worst actor I have ever known or seen'.[14]

Shortly after the premiere of *The Wicked World* Marie Bancroft contacted Gilbert; she was arranging a private entertainment to be performed at the Prince of Wales Theatre on Ash Wednesday, and, as he recalled, 'she asked me to write a wild burlesque for the occasion'.[15] He sketched out a political parody of *The Wicked World*, in which the three visitors to Fairyland were not medieval knights but modern-day politicians – specifically the Prime Minister William Gladstone and two of his ministers, the Chancellor of the Exchequer Robert Lowe and the unpopular Commissioner of Works Acton Smee Ayrton. (Lowe had been in charge of the Education Office when Gilbert worked there; it is tempting to see this as a delayed act of revenge.) The Gladstone government was beleaguered and unpopular, and Gilbert clearly approved of this state of affairs.

His sketch plot, entitled 'Great Britain and Ireland', explains that the action of the play shows the politicians' attempts to introduce the fairies to 'the beauties of a Liberal government'. The fairies are encouraged to form their own government on the Liberal plan, and are individually assigned to 'the very posts they are least fitted for'. For instance, 'Zayda is questioned as to her knowledge of naval matters – She has never seen the sea and don't know a ship by sight – evidently the very person for First Lord of the Admiralty'.[16] Gladstone's government is ridiculed as a penny-pinching concern that has no interest in protecting its country's honour. As in *The Wicked World*, the play ends with the politicians returning to earth and the fairies returning to their original state.

The private performance did not take place, 'owing to a domestic affliction' as Gilbert said,[17] but Marie Litton had previously expressed an interest in producing the piece at the Court Theatre, so Gilbert handed the plot outline to her and she 'gave the plot to Mr. Gilbert à Beckett, who completed it, with some slight assistance from me'.[18] This, at any rate, was Gilbert's official recollection; but the facts show a slightly different picture. Gilbert certainly wrote the sketch plot – a copy of which survives in his hand in the British Library – but he was also more closely involved with the actual writing of the piece (eventually called *The Happy Land*) than he was prepared to state in his autobiography. The surviving manuscripts – the licence copy in the British Library and a revised draft of Act 2 in the Pierpont Morgan Library, New York – are largely in Gilbert's handwriting, and some of the play's best scenes bear the stamp of his style. He was intimately involved in the play's stage management through rehearsals. However, in public Gilbert was most anxious to minimise his involvement in the play's creation. He disguised himself under the pseudonym F. Tomline and denied authorship when asked. His reasons were twofold: firstly, he felt it would not do to be seen parodying his own play which was running at another theatre; secondly and probably more importantly, he wished to distance himself from what was an audacious and technically illegal act.

There was always some kind of censorship of English drama, even in Shakespeare's time, but it was in 1737 that Robert Walpole gave powers of censorship to the Lord Chamberlain – allegedly to stop Henry Fielding from satirising Walpole on stage. The Lord Chamberlain's Office retained these powers until 1968 when all official censorship of drama in the United Kingdom was abolished. Between the years 1737 and 1968, then, all new play scripts – initially at the 'legitimate' theatres in London, later throughout the British Isles – had to be read and approved before they were performed. In Gilbert's time personal allusions to current politicians were not allowed on stage, and it almost went without saying that the same stricture applied to the direct impersonation of current politicians.

The reading and licensing of plays was done not by the Lord Chamberlain himself, but by the Examiner of Plays, who at this time was William Bodham Donne. Donne was a most cultured man: Cambridge-educated, literary-minded and for some years the librarian of the London Library. He was a keen theatregoer and he knew the tradition of English drama as well as anyone and better than most. In 1873, he was 64 years old, on the verge of retirement and, we might speculate, rather worn down by the tide of third-rate drama that he had been obliged to wade through since taking on the post in 1857. He was about to wander blithely into a storm of controversy. A script of the play was submitted to the Lord Chamberlain's Office on 3 February, and was approved five days later as being a general satire without personal allusions.

It seems likely that Gilbert à Beckett wrote the play's more direct topical jokes. A brother of Arthur William à Beckett (with whom Gilbert had clashed over *An Old Score*), he was a mild young man with a satirical temperament, later a stalwart contributor to *Punch* and the man who conceived the idea for the famous Tenniel cartoon 'Dropping the Pilot'. In November 1872 his burlesque *Charles II; or, Something Like History* had been performed at the Court Theatre alongside a revised version of Gilbert's *An Old Score*, now retitled *Quits*. He was known, therefore, to Marie Litton, as well as to Gilbert, who had been a friend of the family since childhood.

One of the actors at the Royal Court, Edward Righton, recalled the play's rehearsals:

I had the honour of stage managing the original production … if, indeed, he can be called stage manager who is entirely guided by the wishes of the author ... The question of how to dress the three male characters was one which exercised me greatly, and Mr. Latour Tomline, the *nom de plume* chosen by Mr. Gilbert ... seemed to have formed no idea on the subject ... Passing down Piccadilly, I saw, in a bookseller's window, some cartoons from *Vanity Fair*, among which were those of Mr. Gladstone, Mr. Lowe, and Mr. Ayrton. It flashed across me like lightning that a 'counterfeit presentment' of the trio would be the very thing for *our* Cabinet Ministers. I communicated my new idea to Mr. Tomline, who caught at it instantly ... My joy at having so gratified an author – not always too easy to please – was considerably discounted by a suspicion, almost amounting to certainty, that from the first it had been his intention to dress his characters in the guise I thought I had sprung upon him.[19]

The first night of *The Happy Land* took place on 3 March 1873 and was a sensational occasion. There was the usual long mid-Victorian programme of entertainment: a curtain-raiser called *Vesta's Temple*, followed by a performance of the eighteenth-century classic comedy *The Jealous Wife* by George Colman the Elder; *The Happy Land* was the last item on the bill of fare, probably starting about ten o'clock in the evening. It was a packed house. Gilbert à Beckett and his brother Arthur had intended to occupy the Royal Box, but at the last moment they found themselves unable to do so because the Prince and Princess of Wales, the Duke of Edinburgh and suite had decided to attend; and so the à Becketts had to be content with a top proscenium box, 'the only unoccupied places in the house'.[20]

The first scenes of the new burlesque went well enough, in which the fairies discuss the wicked world below. The King of the Fairies is visiting England as a guest of royalty, and they discuss the fact that he is being put up at Claridge's hotel rather than being invited to stay at one of the royal palaces. One of the fairies comments: 'But it must be rather an expensive process in the end,' and another replies: 'Social economy means spending a penny to save a pound. Political economy is spending a pound to save a penny.'[21]

This sally must have been embarrassing enough for the occupants of the Royal Box, but there was worse to follow. Edward Righton was behind the scenes, dressed as Ayrton, alongside two colleagues made up as Gladstone and Lowe; and Righton recalled that as the stage machinery worked and the three men rose through the clouds of Fairyland into the sight of the audience:

there burst upon us another gale of boisterous merriment, which increased and increased in volume as we rose higher and higher, until the three figures from *Vanity Fair* stood on the stage; then the applause resembled the roaring of cannon or claps of thunder, and this was renewed when we did a little break-down step at the end of each verse of our trio –

'We are three most popular men,
I'd like to know who'll turn us out.'[22]

The direct caricaturing of living politicians was forbidden, and to break the interdiction was an achievement in itself; but to do so with such panache, and to show Gladstone and his colleagues demolishing themselves in song and dancing the most vulgar of burlesque dances at the same time: that was delicious. It is tempting to see an echo of this moment in some of the later Gilbert and Sullivan operas, when the Lord Chancellor or the First Lord of the Admiralty are made incongruously to dance and dance in their official robes.

A later speech made by 'Mr. A.' (Ayrton) to the fairies appears to sum up Gilbert's attitude to the workings of government:

> My dear, it's one of the beautiful principles of our system of government never to appoint anybody to any post to which he is at all fitted. Our government offices are so many elementary schools for the instruction of ministers. To take a minister who knows his duties, and to send him to an elementary school to learn them, is an obvious waste of educational power. Nature has pointed you out as eminently qualified for First Lord of the Admiralty, *because* you don't know anything about ships. You take office – you learn all about ships – and when you *know* all about ships, the Opposition comes in, out you go, and somebody else, who doesn't know anything about ships, comes in and takes your place. That's how we educate our ministers. [23]

The piece ranged between sophisticated criticism of the political system and broad mockery of the personal attributes of Gladstone, Ayrton and Lowe. No punches were pulled, right down to the final chorus in which the cast pointedly sang: 'Poor Britannia,/Although she rules the waves,/Britons ever, ever, ever,/ Shall be slaves.' [24]

The audience was wild with enthusiasm, and a good deal of political feeling was aroused, but the royal party was not so ecstatic. *The Graphic* reported that 'the amusement of the Royal party at the ridiculous position of respected Cabinet Ministers was as undisguised as the delight of the audience' (8 March 1873). But *The Era* saw their behaviour differently: the prince was 'placed in a peculiarly delicate position, and was naturally forced to smother the laughter that was inevitable from a very amusing entertainment' (9 March 1873).

The prince was not happy. His private secretary Francis Knollys wrote a strongly worded letter on his behalf to the Lord Chamberlain the next day:

> His Royal Highness has rarely if ever brought under your notice as Lord Chamberlain any criticism of his own upon any play, but he cannot in the present instance refrain from calling your attention to the Piece in question, the whole object of it apparently being to bring into ridicule and contempt certain members of the government. A fair amount of criticism on the stage of the Public men of the day no one could object to, but His Royal Highness thinks

that if you went to see 'Happy Land' you would agree with him in opinion that in this case all legitimate bounds have been passed and that what is called 'chaff' has degenerated into licence.[25]

On the evening of 5 March the Lord Chamberlain, Lord Sydney, visited the Court Theatre himself to see *The Happy Land*. Afterwards, he noted that 'nothing could be more offensive'.[26] Next day, the might of the Lord Chamberlain came down heavily upon the Court Theatre. Its acting manager was interviewed by Donne, accompanied by Spencer Ponsonby, the comptroller of the Lord Chamberlain's department and Donne's immediate superior. But the acting manager seemed to know little or nothing, and they dismissed him with a letter, addressed to Marie Litton, withdrawing the Lord Chamberlain's licence for the play. She fired off a reply and, hot on its heels, travelled to St James' Palace herself to try to sort things out. But she was told on arrival that nothing could be done until the licence copy of the play was compared with the prompt copy.

What followed was a little farce appropriate to the subject. Marie Litton secured the theatre's prompt copy of the play and sent it by messenger to William Bodham Donne's private house. However, Donne was in the meantime waiting at his office in St James' Palace, having located the licence copy of the play. Here he stayed until the end of his working day, about four o'clock. Then he went home, and there he found the Court Theatre's messenger waiting with the prompt copy. The licence copy, meanwhile, had been left back in his office at St James' Palace. It was now too late in the day to decide the fate of *The Happy Land*, and the Lord Chamberlain sent a message to Marie Litton saying that the play could not be performed until they had reached a verdict. Unfortunately, by the time she got this message the doors of the Court Theatre were open and the public were arriving.

Marie Litton was clearly a young woman of great courage and judgement; born in 1847, she was in her mid-twenties at the time of this episode, and already the successful manager of a major London theatre. Faced with a crowd wanting only to see the Royal Court's new satire, she made the difficult and courageous decision to let the performance go ahead.

In an attempt to appease the Lord Chamberlain, the three men did not wear their caricature make-up. However, to ensure the audience knew what they were missing the management distributed a notice stating: 'Miss Litton begs to inform the public that the Lord Chamberlain has forbidden Messrs. Fisher, Hill, and Righton to make up their faces in imitation of Messrs. Gladstone, Lowe and Ayrton.'

The house was packed. Before the performance, Edward Righton delivered a speech:

You are probably aware that the *Happy Land* is a good-humoured political skit directed partly against the recent doings of the present Ministry, partly against the system upon which the Ministers are appointed. It is, in fact, precisely the kind of satire which you are accustomed to laugh at, week after week, in *Punch* and the other comic papers.

He explained the situation in somewhat inflammatory terms, describing the Lord Chamberlain's intervention as 'official intolerance'. He added: 'the manager had one of two alternatives open to her – either to play the piece in the face of this most arbitrary and tyrannical opposition or to close the theatre altogether. Having regard to her duty to the public … she has selected, at all hazards, to play the piece this evening.'[27]

On the next day, Friday 7 March, Marie Litton went to St James' Palace again to be grilled by Spencer Ponsonby. It was now becoming clear how this whole farcical episode had happened. The script which the Lord Chamberlain's Office had approved in February was substantially different from the version performed at the Court Theatre in March. The Lord Chamberlain's men had spent the evening of 6 March compiling a list of differences between the licence copy and the prompt copy, and had ended up with a list nineteen pages long. Marie Litton admitted to Spencer Ponsonby that the whole business had been 'a "try on" to which she had been urged by the Authors'.[28] It seems that Gilbert and à Beckett had prepared a kind of dummy script for the Examiner of Plays to read, and that a good deal of personal satire was added during rehearsal. Marie Litton 'expressed regret at what had occurred, and begged that the piece might be allowed to be performed as originally licensed, promising to adhere *verbatim* to the text, and to avoid anything which should convert the general allusions to personalities'.[29] The Lord Chamberlain's Office agreed to this. There was no performance of the play on Friday 7 March, but it was back on the boards the following night.

Friday 7 March also saw a letter appearing in the *Daily Telegraph*, signed 'F. Latour Tomline', and responding to the paper's review of *The Happy Land* which had appeared on 5 March. The *Telegraph* reviewer (probably Clement Scott) had been delighted to see 'so bright, so cheerful, and so well acted a play as "The Happy Land"', but had questioned the principle of putting satire upon the stage: he argued that stage satire was unlike the printed equivalent because it did not allow for a right of reply from the politicians. Tomline, however, disagreed:

These gentlemen have a right to appeal (such as it is) at the Court Theatre. They can come into the stalls and hiss. But the imagination refuses to picture Messrs. Gladstone, Ayrton, and Lowe standing in front of a stationer's window, and hissing a 'Punch' cartoon. Such an act would be wholly undignified.

Tomline admitted there was a case for banning stage satire, but as he most reasonably pointed out, it did not apply in the present instance:

The soundest objection to the conversion of the stage into a political arena is, I think, to be found in the fact that pieces produced to further political ends would, in many cases, excite riot and dissension among the audience. That objection certainly does not hold in the case of 'The Happy Land,' for the audiences have, at each representation, expressed the most enthusiastic and unqualified approval of the nonsense set before them. We were careful to confine ourselves to topics concerning which there could scarcely be two opinions, and I think we were entitled to reap the benefit of our discretion.

On the same day, Fred Clay (who was, as well as a composer, private secretary to the Liberal MP and joint secretary to the treasury George Grenfell Glyn) wrote to Gilbert ('Dear Gilbertides'), asking for his confirmation that he had not written *The Happy Land*:

A meddlesome ass writes to my chief that he has good reason to believe that the new Burlesque brought out at the Court was written by *you* ... It occurs to me that I have taken on myself to state a fact as to the truth of which I am wholly ignorant – but I take it for granted you had no hand in 'Happy Land' so I have written to say so.[30]

Gilbert wrote two letters in reply which are preserved amongst his correspondence at the British Library, probably alternative drafts of what he eventually sent to 'Claydides'. In the draft dated 7 March he wrote:

As you ask me a question point-blank, I am bound to reply to it point-blank. The general scheme of the piece occurred to *me*, but not wishing to be identified with a burlesque on my own work, I imparted it to à Beckett, who agreed to write the piece but having a delicacy about assuming the entire authorship of a piece suggested by another person, he expressed a wish to have a second name joined with his own. Hence 'Tomline' – under which pseudonym I wrote some articles many years ago. I need not say that I wish my 'anonymity' respected.

The second letter, dated 8 March, was briefer, stating that Gilbert had handed the idea of the play to Marie Litton (not à Beckett) and added (inaccurately) that 'I have no pecuniary interest whatever in the piece'.[31]

By now the whole affair was public property, and there was a good deal of discussion in the newspapers concerning the pros and cons of stage censorship. A leader in *The Times* (8 March) stated: 'we are not prepared to dissent from [the Lord Chamberlain's] implied opinion that it is going beyond a joke to exhibit scenes which must inevitably foster a vulgar contempt for authority as such.' However, *The Graphic* (15 March) commented witheringly on those 'who fancy they can discern essential differences between the case of caricatures in *Punch* and caricatures on the stage', adding that the history of stage censorship abounded with 'examples of the vexatious, paltry, and irritating meddling of the official licensers of plays'. On 10 March Sir Lawrence Palk asked a question in the House of Commons about the suppression of the play, and received an uninterested answer from the Home Secretary. There was talk and flurry; then the excitement died down and nothing happened. It was, in all, a very British scandal.

The success of the play itself was assured. The actors were now obliged by law to perform the rough draft of the script that had been approved by the Lord Chamberlain and not to be made up as any recognisable politician – but this made no great difference. It ran at the Court through to July, when the company and two others toured the country, taking *The Happy Land* to the main provincial towns (where the forbidden make-up mysteriously reappeared). On 14 October the play returned to a newly redecorated Court Theatre, where it stayed for a month before finally disappearing from the boards. Unappealingly, Gilbert wrangled with Marie Litton over the money for the play; it seems he was splitting the authors' share equally between himself and à Beckett. A letter from Marie Litton dated 18 October suggests that relations were strained:

> I enclose you a cheque due for 'Happy Land' … I asked you a simple question, whether you would take less per night for the 'Happy Land' (an arrangement which is quite customary in the profession) … I do not say one word against you refusing to take less but I *do* protest against your writing to me as if I were a mere dependant on your consideration and liberality.[32]

Gilbert does not come out of *The Happy Land* affair smelling entirely of roses. Though he was clearly the play's primary author, he took extreme care to ensure the fact did not become public. This was Gilbert in his role as competitor in the foot-race of life, jostling his rivals and using every method to get ahead of the pack. He had money to make and a reputation to gain and he did not want anything to get in the way. It was Marie Litton who took the risks and made the bold decisions; it was she, then, who was the hero of the hour.

But, as ever, the issue is not quite so simple. Gilbert was ambitious, but he also had an anarchic streak which acted in opposition to his material interests. It would have been safer from his point of view not to have written *The Happy Land* at all – but something, possibly a simple sense of mischief, spurred him to do so. As Annie Thomas had noticed, the fiercely independent Gilbert had to feel he was his own master and he deeply resented coercion from any source. To be forced to submit his plays for the approval of a civil servant at the Lord Chamberlain's Office must have galled him greatly. He had expressed his resentment previously in a letter which appeared in *The Daily News* on 12 January 1872:

Mr. Donne has, on three occasions, taken objection to passages in my plays. As I consider that I am quite as well qualified to judge of what is fit for the ears of a theatrical audience as he can be, I have systematically declined to take the slightest notice of his instructions.

It was this anti-authoritarian streak in Gilbert's make-up that led to the writing of *The Happy Land*; and it was this same streak that now encouraged him to write another play, under the pseudonym F. Latour Tomline, entitled *The Realm of Joy*.[33] Announced as 'a very free and easy version of the highly successful Palais Royal Farce, *Le Roi Candaule*', this short afterpiece is set in the box lobby of a theatre during the performance of a scandalous play. In the original French version, the scandal was sexual in nature; in Gilbert's version, naturally, it is political. Audiences flock to see it because it is shocking. As the box-keeper says:

A more disgraceful attack upon high minded and estimable public characters was never perpetrated. The authority of the most generally esteemed and unmistakeably indispensable of all our Court Functionaries, I allude to the Lord High Disinfectant – is publicly set at naught and his office is declared night after night to be nothing better than an unnecessary mockery. Society is furious, Society loves its Lord High Disinfectant. It regards him as a discreet and loving father who shall determine what it is fit for them to hear, and they have no words of contempt sufficiently strong for the irreverent hacks who have dared to defy his authority ... Society is loth to believe in such audacity on mere hearsay, and flocks to the theatre in thousands to witness the appalling spectacle for themselves.[34]

When the script was submitted to the William Bodham Donne for approval in October 1873, he passed it on to the Lord Chamberlain with a note pointing out that the author was 'the same Mr Tomline, who is the principal author of *The Happy Land* and who, I think your Lordship cannot fail to perceive, intends in this burlesque to single out the office of the Lord Chamberlain for the special aim of his satire'. But the Lord Chamberlain, probably realising that the publicity over *The Happy Land* had done the department nothing but harm, merely sent it back, advising: 'the play sent to be read may be acted ... you can make the usual corrections.' Donne wrote an angry letter to Spencer Ponsonby to let off a little steam: 'What "the usual corrections" can be in a piece so utterly *incorrigible*, and so obviously meant to be an official, if not a personal insult, passes my understanding.'[35] And then he passed the script, as requested.

The Realm of Joy, first performed at the Royalty Theatre (under the management of Henrietta Hodson) on 18 October 1873, went down well, though *The Observer*, for one, considered the satirical element to be its least interesting aspect: 'The real fun of the thing has nothing whatever to do with its being a "political recantation" as was stated on its original announcement; and when the house explodes with merriment it is always over the intensely funny situations of the original "Roi Candaule'" (19 October 1873). Whatever the reason, however, it ran at the Royalty for a very decent 112 performances.

F. Latour Tomline also translated Labiche's great farce *Un Chapeau de paille d'Italie* (*An Italian Straw Hat*) as *The Wedding March*, and it was seen at the Court Theatre from 15 November through to the following March. Gilbert always viewed the success of this piece with something between amusement and annoyance, as a letter in the *Times* on 17 January 1879 suggests:

> I translated the piece known to the English public as *The Wedding March* in two days, and I have received from various sources between £600 and £700 for it. I have been complimented, over and over again, by dramatic critics on the humour of that play, although I had no more to do with its humour than with that of the *Eunuchus*, which I translated (very freely, I believe, and under compulsion) at an early age. I have never regarded myself as the author of either play.

One last event from the year 1873 may be recorded as a coda to this strange, eventful history. After considerable delay, on 27 November, Gilbert's action for libel against Frederick Enoch, the publisher of the *Pall Mall Gazette*, was finally heard at the Court of Common Pleas.[36] The Attorney-General, J.C. Mathew, acting for Gilbert, asserted that the *Gazette* had a personal vendetta against Gilbert as a writer: 'whenever one of Mr. Gilbert's plays was noticed favourably his name was not mentioned; but whenever there was an unfavourable notice his name was mentioned.' The article in question (the criticism of *The Wicked World* signed 'Amuetos' which appeared in the *Gazette* for 23 January 1873) charged Gilbert with 'writing what was coarse, vulgar and indecent'. Witnesses were called – well-known actors, critics and dramatists – and gave evidence that *The Wicked World* was, in the words of *The Times* critic John Oxenford, 'a remarkably inoffensive piece'. The Attorney-General asserted that 'Amuetos' was unique in finding coarseness and indecency in the play, and this being the case, 'surely Mr. Gilbert was not to suffer on that account'. The *Gazette's* defence was that, whether the criticism was justified or not, it did not go beyond the bounds of legitimate comment and was not a personal attack, and therefore could not be considered a libel. After much examination and cross-examination, the case was wound up. The jury, deciding that both Gilbert's play and the letter by 'Amuetos' were innocent, returned a verdict in favour of the defendant (*Pall Mall Gazette*). Gilbert had to pay the defendant's costs, but he was not unhappy. His play had been declared free of indecency. Honour was satisfied.

10

THE END OF THE BEGINNING (1874–75)

Gilbert knew he had gone as far as he could go with his fairy comedies. He had written to Buckstone on 10 January 1873, just after the premiere of *The Wicked World*: 'it won't do to work "Fairy Comedies" "*ad nauseam*"',[1] and Buckstone agreed. Gilbert took time to devise and write a strong drama – modern in theme, setting, dialogue and attitude – tailored to meet the requirements of the Haymarket company. It was called *Charity*.

The title of the play came to seem heavily ironic in view of Gilbert's own conduct. Buckstone, old and deaf and perhaps a little confused, kept arranging to meet Gilbert to discuss the play, and then missing the appointments; finally, he arranged to produce another man's play instead of *Charity*. Gilbert wrote to Buckstone on 17 November 1873:

> I will not dwell upon the deliberate character of the insult you have placed upon an author who has worked laboriously & conscientiously for you for nearly four years … I hereby warn you that if my piece is not put into rehearsal forthwith & produced as soon as it is ready I shall place the matter in the hands of my solicitors.

Buckstone wrote back rather plaintively on the same day: 'I presumed I was suiting your convenience by giving you more time – I do not want to argue.' To which Gilbert replied tartly: 'If in producing another Author's 3 act play at a time when you were under contract to produce mine, you intended to do me a personal favour, you might have paid me the compliment of consulting me as to whether I considered such a proceeding "a favour at all".'[2] The play went into rehearsal under a state of uneasy truce, and was premiered at the Haymarket on 3 January 1874 (in a triple bill between *The Crimson Scarf* and *Raymond and Agnes; or, The Bleeding Nun of Lindenberg*).

The play, written in four acts, concerns the rich widow Mrs Van Brugh, who does much good in her community by helping anyone in distress, without any regard to denomination or creed. Mr Smailey, the local Pillar of Society, resents this irreligious goodwill, especially when Mrs Van Brugh decides to employ in her household Ruth Tredgett, a disreputable 'tramp' who has lived as a thief and as 'what gentle-folks thinks is wus than a thief'.[3] In an extraordinary scene she and Smailey meet and it emerges that Smailey had seduced and abandoned her twenty years before:

Ruth. ... I'm kinder curious to hear what *you've* got to say about a woman o'my stamp. I['m] kinder curious to hear wot Jonas Smailey's got to say about his own work.

Mr. S. We meet in a strange way after so many years.

Ruth. Yes; we do meet in a strange way. Seems to me it's suthin' of a topsy-turvy way. But it's a topsy-turvy world, ain't it?

Mr. S. (*recovering himself, with bland dignity*). I have no desire to press hardly on a fellow-creature—

Ruth. (*quietly*). Come, that's kind, anyhow.

Mr. S. Perhaps, after all, you were not entirely to blame.

Ruth. Well, p'raps not.

Mr. S. Perhaps I myself was not altogether without reproach in the matter. But in my case allowance should, in common charity, be made for follies that arise from extreme youth and — and inexperience. I was barely forty then.

Ruth. And I was just sixteen. Well, I forgive you, along o' your youth, as I hope to be forgiven along o' my childhood.[4]

In this scene Gilbert harnesses his heightened, ironic style to a desperately serious situation, and the result is shocking and blackly funny. Ruth's line 'But it's a topsy-turvy world, ain't it?' was surely a deliberate challenge to those critics who thought Gilbert's topsy-turviness was a retreat into fantasy.

The rest of the play concerns Smailey's attempts to ruin Mrs Van Brugh financially and socially by proving she was never formally married to her late husband. Subplots and machinations lead, at last, to the downfall of Smailey and to Mrs Van Brugh's final determination to emigrate to a foreign colony where she will, she hopes, meet with greater Christian charity than she could in her own land.

It was clear from the first night that the play would not equal the fairy comedies in success. The critics were uniformly critical. *Lloyd's Weekly Newspaper* gave perhaps the harshest of the verdicts: '*Charity* is a mistake, both in its theme and treatment, and cannot add to the reputation of the author' (11 January 1874). *The Observer* was kinder, but still disappointed:

Clever, intellectual dialogue, the language of a scholarly writer, now and then the action and situation that come out of high dramatic purpose and capacity —

all this we had, and much more; but on the whole the work was not complete; the intention was not clear; the end not equal to the splendid promise of the opening scenes. [4 January]

In general, the critics considered the plot to be too involved and some of the characters (especially Smailey) too impossible. It was a daring experiment, and contained some scenes which should be compared for ironic force with Bernard Shaw twenty years later; but the play as the whole left the audience unsatisfied and perhaps rather puzzled. It did not last long, surviving only until 14 March.

At the Royalty, meanwhile, Gilbert was preparing another play – a dramatisation of Annie Edwardes' 1871 novel *Ought We to Visit Her?*, which also satirised mid-Victorian attitudes to women. The theme is a simple one: the social ostracism that an actress experiences in the county set of her well-born husband and her spirited reaction to the situation. The adaptation was made at the request of Henrietta Hodson, the manager of the Royalty, but the themes were congenial to Gilbert in any case, as the contemporaneous *Charity* suggests.

Henrietta Hodson also played the lead role in the play. Her personal situation was a highly unconventional one and had some parallels with the heroines of both *Ought We to Visit Her?* and *Charity*. She had married a Bristol solicitor named Richard Pigeon in 1864, but soon became estranged from him. In 1867 she met the maverick journalist and politician Henry Labouchère, and by 1874 they had been living together for several years. They were unable to marry because her husband was still living and any divorce would have cited Labouchère as co-respondent, destroying his political career.

From the first, Henrietta Hodson's relationship with Gilbert was strained. She wrote:

In 1874, I saw a good deal of [Gilbert], as I was then the Lessee of the Royalty Theatre, and he wished to write a play for me. He told me that, somehow or other, he had invariably quarrelled with every one with whom he had been professionally connected, and I took great pains to prevent giving him any cause for quarrel with me. I agreed with him in all that he said, and I concurred with him in all his opinions. When he complained, that Shakespeare had statues elevated to him, whereas he, who was in every way Shakespeare's superior, had none, I went so far as to console him with the assurance that, if he would only be patient, there could be no doubt that he too would live to see his own statue. When he abused all other dramatic authors, all critics who did not praise him, and the numerous actors and actresses with whom he had had disputes, I did not defend them. Even when he told me stories, how he had 'humiliated' actresses, who had dared to resent his unprofessional behaviour, I kept my indignation to myself, and uttered no protest. When he said, that Miss Robertson had ventured, at a dinner party, to observe, that she did not like one of his plays, in which she was acting, and that, before he forgave her, he had forced her to cry and humbly sue for pardon, I merely replied, that any one who questioned his great ability must be insane. Thus I kept on good terms with him.[5]

Clearly it never occurred to her that this subservient conduct was in fact the worst way to keep on good terms with him. Some of the opinions attributed to Gilbert seem to have been misunderstood by Henrietta Hodson. For instance, it appears Gilbert had no great belief in his own brilliance as a writer but he did hold the (not unique) opinion that Shakespeare was vastly overrated. It seems possible that Gilbert regarded Miss Hodson as something of a figure of fun who would take seriously anything he said. When, in 1877, she published the account of her relationship with Gilbert which is here quoted, Madge Robertson's husband W.H. Kendal rushed to write to *The Era* (6 May 1877), insisting that the pamphlet contained 'untrue statements concerning my wife' and adding that Gilbert had written to her assuring her that 'Miss Hodson's statement [about what he had said] is utterly false'. The Kendals had no reason to defend Gilbert if they did not wish to, as he had quarrelled with them and they were not on speaking terms. However, it is true that Gilbert enjoyed being the dominant male in any gathering and took great pleasure in demonstrating his superiority over others, with varying degrees of humour and irony. The broad outline of events described by Henrietta Hodson is probably accurate, even if the details are exaggerated. Gilbert, accustomed to the rough humour of the Savage Club and the Arundel, did not always adapt to his surroundings as easily as his more sociable contemporaries.

According to Henrietta Hodson, the rehearsals for *Ought We to Visit Her?* went smoothly without any argument at all until the day before opening night. Gilbert, however, remembered disagreements throughout the rehearsal process. During the last rehearsal, according to Henrietta Hodson:

suddenly Mr. Gilbert jumped up, and commenced pulling his hair and dancing like a maniac. 'Look,' he said, 'at that man reading a newspaper;' and he pointed to Mr. Bannister, who was rehearsing the reading of a newspaper on the stage. 'Do, pray,' I said, 'let the rehearsal go on quietly, and if anything goes wrong, make a note of it, and we will go all over it again.' On this, he put on his hat, and, without a word, walked out of the theatre.[6]

This incident hints at the real point of disagreement between them: Gilbert insisted on being in absolute control in rehearsals (especially the vital last dress rehearsal), while Henrietta Hodson seems to have assumed that she, as 'leading lady', was in a position to direct proceedings.

Gilbert made the mistake of gossiping about all this to his friends in the theatrical world – particularly to Marie Litton. Henrietta Hodson heard that Gilbert had been spreading slander about her and threatened him with an action. On

4 February 1874 Gilbert wrote to Marie Litton a letter which suggests a genuine bewilderment about what he could have said to provoke such a result:

> I have received a letter from Miss Hodson's attorneys threatening me with an action for slander on the ground that I attributed 'obscene and disgusting language' to her in my conversation with you. As I am certain that she must be acting under some misapprehension, I shall be much obliged if you will kindly let me know what you said to Miss Hodson in reference to our conversation concerning her, that could possibly bear such an interpretation.
>
>   I am prepared to admit that I said that Miss Hodson used the ridiculous expression 'floody bool' in reference to me & that she told me at the last rehearsal 'not to stand growling there, but to go home & go to bed' as that was the best place for me.[7]

The action did not take place; instead, on 3 March 1874 Gilbert very unwillingly signed a statement of apology:

> I never intended to make the least imputation upon your character as manageress of the Royalty Theatre … I never intended to attribute to you the use of language inconsistent with your position as a lady. I further desire to express to you my sincere regret that in a moment of great excitement I should have used words that have offended you, and I trust you will accept this retractation.[8]

There, for the moment, the incident rested; but deep and bitter resentments remained.

Ought We to Visit Her? was better received by the critics than *Charity*, but it was not much more successful, lasting only until 14 April.

Sometime in the autumn of 1873, Gilbert was approached by Carl Rosa, who earlier that year had set up an opera company to perform works in English. Gilbert was asked to provide the libretto for a short companion piece in a season of opera projected for the start of 1874. Gilbert responded by taking a one-page skit called 'Trial by Jury' which he had written for *Fun* in 1868 and expanding it.[9] This operatic version of a trial for breach of promise of marriage had its roots in the Bancrofts' mock trials in Liverpool in 1866. He made the idea his own, satirising the legal system as he had experienced it. Unfortunately, the scheme fell through because Rosa's wife, the singer Euphrosyne Parepa-Rosa who had been projected to star in the little opera, died in January 1874.

Gilbert's temper was deteriorating rapidly. He was quarrelling with everyone, and his plays were becoming more crabbed and full of vague regret. His short musical play *Topseyturveydom*,[10] with music by Alfred Cellier, was first performed as part of the opening night of the new Criterion Theatre, on 21 March 1874. It took the topsy-turvy principle to its extreme, combining fantasy, nonsense and satire in a narrative which followed a Conservative MP on a journey to a strange land where 'although everything here is the exact opposite of everything there, yet there isn't as much difference as you may think'.[11] The result was so bizarre as almost to prefigure the absurdist dramas of Ionesco eighty years later, and seemed to suggest a mood of disorientated bewilderment with human behaviour. But it was, in Gilbert's mind, a very minor piece, and thirty years later he had completely forgotten it. He told T. Edgar Pemberton around about the year 1903: 'I never saw *Topsyturveydom*. If you happen to have a copy of it and could lend it to me for a few hours it might suggest some reminiscences: as it is I don't even know what the piece was about!'[12] His wife Lucy, however, remembered it clearly even in the 1930s, and considered that 'the humour was above the heads of the general public'.[13] *Reynolds's Newspaper* noted (29 March 1874) that the audience 'hissed freely' on the first night; and the little afterpiece survived for less than a month before being quietly dropped.

His short play in two acts *Sweethearts*, first performed at the Prince of Wales Theatre on 7 November 1874 in a double-bill with Robertson's *Society*, was entirely different in tone: a sensitive and perfectly balanced little piece which could almost (but not quite) be called sentimental. In this play, again, there is a perception of something lost or missed, though the tone is not harshly satirical, but regretful and human. In Act 1, set in the year 1844, a young couple meets for the last time before he goes off to India. He is sentimental and effusive in his declarations; she is light and flirtatious and unfeeling. He urges her to pick a flower for him to keep, which he will keep and prize; he gives her the rose from his button-hole, which she casts aside carelessly. And he leaves for India. When he is out of sight, her manner changes suddenly and she bursts into tears. Act 2, which takes place thirty years later, shows the girl grown into a middle-aged spinster, and the boy into a weather-beaten Anglo-Indian gentleman. They meet again, and slowly they recall the events of their youth. The man forgot his love before the ship reached India and he threw away his treasured flower; but she kept the rose from his buttonhole carefully pressed. The play ends with the two deciding to pick up the romance where they left off.

It is a drama of character rather than plot or ideas, and, simply and without fuss, it touches the heart. As such, it is unique in Gilbert's output. One night, Squire Bancroft noticed a man sitting close to the stage who was unable to control his emotions during the second act. Finally the man turned to his neighbour and exclaimed audibly, 'Yes, ma'am, I *am* crying, and I'm proud of it!'[14]

The play was received with enthusiasm. At the end of the first performance, first the actors were cheered to the rafters, and then the author was called for by general acclamation. Gilbert was not in the building to hear them, having started his practice of not seeing his own plays; but the reviews must have helped to compensate. *Sweethearts* turned out to be his most successful play of the year; it remained on the programme at the Prince of Wales through to the following April.

At about this time Gilbert wrote a short burlesque of *Hamlet* in the classic style, entitled *Rosencrantz and Guildenstern*. It was written for the Court Theatre and even got to rehearsal, but, as Gilbert told a correspondent some years later, 'from circumstances into which I need not enter the performance did not take place'.[15] The nature of these circumstances is not known, but it seems possible that Gilbert had one of his periodic rows with the management. However, the piece did not get thrown into a drawer and forgotten. On 20 November 1874, Tom Hood, the editor of *Fun*, died of a liver complaint. Like many of the *Fun* crowd, he lived boisterously and recklessly, and he died too young. As a favour to the old magazine in this time of crisis, Gilbert allowed *Rosencrantz and Guildenstern* to be published in *Fun* over the course of three weeks in December, and drew two Bab illustrations to accompany the columns. It is a magnificent parody of Shakespeare and Shakespearean productions, and contains a pithy summary of the vexed arguments about Hamlet's character: he is 'idiotically sane,/With lucid intervals of lunacy'.[16] This was to be Gilbert's last contribution to *Fun*, the paper that had given him his first chance as a writer.

Gilbert's Bab-illustrated story in the Christmas number of *The Graphic* that year, 'The Story of a Twelfth Cake', returns to the theme of regret, though in a farcical vein. Tommy Williamson, a confectioner on the Borough Road, is threatened with a trial for having deserted from the Highlanders some years ago; in order to avoid this he takes up an offer provided by a fairy to have three chances to change his past and make things better. His wishes, of course, only make his situation a hundred times worse, until he makes his last wish, which is to eliminate from his life his acquaintance with the fairy who gave him the wishes in the first place. It is a brilliantly original story (anticipating the familiar science-fiction idea of 'alternative universes'), told in a coolly ironic style with a harsh undertone.

There was a growing feeling that Gilbert's moment of greatness had been and gone. There is nothing so passé as last year's sensation. *The Hornet* took to referring to him as 'dead Gilbert', and an article in *London Society*'s series of 'Notes on Popular Dramatists' in January 1875 deliberately struck another nail into his coffin:

It is but a very short time since Mr. Gilbert promised to take a position second to no dramatist of the day. His plays were to be seen in all directions; managers clamoured for more; and the first representations of his works were attended by the recognised leaders of literature and art. The public applauded and the newspapers praised ... and when each new play was announced his admirers hoped that his acute faults would have been overcome, and his weaknesses strengthened. His admirers have been disappointed. The faults seemed to have become chronic; interest in his plays diminished; the critics, disinclined to keep on for ever hiding blame and encouragingly giving praise, spoke freely, and acknowledged that Mr. Gilbert had not done what was expected ...

Whether it is that managers have grown shy of trusting their fate to Mr. Gilbert's hands, or whether he himself is angry at the cool reception his work has lately experienced, we are not able to judge. The only way we have of estimating a dramatist's position is by noticing the number of plays he produces and the effect they create; and by this standard Mr. Gilbert at the present moment cannot be regarded as a successful writer ...

A play, to be effective, must win the sympathies of the audience, and it is here that, as a general rule, Mr. Gilbert completely fails. We do not insist that every pair of lovers should be united before the curtain falls; but we do insist that some of the characters should possess generous impulses, should excite our sensibilities by the exhibition of some little tenderness and good feeling. Mr. Gilbert's creations are generally cynical, and sometimes brutal, in their behaviour. They are constantly out of harmony with the spectator; few of them betray that generosity and nobility of spirit which arouses and enchains interest. [17]

It was true: Gilbert had not done what was expected of him, and his plays found themselves out of harmony with their audiences. He could not dance to their tune. Fiercely independent, he had no choice but to continue to make plays in his own way and damn the consequences. But what did the future hold? What could lie in store for him except stale repetitions of what he had already achieved?

11

TRIAL AND TRIBULATION (1875–77)

The theatre was Gilbert's world. Madge Robertson wrote, 'He loved the theatre. He was happy in it. Rehearsals were the breath of his nostrils.'[1] Acting and drama were what he understood. Music, on the other hand, was a closed book to him, or perhaps an open book in an alien and barely understood language. He had seen the operas of Donizetti and Bellini as he grew up, and he had enjoyed them; and he knew enough to turn these old operas into burlesques. However, as he said, 'I suppose I may claim a fairly accurate ear for rhythm, but I have little or no ear for tune'.[2] His inability to sing was legendary. Though many of his works for stage thus far had included music and songs, they were merely plays with music, and they were performed by actors and entertainers, not trained singers. Even *Thespis*, which had called itself an opera, had been performed by burlesque actors, many with little or no voice.

But all this was about to change.

Richard D'Oyly Carte was the founder and manager of an operatic and concert agency based in Charing Cross, with a large client list of singers and instrumentalists and other musicians. His clients included Jacques Offenbach and Charles Gounod. He was born in 1844, so he was younger than either Gilbert or Sullivan, but by 1875 he had already achieved much; and he was determined to achieve more. He had a great ambition: to found and nurture a school of native English opera. The son of a musical instrument maker, he had distinct musical leanings himself. He wrote a handful of comic operas and parlour ballads before the public's reaction of almost complete indifference finally discouraged him from further effort in that direction. In the early 1870s he moved into theatre management. He took the Opera Comique in 1874 and attempted to establish it as a permanent house for light opera, with works by Lecocq and others. But the scheme fell through and he terminated his lease of the theatre the same year.

One of his clients, the singer Selina Dolaro, formed her own light opera company and took over the Royalty Theatre at the beginning of 1875, with

Carte managing the front-of-house business. They opened on 30 January with Offenbach's *La Périchole* and a curtain-raiser called *Awaking*.

However, they were having some problems with the opera's companion pieces. A month later, on 27 February, *Awaking* was replaced by two brief items, *A Good Night's Rest* and *Cryptoconchoidsyphonostomata; or, While It's To Be Had*. The latter was apparently something of a stop-gap, dependent on the availability of its main performer Charles Colette, who was on loan from the Prince of Wales Theatre.[3] It is clear that the company (Carte in particular) was in search of a high quality replacement. And Carte remembered *Trial by Jury*. Gilbert had met Carte the previous year, during the latter's time at the Opera Comique, and had mentioned his little opera libretto. Carte had not been able to do anything with it then; but now its time had come.

Sullivan's account of what happened next has often been quoted but has never been bettered:

> It was on a very cold morning … with the snow falling heavily, that Gilbert came round to my place, clad in a heavy fur coat. He had called to read over to me the MS. of 'Trial by Jury.' He read it through, and it seemed to me, in a perturbed sort of way, with a gradual crescendo of indignation, in the manner of a man considerably disappointed with what he had written. As soon as he had come to the last word he closed up the manuscript violently, apparently unconscious of the fact that he had achieved his purpose so far as I was concerned, inasmuch as I was screaming with laughter the whole time.[4]

Sullivan wrote the music in a matter of days, and the cast was assembled and the opera was rehearsed in a couple of weeks. Its first performance took place on the evening of Thursday 25 March, as an afterpiece to *Cryptoconchoidsyphonostomata* and *La Périchole*. It was nearly eleven o'clock by the time the piece began, but the audience was in good humour and *Trial by Jury* went down very well indeed, keeping the crowd in a state of 'unceasing and almost boisterous hilarity' throughout.[5] Both Sullivan (who conducted) and Gilbert (who did not) were enthusiastically called for as the curtain fell. This time, in contrast to the first night of *Sweethearts*, Gilbert was present and able to respond to the call.

The reviews were uniformly enthusiastic. There was much comment on the audacity of the concept: 'We live in an age of dramatic novelties,' *The Era* said (28 March), 'but we venture to say there are few who would have expected to hear of *Trial by Jury* treated as a dramatic cantata … Great curiosity was naturally felt as to the manner in which Mr Gilbert would deal with this unprecedented libretto.' Gilbert's jokes and conceits were repeated with great relish and his jibes at the rich attorney's elderly, ugly daughter laughed over most heartily. The unity of his words with Sullivan's music was praised in extraordinary terms: *The Times'* critic wrote (29 March) that 'it seems, as in the great Wagnerian operas, as though poem and music had proceeded simultaneously from one and the same brain'.

Though the characters of the two men were radically different, there was something in their art which chimed together. Gilbert saw the things people did and found them absurd, and Sullivan, seeing the same things, found them humorous. Sullivan was able to laugh at the quirks of Victorian society without sharing Gilbert's sense of resentment or alienation. As a result, Sullivan's music was able to give Gilbert's words a warmth which they often lacked, and audiences responded.

But if Gilbert needed his Sullivan, then Sullivan also needed his Gilbert. Sullivan was a man of great conviviality and humour, but these aspects of his character found little outlet in his 'respectable' works: his cantatas, concert overtures and hymns. His Leipzig training gave him form and discipline, but his puckish side also clamoured for expression. His operas with Burnand were the first to release that other aspect of his temperament, but Gilbert went deeper than the easy-going, conventional Burnand could ever manage.

Trial by Jury survived on the Royalty's programme through to June. It was then taken on tour for the summer, and in the autumn brought back to the Royalty, where it remained to the end of the company's season in December. It was a firm favourite with audiences. Carte, still mulling over his grand plan for the creation of English opera, took note of this fact and laid it to one side for future reference.

For Gilbert, *Trial by Jury* was a very minor diversion in a still frenetic working life. Marie Litton had left the Court Theatre in March and taken a lease on the St James' Theatre instead; and Gilbert had written a three-act farce for her, *Tom Cobb*, based on his previous short story 'Tom Poulton's Joke'. It is an uproarious piece of nonsense, with no overt purpose other than to provoke laughter. It opened on 24 April to generally positive reviews: *The Times* declared that it contained 'more wit, humour, and truthful satire than would go to the making of half-a-dozen ordinary comedies' (26 April 1875), though *The Graphic* rather sniffily complained about the story's improbable and impossible elements. The play ran until the close of Marie Litton's season at the St James', at the end of June (when it briefly shared the bill with Sullivan's one-act opera *The Zoo*). Most of the major London theatre companies traditionally left the capital and toured the provinces during the summer; for this reason it is not always wise to judge the success of a play by the length of its London run, especially if it premiered in the late spring or early summer months. So it is true that *Tom Cobb* ran for only fifty-three performances at the St James', but it was well received, earning a second laudatory notice in *The Era* on 13 June, just as the run was nearing its close ('one of the most amusing and extravagant productions of Mr Gilbert's witty and facile pen'); it was later revived in a successful touring production.

He wrote one more piece for the German Reeds, entitled *Eyes and No Eyes*, and in the summer he trained with the Royal Aberdeenshire Highlanders in Scotland. There was talk of his writing a new piece with Sullivan, and it was not only Richard D'Oyly Carte who was making the suggestion: Carl Rosa was making noises, as was another manager, Charles Morton. But Gilbert had other priorities, and maybe the right offer had not been made. At any rate, nothing happened on that front just yet. In the autumn Gilbert was occupied heart and soul in writing his first completely serious play, the blank-verse tragedy *Broken Hearts*. This strange, remote piece is set on a tropical island where a group of broken-hearted women live in retreat from the world, diverting their affections towards inanimate objects such as a sundial and a fountain. A handsome prince is cast ashore, destroying their peace of mind, and one of their number finally dies, killed by the anguish of love. It was perhaps Gilbert's most personal work. Writing it consumed all his time and energy. He was dismayed to find, in the middle of the process of composition, that he was being called up for jury duty. This could not be contemplated: 'a possible six weeks at the Pleas was not to be entertained for a moment,' as he later explained. 'A practising barrister is exempt from jury service, but I had not practised for some years, and my name had somehow found its way onto the jury lists. Still I *was* a barrister, and this fact stood me in good stead.'[6]

It so happened that a gruesome murder case had just come to light. Henry Wainwright, a brush-maker on Whitechapel Road and a great follower of all things theatrical, had killed his mistress, a young woman called Harriet Lane. For some time he hid the body under the floor of his warehouse, but after some months it became necessary to move the body to a safer location. Enlisting the help of his brother Thomas, he dug up the remains and bound them up in two packages of American cloth, and on the morning of 11 September 1875 he tried to transport them across London by cab, to be reburied in a building owned by his brother. This amazingly stupid plan went wrong: the body was discovered in transit and he and his brother were arrested.

A friend of Gilbert's, a Mr Besley, was acting as defence counsel for the Wainwright brothers. Gilbert wrote to Besley, asking him as a favour to instruct Gilbert as a junior brief in the case. Gilbert recalled: 'In two days' time I received my brief, duly marked with a fee of £10 10s., which was just their fun.'[7] On 12 and 13 October 1875, Gilbert attended the police court hearings, cross-examined a couple of witnesses, made sure that, as a practising barrister, he would not be called up for jury duty and that was that. But the thing that astonished him most about the whole business was the moment when the two defendants were placed in the dock, and Gilbert looked up and saw, in Henry Wainwright, the man he had first seen at Tom Robertson's funeral, reminding him so forcibly of Robertson himself. Wainwright had obliquely inspired one of Gilbert's funniest plays; and now he was about to be tried, found guilty and executed.

Gilbert finished *Broken Hearts* in the early hours of 15 November, and rehearsals began very shortly afterwards. It was to be produced at the Court Theatre, now under the management of his old friend John Hare, with a cast that included the Kendals. The rehearsals were unusually stormy. 'Hare and W.S. Gilbert ...' Madge Robertson wrote, 'were both in the habit of losing their tempers every minute and recovering them in half a minute. I used to call them "The Rapids".'[8]

Their tempers were not made any the cooler by the fact that Hare preferred to stage-manage the plays he was associated with and, of course, Gilbert insisted on stage-managing his plays himself. One day they blazed at each other and then both stormed out of the rehearsal. They strode down the road and into the local underground station. They waited for the train, resolutely ignoring each other, but when it finally puffed in they both made for the same door.

'Naturally,' as Madge Robertson wrote, 'as the door was too narrow to admit both at the same time, neither could get in. Suddenly, Gilbert's strong sense of humour came to the rescue of the absurd situation. He burst out laughing.

'Hare looked at him, and in his turn, burst out laughing. Each took a step back from the train and at the same time held out his hand to the other. They shook hands warmly and together they returned to the theatre.'[9] They were met at the stage door by Madge Robertson, who rather relished letting them know that the rehearsal could not continue as everyone else had gone home.

Not all their arguments ended so well, however. For some years afterwards Gilbert refused to speak to Hare or the Kendals, simply as a result of disagreements during the production of *Broken Hearts*. The play opened at the Court Theatre on 9 December. The audience cheered Gilbert and Hare enthusiastically at the end. The play was received with general approval by the critics – *The Era*, for instance, calling it 'more of a poem than a play' (12 December) – but others found the subject matter excessively unreal: 'we turn with impatience from the absurd and impossible natures which are assigned to [these women]', *The Times* complained (13 December). The play had a run of seventy-eight performances, lasting until 10 March. It was neither a dead failure nor a great success.

It was nearly the cause of a split with two of Gilbert's oldest friends, when Burnand happened to make a joke to Clement Scott about going to see *Broken Parts*, and Scott repeated it in an article. 'Burnand's attempt at wit is silly and coarse, and your desire to bring it into prominence in the worst possible taste,' Gilbert told Scott in a letter.[10] But their friendship (for the moment) survived.

Just as the year was closing, another of Gilbert's bids for immortality appeared: a volume of his *Original Plays*, published by Chatto & Windus in a form designed to be kept and read as literature. Most plays were (and are) published in flimsy acting editions, designed to be used in the process of rehearsal rather than to be read as a novel is read. But Gilbert had other plans for his works; he had been meditating a 'respectable' volume of his best plays for at least a year. Gilbert drew up a list of the titles to be included: *Charity, Sweethearts, The Wicked World, The Palace of Truth, Pygmalion and Galatea* and *The Princess*. In the end, *Sweethearts* was dropped for copyright reasons, and in its place appeared *Trial by Jury*. He originally intended to draw a number of woodcuts to accompany the plays. Chatto & Windus liked this notion very much, telling him, 'The book will not stand anything like so good a chance without illustrations with them'.[11] But in the end the idea was dropped; it does not seem to have affected sales.

The reviews were mixed. This was an opportunity to take an overview of Gilbert's *oeuvre*, to judge his worth as a writer. 'It is one thing to concoct a drama which shall for an unconscionable number of nights fill the higher-class theatres, it is quite another to appeal to the thinker in his study,' said *The Graphic* (4 March 1876):

> On the whole, then, the plays are failures in a literary point of view ... they are pervaded throughout by a low tone of morality. We do not use the phrase in its vulgar acceptation, but in its essential sense ... there is, underlying all the fun and pathos of the dramatist's work, a bitter spirit of cynicism which is as shallow as it is untrue ... Take 'The Wicked World.' The moral – if there be one – is that men are sensual, heartless brutes, and that women are frivolous, spiteful fools.

The Examiner was more kindly (22 April 1876): 'This is a very charming volume,' its critic wrote. 'It has the stamp of originality upon it in every page.' The critic went on to argue that while Gilbert could not be called a poet if the word referred to the beautiful use of words – 'Mr. Gilbert's blank verse has actually no beauties' – he could still claim the term if it could refer to beauty of form: 'we can call to mind only one among our contemporary poets whose gift of form would have enabled him to fashion anything so symmetrically beautiful as *Pygmalion and Galatea*.'

A later review of the book from *The Theatre* on 26 June 1877, shrewdly suggested that Gilbert was undergoing a transitional period in his career: 'It is probable that Mr. Gilbert's name will live in association with efforts not to be included in any collection of his plays which can yet be made.'

The year 1876 was indeed a transitional year for Gilbert, more notable for what happened outside the theatre than in it. In every aspect of his life – domestic, familial and professional – there was a sense of change, disruption or strain.

In the latter months of 1875 Gilbert had been occupied in writing a play for the actor E.A. (Ned) Sothern, who was taking over the management of the Haymarket for a while. This play, first called *Abel Druce* and then *Dan'l Druce, Blacksmith*, proved troublesome, and Gilbert finished it later than expected. Sothern was a truly cosmopolitan actor, spending as much of his time acting in the United States as he did in Britain, and in fact he had become a naturalised American. His early success as Lord Dundreary had forced his career into a single groove of 'eccentric' comedy, but Sothern was always attempting to find a new success which would allow him to move into new areas. Gilbert's play, set during the English Civil War, was a variation on the theme of *Silas Marner* written in the historical-drama mode, and was clearly intended as a way of showing Sothern in a more serious histrionic light than previously. Sothern's season at the Haymarket finished at the end of January, and Gilbert had still not managed to finish the play to his satisfaction by the time Sothern returned to the States. It seems Gilbert handed the play, on completion, to Buckstone, who was back at the Haymarket. It was scheduled for production at Easter, with the much-admired actor Hermann Vezin in the title role; but, as a paragraph in *The Era* noted on 19 March, the date of the production remained 'not definitely settled' as Easter approached, and was in the end postponed.

At the same time, Gilbert remained in contact with Sullivan. They were in active negotiation with managers regarding the terms of their next collaboration. They wrote jointly to Charles Morton on 7 February 1876, stating these terms. Nothing happened. At the same time they were contemplating writing a one-act opera-bouffe for Richard D'Oyly Carte, but this too came to nothing because of delays on Carte's side. A proposed revision and revival of *Thespis* for Carte had previously been dropped for the same reason. A little later, in May and June, there was serious talk of the two men revising *The Wedding March* as a comic opera, with Arthur Sullivan's brother, Fred, acting as manager supported by the music publisher Thomas Chappell. Gilbert wrote to Fred Sullivan on 14 May assuring him that 'the piece will be finished, as far as I can see, by the fifteenth June',[12] and *The Era* on 11 June suggested that the project was substantially advanced. But it did not progress to production.

In the meantime, however, Gilbert had other problems to worry about: specifically, his parents. William and Anne Gilbert lived with their unmarried daughters Florence and Maude at 14 Pembridge Gardens, Notting Hill, their married daughter Jane Weigall having moved to Salisbury. The relationship between the father of the family and his wife and daughters had strained to breaking point. Gilbert Murray, an Australian cousin who heard the tail-end of the story from relatives, recalled being told what had caused the final breach. William Gilbert had come home one evening to discover the house preparing for a party. He was outraged: why had he not been told? The reply came that he did know, he had been told. Whereupon he ordered his wife and daughters to bed, had the party preparations put away and turned away the guests as they arrived. 'After that,' Gilbert Murray said, 'he lived at his club.'[13]

Gilbert tried to intercede and bring about a reconciliation, but his mother wrote to him coldly that she and her husband had 'determined never to live together again'.[14] Gilbert was, it must be admitted, not an ideal choice as negotiator, and he soon discovered that 'my proffered interposition was rejected by both sides'.[15] He found himself in a position of delicacy with which he was completely unequipped to deal. But, clearly distressed by his parents' separation, he was determined to do the best thing by them both.

William Gilbert had suffered a physical collapse shortly after leaving his wife, and for some time he was thought to be near death. He had assigned £400 a year and the house to his wife, and a total of about £400 a year to his daughters; but his doctors said that illness had left him unable to write for profit in the future, leaving him with a net income of only about £150–160 a year. By the end of

May 1876 he was convalescing at his daughter's house in Salisbury, and Gilbert wrote to his mother on his father's behalf, imploring her either to forego some of her income or to allow her estranged husband to live separately in two rooms in her house. She refused both alternatives, and William Gilbert spent the rest of his life with his daughter and son-in-law in Salisbury, frequently visiting his son in London.

When Gilbert Murray got to know William Gilbert the following year, he found the old man surprisingly congenial: 'tall, handsome, white-bearded and formidable to grown-ups, [he] was a delightful companion to a child, especially a rather bookish and high-brow child like me.' The old man's memories of far-off lands and his descriptions of 'peculiar forms of insanity' were irresistibly fascinating to the boy.[16] But other aspects of the situation were less attractive. Both William Gilbert and his estranged wife were frequent visitors to the Murrays, and if they chanced to call on the same day they had to be received in separate rooms. Another relative, Margaret Edwards, tried to reconcile the two, but the only result was that they both quarrelled with her, necessitating the setting aside of three rooms – 'a device at which the Gilberts laughed cheerfully while dear Aunt Margaret ... was distressed'.[17] The Gilbert family rather revelled in dissension, it seems.

W.S. Gilbert and Lucy, meanwhile, were planning a less traumatic change of address. In spite of his recent reversals, Gilbert remained one of the most successful playwrights of his generation and his increasing wealth made possible a move from Essex Villas into a more luxurious home. The Boltons in South Kensington was a prestigious new development; the singer Jenny Lind was to be the Gilberts' new neighbour. They moved into 24 The Boltons towards the end of July, having arranged for some alterations to the house beforehand, including the installation of double-glazing to shut out the sound of local bells. Gilbert, always sensitive to noise, knew he could only work in conditions of absolute quiet.

A comic opera he had written with Fred Clay, *Princess Toto*, was being performed in the provinces, starting in Nottingham on 1 July and proceeding to Manchester, Bradford, Edinburgh, Birmingham and Liverpool, before settling down to a (brief) London run in October. Though entertainingly silly, the opera did not catch on; but as Gilbert had sold the rights of the piece to Clay in June and was not involved in mounting the production, he probably did not care very much about it either way.

Of more immediate interest to him was the long-delayed production of *Dan'l Druce, Blacksmith*, which took place on 11 September. The play was received warmly by the first-night audience and by the critics. 'After many theatrical failures,' *The Examiner* (16 September) began its review with an almost audible note of relief, 'there is at last one great success'. It was a common complaint that Gilbert tended to intrude grotesque and inappropriate elements into his serious dramas, but here, at any rate, he had managed to subdue the tendency and earn the approval of his audience. 'In *Dan'l Druce* … [Gilbert] is thoroughly human, and, instead of holding up the follies of his fellow man to excite our ridicule, he bespeaks our warmest sympathies for him in his temptations and his trials' (*Era*, 17 September 1876). Druce is a miser whose hovel, in the aftermath of the Battle of Worcester, is intruded upon by two soldiers who steal his gold and leave in its place a foundling child. This apparently miraculous event redeems his life, and the remainder of the play explores the nature of that redemption. The critics grumbled at the coarse humour of one of the characters, Reuben Haines, but they were inclined to forgive even this blemish on an appealing human drama.

The honours did not belong to Gilbert alone. It was Vezin's moving, powerful performance as Dan'l Druce that electrified the house. *The Era* wrote that 'Mr Vezin's greatest triumph … was in the third act, with Dan'l Druce reconciled to his troubles, repressing his tears, stifling his emotion, hiding his grief, and resigning his treasure to other hands', a powerful, nuanced performance that 'called forth a storm of cheers such as has not been heard within the walls of a Theatre for a very long time'. However, Gilbert shared some of the glory and a 'shout of acclamation' (*The Era*) greeted his appearance at the end of the play.

At the same time, another drama was also developing at the Haymarket, but behind the scenes. In July 1876 Buckstone had arranged to take on Henrietta Hodson as the company's leading lady for three years, starting in October of that year. But *Dan'l Druce* was proving to be a success, with Marion Terry in its leading female role, and Henrietta Hodson was not able to take up her engagement until the programme was changed. In November, Gilbert suggested to Buckstone that *Dan'l Druce* could be followed by a revival of *Pygmalion and Galatea*; Buckstone agreed to this and drew up a proposed cast list for the revival, including Miss Hodson as Cynisca.

The subsequent events became the subject of heated dispute. However, according to his later account Gilbert had 'no idea that Miss Hodson was a member of the company. In fact, I believed that Mr Buckstone proposed to engage her specially for the part.'[18] This was, Gilbert considered, out of the question after their previous dispute at the time of *Ought We to Visit Her?* 'By my agreement with Mr Buckstone the cast of the piece was left entirely in my hands, and it will be readily understood that, in the interests of the Theatre, I preferred a lady to whom I could communicate my views, to one with whom I was not on speaking terms.'[19]

Gilbert had taken a violent dislike to Miss Hodson. Buckstone 'used every argument and pressure' to persuade Gilbert to accept her, but Gilbert was adamant.[20] On 13 November he had met a fellow playwright, Frank Marshall, at the first night of the farce *Hot Water* at the Criterion Theatre. Marshall taxed him with the question of whether Miss Hodson was to play in *Pygmalion and Galatea*. Gilbert replied: 'Do you think after the way in which she had behaved to me I would let her play any part in one of my pieces?'[21] Marshall wrote to Miss

Hodson relating this incident, explaining that he had remonstrated with Gilbert on the matter, without success. Miss Hodson took the matter to her solicitors, who wrote to Gilbert on 27 November notifying him that she intended bringing an action of slander against him. Gilbert wrote back to her two days later, assuring her that he was perfectly willing to accept her in the play 'if you are willing to meet me, for the purpose of this rehearsal, on friendly terms', adding that 'I had no idea, until yesterday, that you were still engaged on the staff of the Haymarket Theatre'.[22] So the action was retracted and it was finally decided that Miss Hodson was to play Cynisca (and Marion Terry, Gilbert's current favourite, was to play Galatea). *Dan'l Druce* ran until 19 January 1877, *Pygmalion and Galatea* taking its place the following night.

Gilbert had asked Henry Howe (the stage manager at the Haymarket, who also played Leucippe in the production) to keep an eye on his behaviour through the rehearsals for *Pygmalion and Galatea*, and to let him know if he should behave discourteously towards Miss Hodson. The rehearsals were, as might have been predicted, fraught with tension. Miss Hodson later insisted that Gilbert's behaviour to her was in fact a 'studied insult' throughout: he invited guests (including his father) to the rehearsals and talked with them while she was attempting to rehearse, ignoring her completely.[23] But it is difficult to reconcile this with Gilbert's well-known insistence upon rehearsing every move and inflection of a play until they became instinctive.

The play was performed and was received warmly by the critics, greeted, indeed, as an established classic and an old favourite. Marion Terry delighted audiences as Galatea, and Buckstone returned to his role as Chrysos. Gilbert was pleased with Marion Terry's performance, writing to her on 21 January:

> I was in every way charmed & delighted with your performance of 'Galatea' last night. The simple artless grace of the whole embodiment gratified me inexpressively. It has never before happened to me to have an idea so completely realized. And as you know me to be an opinionated & crotchety fellow, the best proof I can give you that I am in earnest is to tell you that I have absolutely no criticism to make on the performance.[24]

Henrietta Hodson's performance as Cynisca was much praised, *The Daily News* suggesting that she displayed 'greater power than she has ever yet shown in any of her impersonations' (22 January 1877). The play lasted until 6 April.

Henrietta Hodson later alleged that Gilbert more or less bullied Buckstone into producing his plays, that the plays ran at a substantial loss and that they were effectively ruining the Haymarket. The actors were asked to accept half-pay. They played a bad new comedy called *Fame* for two weeks and then *The Palace of Truth* took its place (to excellent reviews). Henrietta Hodson was not in the cast, though Marion Terry was.

This was, for Miss Hodson, the final straw. She was the company's leading lady but she was being excluded from the Haymarket's plays again and again. She had been advised by her solicitors that she could not bring an action against Gilbert, so instead she appealed to the informal court of public opinion. She put together a pamphlet detailing all her grievances against Gilbert and, towards the end of April, distributed it amongst the theatrical profession.

It is probable that this pamphlet was written in collaboration with the journalist Henry Labouchère, with whom she was living. His main contribution was probably to make a bad situation worse. He delighted in being a maverick and a truth-teller. 'In sending me into the world,' he said, 'nature sent a person without prejudice or bias and consequently absolutely impartial.'[25] He was later to draft the so-called 'Labouchère Amendment' to the Criminal Law Amendment Act of 1885, which, by outlawing 'gross indecency', led to the prosecution of Oscar Wilde; his only subsequent regret was that Wilde's punishment of two years' hard labour was too lenient. He revelled in controversy and rather courted libel actions than otherwise. Traces of his influence may be found in the pamphlet, which pushes its accusations to the extreme, presumably in an attempt to provoke Gilbert to take the legal action that Miss Hodson could not.

The pamphlet accused Gilbert of persecuting Miss Hodson, of humiliating actresses such as Madge Robertson (though, as we have seen, W.H. Kendal denied this accusation), of taking over the Haymarket and pushing it to the brink of ruin. It more than implied that Gilbert was insane ('He appeared to be in a condition approaching to madness').[26]

During the course of May, Gilbert replied to her allegations, in *The Era*; and Miss Hodson responded to his replies, in *The Era*; and Gilbert replied to her replies to his replies, in *The Era*; and so on. Gilbert denied many of her accusations and printed letters from Buckstone and Howe contradicting her version of events, but this had no appreciable effect. Both parties talked boldly of legal action, and nothing came of it.

Labouchère gleefully commented upon the controversy in the paper he had founded earlier that year, which he typically called *Truth*. Gilbert wanted to bring proceedings against the paper but his solicitors advised against it: 'The articles and notices before me show clearly enough that the writer is an adept in the art of offensive comment and criticism and that he has done his best to annoy and insult Mr Gilbert. But I am of opinion that proceedings ... would not be successful.'[27]

Hodson's pamphlet asserted that Gilbert's plays lost substantial amounts of money: 'On "Dan'l Druce" the loss was above £1,000; on "Pygmalion," after a few weeks, the loss was about £150 per week.'[28] In a letter to *The Era*, she went further: 'I maintain that, not only on "Dan'l Druce," but, upon every other piece of Mr Gilbert's that Mr Buckstone has produced, or revived, there has been a heavy loss.'[29] This was an outrageous statement, and deliberately so; it suggested that every one of Gilbert's most widely admired plays for the Haymarket, *The Palace of Truth*, *Pygmalion and Galatea* and *The Wicked World*, as well as the admittedly unsuccessful *Charity*, was a financial disaster; in which case the question arises why Buckstone kept asking Gilbert for more such disasters.

It does appear to be true that by the time of these last revivals in 1876–77 the Haymarket was losing money hand over fist; but this had more to do with the failings of its old and ailing manager than with the machinations of a playwright. For instance, Robert Buchanan's play *A Madcap Prince* had been performed with reasonable success at the Haymarket in 1875, but Buchanan had to issue Buckstone with a writ before he got his money for it.[30] The sad fact is that Buckstone was no longer fit to look after the business of the theatre. He had suffered sun stroke in 1872 or 1873, and as a result, he complained, 'my head is so queer'.[31] In 1876 he suffered an indisposition that kept him off the boards for months; he did not perform in *Dan'l Druce*, though the part of Reuben Haines seems to have been written for him. Buckstone should have retired two or three years before he finally did, later in 1877.

When two people dislike each other intensely, it is often irrelevant to try and apportion blame. It is not a matter of right or wrong: it is a force of nature. Henrietta Hodson wrote to Gilbert in February 1877:'we seem to be playing at a sort of "cross purposes and crooked answers" game',[32] and she was right. They misunderstood each other completely. If Gilbert cracked a joke, she took it seriously; if he decided he could not work with her, she interpreted it as an attempt to force her out of the profession. On the other hand, if she tried to ingratiate herself with him, he considered it sycophancy; if she insisted on her rights as leading lady, he took it as an affront to his position in the theatre. They should not have been forced together; and if they had, it should not have been in a theatre where the supposed controlling force was an old man who wanted nothing but peace and quiet.

The natural and inevitable result of this public war of words should certainly have been a lasting injury to Gilbert's career. Who would work with such a man as Henrietta Hodson had shown him to be? But, strangely, it was at precisely this point that the plunge was finally taken, and Gilbert became a primary force in the theatrical venture that was to make him rich and famous beyond all expectation.

1 William Gilbert by Alfred Weigall (Reproduced with the kind permission of Thames & Hudson; the whereabouts of the original painting are unknown)

2 W.S. Gilbert in 1873. Photograph by Window & Grove (Peter Joslin Collection)

3 T.W. Robertson (Peter Joslin Collection)

4 Clement Scott (Peter Joslin Collection)

MEN WE MEET.

BY THE COMIC PHYSIOGNOMIST.

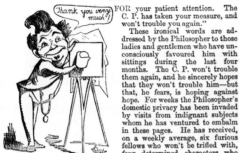

"FOR your patient attention. The C. P. has taken your measure, and won't trouble you again."

These ironical words are addressed by the Philosopher to those ladies and gentlemen who have unconsciously favoured him with sittings during the last four months. The C. P. won't trouble them again, and he sincerely hopes that they won't trouble him—but that, he fears, is hoping against hope. For weeks the Philosopher's domestic privacy has been invaded by visits from indignant subjects whom he has ventured to embalm in these pages. He has received, on a weekly average, six furious fellows who won't be trifled with, four determined characters who don't intend to stand this sort of thing, five demonstrative souls who propose to show him what is what, two mild gentlemen who think it is really too bad, and a hundred and twenty-seven practical fellow-creatures who don't want to bring the Philosopher before a public tribunal, if a fair compromise can be arrived at. Besides those of whom he has actually treated, he occasionally receives visits from people who think it likely that their turn will shortly come. It is customary with these folk to get the C. P. into a corner, and there to bind him over with fearful threats, and in fancy sums, never to allude to them, directly or indirectly, in any periodical for which he may happen to write.

It will be seen that if this sort of thing goes on much longer (and the nuisance is increasing daily), the C. P.'s sphere of action will eventually become so narrowed as hardly to leave him any elbow-room at all. He took every means in his power to abate the inconvenience to which he was subjected. He first referred the matter to Sir WILLIAM BOVILL and Sir HUGH CAIRNS, who were particularly requested to say whether there was any legal authority in the C. P. to disperse by force any person who should visit his private residence with the view of inducing the Philosopher to refrain from publishing his portrait in this journal.

Their answer was that there was no such authority for any practical purpose. They stated that when persons have once obtained peaceable entrance into his house they can only be ejected after notice served on, or brought home to each individually. Publication, they say, is not enough, and an express warning must be shown. The C. P. must turn them out in the *molliter manus imposuit* fashion. The C. P. cannot go up to a trespasser and threaten to knock him down if he does not go out; and no deadly weapons can be employed. In no case may he legally clear his house by a charge—he can simply hand them out, man after man.

The C. P., acting upon this advice, handed them all out, man after man, but still they came. So he took the final step of issuing a proclamation, keeping dark the advice that he had received from the eminent legal authorities above-mentioned. The proclamation assumed that every necessary power of massacre was vested in him, and that he should put that power into operation if necessary. But notwithstanding this, they still came. So the C. P. was obliged to admit that the proclamation was only a dodge of his—a threat that he dared not carry out. He feels that by adopting this cowardly course he has covered himself with confusion, and deeply compromised the admirable journal to which he is attached. He will probably be "struck off the list of its contributories," but he don't care. He is utterly indifferent. Why is he indifferent? Listen.

Time was (not many weeks since), when x pounds a week were a matter of moment to him. It was worth his while to work hard for that sum, for it went far towards defraying his weekly breakfast bills. But that squalid era has passed away from him, for ever. In the course of these papers, he found occasion to make several appeals to a class of beings to whom a reasonable appeal is never made in vain. He alludes to the Maidens of England. To those appeals, the Maidens of England responded like one man. It cut the Philosopher to the heart to reflect that he could only distinguish one of them at a time. Polygamy is, at present, out of favour in England, and while this unfortunate state of things exists, they will have to await their turn. He selected the loveliest and the wealthiest, and married her half-an-hour ago. No cards. As soon as he is a widower, he will marry the next loveliest and the next wealthiest—and so on through the list. He has found it impossible to reply individually to all applications, and he begs that in cases where no answer has been received, silence will be considered a respectful negative.

He is now about to start, *viâ* Folkestone and Nijni Novgorod, for Bokhara, for his honeymoon. When he returns he will be happy if the Editor and contributors will call upon him now and then. A chop and a knife and fork, in the servant's hall, will always be at their disposal. Now he's off.

NOW AND THEN.

Now and then, not very often,
  We have sun in May and June,
Now and then our feelings soften
  To a man who sings in tune.
Now and then, one's friends won't tarry,
  Smoke and keep us up all night;
Now and then some people marry
  And seem disinclined to fight.

Now and then the man we've trusted
  Doesn't turn out quite a rogue;
Now and then our rooms get dusted,
  And we tolerate a brogue.
Now and then an English lady,
  For a whim, or pique, or "fad,"
Changes grace for manners shady
  In the household of a cad.

Now and then relations find us
  Come to stay a week in town;
When we leave our gamps behind us,
  Now and then the rain comes down.
Now and then, by dint of struggling,
  Flirts, like fish, get off the hooks,
Now and then, instead of smuggling,
  Friends *return* our precious books.

Now and then we reach the station
  In good time and full of breath,
Disappointments and vexation
  Seem to dog us to our death.
I am not prepared to state now
  How it is with other men,
I can only bow to fate, now—
  Happy? Yes—but now and then!

Foreign Affairs.

WHAT the French may naturally expect from L.N. (*Hélène*), after the Exhibition of *Paris*—a Ten Years' War.

5 Gilbert's last column as the Comic Physiognomist. *Fun*, 18 May 1868 (Author's Collection)

6 Marie Litton in 1874.
Photograph by Window & Grove
(Peter Joslin Collection)

7 Scene from *Sweethearts*,
Act 1. *Illustrated London News*,
21 November 1874 (Author's
Collection)

8 Lucy Gilbert. Panel photograph by Robert Johnson (The Pierpont Morgan Library, New York)

THE GRAPHIC

AN ILLUSTRATED WEEKLY NEWSPAPER

NO. 682.—VOL. XXVI.
Regd at General Post Office as a Newspaper]
SATURDAY, DECEMBER 23, 1882
WITH EXTRA SUPPLEMENT [
PRICE SIXPENCE
Or by Post Sixpence Halfpenny

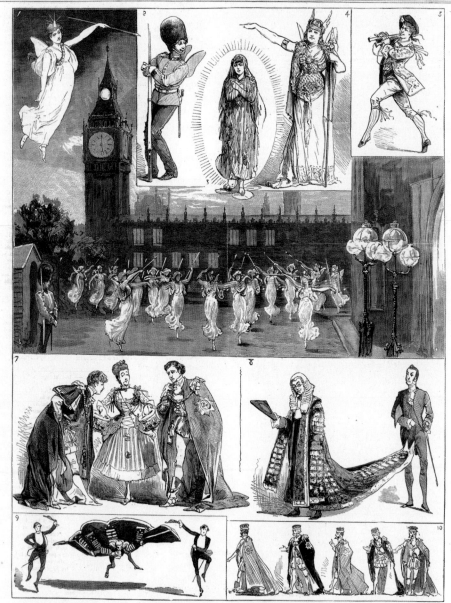

1. Leila (Miss Julia Gwynne), One of Strephon's Aunts.—2. Private Willis, Grenadier Guard (Mr. Manners).—3. Iolanthe (Miss Jessie Bond) : The Life and Soul of Fairyland, Returning from Penal Servitude.—4. A Very Influential Fairy (Miss Alice Barnett).—5. Strephon, M.P. (Mr. R. Temple).—6. Act II. Fairy Invasion of Palace Yard.—7. Phyllis, a Ward of Court (Miss Braham), Sees Nothing in the Coronets of Lords Mountararat and Tolloller (Messrs. Barrington and Lely).—8. A Highly Susceptible Chancellor (Mr. George Grossmith).—9. "Faint Heart Never Won Fair Lady."—10. Pillars of the British Nation.

"IOLANTHE" AT THE SAVOY THEATRE

9 Scenes from *Iolanthe*. From *The Graphic*, 23 December 1882 (Peter Joslin Collection)

GILBERT WITH HIS LAW-SUIT ON.
"Sir Arthur Sullivan seems to have stood quite aside."
Vide Mr. Justice Lawrance, in recent case.

10 'Gilbert with his law-suit on.' From *Judy*, 10 September 1890 (Peter Joslin Collection)

11 Arthur Sullivan (Peter Joslin
Collection)

12 Gilbert in later years (Peter
Joslin Collection)

A VERY ENGLISH OPERA (1877)

Richard D'Oyly Carte had secured the financial support of a number of backers, and had set up the Comedy Opera Company (Ltd) in support of his scheme to establish in London 'a theatre which shall have for its staple entertainment light opera of a legitimate kind, by English authors and composers'.[1] His plan was to recruit a pool of composers and librettists in aid of his grand scheme, including Alfred Cellier, Fred Clay, Frank Burnand and James Albery. But his great guns were Gilbert and Sullivan, and these were the men he approached to provide the company's first production. On 4 July 1877 they signed a contract for the creation of an opera in two acts, and composer and librettist set seriously to work.

Gilbert and Sullivan already had significant experience of working together. Apart from *Thespis* and *Trial by Jury*, they had also written three drawing-room ballads (including a ballad version of *Sweethearts*) and also, apparently, part of the abortive *Wedding March* opera. They had, by now, a good working knowledge of each other's qualities. And in creating this new opera, which was to be called *The Sorcerer*, for the first time they had leisure to discuss the nature of what they wanted to create before they did it. For instance, Gilbert's libretto for *The Sorcerer* has less dialogue and is more developed in its sequences for music than any of his previous libretti except *Trial by Jury*. It is not a mere succession of songs and ballads separated by long passages of dialogue, like *Princess Toto* for example; it contains several scenes conceived in entirely musical terms, such as the parodic incantation scene. This suggests a significant influence by Sullivan on Gilbert's work.

Gilbert, Sullivan and Carte all had rather different ideas of what they wanted to achieve. Carte's ambition was quite simple: 'The starting of English comic opera in a theatre devoted to that alone was the scheme of my life,' he later wrote to Gilbert and Sullivan.[2] Sullivan, too, had his ambitions, though when he expressed them in an interview in 1885, he implied that for the most part he had not yet had the opportunity to fulfil them:

The opera of the future is a compromise. I have thought and worked and toiled and dreamt of it. Not the French school, with [its] gaudy and tinsel tunes, its lambent lights and shades, its theatrical effects and clap-trap; not the Wagnerian school, with its sombreness and ear-splitting airs, with its mysticism and unreal sentiment; not the Italian school, with its fantastic airs and *fioriture* and far-fetched effects. It is a compromise between these three – a sort of eclectic school, a selection of the merits of each one.

He spoke of this, with a presumably unconscious echo of Carte, as 'the dream of my life'.[3]

As for Gilbert, many years later he recalled having discussed with Sullivan the question of reviving English comic opera at a time when it had 'practically ceased to exist', except as adaptations in the burlesque style of Offenbach and other French composers. They had agreed that their own efforts would be of an entirely different character: 'We resolved that our plots, however ridiculous, should be coherent, that our dialogue should be void of offence; that, on artistic principles, no man should play a woman's part and no woman a man's.'[4]

The three men entered into their joint project with different expectations. But they latched on to a shared concern, the notion of Englishness (a word which, to them and many other Victorian English people, was synonymous with Britishness), and, to begin with at least, emphasised it as their defining idea. To Carte it meant light opera written and performed by English talent; to Sullivan it meant finding a new style of opera that was neither French nor German nor Italian; to Gilbert it meant cleaning the stage of French licentiousness.

Gilbert bore this idea of Englishness in mind when casting round for the new opera's subject. A significant number of his previous libretti been set in the conventional territories of European operetta: *The Gentleman in Black* (a collaboration with Fred Clay dating from 1870) had been set in a German village, *Thespis* on Mount Olympus and *Princess Toto* in a fairytale kingdom. He certainly had no personal objection to such settings. But now he chose to place the new opera in the most English location possible: an English village complete with local squire, vicar and tenantry.

He took a short story entitled 'An Elixir of Love', which he had contributed (with Bab illustrations) to *The Graphic*'s Christmas Number at the end of the previous year, and set about refashioning it into a comic opera framework. The story adapted itself well. In the village of Ploverleigh, the well-born Alexis Pointdextre (tenor) is on the verge of marrying his well-born sweetheart Aline Sangazure (soprano) when Alexis, who is a well-meaning reformer of life's ills, reveals that he has invited to the village a prosperous tradesman-sorcerer (comic baritone) who will distribute a love potion among the villagers (chorus), thus generating love matches between the social ranks and promoting general harmony. The result, as any Victorian would affirm, is inevitable: anarchy, as all kinds of ill-assorted couples decide to marry without regard for rank or wealth. Order is restored only when the sorcerer yields his life to the demon Ahrimanes, thus reversing the effects of the potion.

At about the same time – probably just as the Henrietta Hodson controversy was reaching its crisis – Gilbert was occupied in writing another stage work, his last play for the Haymarket and his masterpiece in the field of non-musical drama. *Engaged* is an extraordinary play, the culmination of everything he had written before but quite different in atmosphere and intensity. It can be seen as a cry of rage, a brutal satire on modern morality, a farcical burlesque, a huge practical joke, a piece of abject nonsense: any or all of these things. In style it is similar to *Tom Cobb*, though it is longer, more developed and more biting. In intention it is similar to that of *An Old Score*, though translated into the realm of farcical comedy. Indeed, the comment that Gilbert wrote into his self-parody of *An Old Score* – 'every one in the piece (as far as I can judge) would do anything for money' – sounds very much like the starting point for *Engaged*.

The play begins with an outrageous bluff. When the curtain rises on the first scene, the garden of a cottage in the Scottish lowlands, it seems as if we are about to witness a sentimental drama of rural life along the lines of *Dan'l Druce*. A tender love scene takes place between the pretty lowland lassie Maggie and her handsome lowland lad, Angus, interrupted only by the entrance of her benevolent old mother Mrs Macfarlane; but before long they start saying strange and disturbing things:

> Yes, I'm a fairly prosperous man. What wi' farmin' a bit land, and gillieing odd times, and a bit o' poachin' now and again; and what wi' my illicit whusky still – and throwin' trains off the line, that the poor distracted passengers may come to my cot, I've mair ways than one of making an honest living – and I'll work them a 'nicht and day for my bonnie Meg!⁵

From this moment Gilbert seems determined to make his work more brutally disorientated than ever before: the honest lowland lad sells his fiancée to a stranger for £2; a baby-talking young woman proves to have more financial acumen than any other character in the piece; her benevolent papa is a selfish, greedy old rogue, who at one point tries to convince another character to commit suicide; and everyone acts throughout from the lowest, most mercenary motives. As in *The Palace of Truth*, they speak brutal truths as if they are polite fictions: 'Belvawney, I don't want to hurt your feelings, but I will not disguise from you that, not having seen you for three months, I was in hopes that I had got rid of you for ever.'⁶ And in the middle of it all there stands the anti-heroic figure of Cheviot Hill, rude, boorish, stingy and a serial flirt, appalling and strangely likeable:

> I wonder if I'm taking a prudent step. Marriage is a very risky thing; it's like Chancery, once in it you can't get out of it, and the costs are enormous. There

you are – fixed. Fifty years hence, if we're both alive, there we both shall be – fixed. That's the devil of it. It's an unreasonably long time to be responsible for another person's expenses. I don't see the use of making it for as long as that. It seems greedy to take up half a century of another person's attention. Besides – one never knows – one might come across somebody else one liked better.[7]

Gilbert had been cynical about human behaviour before, but never so concentratedly or relentlessly. It is tempting to link this fact with the terrible year he had just experienced, which had seen both the break-up of his parents' marriage and Henrietta Hodson's devastating attack on his reputation. Viewed in this context, the play is remarkably controlled, but it contains a new undercurrent of bitterness.

It was produced at the Haymarket, now under the management of J.S. Clarke after the retirement of Buckstone. The first night took place on 3 October 1877, with a cast including George Honey as Cheviot Hill and Marion Terry as Belinda Treherne. 'There was but a poor house,' *Lloyd's Weekly Newspaper* reported (7 October), and the audience was oddly divided in its opinion of the piece: 'though the laughter was abundant, it was not general, many expressions of disapproval were heard, and when the curtain fell, Mr. Gilbert did not answer the partial call made for the author.'

The critics had something of a field day over the piece.[8] 'It is not often,' said *The Echo* (10 October):

> that a piece is received with so mingled an outburst of cheers and dissatisfaction, and this was not surprising considering the opposite qualities it possesses; for Mr. Gilbert seemed to have given his audience a draught of champagne of the finest vintage, which was no sooner to their lips than they found it was marred with dashes of sulphuric acid and the most nauseous bitter he could find.

The *Daily Telegraph* (6 October) was most impressed by Gilbert's power as a satirist: 'he strips off the outward covering concealing our imperfections, and makes us stand shivering. The failings we are aware of, the thoughts we scarcely dare utter are proclaimed to the world and diagnosed by this merciless surgeon.'

The *Morning Advertiser* (6 October) called the play 'a violent burlesque upon everyday existence and a fantastic mockery of life as we know it'. The *Sunday Times* (7 October) complained that 'In *Engaged* Mr. Gilbert is more cold-bloodedly cynical than any human being has ever shown himself in the drama', while *The Figaro* (10 October) indulged in a long and violent diatribe against its morality and humour:

> From beginning to end of this nauseous play not one of the characters ever says a single word or does a single action that is not inseparable from the lowest moral degradation ... We do not believe that, except among the most repulsive

comedies of the seventeenth century, or in the very lowest specimens of French farce, can there be found anything to equal in its heartlessness Mr. Gilbert's latest original work.

The 'Captious Critic' of the *Illustrated Sporting and Dramatic News* (20 October) was baffled by all this outrage at a play which he called 'the cleverest comic work that has proceeded from Mr. Gilbert's brilliant pen'. *Engaged* was simply 'a whimsical, satirical, exquisitely humorous extravaganza. Where is this bitter, heartless cynicism they talk so much about? I cannot find it.' But he considered that the critical reaction to the play contained its own moral: 'The fact that this farcical comedy has had the effect of initiating a certain kind of playgoer into the strongest expressions of condemnation, and of arousing in another kind of spectator the liveliest admiration and eulogy is the surest proof that it is an unique and remarkable production.'

The play lasted for 110 performances and was one of the highlights of the theatrical season. Gilbert was happy with the entire cast – except George Honey, who was too self-consciously 'funny' as Cheviot Hill. Gilbert wrote a prefatory note to the printed edition of *Engaged* nine days after the premiere, possibly in reaction to Honey's performance:

> It is absolutely essential to the success of this piece that it should be played with the most perfect earnestness and gravity throughout. There should be no exaggeration in costume, make-up, or demeanour; and the characters, one and all, should appear to believe, throughout, in the perfect sincerity of their words and actions.[9]

He expressed his opinion of Honey's performance more frankly in a letter to E.A. Sothern on 16 December 1877:

> Honey is simply damnable – self conscious & extravagant – & dressed & made up like the late Mr. Wright – loud check suit yellow wig &c. All the other parts are played admirably but then I had full control over the other members of the company … People are beginning to find out, over here, that an 'eccentric' actor need not let the audience know that he *knows* he is eccentric. Of course *you* know that, & so do half a dozen others, but the lesser lights of the stage are beginning to understand it now, & it is quite a revelation to them. Honey, however, has yet to be enlightened.

He told Sothern in the same letter, 'I fancy I have struck a vein that can be worked profitably', and hinted: 'If you care to have a piece of the same class, I should like to know *at once*.'[10]

But there were other claims on his time. It had originally been agreed that his opera with Sullivan would be performed in September; but Sullivan did not have the music ready and the date was put back first to the end of October, and then to the middle of the following month. It finally came before the public at the Opera Comique on 17 November.

The Opera Comique was an unsatisfactory theatre in many respects, located between Holywell Street, Wych Street and the Strand, with a warren of tunnels and passages connecting it with its various entrances. It was cramped back-stage and its dressing-rooms looked out on to Holywell Street, a thoroughfare notorious throughout the Victorian period for the sale of obscene prints and publications. No, it was far from perfect. But it was the best Carte could command for the moment, and perhaps even then he was contemplating the building of a new theatre which would be designed, when the time was ripe, to house the operas he wanted to produce.

It was only in the last days of October that the casting of the piece came together. Several experienced operatic singers were engaged: Richard Temple, Giulia Warwick, George Bentham and Alice May. Mrs Howard Paul, a well-known actress and entertainer, was engaged to play the aristocratic Lady Sangazure, and two young men she had worked with were also brought on board, at least partly at her recommendation: George Grossmith and Rutland Barrington.

Grossmith was a small, slight man with a sensitive, humorous face. He had little stage experience, but was known for his comic songs and recitations at 'penny readings', church halls, literary institutes and branches of the YMCA. Sullivan approved of his voice, and Gilbert liked him as well, much to Grossmith's surprise. Grossmith was to be cast as the sorcerer himself, John Wellington Wells, but, as he said to Gilbert, 'For the part of a Magician I should have thought you required a fine man with a fine voice'. Gilbert looked at him humorously and replied, 'No; that is just what we don't want'.[11] Grossmith hesitated for several days before accepting the role, because taking up the wicked stage would mean an end to his income from the YMCA and other religious institutions. His mind was made up when he received a letter from Mrs Howard Paul: 'do not fail to accept the part of the "Magician" in Gilbert and Sullivan's new play. It is a splen-did part – better than you think, I fancy – and the "patter song" is great in its way.'[12] Grossmith took her advice. Mrs Howard Paul celebrated by inviting him and Barrington and a few others to a fireworks display at her house at Bedford Park on 5 November.

Rutland Barrington, larger and more physically staid than Grossmith, was nervous at the prospect of portraying a comic vicar on the stage – a daring idea at that time. He shared his fears with Gilbert, telling him that he thought the audience would either take kindly to him or hoot him off the stage. 'I quite agree with you,' Gilbert replied.[13]

Barrington recalled:

The great initial idea [of the Company] was that every soul and every thing connected with the venture should be English. It was to be a home of English talent, and so strong was this feeling that two choristers, whose names were never likely to appear on the programme, renounced their Italian titles and became Englishmen for the express purpose of being associated with such an enterprise ... I remember feeling great distress at the risk run by my old colleague Dick Temple, who would use the 'Italian production,' which unfortunately there was no mistaking. However, I was soothed by noticing that it gradually left him during the course of rehearsals.[14]

The production was put together in some haste: the rehearsal period can only have taken two weeks or even less. But the first night was an outstanding success. It was attended, in the words of *The Era* (25 November), by 'All musical London, or rather that portion of it which by hook or by crook could obtain a seat at the Opera Comique Theatre'. The programme of the evening began at eight o'clock with a one-act operetta by Alfred Cellier and Arthur Cecil, entitled *Dora's Dream*. *The Sorcerer* followed, starting at about 8.45. The *Pall Mall Gazette* noted (19 November) that Gilbert and Sullivan 'have evidently worked together in full sympathy and one will'. One of the highlights of the night was Grossmith's performance as Wells, singing his patter song with aplomb and introducing a comic run into the incantation scene which provoked 'shouts of laughter' according to *The Era*.

The opera was a novelty in its style, as some of the critics noted. *Lloyd's Weekly Newspaper* decided it was not so much a comic opera as 'a caricature upon serious opera', while others called it an extravaganza or a kind of burlesque. The mere fact that this particular comic opera was set in the present day and was costumed accordingly was a matter for comment and laughter. Both authors of the piece were enthusiastically called at the end; it was a success.

It seems that its creators were thinking in terms of writing a successor, if not on the opening night then not long afterwards. On 27 December, less than two months later, Gilbert was writing to Sullivan enclosing 'a sketch plot of the proposed Opera'. It would, he said, contain a great deal of fun, 'Among other things a song (kind of "Judge's Song") for the First Lord – tracing his career as office boy in cotton broker's office, clerk, traveller, junior partner & First Lord of Britain's navy. I think a splendid song can be made of this.'[15]

He was right.

13

HARLEQUINADE (1878)

Gilbert kept a diary through the year 1878. A skeleton record of his daily activities, it is by turns informative, intriguing, infuriating and illegible. As an account of his emotions and attitudes it is nothing, but as a factual record of what he did each day it tells us much.

He was occupied, as usual, with several different projects. On 1 January he lunched with Henry Neville and Lord Londesborough – respectively the leading actor and the lessee of the Olympic Theatre – proposing a play about Faust and Marguerite. Then there is a note: 'D'Auban in afternoon.'[1] This refers to the Beefsteak Club's projected amateur pantomime of *The Forty Thieves*, which was to be jointly written by Gilbert, Byron, Burnand and Robert Reece and performed for charity as an afternoon performance at the Gaiety. The scheme was co-ordinated by John Hollingshead, and John D'Auban, the choreographer for many of the burlesques and pantomimes of that era (also of *The Sorcerer* and all its successors), patiently taught the necessary dance steps to those amiable Beefsteak members who had put themselves forward to perform. Gilbert himself had agreed to attempt the role of Harlequin, to the 'relief and general astonishment' of the other members.[2] Though his fellow Beefsteakers had no previous inkling of it, this represented the fulfilment of one of Gilbert's most deeply cherished dreams, a dream extending back to his earliest childhood. He was 41 years old and, it may be assumed, not as nimble of limb as he used to be, but he threw himself into the task with tremendous energy and determination. Even before the rehearsals began in mid-January, D'Auban was coming round to Gilbert's house to coach him in Harlequin's leaps and pirouettes.

Those first two weeks of January were mainly occupied with learning his Harlequin business, writing his scene for *The Forty Thieves*, and liaising with Carte's Comedy Opera Company with regard to the new opera. For instance, on Tuesday 8 January he met up with Rutland Barrington and read the plot to him, and later in the same day picked up his new Harlequin costume and dined in it (one can only guess at Lucy's reaction). Two days later, just before another session with D'Auban, he sat down and wrote the opera's opening chorus.

On 17 January he read the plot to Carte (who was 'much pleased') but then, in counterbalance, was left badly bruised after his day's Harlequin practice with D'Auban. Rehearsals for the pantomime began at the Gaiety the following day. This was to prove a gruelling daily schedule of afternoon rehearsals, with frequent additional sessions beginning at midnight and going on until two or three o'clock in the morning. But even this, it seems, was not enough to occupy Gilbert. He had another project coming to the boil, as the entry for 23 January shows. In the morning he 'Worked at opera'; in the afternoon he 'went to Gaiety pantomime [rehearsal]'; and in the evening he 'prepared parts of Neerdoweel'.

Gilbert had been working on *The Ne'er-do-Weel* for a long time. The play had its origins back in February 1876, when Ned Sothern had written to Gilbert requesting him to write 'a play of modern times with strong pathetic interest' for Sothern to star in at the Haymarket.[3] After some bargaining, Sothern agreed to pay Gilbert 2,000 guineas for full rights to the play for ten years. Gilbert created a story concerning a well-born young man who, after being deserted by his fiancée, gives up his prospects and becomes a poor and broken-down wanderer, until by chance he runs into an old friend who offers him a secretaryship. At the same time he encounters the woman who had destroyed his life by marrying another; she is now a widow and she still loves him. The plot is concerned with the hero's attempts, in these circumstances, to do the right thing according to the code of honour of the day.

By July 1876 Gilbert had sketched out the play in full, though this was followed by some fretful wrangling over the details. Sothern wanted his hero and heroine to remain 'respectable' – a matter which did not concern Gilbert so much. Sothern did not want his character to be too much of a vagabond: 'Care should be taken not to break him down *too* far – let him always be a gentleman.'[4] Furthermore, he was worried about the heroine's situation as a widow: 'Couldn't Callendar have died of heart disease or some accident the very day of his marriage with Marion? I think the sympathy of the audience will go much more with the hero and heroine if the marriage has not been actually consummated … I do want Marion *pure*.'[5] Gilbert would have none of this nonsense:

> I don't see that her virginal condition would be particularly exalted by the fact that, owing to an unforeseen accident, her husband was prevented from consummating the marriage. I am afraid that, in dealing with a widow, one must accept the fact that if she is still a virgin, it is her husband's fault rather than her own.[6]

It seems peculiarly Victorian that the issue should have arisen at all.

Gilbert wrote *The Ne'er-do-Weel* in the latter half of 1876. Sothern was not happy with it when he read it in January 1877, and he soon decided that the play was not for him. Gilbert took back the rights and arranged for it to be produced at the Olympic Theatre in February 1878, with Henry Neville in the starring role. On 24 January 1878 he read the piece to the cast, and, as he noted in his diary, it was received with 'great applause'. Rehearsals for the piece began shortly afterwards.

Marion Terry, one of the acting family of Terrys and a younger sister to Ellen Terry, was a protégée of Gilbert's at this time. He did much to promote her career, coaching her acting privately and casting her in his plays whenever possible (including the prospective *Ne'er-do-Weel*). She frequently met with the Gilberts socially and often stayed at their house overnight. Gilbert clearly felt a great deal of affection for her. This affection seems to have been of the *Pygmalion and Galatea* type, the tenderness of a creator towards what he feels he has created.

Certain entries in Gilbert's diary from about this time are marked with an X in the margin. They appear to indicate visits to various locations in London. Uxbridge Road (often abbreviated to UR) appears most often, with Notting Hill (NH) close behind. Other locations referred to include Gloucester Road, Latimer Road, Westbourne Park, High Street Kensington and Bayswater Road. These were, in fact, all underground stations in the vicinity of Notting Hill and Kensington. Temple, a station in central London, also appears, as does Drury Lane (which was not a station). Marks also appear against journeys by cab without a destination being noted.

Many of these marks are clearly connected with Marion Terry (referred to as 'MT' in the diary). Michael Ainger has suggested[7] that they indicate occasions on which Gilbert escorted Marion Terry home from a rehearsal or a performance. Ainger has also suggested that Gilbert entered the marks into the diary at a later date, after a row with his wife, who may have felt he was being 'overprotective' towards his pretty young protégée.

It is true that many of the locations mentioned in the diary (though not all) were underground stations within walking distance of Marion's home.[8] It is also true that the majority of the entries marked with an X (though not all) are placed after rehearsals or performances at which Marion would have been present. Some, however, are associated with entries in which Marion's presence is not stated or implied; for instance, on 28 February the diary entry reads (in part): 'In afternoon called with Mrs on Fairs [John Hare] – afterwards walked with her to Sloane St – then in cab to Drury Lane – then home to dinner.' There is an X against the line referring to Drury Lane.[9] Similar visits to Drury Lane without an assigned reason took place on several other occasions, for instance on 28 March: 'Then to Olympic – moderate house – piece going well. Then to Op Comique – persuaded Carte not to close till Passion Week – then to Drury Lane [X in margin] Home in Hansom.'

It is natural to suspect a sexual meaning to these mysterious markings, though it would be unwise to carry these suspicions too far without definite evidence.

Gilbert's attitude to sexual relations was fastidious, even prudish, though he was capable of 'Rabelaisian' humour in the all-male atmosphere of London clubland.[10]

However, it does seem that Gilbert's relationship with Marion Terry created some tension. The entry for 7 February notes that Gilbert 'went with Mrs & MT to Opera Comique [*The Sorcerer*] – abominably played to fair house – went badly … then took them to Notting Hill Gate station. Mrs three-cornered, going home.' Gilbert's use of the eccentric word 'three-cornered' (which he would also write into the new opera) seems like a jocular attempt to gloss over the dispute. Was he showing himself to be too affectionate in his behaviour to Marion?

In the meantime, the performance of *The Forty Thieves* approached. Like many others in the cast, Gilbert had been rehearsing his moves at every available moment. A fellow cast member recalled:

> You had only to go into the Beefsteak Club at any time after the doors were open and you would find 'Odger' Colvile, as we called him, Archie Stuart-Wortley, W.S. Gilbert, your humble servant, and others connected with the 'show,' practising harlequin leaps over the fire-screen on to the sofa, doing scraps of dances in the corners, and arranging details of proposed business over a hastily swallowed meal … [Gilbert] never missed an opportunity of going through the 'animations,' or pirouetting, or doing something to perfect himself, when in sufficient privacy or only in company of his fellow-workers.[11]

His hours of obsessive practice stood him in good stead in after years: he took great pride in twirling himself into the standard Harlequin poses for the edification of women and children.

The Forty Thieves, performed at the Gaiety on the afternoon of 13 February, was a great success. That first performance alone brought in over £600. Gilbert's own performance was a highlight of the event. A poem describing the occasion, probably by H.J. Byron, appeared in the periodical *Mirth* shortly afterwards:

> There was laughing and cheering, and shouts of surprise,
> As Gilbert in glittering garb met our eyes;
> And when the 'positions' he showed well he knew,
> A thrill of astonishment ran the house through …
> And Gilbert through all danced and postured with grace,
> With a very determined expression of face.[12]

The performance was so successful, indeed, that they repeated it twice: at the Theatre Royal, Brighton, on 9 March, and at the Gaiety again on 10 April. The Brighton performance was attended with a small drama when, with three days to go, Gilbert suffered an attack of the gout that was to plague his later years. He even sent Hollingshead a telegram warning him that he might not be able to perform on the Saturday. But in the event the gout disappeared and Gilbert's Harlequin danced and twirled as successfully in Brighton as in London.

Faint glimmerings of Gilbert's relationship with his wife can be found in the diary. The facetious decision to refer to her as 'Mrs' tells us something; the long evenings he spent at the Beefsteak Club, before returning home in the small hours, tells us more. But on the other hand they went shopping together (as on 26 February when Lucy went for a fitted hood) and they holidayed together. Later in the year there is frequent record of walks and other excursions accompanied by 'Mrs'. She was interested enough in his work to attend one of the night rehearsals for *The Forty Thieves* (11 February). They were close enough, and they cared enough, to have rows (7 February: 'Mrs three-cornered'; 11 July: 'met Mrs at station – I was rather late – caught it'; 6 October: 'Row'). They dined with friends, and friends dined with them; Lucy acted the role of society hostess with aplomb.

The first night of *The Ne'er-do-Weel* took place at the Olympic on 25 February. It was a fiasco. The piece went well through the first act, which was beautifully written; but the second act foundered on a scene in which a character attempts to steal some letters from the library of a country house, only to be caught by the hero, and then forced to hop out of the room bound hand and foot. This obtrusively farcical scene was greeted with 'disapproval ... expressed with a vigour and clearness rarely to be met with in the present day' (*The Times*, 28 February 1878), and the rest of the play was disrupted with similar expressions of dissatisfaction. The critic of *Lloyd's Weekly Newspaper*, reviewing a performance later in the week, relayed the information that the author had been hissed after the first performance and that 'there was a good deal of derisive laughter' during the second, before adding that at the end of the night he attended 'the curtain fell amid a silence that was not disturbed by the appearance of one of the company' (3 March 1878). Gilbert went to the Olympic on the evening of 28 February and reported a 'wretched house'. On the following morning he drafted an advertisement announcing the withdrawal of the play. He rewrote it as *The Vagabond*, and this revised version appeared briefly at the Olympic from 25 March; but it was generally felt that while the errors of taste had been removed nothing of interest had been added. It lasted only until 18 April before being finally put out of its misery.

Restructuring and rewriting his poor wounded play was not, of course, his sole occupation for March. Richard Barker had, the previous year, set up the Dan'l Druce Company to tour Gilbert's plays round the British provinces, and they were preparing a new season to include *The Vagabond*, *Tom Cobb*, *Creatures of Impulse*, *Sweethearts* and *The Wedding March*. Gilbert supervised several rehearsals of these pieces at the Opera Comique before they set out on tour. And he was still at work on the new piece for Sullivan. On 25 March, the same day that *The Vagabond* was premiered, he called on Sullivan with his new lyric, a song for the First Lord of the Admiralty. The singer Charles Santley was also there. Gilbert read out the lyric, and both men were delighted with it.

14

ALL ABLAZE (1878–81)

H.M.S. Pinafore; or, The Lass that Loved a Sailor, the opera that Gilbert was writing with Sullivan, was quite unlike its predecessors. It is true that, like *The Sorcerer*, it took pains to be 'English' (or British) in atmosphere and subject matter; but its Englishness was of a very different order. This 'entirely original nautical comic opera' teased the nationalistic feelings of an audience trained by the old melodramas to associate British sailors with courage, pluck, the waving of Union Jacks and the thrashing of villains and foreigners. It simultaneously celebrated and parodied that nationalistic spirit, as in the subtly mocking anthem 'He is an Englishman':

> For he himself has said it,
> And it's greatly to his credit,
> That he is an Englishman …
> For he might have been a Roosian,
> A French, or Turk, or Proosian,
>   Or perhaps Itali-an …
> But in spite of all temptations
> To belong to other nations,
>   He remains an Englishman!

The hero of *H.M.S. Pinafore*, unlike that of *The Sorcerer*, is not aristocratic in upbringing but distinctly working class, and honest and straightforward through-and-through. The plot, which derives from a handful of the Bab ballads, is simple to the point of cliché: the humble sailor who loves his captain's daughter and wins her hand against all the odds. Whatever the ironies that may pervade other parts of the opera, the love that these two characters feel for each other is shown as simple and real – another rarity in Gilbert's comic work. The simple romance of the story, the mockery levelled at pompous officialdom, the spectacle and ceremony that come with the naval setting, all converge to help create a piece that would have an appeal not simply to an elite but to the broad mass of people.

Gilbert felt, from very early in the process of creation, that the opera's nautical atmosphere would be integral to its impact. Even as far back as 27 December 1877 he was writing to Sullivan with the suggestion that 'the chorus will look like sailors, & we will ask to have their uniforms *made for them* at Portsmouth'[1] – a somewhat radical departure in a culture where the characters of a comic opera generally looked like nothing on earth. (In the end, this scheme proved too expensive, but Gilbert did ensure the costumes were as authentic as possible.) It was probably Gilbert who organised the day trip to Portsmouth which he and Sullivan took on Saturday 13 April 1878: they toured the historic ships, going on board the *Invincible*, the *Victory* and the *St Vincent*, and Gilbert drew sketches on the last two of these, from which he devised the set for *H.M.S. Pinafore*. Though Gilbert and Sullivan had already discussed the opera on several occasions, and Gilbert had completed most of the lyrics, it was only after the Portsmouth trip that Sullivan felt able to settle down properly to the writing of the music; he wrote to his mother on 19 April (Good Friday) that he was now 'in the full swing of my new work', adding that 'It will be bright & probably more popular than the Sorcerer, but it is not so clever'.[2] The score he produced was full of shanty rhythms and a hearty open-air spirit, possibly influenced by the sights and sounds he had absorbed at the sea port.

The first music rehearsals began on 24 April, while Gilbert and Lucy were taking a brief break from things in Paris, Brussels and Antwerp. He attended the later music rehearsals, familiarising himself with the music and devising business to accompany it, and then he conducted his own stage rehearsals from the beginning of May onwards.

By this time the Comedy Opera Company was beginning to gather together a regular team of reliable performers, with George Grossmith and Rutland Barrington at the core. Both Gilbert and Sullivan knew the team's capabilities and wrote to suit them. Gilbert knew from the start of writing *H.M.S. Pinafore* that he wanted Grossmith to play the First Lord of the Admiralty, and Barrington to play the Captain. (On the other hand Mrs Howard Paul was eased out of the company just before rehearsals began, and replaced in the small role of Cousin Hebe by a young newcomer, Jessie Bond.) Gilbert went into the rehearsal room knowing that he was working with performers who would do their best to do what he wished. In fact, he was now in a position, in which he had rarely if ever found himself in the past, of absolute control over the stage. Carte, unlike Hare for instance, did not interfere in matters of stage management but gave him unquestioned power over all the theatrical aspects of the production: acting, sets, costumes. The performers, unlike many of those he had encountered at the Haymarket and elsewhere, did not seem to resent being told what to do by a mere writer; many of them were singers or entertainers rather than trained actors, and so were more amenable to being taught the elements of Gilbert's unique style of comedy.

Some of the company's best-known players recalled Gilbert's rehearsal techniques. George Grossmith wrote:

> Mr. Gilbert is a perfect autocrat, insisting that his words should be delivered, even to an inflection of the voice, as he dictates. He will stand on the stage beside the actor or actress, and repeat the words with appropriate action over and over again, until they are delivered as he desires them to be. In some instances, of course, he allows a little license, but very little.[3]

Jessie Bond, who admired Gilbert greatly, understood what he was trying to achieve:'No striving for individual effect was allowed to interfere with the ensemble, no horse-play was permitted to vulgarize or disturb the action. Nothing must interfere with the balance of the whole, and its presentation according to the perfect principles of art.'[4] Grossmith relished the chance to improvise on stage rather more than Gilbert did, but he realised the value of Gilbert's techniques:

> He has great patience at times; and, indeed, he needs it, for occasionally one or other of the company, through inaccurate ear or other cause, will not catch the proper action or inflection … Gilbert has nearly been driven frantic (and so have the onlookers for the matter of that) because a sentence has been repeated with a false accent … The performer frequently gets the credit which is due to Mr. Gilbert, and to him absolutely.[5]

At last the piece was ready, and the first night took place on Saturday 25 May. Gilbert recorded in his diary: 'Rowdy gallery, singing songs &c. Piece went extremely well – I went in & out three or four times during evening. Enthusiastic call for self & Sullivan. Then to Bfst [Beefsteak].' The reviews were generally favourable and everyone enjoyed the piece's broad fun, but there was an undercurrent of disappointment that Sullivan should, in the words of *The Times* (27 May),'confine himself … to a class of production which, however attractive, is hardly worthy of the efforts of an accomplished and serious artist'.

The timing of the production was risky. High summer (July and August) was traditionally the 'dead season' in the London theatres, the period in which the more established companies (such as that at the Haymarket) shut up the theatre or leased it out, and toured the provinces.[6] London 'society' left the capital for the country, Europe or the seaside. Any productions continuing through the summer expected reduced audiences as a matter of course, especially during a heatwave. *H.M.S. Pinafore* had been running for little more than a month when it entered this dangerous period. The board of the Comedy Opera Company began to get nervous at the reduced takings. One member of the board, Edward Bayley, wrote to Carte on 6 July: 'I hope you will get Gilbert and Sullivan's agreement to break at once ... I object to putting my head in a noose.'[7] Carte held firm, however; it was probably a settled part of his long-term strategy to struggle through the lean summer and wait for the upturn in September.

At this time the most successful plays were beginning to run for longer and longer. Anything over 100 performances was still considered a hit, but H. J. Byron's *Our Boys*, which had opened in January 1875, was still going strong, as was James Albery's scandalous French adaptation *Pink Dominos* (from March 1877). It may be that Carte had recognised in *H.M.S. Pinafore* the same long-running qualities, provided everyone kept their nerve through the temporary downturn.

There were hardships. The company agreed to take reduced salaries when the takings were down. On 9 August Carte rewarded their loyalty with a picnic at Windsor, followed by a trip up the river to Cliveden in a fleet of steam launches. Gilbert was there, though typically his diary entry fails to record whether he enjoyed it or not.

Sullivan, conducting a series of Promenade concerts at Covent Garden at about this time, included an orchestral selection from *H.M.S. Pinafore* arranged by Hamilton Clarke, and this certainly helped to remind audiences of the opera. By the autumn, audience figures were up, the board stopped complaining, and it became clear that the opera was indeed a success.

Gilbert, meanwhile, was feeling a little restless. On 30 June he had 'suggested to Mrs to take tour round world'. This did not happen; they had to content themselves that summer with a few weeks at Margate, Havre, Trouville, Dieppe and (of course) Boulogne. But he felt the lure of the sea, perhaps stirred by the atmosphere of the opera, and on 11 September he bought a yacht, which he called the *Druidess* after one of his early burlesques. He spent a few days trying it out off the coast of Kent, but was back home by 16 September. In October he decided to study navigation, so perhaps his maiden voyage had been problematic in that respect.

On Friday 20 September Gilbert called on Sullivan and, as he recorded in his diary, 'urged him to do another piece for Op. Com.', adding that Sullivan 'Half-consented' to this. Gilbert was eager to continue with an association that was proving so financially and artistically successful, but Sullivan was more ambivalent, well aware of the critics who complained at his stooping to such frivolous work. But, all the same, Sullivan went from half-consent to consent. On 23 September Gilbert, Sullivan and Carte met at Covent Garden and went together to the site of the theatre that Carte was already planning, which would be built to house the native English operas he had always dreamed of, the operas it was now clear only Gilbert and Sullivan could write. They visited each other several times over the next few months (for instance on the evening of 4 November Sullivan called at 10.30 in the evening and remained until three in the morning) and on 8 December Gilbert was at work on the plot of a new operetta, going over to see Sullivan on the evening of the same day and discussing the piece into the small hours.

On 16 November he wrote an article for *The Era Almanack, 1879* called 'A Hornpipe in Fetters'. In it, he argued that while critics condemned native English plays for lacking 'the vigorous dramatic interest that characterizes many successful French pieces', this is primarily due to 'the very serious restrictions under which we labour'. These restrictions meant 'that no married man (in an original piece) may be in love with any body but his wife, and, in like manner, no single lady may see any charm in a married man' and, while Gilbert was at great pains to insist that 'the principle upon which it is founded is right enough, so that it be not pushed to a prudish extent', he objected to being debarred from writing about such things and then being criticised for insipidity.[8]

Perhaps Gilbert was brooding upon the failure of his most serious plays of modern life, *An Old Score, Charity* or *The Ne'er-do-Weel*, and contrasting this with the raging success of the entertaining but morally bland *H.M.S. Pinafore*:

> The story of an honourable young man in love with a blameless young lady – separated from her by unsympathetic parents, who urge their daughter to marry a wealthy villain – the ultimate discomfiture of the villain by the discovery that the honourable young man is heir to the very estates upon which the villain founded his claims to the blameless young lady's hand – is a kind of plot that may possibly be made faintly interesting, but cannot be compared in dramatic value with plots of the unpleasant but exciting class to which *Frou Frou* and *Le Supplice d'une Femme* belong. The fetters in which we are required to dance our dramatic hornpipe are increasing in number and in weight.[9]

The critical reaction to *Engaged* was also fresh in his memory, and he took his revenge in a moment of sarcasm:

> It has recently been discovered by many dramatic critics that satire and cynicism are misplaced in comedy, and that the propriety of repartee is to be estimated by the standard of conversation in a refined drawing-room. It is fortunate for Sheridan that this ukase had not been pronounced when he wrote *The School for Scandal*.[10]

For much of 1878 Gilbert had been occupied in the writing of his version of the Faust story, which he called *Gretchen*. He finished it on the night of 14 December and it was produced at the Olympic on 24 March 1879, with Marion Terry in the title role. The first-night audience received the play well and applauded the author before the curtain, but reviews were lukewarm at best. There was much discussion of the play's relationship to Goethe's *Faust* and of a note by Gilbert published in the programme in which he expressed the hope that 'in preferring to remodel, for purely dramatic purposes, the entire story of Gretchen's downfall, I shall at least be absolved from a charge of intentional irreverence towards the grandest philosophical work of the century'. The critics generally agreed that, however reverent the intention, the result was far below the level of the original. *The Graphic* was representative in reporting that 'the story fails … to awaken any deep interest' (29 March 1879). The play was soon playing to half-empty houses. It survived for only three weeks.

Gilbert remained proud of the work and almost immediately prepared a published edition, luxuriously designed, printed and bound by Newman & Co., which appeared in June the same year, prefaced with a bitter note in which he blamed the short run of the play on the Olympic Theatre's lessee, Lord Londesborough. The volume was reviewed by several journals. *The Graphic's* verdict (21 June) was enthusiastic: 'it is by far the finest and most satisfactory work yet published by the author.' But *The Examiner* (21 June) was condemnatory, calling the play 'dreary' and concluding: '[Gilbert] has not even mastered the poetic vocabulary, and we trust "Gretchen" will be his last experiment in what writers call the "modern poetical drama."' *The Examiner's* wish was granted: Gilbert wrote no more serious blank verse plays.

The first-night review of *Gretchen* in *The Era* (30 March) had referred to Gilbert's 'Success – brilliant success – in the walks of comic opera'. This was no exaggeration. The popularity of *H.M.S. Pinafore* did not wane but rather went from strength to strength. In November 1878 it had been performed for the first time on the far side of the Atlantic Ocean, in Boston, Massachusetts, and since then the absurd little entertainment had caught hold of America's imagination to an amazing extent. Productions proliferated, the songs were sung and whistled everywhere, and the jokes ('What, never? Well, hardly ever!') became catchphrases parroted high and low. There was, at this time, no international copyright law between the United Kingdom and the United States, and Gilbert, Sullivan and Carte were not entitled to a penny of the profits gained by any of the American productions – much to their displeasure. After some debate they decided on an audacious course. If they had no claim to the profits from productions put on without their consent, they could at least show the Americans how it should be done. They could show them a production that would use Sullivan's orchestrations and Gilbert's stage management. They could go to the United States themselves, taking with them a complete company of performers, and organise a production of a thoroughly authentic *H.M.S. Pinafore* in one of New York's major theatres.

Gilbert was, at first, anxious about the project. Carte discussed the matter with Gilbert and Sullivan on 24 April; they were to start for America on 7 October, and they were to share the profits equally between them. On 3 May Gilbert saw Carte at the Opera Comique and, as he recorded in the diary, 'Stated my fears as to American tour'.[11] He probably thought the project risked too much, and with no certain result. However, whatever his fears, Carte succeeded in allaying them.

This was an extraordinary time for everyone involved with the operas, but one may argue that it was especially extraordinary for Gilbert. Practically all his life he had struggled to make his way in the world, from his interrupted education to his years as a journalist on *Fun*, when he watched his contemporaries getting chances for stage work that consistently passed him by, through those years when he made up his lost time by bullying his way to the top of the dramatic profession, systematically alienating the leading lights of the acting profession as he did so. And now, suddenly, all antagonism seemed to fall away; he was in undisputed command of a team of performers who eagerly followed his instructions, in partnership with a theatre manager who was happy to leave all theatrical decisions in his hands and a composer who understood his jokes and softened the rough edges of his words; he was rewarded with the praise of the critics, popular success, a stage work running much longer than any previous work of his had even approached, and unprecedented wealth and fame.

A bizarre incident took place at the Opera Comique on 31 July which demonstrates the unique success of *H.M.S. Pinafore* and the lengths to which people would go in order to retain a slice of it. Carte was planning to free himself of the directors of the Comedy Opera Company, who had done nothing but hamper everyone with their cautious outlook and who had become an unnecessary evil now that *H.M.S. Pinafore* was pouring money into the pockets of Gilbert, Sullivan and Carte. The triumvirate could manage very well without their inconvenient backers. There had been a break in the opera's run at the end of December 1878, the Opera Comique Theatre being closed in order to make improvements to the drains, and when it reopened at the beginning of February 1879 it was under a new six-month lease organised by Carte. At the beginning of July, as the lease was approaching its expiry date, the Comedy Opera Company was given notice of the cessation of their rights in the piece. But the company disputed this claim and decided that the rights, far from reverting to Gilbert, Sullivan and Carte, actually reverted to them. They arranged to set up their own rival production at the Imperial Theatre to open on 1 August and hired a cast accordingly. However, they lacked the necessary set, and it was their contention that the set used at the Opera Comique was theirs by right.

Therefore, on the evening of 31 July, the last night of the six-month lease, Edward Bayley, Frank Chappell and Collard Drake of the Comedy Opera's board appeared at the Opera Comique accompanied by Chappell's solicitor brother Cecil and what Gilbert described as 'a mob of 50 roughs'.[12] (Carte was in America making arrangements with theatres and Sullivan was on the Continent, so Gilbert was the only one of the three still in town.) The situation was tense and boiled over into violence as the intruders tried to take possession of the set while the performance was still taking place. The stage manager Richard Barker was pushed down a lethally steep flight of stairs in the scrimmage, but escaped permanent injury. A panic started to spread amongst the performers and then the audience.

However, Grossmith stepped forward and gave a reassuring speech, and the performance struggled to a conclusion as the police arrived.

The legal situation following this event was far from clear and took some months to work out. But the end result was that Gilbert and Sullivan came to a new agreement with Carte, whereby each of the three put in an equal investment of £1,000 and in return received one-third of the profits of their operas, after the payment of expenses. The Comedy Opera Company was effectively finished; D'Oyly Carte's Opera Company was born.

Gilbert was engaged on two major projects: a farcical comedy for Sothern based on 'The Story of a Twelfth Cake' and the new opera with Sullivan. The latter was being developed from an earlier idea for a one-act opera bouffe which had come to nothing.[13] Sullivan explained the essentials of the plot in an interview with the *New York Times* (1 August 1879):

> An old gentleman returns home in the evening with his six daughters from a party. Nice bit of soft music takes them off for the night. Then a big orchestral crash, which introduces six burglars. They commence their knavish operations in a mysterious chorus, lights down. Presently the old gentleman thinks he hears some one stirring; comes on; of course, sees nobody, though the burglars are actively at work. The noise is only the sighing of the wind, or the gentle evening breeze. The old gentleman and the burglars performed a bit of concerted music, and in due course the six ladies enter. The six burglars are struck with their beauty, forget their villainous purposes, and make love. Chorus of burglars and old gentleman's daughters, whose announcement that they are 'wards in Chancery' creates great consternation among the bandit lovers. Then there is the policemen's rescue and other humorous conceits of Gilbert, which I hope and believe will be as funny as anything in the *Pinafore* or the *Sorcerer*.

On 25 October, two weeks after the date originally planned, Gilbert and Sullivan set sail for New York from Liverpool on board the *Bothnia*, accompanied by their conductor Alfred Cellier, their new soprano Blanche Roosevelt and her husband. Lucy was left at home. Carte was to follow with the rest of the company a week later. On arrival in New York on 5 November, Gilbert and Sullivan were met by that most American of phenomena: an interviewer. The concept of interviewing was still a little unfamiliar in Britain, but both men were to become habituated to it in the coming years.

'Mr. Gilbert,' the *New York Herald* journalist wrote:

> is a fine, well-made, robust man apparently of 45, above the medium stature, with the brightest and rosiest of faces, an auburn mustache, and short 'mutton-chop' whiskers, tipped, only slightly, with iron gray, large and clear blue eyes, and a forehead of high, massive, and intellectual cast. His voice has a hearty, deep

ring, and his utterance is quick and jerky – as though he were almost tired of keeping up this business of saying funny things, which everybody more or less expects of him.

They submitted to the process of interviewing with good grace. Gilbert grumbled that he considered it hard to find 'that a frothy trifle like this should have so far exceeded in its success the work which one has held in far more serious estimation'. He was happy, however, to discuss their next opera and expound his theories of comedy along the way: 'the treatment of the new opera will be similar to that of "Pinafore" – namely, to treat a thoroughly farcical subject in a thoroughly serious manner. That has been my idea all along.' 'It's the story of a modern Zampa,' Sullivan added, 'of pirates and escapades of 200 years ago, which, if dressed up in our modern clothes, must seem very absurd'.[14] So at some point between August and November drab burglars had been transformed into picturesque pirates. It was, undoubtedly, an improvement.

The two men were feted by New York. In London they were part of the scenery, prominent workers in their fields, but rather taken for granted. Here they were exotic celebrities. On 8 November a dinner was given in their honour at the prestigious Lotos Club. The club's president, Whitelaw Reid, praised them for writing a piece that provided 'wit without dirt', and Gilbert replied with a well-received speech:

> I have read in some journals that we have come over here to show you how that piece should be played, but that I disclaim both for myself and my collaborateur. We came here to teach nothing – we have nothing to teach – and perhaps we should have no pupils if we did. [Laughter.] But apart from the fact that we have no copyright, and are not yet managers in the United States, we see no reason why we should be the only ones who are not be permitted to play this piece here. [Laughter and applause.]

He announced that they would also be producing their new opera in New York, and that one of their purposes in performing *Pinafore* first was 'to prepare the audiences for the reception of our new and highly preposterous story'.[15]

The Lotos Club dinner was a moment of relaxation before the work began. They had an opera to rehearse, and they had only three weeks to do it. However, it was done, and Sullivan even had time to travel to Boston to conduct a performance of his oratorio, *The Prodigal Son*. The opera's cast was a mixture of principals brought over from Britain and a native New York chorus. The authentic *H.M.S. Pinafore* was premiered at the Fifth Avenue Theatre on 1 December, with Sullivan conducting and Gilbert actually on stage dressed as one of the crew. The occasion was a success and the auditorium was packed, but audience figures fell disappointingly in the next few days. After all, every theatre-goer in New York knew

Pinafore already – why should they see it again? It was evident that the new opera had to be completed and put on as a replacement – and quickly. It was at this point that Sullivan discovered that he had left his notes for Act 1 in London.

What happened next is a matter of dispute. But it is clear that Sullivan had to reconstruct the music for Act 1 in some haste, not to say panic. The completed opera re-used the chorus 'Climbing Over Rocky Mountain' from *Thespis*, and indeed the first pages of this number in Sullivan's autograph score appear to have been physically taken out of a copyist's score for *Thespis*. Gilbert told a correspondent some years later that the chorus was introduced in order to help Sullivan out in his moment of crisis.[16] However, this does not appear to be the case; the chorus seems to have been introduced into the opera at an earlier date in its composition, as is shown by its presence in early manuscripts of the libretto. It has been suggested, indeed, that not only this chorus but also other parts of the score re-use music from *Thespis*. Whatever the truth of the matter, Gilbert and Sullivan worked together closely and hastily in order to compose and rehearse their new opera and have it ready for the end of the year.[17]

The plans for its production were complicated. The opera had first to be performed in Britain, in order to secure the British copyright, so a touring company of *Pinafore* stumbled through a rough read-through at the Bijou Theatre at Paignton in Devon on 30 December, presided over by Carte's invaluable business assistant, Helen Lenoir. The New York premiere could then take place on the evening of 31 December, the hope being that by authorising the first American performance Gilbert, Sullivan and Carte could claim the American legal rights. It was an untried claim, and one that would only be settled in the American courts, state by state, but they felt it was worth the hazard. One precaution they took was to go against their established practice and not publish the libretto. They had consulted a New York lawyer who advised them that if they withheld publication they could argue that any subsequent use of it was a theft of private property, prosecutable under common law. This was not watertight: it could be argued that performance was itself a form of publication. But at least this way they were giving themselves a fighting chance.[18]

The premiere of *The Pirates of Penzance; or, The Slave of Duty* was a great success (in spite of an atrocious performance by Hugh Talbot who, as Frederic, forgot his lines and sang badly). The audience, drawn largely from New York's fashionable society, laughed and applauded and demanded encores throughout, and greeted the authors at the final curtain with cheers. After a month of hard and stressful work (especially for Sullivan) the piece was triumphantly finished, just as the year itself was closing.

It may, as has been suggested, have contained elements not only of the aborted one-act 'Burglars' opera but also of the now-defunct *Thespis*; it certainly borrowed ideas from Gilbert's German Reed entertainment *Our Island Home*. It is the fruit of what was probably Gilbert and Sullivan's closest collaboration. They were thrown together in a strange country, dining out and dining in, rehearsing, discussing the opera and working on it. Gilbert's libretto went through at least two or three radical reworkings in the process of creation, partly as a result of discussions with Sullivan. It is usually said that Gilbert always wrote the words first and that Sullivan's music followed, but the reality was not always so simple. It is a tenable theory that parts of the libretto of *Pirates* were written to fit Sullivan's pre-existing music. It may even be suggested that if Gilbert and Sullivan were working on the opera together in the same room, words and music may have in places been composed more or less simultaneously.

If so, it was a unique occurrence not to be repeated. They were happier working separately, communicating by letter and the occasional meeting to discuss progress. The first inklings of tension between the two men now began to show themselves. While in New York Sullivan grew to resent Gilbert's way of 'chaffing' him, particularly in public.[19] Small irritations became magnified. In spite of this, however, Sullivan continued to appreciate Gilbert's unique talents: 'The libretto [of *Pirates*] is ingenious, clever, wonderfully funny in parts, and sometimes brilliant in dialogue – beautifully written for music, as is all Gilbert does, and all the action and business perfect.'[20]

Gilbert was busy. In December he had been rehearsing not only *Pirates* but also a production of *Princess Toto* (with a new discovery, Leonora Braham, in the title role). It opened at the Standard Theatre on 20 December and played there for a week before going on tour. In the New Year he rehearsed *Sweethearts*, *The Wedding March* and *Engaged* for production at the Park Theatre in February. He probably found time to meet up with Sothern, who was also in the city, to discuss the play he had written. Gilbert and Sullivan were also busy rehearsing three touring companies of *Pirates*. Gilbert threw himself heart and soul into these rehearsals as ever, insisting upon every inflection and acting out the effects he wanted when necessary.

Finally the collaborators were ready to return home, and they left on the *Gallia* on 3 March. They were anxious to introduce the new opera to London as soon as possible, before spring became summer and 'the season' was over. At last, on 3 April, Grossmith and Barrington and the established company were able to assume the roles they had been fitted for. The reviews were mostly enthusiastic, with the exception of *The Times*, which complained on 5 April that Gilbert's libretto contained 'little or no trace' of 'dramatic invention', and sniffed that 'broadly comic pieces, such as the pirates' chorus and the song of the policeman – the latter received with a perfect storm of applause – will be welcome food for street organs and popular minstrels'. But the collaborators could afford to ignore such snipes: the audiences loved it, and it ran for almost exactly a year – not as long as *H.M.S. Pinafore*, true, but over twice as long as *The Sorcerer*.

Sullivan had a commission to write a sacred work for the Leeds Festival, and he had decided to use as his text the Rev. H.H. Milman's dramatic poem *The*

Martyr of Antioch. Unfortunately, he soon found the poem to be impossible in its original form, and in the summer of 1880 he asked Gilbert to edit it for him. Gilbert reduced it to a wieldy size and turned blank verse into rhymed couplets where necessary, even adding a few lines of his own. It was a success at the festival in October 1880, and Sullivan expressed his thanks to Gilbert with the gift of an engraved silver chalice.

Back in the Boltons, life was more leisurely than previously. There was no pressing need to write a play if Gilbert did not wish it. He was rich, and every week more money was coming in on the strength of *Pirates*, even over the dreaded summer months. He had a new yacht, the *Pleione*, which he found a better place to work than at home, for, as an interviewer from *The World* observed in June 1880: 'Afloat there can be no letters or messages, no appointments, no people craving for "five minutes," no rehearsals.'[21] On board the *Pleione* Gilbert was able to write 'with infinite comfort': 'His great coolie dog, Roy, lies down at his elbow … Blank verse, a favorite medium of Mr. Gilbert, comes easier afloat than ashore … Prose is well enough in its way; but blank verse compels severe attention, and rhyming verse is most precious on account of its suggestiveness.' When at home in the Boltons, he worked in the library, with its 'double windows' to ensure absolute silence, usually late at night between eleven in the evening and four in the morning.

Ned Sothern had announced he would be performing in Gilbert's new play, *Foggerty's Fairy*, at the Gaiety in October. Unfortunately, Sothern was growing ill and the play was postponed. In fact, as it turned out, he was more than merely ill. He lingered a while but finally died on 20 January 1881, at the age of 54.

Otherwise, Gilbert's only professional occupation was a leisurely mulling over of the next opera for Sullivan. 'In cabs and railway carriages, aboard ships, or during quiet strolls in the park, the motive of the new venture shapes itself out.'[22] It was to be a story of two men vying for the affections of a chorus of hero-worshipping young ladies. But who were these two men to be? Gilbert thought of making them aesthetic poets, after the fashion of the affected young men in du Maurier's *Punch* cartoons; but he abandoned the idea, fearing that aesthetic costumes for the ladies would be too expensive. No, he decided the two men were not poets but curates, and the women were their adoring parishioners. He mapped out the plot, taking the Bab ballad 'The Rival Curates' as a starting point, and he started to write the lyrics; but he was not quite happy with it. It was, in part, a feeling of being 'crippled at every turn by the necessity of protecting myself from a charge of irreverence'.[23] He was surely also wondering if he had made the correct decision artistically. As he explained to an interviewer some years later: 'Comic opera should appeal to both the eye and the ear.'[24] Were mild, effacing, black-and-white clergymen interesting enough visually to be the central characters of a comic opera?

Finally, on 1 November 1880, he wrote to Sullivan:

> I want to see you particularly about the new piece. Although it is two-thirds
> finished, I don't feel comfortable about it. I mistrust the clerical element. I feel
> hampered by the restrictions which the nature of the subject places upon my
> freedom of action, & I want to revert to my old idea of rivalry between two aes-
> thetic fanatics, worshipped by a chorus of female aesthetics … I can get much
> more fun out of the subject as I propose to alter it, & the general scheme of the
> piece will remain as at present. The Hussars will become aesthetic young men
> (abandoning their profession for the purpose) – in this latter capacity they will
> all carry lilies in their hands, wear long hair, & stand in stained glass attitudes.[25]

Aestheticism was more than an -ism. It was part of a general reaction against the
dour unbeautiful atmosphere of the early Victorian age and an attempt to reclaim
beauty in art, poetry, furnishings, clothes – in everything. For the previous couple
of years *Punch* had been full of cartoons by George du Maurier making fun of the
pretentious 'aesthetic' men and women who had latched on to the movement.
In his pictures tall pre-Raphaelite ladies dote upon long-haired artists against a
background of Japanese fans and tables and vases. An early example from 14 June
1879 sets the tone: a serious young woman asking a commonplace-looking young
man, 'Are you *Intense?*'

By the middle of 1880, du Maurier's drawings had become part of a series,
depicting regular characters as in a situation comedy. In these cartoons, society
figures such as Mrs Lyon Hunter and Mr and Mrs Cimabue Brown act as artistic patrons to such others as 'the great Poet' Jellaby Postlethwaite and 'the great
Painter' Maudle, much to the disgust of characters such as the down-to-earth
Grigsby and the no-nonsense Colonel.

The targets of the satire were the conceit, ignorance and affectation of aesthetic
young fools, as sometimes observed by older and wiser heads. Oscar Wilde – fresh
from Oxford and full of attitudinising about his blue-and-white china – was one
of the targets, but he was far from being the only one. He was very young and just
starting out in life; he was just one oddity in a group of oddities.

The cartoons were a major influence on the opera Gilbert was now writing,
which he was to call *Patience; or, Bunthorne's Bride*. He originally intended du
Maurier to design the costumes, though in the event Gilbert designed them
himself. He named his two rival poets Bunthorne (after Bob Bunnythorne, a
poet in Tom Robertson's 1869 play *Progress*) and Grosvenor (after the Grosvenor
Gallery in London). Some of the reviews took the opera to be a direct crib from
the cartoons: *The Era* (30 April) said: 'It was laughable indeed to see Maudle
looking at his rival on the stage, and Postlethwaite grinning at his counterfeit
presentment in the opera.' The resemblances were merely superficial, however.
Punch's condemnation of the aesthetic fashion was crude and often vicious,

the status quo mocking the outsider. *Patience* contains little or nothing of such hatred; the Philistine is made to appear just as absurd as the aesthete. Indeed, the opera is not really about aestheticism at all; that is just an incidental feature. It is about love and admiration, and the terrible disappointment involved in getting what you want. As Bunthorne says: 'What's the use of yearning for Elysian Fields when you know you can't get 'em, and would only let 'em out on building leases if you had 'em?'

When *Patience* was premiered on 23 April 1881, aestheticism was already a familiar target for stage satire. James Albery's farce *Where's the Cat?*, which opened at the Criterion on 20 November 1880, featured the young actor Herbert Beerbohm Tree as an aesthete who uses words like 'consummate' and 'precious' and enters at one point holding a bunch of lilies. Frank Burnand's *The Colonel*, a direct offshoot from the *Punch* lampoons, opened on 2 February 1881 at the Prince of Wales to great success, portraying the aesthetes as out-and-out hypocrites and villains. *Patience* and *The Colonel* were actually written more or less simultaneously, each author apparently having no idea that the other was also writing a similar piece. But there was room on the London scene for both, as it turned out: *Patience* ran for 578 performances and *The Colonel* for 550.

Patience marked a change in direction for Gilbert's relationship with Sullivan. Quite simply, it had much more dialogue than any of its predecessors. It was more sophisticated dramatically than *Pirates*, and music played a less important role. There was little operatic parody and instead of extended operatic scenes there was a fairly simple alternation of songs and dialogue. All this suggests a shift of focus away from the idea of the Gilbert and Sullivan entertainments being operas and towards their being musical dramas. It may also indicate Gilbert's increasing confidence in the acting abilities of the D'Oyly Carte regulars.

This was the last of the Gilbert and Sullivan operas to be premiered at the shabby and inconvenient Opera Comique. There was a new theatre rising on the Strand, just up from the Thames Embankment: the Savoy. It was finally completed over the summer and it opened with much fanfare on 10 October, the first public building in the world designed to be lit throughout by electricity. *Patience* transferred to the new theatre smoothly, although the set needed to be redesigned to fit the new space and a sight gag about looking into a pool of water had to be changed into one about looking into a hand-mirror.

Carte's dream was at last realised. The success of Gilbert and Sullivan and Carte seemed solid and lasting, and it was destined to continue and grow. But there were tensions. Gilbert distrusted Carte as a businessman and thought he was getting more money than he deserved. (Gilbert was uniquely lucky to find in Carte a man prepared to provide an environment in which Gilbert could realise his intentions without opposition; but he does not seem to have realised this.) Sullivan, unhappy to be occupied with such lucrative but frivolous work, wished to write only one more opera with Gilbert. But Carte had sunk a great deal of money into the theatre and had to be sure of recouping it: Gilbert and Sullivan had to continue.

Gilbert was happy to agree to this, at least for the moment. In December 1881 *Foggerty's Fairy* had at last reached the stage, at the Criterion with Charles Wyndham in the starring role. Despite its inventiveness and the brilliance of its wit, it lasted only three weeks before disappearing. *The Era* (17 December 1881) had been most disappointed by the piece:

> It begins briskly, and all through there are comic ideas and quaint turns of expression such as no other dramatic author could have written. It is only fair to Mr. Gilbert to say that, when these passages occurred, they were greeted with shouts of laughter. They were frequently so odd, so unexpected, as to take the audience by surprise. But the author's power to take his audience by storm is nothing new ... in this comedy he has gone far beyond any previous attempt, for the entire piece is a surprise ... there were times, especially in the third act, when the bulk of the audience must have been profoundly in the dark as to the author's meaning ... In departing from the ordinary standards of dramatic literature Mr. Gilbert appears to have ventured upon a strange ocean, where his barque has been drifted hither and thither without any settled ideas as to what port he could make for.

Gilbert's crazy tale of a man who attempts, with the aid of a slightly dim guardian fairy, to set his life on the right tracks by eradicating an element from his past, was too quirky and original for an audience who simply wanted to enjoy themselves without straining their brains.

Every fresh experience confirmed that the public would take only one thing from Gilbert now, and that was Gilbert and Sullivan. *Foggerty* failed; but there was always another opera to write.

15

THE MAKING OF *IOLANTHE* (1881–82)

Gilbert explained, on several different occasions, his process of writing with Sullivan: 'I first ask myself what things are just then asked for by the public, and try to write up to some one interesting subject. The state of the navy, of the army, aestheticism, and so on, have thus been written about.'[1] He mulls over the story 'in the odd hours of the day or night, until it becomes coherent'.[2] Then he meets up with Sullivan to discuss the proposed subject, 'which, if entertained at all, is freely and fully discussed in all its bearings'.[3] He goes away and draws up the plot as a detailed scenario, which is then discussed again. 'Those passages and situations Sir Arthur thinks unsuitable to musical treatment I either modify or perhaps eliminate altogether. If I find that his difficulties or objections in any way knock the keystone out of my plan I tell him so, and he in turn yields a point or two.'[4] Gilbert writes the plot outline again and again ('Sometimes I do this a dozen times'),[5] developing the details slowly until at last he and Sullivan are satisfied with it:

> I next sketch out quite roughly the dialogue, and then fill in the musical numbers as I feel inclined. I do not attempt to write them in order, but just as the humour takes me – one here, one there; a sad one when I feel depressed, a bright one when I am in a happy mood. When at last all those of the first act are done it is sent to the composer to be set to music, with a copy of the rough sketch of the dialogue to show him how the different songs hang together. I generally like reading it over to the composer, so as to give him my idea of the rhythm, which, as a matter of course, he varies at his pleasure.[6]

While Sullivan is writing the songs for Act 1, Gilbert writes the rough dialogue and the lyrics for Act 2; finally, while Sullivan writes the Act 2 songs, Gilbert polishes up the dialogue to a final version.

It was Gilbert's usual practice to destroy his working notes after finishing with them. Luckily, however, the plot book for *Iolanthe* survives, a handsomely bound volume held in the Pierpont Morgan Library in New York; so it is possible to trace the development of this, arguably his best libretto, from its simple beginnings through to the almost final version of the plot.

It may be useful first to give a plot summary of *Iolanthe* as it finally appeared at the Savoy in November 1882.

Act 1 takes place in an Arcadian landscape. A chorus of fairies enters and engages in fairy revels. They are, however, dissatisfied, for fairy revels have not been what they were since Iolanthe left them twenty-five years ago. She had committed a grave sin by marrying a mortal, and was condemned to death. She did not die, however: their queen commuted her sentence to penal servitude for life instead. The Fairy Queen decides to forgive her and restore her to the fairy band. Iolanthe is welcomed back, and tells her fairy sisters that she has a son, an Arcadian shepherd called Strephon. Strephon comes to see Iolanthe and is introduced to the fairies. He is half a fairy – down to the waist. The Fairy Queen promises to protect him; all he has to do is call, and they will come to his aid. The fairies leave, and Strephon remains to meet his fiancée, the Arcadian shepherdess Phyllis. She does not know that Strephon is a fairy. They are to marry, even though she is a ward of Chancery and needs the consent of the Lord Chancellor – a consent which he refuses to give. At this point the entire House of Peers enters to a magnificent march, along with the Lord Chancellor. They are all in love with Phyllis, but she refuses them. Strephon has a tender scene with his mother Iolanthe, who, being a fairy, looks 17 even though she is several centuries old. The peers spy on them and draw Phyllis' attention to this disgraceful act of treachery. Strephon protests that Iolanthe is his mother, which no one believes. Phyllis spurns Strephon and turns instead to two lords – Mountararat and Tolloller – one of whom she will marry, but she doesn't care which. Strephon, at the end of his tether, calls the fairies to his aid. They decide to take their revenge on the ill-mannered peers by sending Strephon into parliament.

Act 2 takes place in Palace Yard, Westminster, with the clock tower of Westminster visible in the background. A sentry, Private Willis, remains on guard throughout. Strephon is now a Member of Parliament, and with his fairy powers he is able to accomplish everything he wants, much to the outrage of the peers. The fairies are on the verge of falling in love with the peers. The Fairy Queen urges them to resist their inclinations. She admits that she is greatly attracted to Private Willis, but she is strong enough to stand firm. Strephon, miserable at being separated from his loved one, tells Phyllis that he is half a fairy and his mother is a full fairy. She accepts this explanation of his conduct and they are reconciled. They persuade Iolanthe to plead with the Lord Chancellor for his consent. She is reluctant but agrees and pleads accordingly. The Lord Chancellor refuses his consent on the grounds that he wishes to marry Phyllis himself. Iolanthe, horrified, reveals the truth: she is his wife. By making this declaration she condemns herself to death. The Fairy Queen is just steeling herself to execute the punishment when the other fairies interrupt with a confession: they have succumbed to impulse and married all the peers. If Iolanthe deserves to die, so do they. The Lord Chancellor intervenes with a solution. Fairy law states that every fairy must die who marries a mortal. He proposes an amendment: every fairy must die who *doesn't* marry a mortal. This proposal is adopted; the Fairy Queen hastens to marry Private Willis; the sentry and the peers all become fairies; and as the curtain descends everyone is preparing to fly off to Fairyland.

Iolanthe's actual plot is to some extent an irrelevance. The things that are important in the opera, the things that make it memorable as a work of art, are its incidentals, its tone and particularly its visual aspects: the fairies; the Arcadian shepherd and shepherdess; the peers entering in the full pomp of their formal robes, magnificent and ridiculous. (Since *Iolanthe*, it has never been possible to take the state opening of parliament entirely seriously.) All kinds of tone meet and mingle in this opera: whimsy, fantasy, romance, wit and political satire. In the plot books Gilbert can be seen trying to define the opera's imaginative world. At times he seems to be groping in the dark for an object, the shape of which he cannot guess.

His starting point was the Bab ballad 'The Fairy Curate' (*Fun*, 23 July 1870), which begins: 'Once a fairy/Light and airy/Married with a mortal.' A fairy marries an attorney and she bears a son, Georgie, who decides to join the clergy. He becomes ritualistic in his opinions, but his mother objects and flies down to discuss the matter with him. His bishop bursts in upon their tête-à-tête and refuses to believe Georgie's statement that the young lady leaning against his shoulder is his mother. His career ruined, Georgie leaves the Church and becomes a Mormon.

The first entry in the *Iolanthe* plot book runs as follows:[*]

> A Fairy has been guilty of the imprudence of marrying a solicitor. She has been sent to earth on a mission & has fallen in love with a prosaic lawyer of 45. Quite a matter of fact person./She is consequently summoned with her husband (who becomes a prosaic fairy from the fact of his marriage with her) into fairyland-& finally banished from it. [p. 1]

Gilbert continued with this idea for a few lines before trying a different tack:

> Fairy married mortal./She has a grandson – although she is still young & beautiful./Grandson is engaged to young lady/Young lady is courted by Wicked Barrister/Wicked barrister overhears conversation of grandson & grand-

---

[*] Many of the entries in the plot book consist of very short sentences, each on a separate line. When quoting from the plot book, I will indicate line breaks with an oblique stroke.

mother./Tells young lady – young lady denounces him – refuses him accepts barrister/Grandson explains – it was my grandmother./Derisive reception of argument [?]/Explains she is fairy./He is seized for Witchcraft … /He employs barrister to defend him. [pp. 1–2]

For Gilbert, one of the great attractions of the core idea was the association of fantasy (fairies) with the prosaic (solicitors). As he put it in a stray thought on these early pages: 'Fairies, tired of single life, marry mortals./Commonplace mortals.' (p. 2)

He could not decide on the details of the story. He had the abstract idea, but where was it all to take place? Who were the characters? He tried it out with an island of shipwrecked people, but he quickly abandoned them. Next, he returned to the source material and made his hero a clergyman who has 'one secret – only one – He is the grandson of a fairy who has the gift of perennial youth & beauty'. (p. 3) The clergyman is afraid to reveal his secret, and with good reason – when he finally does so he is condemned for witchcraft (an idea that recurs through many of these early notes.) But this little plot quickly dies.

Another attempt:

A body of fairies has come to earth./They have fallen in love with the QCs of Northern Circuit/First Act ends with Marriage & rejoicings./In second act, complicated consequences of this./Husbands become good fairies – to their intense distress/They must no longer shield the criminal/Or adopt the cause of the dishonest./They must be quite straightforward & simple/This ruins them professionally. [p.4]

This set Gilbert thinking on another tack. This was not just a story about setting the fantastic against the prosaic, but also setting unworkable ideals against the unjust practicalities:

Ministry & Ministers – picnic of./They rejoice at party triumphs./Fairies meet/They lament discords arising from politics/Especially from fact that patriots are all actuated by selfish motives/To set this right they determine to go to earth & marry the Government./And so convert them all into good Fairies./This they do, at picnic/Rejoicings … /Opposition furious/Ministry have been influenced by Fairies to bring in a bill for Abolition of parties/Fairies attribute all miseries to artificial division of mankind into lib & con./Ministers bring in bill to this effect. [pp. 4–5]

Having had this brilliant flash of inspiration, Gilbert immediately abandoned it and went back to his previous idea of having the fairies marry barristers of the Northern Circuit. He spent some pages developing the idea. He clearly found it a very funny joke, even though it would never have much appeal to the general public:

Mr. Justice Jones is a pure & excellent judge … /He has a secret./He is the grandson of a fairy, & is himself a fairy/His grandmother has the gift of perennial youth & beauty/As a fairy, his judgements are always immaculate./They are never reviewed [?]/He never receives points/He will not allow quibbles/Or brutal & [word missing?] examination/Or fees to more counsel than one in a case./He cuts forensic eloquence short/[Therefore] He is abhorred by the bar. [p. 11]

About this point, Gilbert seems to have realised that his ideas were linking up with the ideas in *The Happy Land*:

Fairies, miserable at prevailing unhappiness, come & rule on earth./They undertake various practical offices – judgeships &c. are all filled by fairies/All political posts-all civil all military & naval posts./General rejoicings – End of Act 1./In Act 2/General discontent/Rule of fairies perfect./Consequently all disputes at an end./Lawyers have no clients/Barristers not allowed to x examine/Soldiers have no fighting – /Politicians have no aims, because party is abolished./Doctors have no patients, owing to sanitary laws:/No convicts to do work:/In short a millennium is established, & consequently all professions that flourish on human weaknesses wither & die./The bar are more affected than anybody/They combine against fairy rule./Eventually fairies marry bar./ Human happiness secured thereby. [pp. 13–4]

Gilbert was stepping in the right direction. He understood that he was trying to write something which involved large ideas, and these would be represented somehow by the two choruses. The difficulty – one of many – was to try and combine this choral plot with smaller-scale plots for the solo artists:

A fairy has fallen in love with a barrister. She marries him & he becomes, ipso facto, a fairy. She & her husband are summoned to fairy land & banished./He had no idea that he was marrying a fairy/He is a prosaic person with a horror of fairies & everything supernatural./He is extremely annoyed at discovering that she is a fairy/Still more on discovering that he also is one./What will his clients say … /The male chorus should be barristers – /The female chorus should be fairies/All the barristers fall in love with all the fairies/At end of piece, they marry them/And so become fairy barristers. [p. 16]

He continued to explore this idea of an opera about fairies and barristers. Who would the characters be and how would they relate to each other? The barristers would resist the idea of becoming fairies because fairies 'are always compelled to speak the truth, which is fatal to their chance of advancement'. (p. 18) But who were the hero and heroine to be? 'Lord Edward & Lady Agatha are rival claimants to a vast estate./They love each other secretly – but the necessities of

the litigation keep them asunder. Moreover one is a Tory – the other a Radical/
Half the Northern Circuit are retained for Lord Edward/The other half for
Lady Agatha.' (p. 19)

Though Gilbert tinkered with this idea a little longer, he seems to have grown
bored with it and it did not last. He jotted down a few random ideas. First, a
return to the idea that the son of a fairy could be condemned for witchcraft:
'Peter & his family [?] are condemned to death in Act 2/Then, the Mayor who is
also hereditary executioner, is extremely nervous at having to behead Peter/He
is encouraged by Peter.' This very faint foreshadowing of *The Mikado* was then
crossed out. Then: 'Story of Cavalry who are billeted on a Puritan girls school.'
Then: 'Three quaint old men who pass their time in devising practical jokes.'
(p. 20) Having taken these stray thoughts and placed them on paper, Gilbert was
able to set them to one side and continue in other directions.

The next development in the plot book appears from nowhere, almost full
blown, presumably after a productive afternoon of brooding in the park or on
the yacht. It is an early expression of an idea, usually referred to as the 'lozenge
plot', which was to cause much tension between Gilbert and Sullivan in the
coming years:

A troupe of strolling players at an inn./They are going to give a performance/
One of them is a young man (*tenor*) the grandson of a fairy who committed the indiscretion of marrying a mortal, & who was thereby excluded from
fairyland until a descendant should own to her./This is difficult to bring about,
inasmuch as anyone owning to such an ancestry would be liable to be burnt
for witchcraft./The scene takes place outside a booth which is close to a fairy
well – of which the banished fairy is the guardian. It makes everything actually
what it appears to be./A bragging coward becomes a brave man./A spendthrift
becomes as wealthy as he appears to be … /In Act 1 Tenor must get into a difficulty – condemned to be beheaded – through owning to fairy grandmother./
In Act 2 He must get out of his difficulty through operation of water, changing
every one's disposition. For instance – the Mayor (who plays a magician & who
has condemned Tenor to death) becomes a magician and consequently liable to
the same penalty. [p. 21]

It is possible that Gilbert now showed this plot, or something like it, to Sullivan; if
so, Sullivan did not like it, and Gilbert abandoned it – for the moment. Instead his
mind went on another tangent, even more bizarre than the last:

Enter chorus of would be sportsmen [huntsmen], dressed in accurate pink & tops.
They explain that the village is bitten with a desire to become sporting. They are
saving their money to buy the necessary outfit by degrees. At present they have
bought costume – everything but horses – & that when they have got them – &

have learnt to ride them – how jolly sporting it will be! In the meantime, following the fox without hounds or horses, is very good fun for the fox. [p. 33]

At the same time, however, he was developing other ideas which either would
make their way into the finished opera or at least had the potential to do so:
'Agatha gives herself up to the three conspirators saying she will marry one of
them – she don't care which – they must settle it among themselves. Agrees to
call the three Algernon till it is settled which of them it is.' (p. 25) One especially
inspired notion, which had to be abandoned, was that the female chorus should
be not fairies but naiads on the banks of the River Thames (English equivalents to
the Rhine maidens, perhaps).

As a rule Gilbert wrote only on the right-hand pages in the book, but he occasionally added doodles (usually cartoon heads) or brief jottings on the left-hand
pages. A significant entry appears on the left-hand page opposite p. 38, a giant
stride towards the opera as it was to emerge. It begins: 'All the male chorus are
members of the nobility & wear full robes & coronets.' The significance of this
must be emphasised. Gilbert had previously been thinking of the male chorus
as barristers or politicians. Neither group has an especially colourful image
associated with them; perhaps this is one reason why he should have briefly considered dressing the chorus in hunting pink. By stressing the nobles' full robes
and coronets, Gilbert seems to be answering an unspoken question. It was vitally
important that they should be visually arresting. He continues, reworking his old
idea to suit the new chorus:

> The fairies are distressed at the misfortunes of the poor & are under the impres-
> sion that they proceed from the tyranny of hereditary legislation – & a division
> of mankind into parties/Fairy mother induces her son Attorney Genl to intro-
> duce a bill for the abolition of parties. This he is loth to do – but consents./
> Indignation of everyone – as if parties are abolished, their position as patriots
> will be abolished/Fury of peers against son.

This is the core of the opera as Gilbert was about to develop it. It must have
been about the same time that he went to Sullivan to place the idea before him.
Sullivan approved; he wrote in his diary (19 October 1881): 'Gilbert came, and
sketched out idea of new piece. Ld. Chancellor, Com: in Chief, Peers, fairies, &c.
– funny, but at present vague.'[7] Gilbert went away, and, as was his wont, wrote it
up as a more or less complete scenario. The draft in the plot book (pp. 48–54) is
worth quoting at length:

> Sir Herbert Hartright is Attorney General, under a Conservative Administration.
> He loves Lettie, a beautiful girl who keeps an Apple stall in Westminster Hall.
> Lettie is the daughter of a Private in the Guards. Lettie is also loved by the entire

House of Peers – prominent among whom are the Commander in Chief and the Admiral of the Fleet. The only exception (if exception it may be called) is in the case of the Lord Chancellor who struggles with his passion throughout the piece, as Lettie is a Ward in Chancery, & the Lord Chancellor is her constitutional guardian.

Sir Herbert Hartright's progress at the bar has been almost phenomenal. He is only five & twenty & yet he is Attorney General, & a most conspicuous success in that capacity. The fact is that Sir Herbert is the son of a fairy who, having received permission to dwell on earth for a year, fell in love with a mortal & secretly married him. The result was the birth of Herbert, but when Herbert was a month old, his mother's term of absence expired & she had to return to fairy land leaving no trace of her whereabouts. She, however, has never ceased to keep watch over her son, & his astonishing progress at the bar is the consequence of her fairy influence. Her attachment to, & marriage with a mortal has been kept a profound secret from the other fairies, as, if it were known that she had so disgraced herself, she would be banished from fairy land. Sir Herbert's success at the bar is mainly due to his mother's counsels which were to the effect that he should be perfectly upright in his conduct – never take a fee from a client whose case he could not advocate in person – never to bully a witness – never to attempt to hoodwink a judge, always to read his briefs before he came into court, – & in short to carry on his profession not so much as it *is* carried on, as it ought to be.

The Lord Chancellor's song in *Iolanthe*, 'When I went to the Bar as a very young man', follows the details of this last sentence very closely. Sir Herbert Hartright was not to survive to the final version of the opera, but Gilbert's labour in creating the character was not completely wasted.

The piece will probably open with a meeting of the fairies (*Thames naiads*) whose duty it is to watch over & protect all counties through which the river flows. They are very much distressed at the unsatisfactory character of British legislation & attribute much of this to the House of Peers which they consider should be abolished. They discuss the absurdities of hereditary legislation & argue that a man should be a legislator by reason of his own fitness, rather than on account of the fitness of his ancestors. They depute the fairy mother, to beg the Attorney General to bring in a bill for the abolition of the House of Lords – or rather, the fairy mother suggests that she shall be empowered to call on the Attorney General & suggest the Bill to him. To this the fairies agree – not knowing, of course, that the Attorney General is the fairy's son.

The fairy has an interview with her son, of a motherly & affectionate character (she has the gift of perennial youth, & consequently looks about 18). The son, who is devoted to his mother, cannot agree to the Bill. He is a staunch

Conservative, & the legal adviser of the Government, & he cannot consent to abandon his principles, even for his fairy mother. The fairy is much distressed but nevertheless takes an affectionate leave of her son.

At this point in the scenario Gilbert is forced to backtrack. 'This scene has been preceded by the following scenes,' he explains:

A Chorus of the Peers in their full robes & coronets, led by Commander in Chief & Admiral of the Fleet, followed by scene in which the love of the Peers for Lettie is explained. Lettie, (who sells apples & oranges to the Peers, which they eagerly buy & eat) explains that her heart is given to the Attorney General, whose love she gained at the refreshment stall in Westminster hall while the court had risen for luncheon. The peers curse the Attorney General & determine to throw out any bill he may introduce.

Then:

A scene between the Lord Chancellor & Lettie – showing his love for his ward & his struggles to suppress it, from a sense of duty. Lettie then tells him of her love for the Attorney General, & implores his consent ... Although he does not feel justified in urging his own love, he cannot bring himself to consent to her marriage with another – & he takes her away broken hearted.

After this, Gilbert returns to the scene between the Attorney General and his fairy mother:

This scene should be overheard by the Commander in Chief & the Admiral of the Fleet & all the peers – finding Sir Herbert in affectionate converse with a young & lovely woman, they conclude that he is false to Lettie. They denounce him – He indignantly denies it. Lettie enters – sees Sir Herbert in the arms of a young woman &, heartbroken & indignant, repudiates him for ever. In a paroxysm of agony, he tells her that the young woman is his mother. His statement is received with indignant incredulity by Lettie – & with ridicule by the others. The fairy is heartbroken at the discovery – which will ensure her banishment from Fairy Land (all the fairies have entered & denounce her).
 This would end Act 1.

The tale, so far, is told with formal coherence, in complete sentences and long paragraphs, as if to a general reader. At this point, however, Gilbert evidently came up against the fact that he had not completely worked out the rest of the story. The remainder of the scenario, therefore, is headed, 'Ingredients for Act 2', and there is a return to the style of the earlier creative notes written for his private use: '[Lettie] Will marry either Commander in Chief or Admiral/Dont care which/They must settle it between them/In the mean time will consider herself engaged to both./Until they settle – she will call them Algernon.' The two men cannot decide the matter themselves, and so 'Agree to refer matter to her father, the private in the Guard who is on duty on scene./Scene in which they do this/He accepts them both – they kneel – he blesses them/Dancing trio – C.in chief & Admiral all over the stage – Father in his own ground opposite sentry box.' (pp. 52–3)

A note on one of the left-hand pages hints towards another scene 'in which peers are furious at Atty Gen's bill to abolish them/They swear to vote against their own abolition – this purely from patriotic motives/(Patriotic song to this effect)/They have but little hope of success as somehow every Bill Atty-Gen brings in, always becomes law.' (opposite p. 54)

The remainder of the scenario is taken up with the opera's climax and resolution. The very end of the piece is rather different from the final version. It starts with the 'fairy mother' agreeing to plead on behalf of her son to the Lord Chancellor:

Veils herself – has scene with Ld. Chancellor in which she pleads for her consent to her sons union with Lettie/He cannot do it – He is deeply agitated./He confesses that he loves her deeply – passionately, but that several reasons occur to perplex him as to what he ought to do/Fairy unaccountably moved/Implores him to reconsider matter/He cannot – he has long struggled with his passion/He must declare himself – for life is unendurable/He is going now to chambers to give his consent to his own marriage with her./The fairy says Stop – I have a last & most urgent argument – /What is it?/This! She reveals herself – & the Lord Chancellor recognizes in her his long lost wife/He is amazed – enraptured/She tells him that the Atty Gen is his son./Lord Chancellor implores her to remain with him – he has never ceased to deplore her absence./She says that she has broken her vow & is doomed./The fairies enter & denounce her/She points to Lord C & asks if they were married to such as he, would they not yield/They admit that he is beautiful/They agree to pardon her if Ld. C. will become a fairy/He agrees – & a pair of wings springs from his back/Thereupon he agrees to Atty Gen's union with his ward./& he resigns/ Atty Gen becomes Ld C. & nobly abandons his bill for abolition of H of Lds./The Com in Chief & Admiral of Fleet marry 2nd & 3rd fairies & wings spring from their backs/ The other peers pair off with other fairies – the soldier pairing with Fairy Queen – & wings spring from his back.

Thus Gilbert secured a happy ending for everyone with a characteristic piece of logic: if every fairy must die who marries a mortal, the simplest solution is to convert the intended husband into an immortal fairy first. He retained this elegant conclusion right up to the last extant draft in the plot book, though, for some reason, he changed it when actually writing the dialogue.

The scenario has the bare bones of the final opera, but certain elements would change before it reached the stage. It seems obvious in hindsight that an attorney general could never be the ideal hero for a comic opera. He has already reached a pinnacle of power: how can an audience be expected to sympathise with his problems? Transformed into Strephon the Arcadian shepherd, he is much more likeable because he is powerless, and the sudden reversal when he takes over the Houses of Parliament and makes everyone do his bidding is all the more satisfying. But he remained Sir Herbert Hartright until late in the creative process.

In the meantime, Gilbert concentrated on refining the details of the plot. The 'fairy mother' at last acquired a name, Iolanthe, and for a short while she was characterised as a fairy servant, to be introduced at the beginning of the opera handing round refreshments to the other fairies.

Gilbert considered giving the Lord Chancellor's trainbearer a prominent role: he 'never leaves [the Lord Chancellor] – but ... imitates all his movements like a shadow'. (p. 87) Gilbert added on the opposite page: 'When Ld C. is alone he gathers up his train & carries it under his arm. Trainbearer then becomes Ld C's confidant ... Ld C. looks on trainbearer as his conscience – or other self, & speaks to him accordingly.' It was an intriguing idea but not one that Gilbert carried through into the libretto.

Some of the plot notes shed light on Gilbert's attitudes to politics. One passage which he then crossed out reads:

> Certain benevolent fairies, who take a deep interest in human welfare, are distressed to find that British legislators devote weeks of laborious attention to matters of mere abstract importance, utterly neglecting the crying miseries which are at their door, & which spring from the filth squalor & crime in which so large a portion of our population are reared. [p. 67]

This outburst appears to place Gilbert left of centre politically, as does the following little piece of satire: 'Suppose Atty Gen brings in Bill providing that promotion to Upper House shall be by Competitive Examination./Then the Peers are annoyed because ... /A number of clever men will get into House – who will entirely revolutionize its character.' (p. 132) But a separate summary of the same situation nails Gilbert's political views firmly in the opposite direction:

> In his fury at having been deprived of his bride – [Attorney General] is determined to be revenged by bringing in a Bill to abolish all existing institutions with a view of reducing civilization to its elements, reconstructing Society anew on Common Sense principles./The Queen asks – is not a politician – but asks – for information only – whether that is not rather a sweeping measure for

a Conservative/He replies that perhaps it may be regarded in that light – but
he is a deeply injured man – & a radical is only a Tory with a grievance. [p. 106]

There is little doubt that Gilbert was a Conservative at the ballot box, though not
an orthodox one. What perhaps outraged him most about politics was the nature
of the system itself. A passage opposite p. 136 suggests the fairy Iolanthe has not
been a wholehearted influence for good in the world:

> It was she who first divided Mankind into Political Parties … It was she who
> arranged that when one party went out, having got half through their work,
> another party with diametrically opposite opinions should come in & finish it
> … It was she who arranged [?] that the Army should be ruled by a lawyer & the
> navy by a wholesale grocer.

The setting of Act 1 changed from 'Demurrer Park, the residence of Lord
Chancellor' (p. 74) to 'exterior of Lettie's cottage & mill' – Lettie now being
characterised for some reason as 'an attractive little miller who lives with her
mother – a portentous & depressed widow with whom everything goes wrong'.
(p. 77) The setting did not last. The mother disappeared as abruptly as she had
appeared. Her father survived longer – 'a private in Guards … a blunt dull semi
shrewd mechanical soldier' (p. 72) who would be the sentry in Act 2 – but in the
final version Private Willis lost his relationship with Lettie (Phyllis) and she ended
up with no relatives at all.

These later pages of the plot book date from the period during which Gilbert
was discussing the opera with Sullivan. The composer had gone abroad to Egypt
at the end of 1881, returning to London only in April 1882; and while he had
taken a number of Gilbert's lyrics with him it appears he did not do much
with them on the trip. Gilbert developed the plot in many of its details during
those long months. It seems certain that at least some of the later alterations
were prompted by Sullivan, following discussions on his return. For instance, he
cannot have been very excited at the prospect of writing romantic love songs
for an attorney general. It is reasonable to surmise that Gilbert's late decision
to change the name, character and profession of his hero was prompted by
Sullivan. Hence:

> Phyllis is a beautiful young shepherdess (*Watteau*) a Ward in chancery, & 19 years
> old. She is a farmer/Corydon is a shepherd in the employ of Phyllis. He is the
> son of Iolanthe, a fairy who married a mortal, 21 years ago … Corydon is in
> love with & engaged to Phyllis – indeed he is to be married to her in the first
> act. The fact that she is a Ward in Chancery has not deterred him. The whole
> House of Peers is in love with Phyllis, & continually come to her farm to eat
> curds & whey. [p. 100]

Corydon became Strephon – later, disappointingly, returning to his old condition as Sir Herbert Hartright the attorney general, before settling as Strephon for good.

The later developments in the plot book are essentially minor refinements. Gilbert occasionally took off on an eccentric flight of fancy (several pages are occupied with an idea about the fairies disrupting Phyllis' wedding to one of the noblemen), but in general the path lay straight before him. He wrote lyric upon lyric (rather more than the opera needed) and Sullivan set them. The plot book includes several rough lists of these. For instance the following (opp. p. 162), the ticked items presumably being the lyrics Gilbert had written to date:

  1 Sentrys song ✓
  2 Chorus of fairies ✓
  3 Song Queen – about sentry ✓
  4 Entrance of Peers – excited chorus ✓
  5 Song Phyllis A & B, leaving A & B to settle it between them ✓
  6 Song Ld C Sleepless night ✓
  7 Trio Ld C A & B ✓
  8 Song sentry 'Fear no unlicensed entry' ✓
  9 Duet – Phyllis & Atty Gen
10 Trio Ld C. Phyllis & Atty
11 Duet Iolanthe & Atty Gen
12 Ballad, Iolanthe ✓
13 Chorus of Fairies
14 Finale

So it seems the hero was still named as the Attorney General even at this late stage in the writing process.

Gilbert met up with Sullivan several times between July and September, to deliver lyrics and discuss the opera in general. The Gilberts dined with him on 15 September. The two men were on good terms with each other, though there were tensions below the surface. Gilbert had wrangled with Carte over money earlier in the year, and Carte had vented his frustration in a letter to Sullivan in February 1882:

> We often hear people say and I have heard you say that it is difficult to get on with Gilbert and it really is. He takes views of things so totally unlike what any one else would … If a discussion arises he will look at matters solely from his point of view, he will not see them from any other, will be very disagreeable about it … And at other times you know how nice and agreeable he can be. Well – I suppose his exceptional ways are part of his exceptional genius and that he could not write as he does if he were different. After all there is only one Gilbert, and I suppose it is of no use to talk about it.[8]

As usual, Sullivan left the serious work on the opera until the last moment. He could not wind himself up to the right creative tension otherwise. The first music rehearsal for the new opera took place on 12 September, with most of the score still to write. A series of all-night sessions through September and October allowed him to complete the music in time to be shipped to America; they planned to produce the piece simultaneously in London and New York at the end of November.

The rehearsals took place over two months, performances of *Patience* continuing in the evening. The title of the new piece was kept a strict secret, even to the extent of the performers having to refer to Jessie Bond's character as Perola instead of Iolanthe. This seems to have been done partly because the title *Iolanthe* had already been used by Henry Irving and there was some anxiety whether Irving would allow the Savoy to borrow it. The Lord Chancellor was to be played by Grossmith, of course; Jessie Bond's casting as Iolanthe signals her increased importance in the company; Barrington was cast in the comparatively small role of the Earl of Mountararat, while the company's principal tenor Durward Lely played the Earl of Tolloller; and, eccentrically, Strephon was played by Richard Temple (who in previous operas had been cast as such characters as the Pirate King and the villainous Dick Deadeye).

Gilbert and Sullivan first nights seemed to grow more prestigious every year. The Savoy Theatre was a more salubrious place for the great and the good to visit than the Opera Comique could ever have been. There were many titled notables amongst the first-night attendees, as well as other famous and fashionable names, such as the well-regarded Superintendent of the Metropolitan Fire Brigade Captain Eyre Massey Shaw, who was given an excellent seat in the middle of the stalls. Gilbert absented himself as usual from the performance, anxiously pacing the embankment, according to rumour, or taking dinner at one of his clubs, though his wife attended, acting as his eyes and ears.

The opera was presented with a new opulence of effect. The peers' entrance was preceded by a marching band of Grenadier Guards, and the peers themselves were gorgeously arrayed in costumes provided by Messrs Ede and Son, robe-makers to Her Majesty. In Act 2, the Fairy Queen and three other principal fairies had electrical head-dresses that illuminated them in the night scene. It was generally felt amongst the audience that Act 2 dragged rather, but a highlight was an outrageous first-night joke, when the Fairy Queen (Alice Barnett), singing her gorgeous song 'Oh, foolish fay', addressed the final refrain to the middle of the stalls:

Oh, Captain Shaw!
  Type of true love kept under!
    Could thy Brigade
    With cold cascade
  Quench my great love, I wonder!

It was not the custom to plunge the auditorium into darkness during theatre performances at this time; Captain Shaw must have felt very exposed indeed at that moment.

As usual, the libretto was available for purchase. 'The audience followed the words most assiduously,' the *Morning Post* recorded (27 November 1882), 'and the rustling of many leaves turned over at one time reminded the hearer of the old days of oratorio in Exeter Hall, a resemblance which the gravity of the demeanour of many present helped to encourage.' It is strange; one would have thought Gilbert wanted his audience's eyes on the stage and not cast down on his book of words; but so it was and so it would remain through all the Savoy first nights.

The reviews were in general very positive. They acknowledged that the first-night audience had enjoyed themselves greatly and had been generous in their applause. But there was an undercurrent of dissatisfaction. Sullivan wrote in his diary, after conducting the first night as usual, that 'the 2nd [Act] dragged and I was afraid it must be compressed',[9] and almost every critic agreed.

Even the dialogue scene in Act 2 between Mountararat and Tolloller, which is amongst the funniest Gilbert ever wrote, made little or no impact on the first night. In rehearsal Barrington and Lely had found the scene 'so intensely funny that we absolutely could not get on with it for laughing', as Barrington recalled; they became 'almost hysterical over it'.[10] Gilbert said he only hoped the audience would laugh half as much; and his fears were justified. The scene fell flat, *The Daily News* commenting that it 'might well be condensed' (27 November). Fortunately the two actors regained their comic timing later in the run.

Moreover, as *The Graphic* of 2 December 1882 was not alone in observing, both Gilbert and Sullivan were starting to repeat themselves. Gilbert's topsy-turvy fancies were becoming familiar, and Sullivan's beautiful melodies were starting to sound like old friends. The Gilbert and Sullivan operas were a success, and people wanted more, but did they want more of the same or something different?

The height of Gilbert's creativity had taken place ten years before, at a time when he had rather taken it for granted. When (as often happened) he wrote something different and unexpected, the reaction had not often been encouraging. Gilbert was now a slower writer and a more careful one. He took many months to write a piece which a decade earlier he would have dashed off in a matter of weeks. The result was more polished and perhaps more durable than he would have made it at an earlier time. The raw surface of his satire was now smooth; the comfortable Savoy audience laughed without qualm. Times had changed greatly since the raucous first night of *The Happy Land* in 1873. Some of the critics objected to Strephon's song 'Fold your flapping wings', with its coarse allusions to poverty and misery: 'Take a tipsy lout/Gathered from the gutter – / Hustle him about – /Strap him to a shutter … /He's a mark of scorn – /I might be another,/If I had been born/Of a tipsy mother!'[11] However, Act 2 was agreed to be too long, so out the song went.

The prime minister came to see the opera on the night of 4 December, as Sullivan's guest. Gladstone wrote a gracious thank you letter to Sullivan two days later: 'Nothing, I thought, could be happier than the manner in which the comic strain of the piece was blended with its harmonies of sight and sound, so good in taste and so admirable in execution from beginning to end.'[12] No mention, of course, of the piece's mocking satirical strain, which may not have been so pleasing to the grand old man:

> When in that House [of Commons] M.P.'s divide,
>   If they've a brain and cerebellum, too,
> They've got to leave that brain outside,
>   And vote just as their leaders tell 'em to.
> But then the prospect of a lot
>   Of dull M.P.'s in close proximity,
> All thinking for themselves, is what
>   No man can face with equanimity.

16

A NATIONAL INSTITUTION (1884–89)

On 22 May 1883, five months after Gladstone's attendance at *Iolanthe*, Sullivan was knighted. Gilbert, naturally, was not. It would have been unprecedented for a dramatist to be so honoured, and it would be most unreasonable for Gilbert to expect it. But, unreasonably or not, he was unhappy to find he had been passed over.[1]

He was not, in fact, doing so badly for himself. The census taken on 3 April 1881 shows that he employed a butler, the Limerick-born Patrick Lynch, as well as three other servants, Ellen Simons, Eliza Pidgeon and Jessie Ann Warner: a most respectable domestic household. In the same year he had a new yacht, *Chloris*, made for him by the ship-builder John Harvey, and in the autumn of 1883 the Gilberts moved house again to another South Kensington address, 19 Harrington Gardens (later renumbered 39). It was a larger and more opulent home than 24 The Boltons, 'said to be splendid beyond anything yet achieved by a dramatic writer out of his own work', according to the *Pall Mall Gazette*,[2] and designed to Gilbert's own specifications in a heavy Victorian style, with oak panelling, beams and staircase. There was an inglenook decorated with seventeenth-century Dutch tiles, and in the drawing room there was an elaborate alabaster chimney-piece. There were four best bedrooms, five secondary bedrooms and four bathrooms. The house was illuminated with the new electric lighting, and had its own electricity generator in the basement. It boasted a telephone and double glazing. Gilbert had also designed the eccentric inscriptions above the doorways: 'All hope abandon, ye who enter here' above the dining room, and over the drawing room the more encouraging, 'And those things do best please me/That befal preposterously'. His growing art collection (Tintoretto, Van der Capelle, Nicolaes Maes) found a home in this miniature palace. He wrote in the luxurious library; when he wrote a letter he had only place it in a letterbox and it would slide down a chute directly to the butler's pantry for the latter to post. The Gilberts entertained their friends and were entertained by them. They gave Christmas parties for their friends and their friends' children, and the Christmas tree was illuminated with electric lights. They organised private dramatic entertainments. In the summer months, they took houses outside the city: at Eastbury to the north-west of London, for instance, or Breakspears at Uxbridge. They played tennis and croquet. They were living the good life.

One weekend, the young actor Herbert Beerbohm Tree was staying with the Gilberts, along with the painter Luke Fildes. Tree and Fildes were walking in the garden on the Sunday morning when Tree had an idea: 'Let's have a lark with old Gilbert!' he exclaimed. He took some mulberries from a nearby bush and smeared his face with them, producing an effect of lacerated flesh, and lay on the ground with his eyes closed. Fildes obediently rushed back to the house, crying out, 'Gilbert, Gilbert, come at once. Poor Tree! Poor Tree!' Gilbert hurried out and, seeing Tree apparently unconscious and horribly wounded, muttered, 'My God! My God!' Upon which Tree opened an eye and winked. Gilbert said nothing, but turned on his heel and returned to the house, furious. The party broke up early that weekend but somehow his friendships with Tree and Fildes survived.[3]

Gilbert and Tree were very different personalities, but they remained on good terms until Gilbert's death: probably because of Tree's easy-going personality. Gilbert disliked Tree's acting style; he told Frank Burnand: 'I like *him* very much, but I detest his art.'[4] He made many jokes against the actor – his description of Tree's *Hamlet* in 1892 as 'funny without being vulgar' became instantly famous – but Tree laughed them off and even circulated the *Hamlet* story himself.

Gilbert's work with Sullivan continued apace. The composer's determination to write no more Savoy pieces was apparently forgotten. The previous November, on the day of the *Iolanthe* premiere, he had suffered a financial disaster, losing £7,000 in the process and he needed to continue with Gilbert and Carte in order to recoup his losses. On 8 February 1883, therefore, Gilbert and Sullivan had signed a new five-year agreement with Carte which allowed the latter to demand a new opera of them at six months' notice. On the same day, Gilbert showed to Sullivan a draft of the first act of their next piece.

Nearly a year later, on 5 January 1884, *Princess Ida; or, Castle Adamant* was first performed at the Savoy. It was far from being Gilbert's finest work, despite some beautiful lyrics. It was not, strictly speaking, a new piece: it was a reworking of Gilbert's burlesque *The Princess* of 1870, retaining much of the blank-verse dialogue but changing the structure from five scenes to three acts, the second rather clumsily being much longer than either the first or the third. Though the opera was received favourably by the first-night audience, the reviews were largely lukewarm. It was spectacular and entertaining, but something was missing, and business fell off quickly. Not three months later, on 22 March, Carte wrote to the two collaborators, giving them their six months' notice for the creation of a new opera. Sullivan had left England for the Continent at the beginning of February, and he replied from Brussels on 28 March with a disturbing resolution:

'it is impossible for me to do another piece of the character of those already written by Gilbert and myself.'[5]

Sullivan also said in the same letter that he had not yet written to Gilbert to this effect because he preferred to discuss the matter with him personally. Carte, however, showed the letter to Gilbert, and Gilbert immediately wrote back to Sullivan to express his 'unbounded surprise' at the news:

> In all the pieces we have written together I have invariably subordinated my views to your own. You have often expatiated to me, and to others, on the thorough good feeling with which we have worked together for so many years ... I am, therefore, absolutely at a loss to account for the decision.[6]

He stressed that they were contractually bound to produce an opera upon Carte's request, and added that he had been hard at work on a new piece while Sullivan was out of the country, writing some lyrics and sketch dialogue, and keeping the composer informed by letter.

Sullivan, now in Paris, replied to this on 2 April:

> I will be quite frank. With *Princess Ida* I have come to the end of my tether – the end of my capability in that class of piece. My tunes are in danger of becoming mere repetitions of my former pieces ... It has hitherto been word-setting, I might almost say syllable-setting, for I have looked upon the words as being of such importance that I have been continually keeping down the music in order that not one should be lost.
>
> And this very suppression is most difficult, most fatiguing, and I may say most disheartening, for the music is never allowed to rise and speak for itself. I want a chance for the music to act in its own proper sphere – to intensify the emotional element not only of the actual words but of the situation.
>
> I should like to set a story of human interest and probability, where the humorous words would come in a humorous (not serious) situation, and where, if the situation were a tender or dramatic one, the words would be of a similar character. There would then be a feeling of reality about it which would give a fresh interest in writing, and fresh vitality to our joint work.[7]

Gilbert's response could have been anticipated; and perhaps Sullivan did anticipate it, having been so anxious to discuss the matter face to face and not by letter. Gilbert wrote on 3 April:

> Your reflections on the character of [my] libretti ... have caused me considerable pain. However, I cannot suppose that you have intended to gall and wound me, when you wrote as you did ... When you tell me that your desire is that I shall write a libretto in which the humorous words will come in a humorous

situation, and in which a tender or dramatic situation will be treated tenderly and dramatically, you teach me the ABC of my profession.[8]

Gilbert simply could not understand Sullivan's problem.

In subsequent letters and discussions, Sullivan's objections focused on the libretto that Gilbert was proposing: a variant on the plot he had proposed to Sullivan before *Iolanthe*, in which a charm such as a coin or a lozenge transforms people into what they are pretending to be. He never liked the plot, though Gilbert held it in great affection and kept re-submitting it. But as Sullivan's letter of 1 April had made clear, the problem ran deeper; he wanted the chance to write a completely different class of piece, where the emotional content was much more prominent. Was he trying to escape the toils of his agreement with Carte? He certainly felt that he had more serious music in him, which the popularity of the Savoy operas was preventing him from writing. But he had to maintain a substantial income: he had relatives and friends and a gambling habit to support. He could not afford to abandon the Savoy.

He drafted a letter to Gilbert on 7 April, writing:

> as I am not compelled to set anything I don't like, it is not very likely that I should have worked so long with you if I hadn't done so with real pleasure ... You yourself on more than one occasion have suggested that we might do something from which the element of burlesque (as the term is generally understood) should be absent, and it is nothing more than this I am now proposing we should carry out. Apart from my own personal feeling in the matter, I am convinced that popularity of our joint work will rapidly decline, as people will say and do say already that we are only repeating ourselves ... Now pray do not say again or think that I cast reflection on the pieces you have already written. I have enjoyed doing them with you and know of no one with whom I can write so sympathetically, but I don't want my interest in our joint work to flag ... A piece of the character and treatment of *Pygmalion and Galatea*, *The Wicked World* or even of a lighter stamp, I feel that I could do with interest and confidence of success.[9]

He arrived back in London on 9 April, immediately phoning Gilbert to arrange a meeting. Gilbert visited him the following day and they talked for two hours, Gilbert submitting his 'lozenge' plot again and Sullivan objecting. The result was deadlock.

Gilbert's problem was twofold: he could not understand the force of Sullivan's objections, and perhaps more importantly he had no alternative ideas to put forward. He proposed to revise the plot to allow for tender emotional scenes. Sullivan agreed to look at these revisions, but he could not pretend to be enthusiastic about them. Gilbert even proposed a radical solution:

What do you say to this – provided that Carte consents. Write your opera to another man's libretto. I will willingly retire for one turn, our agreement not-withstanding. It may well be that you are cramped by setting so many libretti of the same author, and that a new man with a new style will start a new train of musical ideas.[10]

But Sullivan declined this sensible offer. The impasse continued, each man digging in more firmly with each exchange and meeting; until, on 3 May, Gilbert felt obliged to write to Sullivan that 'I must state – and I do so with great reluctance – that I cannot consent to construct another plot for the next Opera'.[11] Sullivan, equally reluctantly, agreed.

The matter could very easily have ended there, to everyone's resentment and dissatisfaction. But the two continued to correspond, each determined to explain his point of view while showing due respect to the other and trying, tacitly, to find a solution to the impasse. And then, on 8 May, one was found, in the most unexpected fashion. Gilbert gave way. He wrote to Sullivan, suddenly agreeing to the proposal that Sullivan had put forward a month before: 'am I to understand that if I construct another plot in which no supernatural element occurs, you will undertake to set it? I mean a consistent plot, free from anachronisms, constructed in perfect good faith & to the best of my ability.'[12] Gilbert did not say what had caused this change of attitude, but the most probable explanation is the simplest: he had thought of a new plot idea. Sullivan, with great relief, agreed to set such a piece 'without further discussing the matter, or asking what the subject is to be'.[13]

The quarrel sheds a little light on the collaboration and its tensions. The agreement which Gilbert and Sullivan had signed with Carte on 8 February 1883 had a deep effect on them, deeper than perhaps they acknowledged. Sullivan undoubtedly felt constrained and even trapped by it; he squirmed in a brief attempt to escape it. The fact was that Carte had effectively become their employer. He could put in a formal request for a new opera and they were legally bound to write it. The main beneficiary was, of course, Carte; he needed Gilbert and Sullivan effectively tethered to the company at the Savoy if it was to remain a successful enterprise. He had other composers and librettists on his books who provided short companion pieces to the operas, but none of them could hope to command the success of his main attractions. Gilbert and Sullivan were now simply part of a commercial process. Gilbert appears to have been happier with this fact than Sullivan. Throughout his life, Gilbert had always rebelled against any attempt to regulate or coerce him, but he was happy to allow Carte to regulate the creation of the operas – for the moment.

Gilbert later described the creation of *The Mikado; or, The Town of Titipu* in some detail – but without mentioning the painful wrangles that had led up to it: 'A Japanese executioner's sword hanging on the wall of my library – the very sword carried by Mr. Grossmith at his entrance in the first act – suggested the broad idea upon which the libretto is based.' The setting would be Japan and the main character an executioner, to be represented by Grossmith 'as an exception- ally tender-hearted person whose natural instincts were in direct opposition to the nature of his official duties'.[14] Having at last found a use for this idea from the *Iolanthe* plot book, he went on in his usual way trying out and discarding ideas, until he had a workable scenario to show to Sullivan. They discussed the piece and agreed to alterations, and then Gilbert set to work writing. The process took some months, longer than the ailing *Princess Ida* could cover, and in October a revival of *The Sorcerer*, playing alongside *Trial by Jury*, was brought in to tide the Savoy over. Gilbert and Sullivan met regularly, discussing and revising in their usual way. On 20 November Sullivan dined with the Gilberts and was shown a version of Act 1, promising but unfinished. By January 1885, however, the opera was complete enough for rehearsals to begin.

The initial read-through was followed by two weeks of music rehearsals con- ducted by Sullivan or Alfred Cellier, during which Gilbert occupied himself in discussing scenery and costume with the relevant people, arranging the stage management and 'getting the rhythm of the musical numbers into [my] very unmusical head'; and then four weeks of stage rehearsals.[15]

Gilbert had settled on the opera's Japanese setting because Japan was in the air and might be popular with a London audience; however he cannot have antici- pated the opening of a Japanese Exhibition at Knightsbridge in January 1885, organised by a Mr Tannaker Buhicrosan, who brought in about 100 Japanese people to populate a constructed 'Japanese Village'. So Buhicrosan's exhibition and the new Savoy opera advertised each other.

The exhibition would also be invaluable in Gilbert's never-ending quest for accuracy of detail. 'As soon as the stage rehearsals began,' Gilbert wrote:

it occurred to me that the native ladies of the Japanese village might possibly be prevailed upon to teach us some of their dances ... A very charming young Japanese lady came day after day to rehearsal, and went through her dances, piece by piece, until her very apt pupils, Miss Braham, Miss Jessie Bond and Miss Sybil Grey, were pronounced reasonably proficient. It was impossible not to be struck by the natural grace and gentle courtesy of their indefatigable little instructress, who ... never permitted them to see that the spectacle of three English ladies attempting for the first time a Japanese dance in Japanese dress had its ridiculous side. Our verbal intercourse with this fascinating little lady was limited, all the Japanese we could command being, 'Sayo nara' ('good by'), whereas the Japanese young lady (who serves cups of tea in the village tea- house) knew but one English sentence, 'sixpence each'.[16]

More than one last-minute crisis attended the opera. Gilbert decided, during the last dress rehearsal, to cut the Mikado's song. 'It was excellently sung and acted by Mr. Temple,' Gilbert wrote, 'but the merit of his performance seemed only to make the words show to a greater disadvantage by reason of the contrast. So at least I thought, and so thought my *collaborateur* at the end of the rehearsal.' The cut was announced to the cast but the chorus and some pressmen, who had been invited to attend the rehearsal, came to Gilbert to voice their protest at the idea, and Gilbert changed his mind. He admitted quite frankly, 'They were right and we were wrong'.[17]

What was worse, Grossmith's nerves were on end not only during that dress rehearsal but also on the following night, Saturday 14 March 1885 – opening night. He stumbled over his words and his feet, and was, as Richard Barker the stage manager growled, 'a lamentable spectacle'.[18] But even this did not upset the piece. There was the usual fashionable crowd, including the Duke and Duchess of Edinburgh. Gilbert was not in the house, of course: 'I always leave the theatre as the curtain rises on the first act and do not return until the end of the last. With the last rehearsal my functions come to an end. All has been done that can be done, and the fortunes of the play are in the hands of the audience.'[19] He did not have to endure the uncertainties of the first performance, though he was back in the house to hear the cheers at the end and to take his bows alongside Sullivan.

The critics were not as uniformly ecstatic as one might expect. *The Times* (16 March) grumbled that it 'does not in any marked degree differ from its numerous predecessors', adding that the story was childish, and marvelling at Sullivan's ability to fit music to the words allotted to him, 'overcoming difficulties at which a less skilful and perhaps more fastidious musician would stand aghast'. But *The Era* (21 March) was more appreciative, and, in the event, more accurate: 'All London will be talking of the new Japanese opera, and, what is better, will be going to see it. The work is unique, and worthy of the reception it met with, and the labour and talent devoted to the performance.' It was to prove the collaborators' greatest success, even more popular than *H.M.S. Pinafore*, running at the Savoy for nearly two years.

Throughout these years of greatest success, Gilbert appears as a relatively contented figure, finally reaping his reward for all the years of struggle and strife: living in opulence at Harrington Gardens, commanding the stage at the Savoy, travelling to Egypt and other exotic locations, yachting, playing tennis, entertaining friends and colleagues. Like King Gama in *Princess Ida*, he had 'nothing whatever to grumble at'. He was no longer beating on the door of the portal; he was inside and supping of the good things.

But even from this position of comfort, he was not satisfied with everything. He was uneasily aware that he was still unable to do everything in drama that he might want to do. He told an interviewer in January 1885:

[In English drama] Our lovers must be single young men and women, and we are tied down to a happy or comedy conclusion ... You and I and a few others are happy in our domestic and other relations; but is this true of all English people? What the contemporary playwright is asked to represent is not what life is, but what it ought to be … Hence, except in the case of Shakespeare or of French adaptations, English dramatists are driven within the narrow limits of *bourgeois* thought imposed by the survival of Puritanical prejudice.[20]

He made a similar point in a speech to the Dramatic and Musical Sick Fund on 18 February, noting that the content of original English plays was hampered by the necessity of making them morally fit for the ears of a young lady of 15 in the dress circle.[21]

He was now beginning to understand his position under his 1883 agreement with Carte. He tried to secure for himself a larger role in the running of the Savoy, but Carte responded by referring to the terms of their agreement, and on 2 June Gilbert fired back angrily:

As you decline to permit me to have any voice in the control of the Theatre … & point out to me that, by our agreement, I am merely a hack author employed by you to supply you with pieces on certain terms, I have no alternative but to accept the position you assign to me.'[22]

He considered Carte was getting too big for his boots, and his lack of trust in the Savoy Theatre's manager grew in the months and years to come.

But he continued to appreciate Sullivan's role in creating the operas. When, on 18 August 1885, the Baron Ferdinand de Rothschild invited Gilbert to write something in the baron's *Livre d'Or*, he responded with a piece of self-revelation:

I'm a trod-under-hoof young man–
A 'keep-him-aloof' young man–
   A comic libretto-ing,
   Sullivan-debt-owing,
Opera *Boof* young man![23]

As usual, he started thinking about the next opera only a few months after the old had established itself. He mulled it over at home and abroad, and a plot emerged: melodrama, bad baronets and a portrait gallery of ancestors that would step from their frames. The tone would be darker than *The Mikado*. The Japanese opera had had its grim side, true, with a plot hinging on the twin threats of death and torture; but Gilbert had taken care to treat these things as trivial inconveniences: beheading was a punishment to which young men 'usually objected' and burial alive merely 'such a stuffy death'. But in the new piece, with the ugly title *Ruddygore; or, The Witch's Curse*, there would be a vivid description in song of a witch being burnt alive and writhing in the flames. There would be a parade of ghosts and a scene of comic torture. The whole of the second act would be sunk in a literal gloom. The early nineteenth-century costumes would seem drab in comparison with the exotic robes of *The Mikado*. Nothing would be as it seemed: good and bad would be almost interchangeable, characters would switch their affections at a moment's notice and even death would be seen as reversible. *Ruddygore* was a quirky and unpredictable piece. How would the Savoy audience cope with it?

On 18 November 1886, Gilbert turned 50 years old. He was about to sit for his portrait before Frank Holl, one of the most distinguished portrait painters of the day. The finished picture, now in the National Portrait Gallery, is a dark and brooding study. Gilbert sits against a gloomy background in riding clothes, a hunting crop grasped in his hand; his hair is grey and his eyes are hidden in darkness. It does not seem like the portrait of a humorist; and indeed it was not: Gilbert was a serious man at heart, even a gloomy one. He had his demons. His wit was a defence against the world. This is the man who appears in Holl's portrait: serious, introspective and rather isolated.

He was in more cheerful mood in January 1887, when an interviewer from the *Pall Mall Gazette* visited him in the days before the opening of *Ruddygore*. He had just been engaged in burning his manuscript materials for the opera – though the interviewer managed to salvage a pen-and-ink drawing of Mad Margaret in her Act 2 costume to print in the paper. Gilbert talked about the measures taken against American companies who continually tried to steal the operas, about his method of arranging the operas' stage-management on model sets with wooden blocks, about the cost of the new opera's costumes: 'I never do any work in the daytime, except rehearsals, but generally begin writing at 11 P.M., and go to bed at 2 or 3 A.M. I find lemon squash the best liquid to work on. I smoke, but not so much as I used to.'

He even talked of his aversion to seeing his works performed in public:

> Mr. Gilbert has never seen one of his own plays acted for fourteen years, owing to excessive nervousness, which he admits grows upon him every day … however pronounced the success, he adheres to his determination. Only on one occasion has he been persuaded to make the experiment, and then he broke down. The Duke of Edinburgh once sent for him to his box to talk to him on this very peculiarity. Being pressed to stay Mr. Gilbert had no option but to take a seat in the box. But presently he began to feel hotter and hotter, fainter and fainter, and had to beg the Duke to release him.[24]

Savoy opera first nights were now established occasions in society, rivalling the first nights at Henry Irving's Lyceum. The Lord Mayor and Lady Mayoress, Lord and Lady Randolph Churchill, Lord Dunraven, the Earl and Countess of Onslow, Sir Charles Russell, Sir John Millais, Frank Holl, James Whistler, Linley Sambourne, Mr and Mrs Marcus Stone, Mr and Mrs Perugini, Mr and Mrs

Pinero, Frank Burnand, William Archer and Clement Scott all attended to see and be seen. The cast appeared nervous and there were some stumbles. The first act went well, Durward Lely's hornpipe as Dick Dauntless being particularly well received, and it concluded with cheers; but the second act, gloomy and ghost-ridden, was a different matter. The scene in which the portraits step from their frames was clumsily handled, some of the stage machinery jamming at the crucial moment. The sombreness of the scene took some time to wear off, and it was agreed that the rest of the piece dragged. There were the usual enthusiastic cheers at the final curtain, but mingled with these were distinct hisses. The *New York Times* even reported (23 January) that there were shouts of 'Take off this rot!' and 'Give us *The Mikado!*'

Many of the first London reviews were kind: '"Ruddygore," if less original than its predecessor, "The Mikado," promises nevertheless to have a long career at the Savoy Theatre,' *Reynolds's Newspaper* predicted (30 January). But opinions were soon voiced that the title was indelicate, and that the opera itself showed symptoms of creative exhaustion. Everyone knew what to expect of the writer and the composer, and while this was comforting in a way, it was also disappointing. Gilbert's style had become so familiar to regular theatre-goers that nothing he could invent had the ability to surprise any more. What had been shocking ten years ago in a play like *Engaged* was now nothing more than a matter of course. Most people did not trouble to look beyond the surface of what *The Daily News* called Gilbert's 'great patent reversible joke' (26 January) and examine the satirical content. '*Ruddygore* is decidedly the weakest and least satisfactory of Messrs Gilbert and Sullivan's operas,' *The Era* concluded (29 January).

Cuts and changes were hastily made, particularly to the ending, and after a few days it was even decided to change the title. Gilbert, angry at the mealy mouthedness of his contemporaries, sarcastically suggested as an alternative *Kensington Gore; or, Robin and Richard were Two Pretty Men*. It was eventually decided, however, that the title was sanitised sufficiently by the change of a single letter, and it became *Ruddigore* from 2 February on. A story was soon going the rounds: a country clergyman had written to Gilbert imploring him to change the opera's title, as *Ruddygore* was unfit even to be mentioned in the drawing rooms of his friends. Gilbert wrote in reply, insisting that the word had no offensive meaning, adding: 'I am sorry to be obliged to disagree with your contentions, but they would seem to me to be as unjustifiable as if I, in speaking of your "ruddy cheek," were understood to mean your bloody impertinence.'[25]

Ruddigore survived the summer, but in November it was replaced with *H.M.S. Pinafore*. In the meantime, Gilbert had, of course, been thinking about writing a real replacement. He resubmitted his 'lozenge plot' to Sullivan, proposing to modify it to meet any objections. Sullivan still could not work up any enthusiasm for the piece – 'it is a "puppet-show" and not human'[26] – and he was greatly relieved when Gilbert, after a moment of inspiration while waiting for a train at

Uxbridge station and staring at an advert for the Tower Furnishing Co., proposed an opera set at the Tower of London.

As the two men set to work on this, Carte's mind was working in another direction. He was worried about the success of a rival piece, *Dorothy* with music by Alfred Cellier and words by B.C. Stephenson, which was enjoying a long run at the Lyric. He seems to have felt that it was a threat to the Savoy operas, taking from them the distinction of uniqueness. Carte responded by suggesting a bold (or rash) move: to lease out the Savoy Theatre and take Gilbert and Sullivan to a new, larger theatre. He wrote to Sullivan on 13 February 1888, urging him to write to Gilbert in favour of the idea: 'we should not let other *people get ahead*.'[27] There may have been a hidden compact between Carte and Sullivan on this issue; a larger theatre would be more suitable to work of a more operatic character. But Gilbert would have none of it, and he replied to Sullivan's letter courteously but firmly and with great pride in what he and Sullivan had together achieved:

> I can't, for the life of me, understand the reasons that urge you to abandon a theatre and a company that have worked so well for us, and for whom we have worked so well. Carte has his own interests. He lets the Savoy to us for £4,000 a year and now we have made it what it is, he can let it for £6,000 … We have the best theatre, the best company, the best composer, and (though I say it) the best librettist in England working together – we are world-known, and as much an institution as Westminster Abbey – and to scatter this splendid organization because *Dorothy* has run 500 nights is, to my way of thinking, to give up a gold-mine. What is *Dorothy*'s success to us? It is not even in the same class of piece as ours. Is no piece but ours to run 500 or 600 nights? Did other companies dissolve because *The Mikado* ran 650 nights?[28]

He was eloquent and, it seems, persuasive: they stayed at the Savoy. It is telling, however, that he should have identified their partnership as being comparable to Westminster Abbey as a national institution. It was quite true. The premieres continued to glitter with the jewels of London society, no matter how equivocal the reviews might be; the audiences kept their heads reverently bowed as they followed the words in their shilling copies of the libretto; within a few very short years the Savoy had succeeded in becoming one of the prides of London. The wheel of fortune had taken Gilbert a long way from his unhappy beginnings, when he had viewed those who held the strings of government with hatred and had poured scorn upon the great and the good. He was now one of the great and the good himself. He had gained his fame by attacking national institutions and now he was one. What does a satirist do when he becomes the thing he satirises? What does an angry man do when he no longer has cause to be angry?

The fault lines in the partnership showed more and more clearly as the years went by. Gilbert wished to remain at the Savoy, upon the stage of which his will was law. But Gilbert distrusted Carte. Sullivan was tired of Gilbert's 'mechanical' plots and wished to write a true grand opera. Carte encouraged that ambition, but Gilbert resisted it – he knew it would mean surrendering his supremacy to the composer. At a personal level, Gilbert annoyed and exasperated Carte and Sullivan; his abrasive and combative character was too much for them. All this occasionally flared out in trivial but bitter disputes, as when Gilbert, wanting to put on a production of *Broken Hearts* for a few afternoons at the Savoy, with Jessie Bond in the cast, was opposed by Sullivan, who refused to allow the performance to take place. 'I think he is taking a very unwarranted & ill-advised course in interfering – but he is quite within his rights,' Gilbert wrote to Jessie Bond on 17 June 1887. 'P.S. Sullivan did not consult me about lending the theatre to the College of Music – he assumed that, as a matter of courtesy, I should agree – Next year, however, it may be otherwise. WSG.'[29]

On 20 March 1888, Gilbert's mother died after a long illness. Estranged from her for some years, since the break-up of her marriage to his father, Gilbert seems to have found it impossible to express his feelings directly. In the week before her death his behaviour was erratic and volatile, culminating in a senseless row with Carte about a clash between a rehearsal for the approaching revival of *Pirates* and a dinner appointment that Gilbert had made.[30] A brief notice of the death of Anne Gilbert described her as 'a woman of great talent and conversational power', adding that 'her house in London was a well-known musical centre, her eldest daughter [actually the middle daughter, Florence] being a star of the amateur musical world'.[31] She had been living at 14 Pembridge Gardens, Bayswater, with her two unmarried daughters, Florence and Maude, who seem to have shared Anne's estrangement from the men of the family. Jane, the married daughter, remained on good terms with Gilbert, however. Anne was buried in Brompton cemetery. There is no evidence to suggest that the funeral was attended by either her husband or her son.

The revival of *The Pirates of Penzance* was succeeded by *The Mikado* in June, while Gilbert and Sullivan worked on their new piece. The projected date of the first night was put back from September to early October. Sullivan's music was to be more serious and substantial than in many of the earlier operas, and he put more of himself into it. Gilbert's lyrics, too, show more care in their writing, as with the folksong-like 'I Have a Song to Sing, O', the imitation Elizabethan 'Is Life a Boon?' and the beautiful 'Were I Thy Bride'. The latter two of these were written, Gilbert later explained, to prove that 'English is (next to Italian) the very best of all European languages for singing purposes'.[32]

The Yeomen of the Guard; or, The Merryman and his Maid was an experiment. The story, set in the time of Henry VIII, was to be human and straightforward in its emotions, with no topsyturvydom or deliberate anachronism in its writing. It would not even have a completely happy ending. Reports of the change in direction started to emerge in the days approaching the premiere, and by the time of the first performance, on the evening of Wednesday 3 October 1888, the audience was fairly well prepared. Lord Londesborough, Sir Robert Peel and Sir George Grove were among the audience, as well as Richard D'Oyly Carte himself with his wife and business assistant Helen, Rutland Barrington (who for once was not in the cast, having decided to go in for theatrical management), and in the stalls Lucy Gilbert accompanied by Gilbert's father, now a white-haired old gentleman of 84.

It was well received – certainly much better than *Ruddygore* had been. The audience found it difficult to adjust to the absence of topsyturvydom, but Sullivan's refreshingly serious music was much admired. It was noticed that the plot owed much to *Don César de Bazan* and *Maritana*, but the critics were forgiving, acknowledging the skill with which the libretto was put together. The best lyrics were extensively quoted, notably 'Were I Thy Bride', which was an immediate hit. Within days it was reported that tickets for the new opera were to be booked three months in advance.

Gilbert retained his links with the theatre beyond the Savoy. He was known to be a great expert in all things theatrical. He received floods of applications from young aspiring actors. He said, 'I make a point of seeing them all, and if they are prepared with any recitation, I hear them recite. But it very seldom happens that a novice shows sufficient promise to justify me in encouraging him or her to abandon a certain income, however moderate, for the lottery of the stage.'[33]

Sometimes he found a talent that was worth encouraging. Round about the year 1880, John Martin Harvey, the son of the man who had built his yacht *Pleione*, wished to enter the profession. He was granted permission to see Gilbert, who listened to him declaiming a speech from Pitt the Elder, then said: 'Yes. I shouldn't keep your elbows glued to your hips like a duck; get your arms free, but go ahead.'[34] Gilbert introduced the 'young shaver' to several of his acting friends, including Charles Wyndham, and gave the young man's career, which was to be long and illustrious, its first boost.

When the American actor Mary Anderson came to England and took the Lyceum in 1883–84, her portrayal of Galatea in *Pygmalion and Galatea* had been one of the season's highlights. Gilbert had admired her performance, without agreeing with it; he had written to Clement Scott that 'Miss Anderson's conception [of Galatea] is her own & hers alone, & it appears to me to be artistically more beautiful, but dramatically less effective, than Mrs Kendal's'.[35] Very unusually, he did not object to her providing her own interpretation of the role. He wrote to her to tell her how much he admired her talents as an actor:

What I have said of [your] Galatea behind your back, that I have said to your face. I have too profound a respect for you and your art to butter you with empty compliments. When I feel at all, I feel strongly – and your Hermione [in *The Winter's Tale*] has blazed in my eyes ever since Saturday night, and made them *hot*.[36]

Gilbert had written his short play *Comedy and Tragedy* (1884) specifically for Mary Anderson to perform as a companion piece to *Pygmalion and Galatea*.

In 1888, a young singer called Julia Neilson came to him with a letter of introduction and recited a speech from *Pygmalion and Galatea*. Gilbert immediately saw that she possessed 'great and exceptional promise of future excellence as an emotional actress'[37] and recommended her to Mary Anderson. She acted in a charity matinee of *Pygmalion and Galatea* as Cynisca, alongside Mary Anderson's Galatea, and was soon performing in afternoon performances of *Broken Hearts* and *The Wicked World* at the Savoy. Gilbert was so convinced of her ability that he wrote a play for her: *Brantinghame Hall*.

Rutland Barrington, having turned manager, had taken the St James' Theatre, and this is where the play premiered, on 29 November 1888. It was a surprisingly clumsy piece for a theatrical expert such as Gilbert to have written: an old-fashioned, almost melodramatic, play entirely lacking in the verve of *Charity* or *An Old Score*. The first-night audience turned against the play, refusing to warm to Julia Neilson's character, which was written stiltedly and performed nervously. When her husband, shipwrecked and presumed dead, reappeared unexpectedly in the final scene and Julia Neilson, as Ruth, responded with her final line, 'Let us pray!', the audience laughed. Unsurprisingly, the play was a critical failure, and it lasted less than a month, marking the end of Rutland Barrington's excursion into theatre management and sending him into bankruptcy. Unfortunately, it also marked an end to Gilbert's decades-old friendship with Clement Scott.

Scott reviewed the play in the *Daily Telegraph* on 30 November, calling it a 'thin story scantily spread over four acts, a romance without vitality and heart', professing himself baffled at the decision to make the heroine, the daughter of a pardoned convict, 'talk in a lingo compounded of a child's Bible history, a smattering of Holy Writ, and the "Pilgrim's Progress"', and attributing Julia Neilson's stilted performance of the role to over-tuition or nervousness. It was not, on the whole, an over-harsh verdict – *The Era* was even more forthright, calling the play 'a dismal failure' (1 December) – but coming from one of Gilbert's oldest friends, it seemed like treachery.

This, combined with the unfavourable verdicts of many of the other papers, encouraged Rutland Barrington to organise a professional matinee performance of the play on 11 December, to which some of the critics were invited in order to reconsider their verdicts now that Julia Neilson's performance had improved. Scott declined the invitation and Gilbert responded by writing to Edward Lawson, one of the proprietors of the *Daily Telegraph*, asking him to attend instead:

> The savagery of Mr. C. Scott's attack on my piece at the St. James's and on the actress who played the leading part has become a matter of such general comment in theatrical and other circles that I have very little hesitation in asking

you ... to take the trouble to see the piece and to judge for yourself whether, *because I have attempted to write an unobjectionable original English play*, I deserve to be held up *to scorn and contempt*, as though in so doing *I have committed an outrage against human nature.*[38]

Lawson turned down the offer. It began to be rumoured that Gilbert had asked Lawson to have Clement Scott dismissed from the *Daily Telegraph*. Gilbert assumed that the source of the rumour was Scott himself. He wrote to Scott in cold fury:

I am determined not to expose myself again to your insolent gibes. I have writ-ten my last play, & I have no doubt that it will gratify you to know that you have driven me from a stage for which (in our days of friendship) you have so often declared that I was pre-eminently fitted to write. If it be any additional satisfaction to you to know that in your determination to make your onslaught as thorough as possible, you have crushed the hope out of the life of a poor girl who, paralysed with nervousness, was appealing − practically for the first time in her life − to the men who were to decide her destiny − you are most fully entitled to it.[39]

The affair went public, much to the delight of the newspaper gossips. When Gilbert's letter to Lawson was quoted, including his claim that 'I am in the habit of "taking punishment" [from the critics] quietly', he was held up to ridicule in *The Era* and elsewhere. Gilbert threatened Scott with a libel action, though it did not in the end take place.

He was interviewed by the *Pall Mall Gazette* after his statement about having written his last play was made public. 'In saying that I shall write no more plays,' he said:

I use the word in its academic sense − as a dramatic composition of a more or less ambitious order. Mr. Scott has settled this for me. He has the distinction of having driven me from dramatic work of that class ... I am under contract to write another libretto for the Savoy, and I hope it may not be my last. They are usually dealt with by the musical critics, who are not, as a rule, disappointed dramatists.[40]

Gilbert and John Hare had renewed their friendship back in 1884, after years of estrangement. More recently Hare had expressed an interest in building a new theatre, and Gilbert had offered to build it for him. A site behind the National Gallery was chosen. In the course of 1888 it began to rise from its foundations. Gilbert had firm views on what a theatre should be: electrically lit; the stalls and the pit should be under ground level, on the theory that in the event of fire and panic it is safer to go up than down; private boxes should be dispensed with (but the new theatre would retain boxes because influential people liked them); footlights should be abolished and replaced with electric lights at the sides of and above the stage.[41] The building of the new theatre – which they called the Garrick – was not without its problems, but it opened triumphantly on 24 April 1889 with Pinero's new play *The Profligate*, under the management of John Hare.

In the meantime, Sullivan had begun discussing with Gilbert the possibility of a new opera. 'I explained', Sullivan wrote in his diary on 9 January 1889, 'that I wanted to do some dramatic work on a larger musical scale, and that of course I should like to do it with him if he would, but that the music must occupy a more important position than in our other pieces … Also that I wanted a voice in the *musical construction* of the libretto.'[42] Gilbert mulled over the proposition and replied with a polite but firm refusal:

> while I quite understand and sympathize with your desire to write what, for want of a better term, I suppose we must call 'grand opera,' I cannot believe that it would succeed either at the Savoy or at Carte's new theatre unless a much more powerful singing and acting company were got together than the company we now control. Moreover, to speak from my own selfish point of view, such an opera would afford me no chance of doing what I best do – the librettist of a grand opera is always swamped in the composer. Anybody – Hersee, Farnie, Reece – can write a good libretto for such a purpose; personally, I should be lost in it.[43]

Gilbert's objections were all, from his point of view, reasonable. The most practical reason why he could not provide a 'grand opera' libretto was glanced at very briefly in a later paragraph: 'From me, the press and the public will take nothing but what is, in essence, humorous'[44] – a fact of which Gilbert had been painfully reminded two months before. He added the suggestion that Sullivan write his opera with Julian Sturgis – a suggestion which Sullivan took up not long afterwards.

Sullivan wrote from Paris on 12 March:

> I have lost the liking for writing comic opera, and entertain very grave doubts as to my power of doing it … You say that in a serious opera, *you* must more or less sacrifice yourself. I say that this is just what I have been doing in all our joint pieces, and, what is more, must continue to do in comic opera to make it successful.[45]

This letter filled Gilbert with 'amazement and regret'. He could not believe Sullivan saw himself as having sacrificed his art in all their joint works. 'You are an adept in your profession, and I am an adept in mine. If we meet, it must be as master and master – not as master and servant.'[46] It was a small disagreement blown out of proportion, a flurry in which each man asserted the primacy of his own art; and it was easily resolved. Sullivan made his decision: to write his 'grand opera' and also a new Savoy piece. 'I understood from Carte some time ago,' Sullivan wrote on 8 May, 'that you had some subject connected with Venice and Venetian life, and this seemed to me to hold out great chances of bright colour and taking music. Can you not develop this with something we can both go into with warmth and enthusiasm?'[47] The result, not coincidentally, was a comic opera in which Gilbert looked after Sullivan's musical requirements with a new sense of consideration; the first twenty minutes consist of a continuous musical sequence introducing the characters and setting the sunny, optimistic tone of the whole and many of the lyrics are deliberately simple, even effacing.

The new opera, *The Gondoliers; or, The Kind of Barataria*, was premiered on 7 December 1889. It was yet another glittering Savoy first night. Rutland Barrington, back in the company after his debacle at the St James' Theatre, was greeted with a storm of applause on his first entrance. The quartet 'Then one of us will be a Queen' was received enthusiastically, and when the performers hesitated as to which verses to encore, voices from the gallery called out, 'All of it!' Grossmith had left the company, but even his absence from the cast did not dampen enthusiasm. The piece's success was beyond doubt. It was funny and romantic and not too satirical.

Gilbert wrote to Sullivan the next day: 'I must again thank you for the magnificent work you have put into the piece. It gives one a chance of shining right through the twentieth century with a reflected light.'[48] Sullivan replied: 'Don't talk of reflected light. In such a perfect book as "The Gondoliers" you shine with an individual brilliancy which no other writer can hope to attain.'[49] *The Gondoliers* was assured of a long run, and Gilbert and Sullivan, relieved, set to one side the underlying tensions in their relationship – for the moment.

17

THE BITTER END (1890-96)

On 20 December 1889, two weeks after the first night of *The Gondoliers*, Gilbert and Lucy left England for a trip to India. Only a few days after their departure old William Gilbert suffered a stroke; he rallied for a few days but died on 2 January 1890. There is, as so often, a blank in the record where Gilbert's emotional reaction ought to be. No letters relating to the event survive. Gilbert and his wife were not able to attend the funeral for they had already travelled as far as Egypt. They toured India – Colombo, Candy, Calcutta, Darjeeling, Bombay – before arriving back in England in the first week of April.

Almost the first thing Gilbert did on his return was to ask for details of the preliminary expenses for *The Gondoliers*. He did not like what he saw: the figures amounted to £4,500, including what he considered excessive figures for items of set and costume and £500 for new carpets for the front of the house. (Carte later told Gilbert that the actual figure for the carpets was £140, adding caustically that 'this is a fair sample of the general inaccuracy of your letters'.)[1] Under the terms of their agreement, Gilbert and Sullivan were to receive one-third of the profits from the production after the expenses had been paid, including repairs incidental to the performances, but Gilbert alleged that replacing front-of-house carpeting should not be included in such expenses. Enraged, he went to see Mr and Mrs Carte on 21 April to discuss the matter.

It is clear that Gilbert was spoiling for a fight. His father had died and he had not been able to see the old man laid to rest; he was suffering from gout; he had just received new evidence of Carte's unprofessional methods. He laid his grievances before Richard D'Oyly Carte, saying first that Carte had allowed the carpenters and others to overcharge for their services, and then that the new carpet should not have been listed among the incidental expenses. Gilbert said all this in a 'violent and insulting way', Helen Carte recalled in a letter to Gilbert, and he addressed Carte 'in a way that you would not have used to an offending menial'.[2] Richard D'Oyly Carte refuted these allegations. Gilbert insisted upon them and added that he would not write another opera unless a new agreement was drawn up. Carte said the only alteration he would make to the agreement was to put up the rent of the theatre from £4,000 to £5,000. This led to either Gilbert or Carte saying that Gilbert would write no more for the Savoy, upon which Gilbert stormed out with the parting remark that it was a mistake for Carte to kick down the ladder by which he had risen.[3]

Gilbert wrote an affable letter to Sullivan the next day explaining the situation ('My dear S/I've had a difficulty with Carte')[4] and appealing to the composer for his support. But Sullivan was not in a position to give that support, even if he wished to. Carte was building a new theatre, an opera house, which was to open with Sullivan's long-anticipated 'grand opera'. Carte was allowing Sullivan to fulfil his dream. Sullivan attempted to mediate, agreeing with Gilbert that the expenses appeared to be high but adding that this was probably inevitable. A flurry of letters followed between Gilbert, Sullivan, Richard and Helen D'Oyly Carte, Gilbert insisting upon a new agreement, Sullivan agreeing but suggesting a delay first, as the success of *The Gondoliers* meant that a new agreement would not be practically necessary for some months. A meeting between all parties was suggested, but Carte wrote to Sullivan on 5 May that he could not agree to it; Gilbert's insulting attitudes had not changed and Carte could not meet him and pretend there was no problem. On the same day Gilbert wrote to Sullivan: 'The time for putting an end to our collaboration has at last arrived … In point of fact, after the withdrawal of *The Gondoliers*, our united work will be heard in public no more.'[5] Sullivan received this letter the next day, and wrote in his diary: '*nothing* would induce me to write again with him. How I have stood him so long!! I can't understand.'[6]

It is not necessary to trace every step of the bitter wrangling which ensued. The conflict of temperaments had risen to the surface at last. Sullivan wished to pour oil on the troubled waters between Gilbert and Carte, while Gilbert preferred to set the oil ablaze and was offended that Sullivan did not wish to hold the matches. Gilbert accused Sullivan of 'marked discourtesy' – 'consistent hostility, veiled or otherwise' – 'contemptuous indifference' and 'placidity in tolerating insults inflicted on [Gilbert]'[7] – charges which Sullivan refuted, adding that his efforts at bringing about a reconciliation with Carte had been hampered by Gilbert's 'imperious will'.[8] Gilbert, of course, denied that he possessed such a thing.

The press had somehow got wind of the breach; Malcolm Charles Salaman of the *Sunday Times* had asked Gilbert to provide a statement. On 15 May Gilbert drafted a polite and, he assumed, inoffensive reply:

I have nothing to say beyond what is already known – that Sullivan, having resolved to divert himself to Grand Opera – at all events for the present – has neither time nor inclination to undertake work of a lighter order. Apart from this we both think it advisable that we should stop on a marked success.⁹

He sent a copy to Sullivan and was perhaps surprised by the vehemence of Sullivan's reaction: 'I have steadily refused to be interviewed or to furnish any information with reference to our break-up, intended for publication,' Sullivan wrote:

> the ways of modern journalism are to me detestable. I should therefore strongly advise you to tell Mr Salaman and others that our collaboration had ceased for reasons into which it was not necessary to enter. For I must protest against your proposed note to him, which implies that *I* broke up the collaboration.¹⁰

Gilbert acceded to this request and immediately wrote an alternative, and rather less polite, letter to Salaman: 'I hope you will not think me discourteous, but Sullivan & I have agreed that the public are not concerned with the reasons that have actuated us in ceasing to collaborate. More than this I am not at liberty to say.'¹¹

The *Pall Mall Gazette* of 20 May 1890 reported that the breach was due to 'the development of Mr. Carte's grand opera schemes' (which Gilbert immediately denied) and added: 'One of Mr. Sedger's first productions at the Lyric Theatre will be a comic opera from the joint pens of Messrs. W.S. Gilbert and Alfred Cellier.' This was true: Gilbert had lost no time before making new arrangements for his future career as a librettist.¹² Cellier was a natural second choice, a lifelong friend of Sullivan who had been Carte's musical director during the company's Opera Comique years and the composer of *Dorothy*. The plot of the new opera had already been decided upon. It was, in fact, to be the much-delayed appearance of the 'charm' plot which Sullivan had been rejecting for the past eight years.

As if all this were not enough, Gilbert was arranging another important change in his circumstances. It was announced in the first week of June that he had bought a luxurious mid-Victorian Tudor manor house called Graeme's Dyke at Harrow Weald, and that he was making arrangements for the sale of 39 Harrington Gardens. As the *Pall Mall Gazette* observed (7 June): 'Here is a chance for a millionaire who wants a town house on a magnificent scale … Topsyturvy Palace is as much the creation of [Gilbert's] own brain as the "Palace of Truth."'

It seems almost as if Gilbert was deliberately making a break from his old existence. He destroyed the alliance that had made his fortune, and arranged to move away from London where he had lived all his life, and set up a new collaboration with another composer – his first non-Sullivan opera since *Princess Toto* in 1876. And all this took place within two months of his arrival back in England from India. The suspicion must arise that he was reacting to something that happened while he was away – probably his father's death. He had never felt able to express his emotions directly; how could he express his grief at the loss of the crotchety, irascible old man who, for good or ill, had formed him? So he raged against Carte, whom he had never trusted, and sold Topsyturvy Palace and found a country retreat away from his enemies in London.

No 39 Harrington Gardens was sold by auction on 16 July. The Gilberts took their usual summer home, Breakspears in Uxbridge, while preparing to move into Graeme's Dyke. Gilbert and his solicitors looked further into the Savoy accounts and in the process found further cause for dispute. During the course of July, Gilbert's solicitors asked the Savoy Theatre for the quarterly accounts for the period ending on 4 July. There was a delay in replying to this request, partly on the advice of Carte's solicitors and partly because Carte was seriously unwell and wished to regain his health with a trip to Hastings. On 30 July Gilbert's solicitors issued a writ notifying Carte's solicitors that an application for receivership was being made. The next day they added that if the exact sum due to Gilbert was not known a payment of £2,000 should be made to him immediately 'on account'. There was a delay in paying this sum due to the intervention of a bank holiday. The dispute escalated. Affidavits were sworn on all sides and the case for the appointment of a receiver came to court on 27 August, but had to stand over for a week because Gilbert had gone to Carlsbad to take the waters – his gout had flared up.

On 3 September the case was finally heard in the Vacation Court before Mr Justice Lawrance. The end result of the session was simple. The application for receivership was rejected and Carte's solicitors undertook to deliver the 4 July accounts and to pay over any outstanding sums.

The essential triviality of the issues, as compared with the lengths Gilbert had gone to in order to resolve them, was made plain. As Carte's counsel said in court:

> Mr. Gilbert had entirely mistaken his remedy … Mr. Gilbert had become dis-
> satisfied with some items in the accounts delivered in April … Until it was
> settled whether certain items were to be included or excluded it was impossible
> to say what form the July account was to take. Instead of adopting the simple
> remedy of taking out a summons to have a proper account, Mr. Gilbert elected
> to take the present harsh proceedings.[13]

Applying for receivership was simply not the right way of responding to the errors discovered in the accounts. There was no need for a court case at all, and all it had achieved was to lay bare the differences of the three men to an interested public.

Gilbert's motives throughout the affair are not clear. It could be said that he had too many. The explosive meeting of 21 April was the culmination of long years of distrust of Carte's business methods, but the immediate trigger may have been unresolved grief at his father's death. It has been suggested that he was also motivated by a desire to sabotage Sullivan's projected grand opera; but there is no real evidence for this.[14] It is, however, possible that money worries added to the stress of his situation. As the court case revealed, Carte had paid to Gilbert over the past eleven years around £90,000 in fees and royalties for the operas, an enormous sum; but the purchase of Graeme's Dyke cost Gilbert £30,000. The house move was no small deal.

Gilbert's resentment of Carte went deeper than mere financial distrust. He felt that he himself ought to be in charge of the Savoy instead of Carte, a man whose contribution to the success of the operas he never really understood. Gilbert felt, indeed, that he and Sullivan did not need Carte at all. He had sworn an affidavit on 1 September 1890 in which he stated that he 'discharged all the intellectual functions of management [at the Savoy], whereas the defendant Richard D'Oyly Carte had merely to attend to minor and inferior matters of organization and routine', adding that 'I have always demanded to be recognised as one of the managers of the theatre'.[15] The bitterest pill of all as far as Gilbert was concerned may have been the fact that Carte should have the power to command him to write a libretto at six months' notice.

After it was all over, on 6 September, Gilbert wrote to Helen Carte:

> You will no doubt be surprised at receiving a letter from me and still more surprised when you find that it is an overture of reconciliation. But we have so thoroughly understood and appreciated each other in byegone days that I cannot believe that, notwithstanding what has passed, you and your husband can be anxious to maintain the unhappy relations that now exist between us … I propose that we should all withdraw the angry expressions which under the influence of strong irritation we may have used, and generally look upon byegones as having gone by.[16]

On the same day he wrote to Sullivan confessing, 'I have been miserable since this wretched affair began, & would gladly end it. The notion of your being a defendant in a suit in which I am a plaintiff has thoroughly upset me.'[17] Sullivan replied:

> My old personal regard for you as a friend pleads very strongly to let the past five months be blotted out of our years of friendship as if they had never been lived through – as if the pain and suffering I (and I honestly believe you also) have endured had only been a nightmare. But I am only human and I confess frankly that I am still smarting under a sense of the unjust and ungenerous treatment I have received at your hands.

He continued by attributing Gilbert's conduct to 'a fit of uncontrolled anger greatly influenced by the bad health you were suffering from', adding that 'I am physically and mentally ill over this wretched business'.[18]

Gilbert immediately wrote back from Breakspears regretting that he had 'allowed a sentimental recollection of our long alliance' to obscure the facts of the issue.[19] He reminded Sullivan that his investigations had uncovered an error of £1,400 in four months' accounts and insisted that his actions had been quite correct in the circumstances.

The investigation into the accounts continued; in the meantime Gilbert agreed to meet Helen Carte to go over certain facts. She put these facts before him and Gilbert admitted that they altered his view of the matter and that he would not have made his affidavit had he known them at the time.[20]

The whole absurd, unpleasant affair growled on for several more months. Sullivan had been persuaded by Carte's solicitors to swear an affidavit (2 September 1890) to the effect that there were outstanding liabilities relevant to the Savoy accounts which made it impossible to calculate the profits due to Gilbert. Gilbert now discovered that, on the contrary, the account referred to had been effectively settled eight years before; and this became a serious point of argument between the two men, though Sullivan's affidavit did not actually affect the result of the court case.[21] The bitterness rankled, but slowly, eventually, calm was restored. Gilbert withdrew his legal action against Carte. The partnership lay in fragments but there was at least a possibility of the pieces being reassembled and glued together.

The Gilberts moved in to Graeme's Dyke at the end of September 1890. The property consisted not only of the house itself but also a large estate of farm and woodland. It was indeed, as Harry How observed in his *Strand* interview the following year, a little land of Gilbert's own. Located safely away from the increasingly polluted air of London, it was an enclosed retreat from the world. They were soon settled in; the paintings and the books, all the movable favourites from Harrington Gardens moved in with them. They employed a staff of seven servants in the house and more on the estate. Their butler, John Warrilow, who had previously performed in the music halls, served the Gilberts faithfully through their years at Graeme's Dyke, until his death in 1921. There were cattle, fowl and pigs on the farm, and more animals were to follow; there were vineries; not to mention the hives. He described the extent of his new domain to a visitor: 'I have forty thousand head of live-stock.' The boast was met with protests, but he insisted: 'I have indeed. At least forty thousand; mostly bees.'[22]

It seems that the Gilberts brought back from one of their visits to India, among their souvenirs, two monkeys. At first kept in a cage in a greenhouse, they were eventually given their own monkey house in the grounds. The male of the pair unfortunately died before the house was finished, but the female moved in and a number of other monkeys were bought to keep her company.[23] Among this consignment there was also, by accident, a ring-tailed lemur whom Gilbert called Job. (The Book of Job was one of Gilbert's favourite works of literature.) Job did not relish the society of monkeys and soon came to live in the main house, where he was much petted and spoiled and even had his own little chair.

The Gilberts were readily accepted into local society, becoming firm friends with their neighbours, such as the entomologist Henry Rowland Brown. Less than a year after their arrival, Gilbert was approached with a view to becoming a local magistrate. He accepted, and on 30 May 1891 he was sworn in as a Justice of the Peace in the Middlesex County Sessions. He attended on the bench at Edgware petty sessions regularly for the rest of his life.

A short article appeared in *The Era* on 25 June 1892 describing his duties on the Bench:

> Handsome and well built, with hair fast turning grey, Mr Gilbert has, despite a certain severity of expression, made himself very popular amongst the officials of the Court and the constables generally … On the Bench Mr Gilbert speaks very sparingly, but when he does make an utterance it is to the point, and worth listening to. During the hearing of a case he is ever making pen and ink sketches on the sheet of foolscap before him, not of the people in court, but of fanciful heads. These sketches are much sought after, and when the court rises are eagerly scanned by the officers and others. But whilst so occupied Mr Gilbert is alive to all that is taking place, as he shows by occasionally stopping from his drawing to put a question to the witness … Soon after he had taken his seat on the Bench there was heard a painful case of attempted suicide on the part of a man who had been well to do. That man is now doing well, thanks to the kind heart of the gifted author.[24]

At the end of January 1891, Sullivan's opera *Ivanhoe* finally appeared at Carte's Royal English Opera House, to tremendous acclaim. Sullivan attempted reconciliation with Gilbert, offering him seats for the first night, but Gilbert, still pressing for an apology from Sullivan regarding his affidavit, refused them. Gilbert did, however, attend a later performance on 11 February, writing to Helen Carte afterwards: 'I am, as you know, quite unable to appreciate high-class music, and I expected to be bored – and I was not. This is the highest compliment I ever paid a grand opera.'[25]

At the same time, work on Gilbert's new opera with Alfred Cellier progressed, but very slowly. Cellier was desperately ill with tuberculosis and he spent the later months of 1890 and the beginning of 1891 travelling in warm climes in an attempt to recover his health. While Gilbert was working on his libretto Cellier was in Sicily, Naples, Egypt or Australia. There were problems and misunderstandings, naturally, and Gilbert at one point notified Cellier that the collaboration was over. On 4 February 1891 he showed the libretto to another composer, Goring Thomas. The dispute was patched up after Cellier's return to England in April, Cellier assuring Gilbert that he was perfectly ready and willing to set the libretto. But unfortunately, he was so ill at that point that the letter containing this assurance had to be written by his wife.

Cellier was not, in fact, in a fit state to undertake the labour of writing a comic opera. His illness made it impossible for him to devote more than two or three hours a day to composition. When rehearsals started in September, he unwisely told Gilbert that the music was practically finished. On 25 September Gilbert wrote to Cellier complaining, 'The piece has been in rehearsal for 3 weeks and only four choruses – *and nothing else* – has been supplied.'[26] Music rehearsals had to be postponed. Indeed the first night itself, originally projected for 23 December, had to be postponed only days before the performance because the finale had not been completed. The months of rehearsal undoubtedly put Cellier under a physical and mental strain which his state of health could not cope with, and a filthy fog which hung over London at the end of December, killing several people, added to the forces ranged against him. Cellier died on the evening of 28 December, with his final score, *The Mountebanks*, all but complete.

In the preceding weeks Gilbert, always irritated by the unreliability of other people, had pressed Cellier again and again to finish the score. In an interview for the *Pall Mall Gazette* published on 26 December, he had grumbled about the delays to the production caused by Cellier's dilatoriness. Asked to comment on the music, Gilbert had even been a little embarrassed:

> Well, so far as I know, who have no great pretence to a right judgment in such things, it is very skilful, especially in the orchestration, but throughout I have suffered by a lack of – well, I haven't seen quite as much of Mr. Cellier as I used to of Sir Arthur Sullivan, or as much as I should have liked. In fact, it is that which has so far kept us back.[27]

He seemed, even then, to be hankering after his old collaborator.

When a few days later Sullivan learned of his old friend's death, he wrote to Cellier's brother Frank with furious bitterness, 'I wonder what Gilbert thinks now of his kindly & generous expression about him in his 'Pall Mall' interview … even *he* ought I think to feel a bit sorry now.'[28]

The Mountebanks was finally seen at the Lyric Theatre on the evening of Monday 4 January 1892. Gilbert had attempted to lure several members of D'Oyly Carte's company to perform in the opera (he had intended Bartolo and Nita to be played by Rutland Barrington and Jessie Bond), but in the event only Frank Wyatt and Geraldine Ulmar were persuaded do so. It was warmly received, though Alfred Cellier's death naturally cast a shadow over things and some of the reviewers felt it would be bad taste to criticise the music. Gilbert's libretto was praised as a return to his best style. It was a reasonable success, but it did not prove popular enough to survive through the summer; it closed on 5 August 1892.

The conditions were right for a return to work with Sullivan; *The Mountebanks* had confirmed to Gilbert the fact that there was only one man with whom he could work freely. But distrust and bitterness lingered on both sides – or rather all three sides, for we must include Carte. It was only in November 1892, after months of wrangling over past events and, after a formal reconciliation, of wrangling over new terms for the contract, that Gilbert felt able to write to Sullivan with a sense of relief that almost floats off the page:

> Your frank disclaimer of any intention to reflect upon my honour and good faith takes an immense load from my mind. I had got it, immoveably, into my head that your stipulations arose from doubts on these points, and by dwelling on the subject day and night I have magnified it to the proportions of a nightmare … Let me meet Carte to arrange the terms … Then I can set to work on the construction of the piece and have the first act ready for you by February or March or whenever you feel able to tackle it.[29]

The piece they now wrote was their most openly satirical work, set on the island of Utopia at a time when the king has decided that the island's customs, manners and institutions ought to be remodelled on the example of Great Britain. (Perhaps Gilbert was remembering the early days of the Comedy Opera Company, when Carte had been so keen for everything to be 'particularly English'.) The king's daughters are taught to be modest and prudish ('we don't like it. At least, we *do* like it; but it's wrong'), the army, the navy and the law take on the English style, and it is decided that everything on the island should be turned into a limited company, as this is an infallible recipe for success. Unfortunately, this succeeds so well that all the professions that feed on human misery such as lawyers and doctors are ruined. The only remedy, it is discovered in the final scene, is to introduce the one element they had forgotten, government by party, so that all the reforms brought in by one side will be undone by the other, leading to chaos and confusion and 'general and unexampled prosperity!' The opera was funny and in parts bitter, but there was little romance and the construction was less solid than previous operas; moreover there was little opportunity for Sullivan to allow his music to breathe.

Another factor complicated the piece's composition. Gilbert had discovered a young and pretty protégée, the American singer Nancy McIntosh. She had come to London in 1890 from Pennsylvania, accompanied by her father, who had been involved with a major scandal of the day, the Johnstown Flood. William Ambrose McIntosh, a wealthy industrialist, had been a member of the South Fork Fishing and Hunting Club, which had made alterations to and maintained (or failed to maintain) a dam which finally burst in May 1889, sweeping away several towns and killing 2,200 people. It is difficult to imagine that the decision of William and Nancy McIntosh to come to London a year later was unrelated to this catastrophe, for which the club members were widely blamed.

Nancy McIntosh, having studied voice with George Henschel in London and sung publicly with some success, was introduced to Gilbert; and Gilbert, charmed, recommended her to Sullivan for the new opera. Sullivan was not enthusiastic, fearing her voice was not strong enough, but agreed, and a new starring role, Princess Zara, was created for her.

Gilbert invited Nancy to stay at Grim's Dyke (as he now called his home) for several extended periods, and within a couple of years the arrangement became permanent. Nancy became a member of the household, an unofficial daughter to the childless couple and a safe object for Gilbert's affections. This was to be the last and most satisfactory of Gilbert's Pygmalion-and-Galatea relationships. Lucy liked her, and Nancy liked the Gilberts and Grim's Dyke. The three of them became a stable 'family', each supporting the other.

Work on the opera was not unattended by dispute. The character of an English governess had to be toned down at the insistence of Sullivan. Gilbert's health was in poor shape that year too: gout attacked him viciously. He went to Homburg, vainly hoping that the waters might help; but at least he was able to gain some comfort from his sufferings:

> My right foot (which I call Labouchere) is very troublesome, and I take a vicious pleasure (not unalloyed with pain) in cramming him into a boot which is much too small for him. My left foot (known in Homburg as Clement Scott) is a milder nuisance, but still tiresome, and would hurt me a good deal if he could.[30]

He was no better on his return and attended some rehearsals in a wheelchair.

At length, however, all was complete, and *Utopia (Limited); or, The Flowers of Progress* was premiered at the Savoy on Saturday 7 October 1893. Many of the old Savoyards had left the company so there was no George Grossmith, Richard Temple, Jessie Bond or Leonora Braham; only Rutland Barrington and Rosina Brandram remained of the much-loved stalwarts. As for the audience, the usual glittering crowd – peers and peeresses, politicians, stars of society – laughed and applauded and demanded encores, and the critics were kind. Even *The Times*, which had been harsh in its verdict on many of the earlier Savoy operas, went into raptures: 'the latest [opera] is also one of the best of the set' (9 October 1893). There was the occasional grumble that certain scenes could be compressed, and Nancy McIntosh, treated kindly by most of the press after a clear attack of stage-fright on that prestigious occasion, did not convince everyone of her worth: 'That she is a pretty woman, and so far an attractive addition to the stage was patent the moment she appeared. But ... it is impossible as yet to guess whether she has any gift for acting.'[31] It was widely noticed that the opera had little or no real plot, though for the most part they did not take this as a fatal disadvantage. It was enough to know that Gilbert and Sullivan were together again, and making people laugh.

Utopia, Limited (the title lost its brackets shortly after opening night) lasted until June the following year. The old days of long runs extending over the summer months were now past. Gilbert suggested another opera subject. Sullivan was interested, but as soon as Gilbert told him that Nancy had to be in the cast, he rejected it. Gilbert had to turn to another composer instead, the Yorkshire-born Frank Osmond Carr, already known for his musical-comedy scores such as *Morocco Bound* (1893). The opera they wrote together, *His Excellency*, premiered on 27 October 1894 at the Lyric, where it had a moderate run (162 perform-ances), with a stellar cast including not only Nancy McIntosh but also George Grossmith, Rutland Barrington, Jessie Bond and Alice Barnett. The quietness of Nancy's singing voice was commented upon. Gilbert's libretto was much praised – the birth in the 1890s of light musical comedy had probably made the critics more appreciative of wit and intelligence when it could be found – but Osmond Carr's music suffered from being compared with Sullivan's. The message was clear: Gilbert may work with other composers – in 1892 he had even persuaded Grossmith to write the score for *'Haste to the Wedding'*, his comic-opera version of *The Wedding March* – but the fact remained that, as a setter of Gilbert's words, no one could touch Sullivan.

Gilbert was in his late fifties, and he was starting to look forward to a time when he could retire from stage work altogether. After the *Brantinghame Hall* debacle he had made a solemn vow not to write any more straight dramas, and since then he had written only libretti. In April 1894, tentatively broaching the renewal of work with Sullivan, he had told the composer: 'this is the last libretto I shall ever write.'[32] He was wrong: that particular libretto would turn into *His Excellency*, and there would be a successor. But there was an odour of valediction in the air. The excruciating attacks of gout which assailed him through the 1890s were a constant reminder of the advancing years. He and Lucy took more trips abroad (Homburg, the West Indies, Burma), partly for his health but also, surely, for pleasure. Grim's Dyke was a place for leisure and enjoyment as no town house could be. He and Lucy could afford to enjoy themselves at last.

In the spring of 1895 a development occurred that made another Gilbert and Sullivan opera possible: Nancy McIntosh decided to retire from the stage and concentrate on concert work. Sullivan, who had dreaded the thought of having to write for her, was delighted. By August, Gilbert was able to read a draft plot to Sullivan. 'It comes out as clear and bright as possible', Sullivan wrote to Gilbert. 'I shall be very pleased to set it.'[33]

The Grand Duke; or, The Statutory Duel is not a bad piece. It is full of good things – and not-so-good. Set in a tinpot German Grand Duchy, it concerns the efforts of a local theatrical troupe to take over the country and the farcical conse-quences of their doing so by means of a 'statutory duel', a painless way of fighting duels with a pack of playing cards which leaves the loser legally dead. One of the results is that the central character, Ludwig (played by Rutland Barrington) ends up apparently married to four women. Gilbert was experimenting with the anything-goes atmosphere of the 1890s; his complaints of a few years before that a dramatist was not allowed to show a married man as being attracted to anyone but his wife suddenly seemed very far away. The first-night audience on Saturday 7 March 1896, which included the Lord Chamberlain, Lord and Lady Londesborough, Captain Sir Eyre Massey Shaw, Henry Labouchère and his wife (*née* Henrietta Hodson), the Bancrofts, Jessie Bond and many other luminaries, was as appreciative as on any previous occasion, and many of the critics remained enthusiastic: '"The Grand Duke" may claim to stand in the first rank of comic operas.'[34] But others found it over-long, tired and even a little in bad taste. The public did not flock to see it and it lasted only 123 performances.

Not even its creators really enjoyed working on the opera by the end. Sullivan was worn down by the long rehearsals and left for Monte Carlo immediately after conducting the premiere. 'I arrived here dead beat,' he wrote to Frank Burnand, 'and feel better already. Another week's rehearsal with W.S.G. and I should have gone raving mad. I had already ordered some straw for my hair.'[35]

Gilbert was left in London to pick up the pieces, and to make whatever cuts he could to the over-long opera. His friend Florence Stoker wrote a sympathetic letter to him, and he replied on 9 March to thank her: 'I have had rather a bad time of it, but now that the baby is born I shall soon recover. I pick up very quickly (thank God!) after these little events.' He went on, continuing his metaphor, 'I'm not at all a proud mother, & I never want to see the ugly misshapen little brat again!'[36]

18

THE NICE KIND GENTLEMAN

In his professional life, Gilbert was always determined to show himself as the 'alpha male' of the group. Any challenge to his authority was to be faced down and he was not to be defeated. In his relations with his fellow men he often seemed hard and aggressive. The effect was not pleasant. It was in his relationships with women that the more attractive side of his character showed itself. In their company he did not feel obliged to snarl or thump his chest; he was able instead to relax, to charm and to entertain. His correspondence includes dozens of charming, flirtatious letters to women friends. He seemed especially happy to joke and flirt with them if they happened to be married – presumably because the innocence of the relationship was obvious to all.

In 1882 Herbert Beerbohm Tree had married Maud Holt, a young would-be actress who had then begun an acting career alongside her husband. The Gilberts had been friends with the Trees since about 1886, when Herbert had starred in a revival of *Engaged*. Gilbert corresponded regularly with Maud, addressing her as N.K.L. (Nice Kind Lady) and signing himself N.K.G. (Nice Kind Gentleman), and offering friendly criticisms of the plays they starred in.

After the premiere of *Once Upon a Time* at the Haymarket on 28 March 1894 – an adaptation by Tree and Louis Parker of 'The Emperor's New Clothes', with Tree as the King and Maud in the small role of a basket-maker's daughter – Gilbert wrote to her in a tone of raillery:

[You were] A perfect ray of sunlight whenever you came on the stage. If I were a younger and more enterprising man I would tell you exactly how you looked – and hope for the happiest results … Why does Magdalena [played by Julia Neilson] love the King? He hasn't a redeeming quality. He is a base tyrant of the meanest type. Is it because he shows himself to her in his pyjamas? If I showed myself to ladies in *my* pyjamas could I hope for such a result? If I thought I could – but no – that way madness lies.[1]

But Gilbert had misjudged his tone; it quickly became obvious that the play was a failure and Maud was not in the mood for frivolity. He made amends in his next letter on 3 April:

I am heartily sorry to hear that you are in so low a state about the new piece. How my nonsense must have jarred upon you! I'm really sorry that I played the buffoon at so serious a juncture. I hope you will forgive me – and that you will come down here to do it ... Now do let your husband be advised by me, for once, and produce Tom Taylor's version of *Le Roi s'amuse* – it is called *The Fool's Revenge* – it is badly written but theatrically effective – it is grossly indecent – and in short has every chance of success.[2]

They did not take his advice, however. *Once Upon a Time* disappeared within the month, replaced on 25 April by Sydney Grundy's *A Bunch of Violets* – a much more successful production. Gilbert wrote a letter of slightly modified rapture on 26 April:

Hearty congratulations on a piece that, I hope & believe, will carry you satisfactorily through the season. All the people I heard talking about it seemed to like it & I really think it will 'catch on'. Personally I'm rather tired of people who get themselves into hopeless entanglements & then poison themselves out of them – but the public take poison very kindly just now – though of course it is easy to have too much of it. I was well interested right through & no scene bored me in the least. Neither did the piece seem to want cutting. You did admirably – especially in the acrid scene in Act 3 – no one could have excelled you in this.[3]

Maud took equal care to support Gilbert in his anxious moments. Despite the hard shell he presented to the world he was often tormented with self-doubt. In June 1893, while in the middle of writing *Utopia, Limited*, he received a letter from Maud Tree passing on some encouraging comments which Sullivan had made to her. Gilbert replied gratefully:

16 June '93.

My dear N.K.L.

Thank you, really, for your letter which was written, I know, out of sheer good nature and good will – and intended to put me into better heart with my work. Well, it has done so, and so your kindly object has been attained. Probably you don't know how highly I value any indication of interest on your part in me and my work.

Sullivan never says much to me, and what he *does* say I usually knock a lot off of, for discount. But what he said to you he, no doubt, meant and it is very gratifying to know that he thinks so well of what I have done. I have made two attempts to pick up the dropped threads, but so far in vain. Before I make a third attempt I shall read your kind letter again, and that will give me heart. I don't think I am a vain man or I shouldn't have so poor an opinion of what I do.

We enjoyed your visit immensely – it was kind of your husband to come. I sincerely hope you don't find us so humdrum as to prevent your coming to make a stay with us.

Yours affectionately

W.S. Gilbert[4]

Lucy Gilbert's letters to Maud (both before and after Gilbert's death) also address her as N.K.L. – and, confusingly, Lucy tended to sign these letters 'N.K.L.', 'N K L Senior' or 'Old K L.' She enjoyed the pet names Gilbert and Maud had for each other and did not object to their affectionate relationship.

Replying to Maud's request for advice about how to thank Lucy for something, Gilbert wrote (10 December 1908):

What a task you have set me! How the divil can I do it? To suggest to *you* what to say in thanking my own wife! If it were anybody's else I might conceive something (no double entente intended). And you! The wittiest woman in the world to apply to my worn out brain for suggestion! Why I'm in my dotage – & you know it for you never come near me – nor let me come near you.[5]

This was, for Gilbert, dangerously risqué, but he probably thought he was so old that he could get away with it. As he had written to another female correspondent six years earlier: 'It is so delightful to have attained a time of life when one can feel quite sure that there is not the remotest chance of being a snake on another man's hearth. One feels *so* safe and (involuntarily) good.'[6]

Lucy appears to have tolerated and even looked indulgently upon Gilbert's admiration of pretty women. The letters which he occasionally wrote to his wife when they were apart are undemonstrative in their affection. His confession to her, in a letter written from Paris shortly after their marriage, that 'I don't much like being a bachelor – and I find a difficulty getting up in the morning … I wish you were here, old girl'[7] is about as warm as he got. His letters to Lucy are chatty and friendly, but without the flirtatious aspect that he showed to his lady-friends. He rather took her for granted sometimes; for instance, in a letter written on a cruise to Greece in the autumn of 1910 he said: 'Give my best love to Nancy', forgetting to ask her to reserve any love for herself.[8] But there was real affection all the same, and they showed great love and loyalty towards each other throughout their lives.

Florence Stoker (*née* Balcombe), twenty-two years younger than Gilbert, was one of the great society beauties of the time. George du Maurier considered her one of the three most beautiful women he had ever seen. At one time romantically linked with Oscar Wilde, she married Bram Stoker in December 1878, the same month that Stoker became Henry Irving's acting manager at the Lyceum. Gilbert became friendly with Bram, but much friendlier with Florence.[9]

Gilbert's relationship with her appears to have been as innocent as with Maud Tree, but he did not want their friendship to be generally known. When one of his letters to her was returned to him, he was outraged and wrote to her (7 May 1897) that he was going to complain to the post office. 'I would write a letter to the Times, only it would never do to allow it to be publicly known that you & I were in correspondence.' Other letters show his more playful side:

14 June 99

My dear Mrs Bram,

Of course & with the greatest pleasure. I have wired to the Savoy people to send you two stalls for tomorrow (Thursday) night.

How delightfully quickly we are skimming through the tedious summer weather!–in a week the days will begin to draw in & we shall be through cheery autumn & right into delightful winter before we know where we are! *This is strictly in confidence.*

Always sincerely yours
WS Gilbert

In the autumn of 1900 he was incapacitated with arthritis and gout. He wrote to Florence in a comparatively serious vein, showing his appreciation of her kindness towards him:

21 Oct 1900

My dear Mrs Bram

Thank you heartily for your very kind letter & also for the exhaustive catalogue of books – which will be most useful to me.

I feel that I shall never be sufficiently grateful to you for your self-denying kindness in spending three days with a helpless invalid – you, whose society is so much sought – & who can spend your time as agreeably as any lady in London.

I'm afraid I can't boast of being any better. I suppose I must give up all hope of improvement until I reach Egypt – which is, after all, but a forlorn hope – & I'm quite prepared to find myself a cripple for life.

I was not sanguine about [Robert] Marshall's play [*The Noble Lord*] when I read it. It was too mechanical in structure to be likely to catch on. But the papers talk nonsense when they say it ought to have had a vein of serious interest in it – a piece of that kind should be chaffy & irresponsible right through.

I've rashly undertaken to stagemanage six rehearsals of Patience next week. I don't know how I shall get through them. I shall put up at the Savoy Hotel & be carried thence to the stage & back. But it will be a serious trial to me.

My wife sends her love & I would send mine if I dared.

Always truly yours

WS Gilbert

P.S. Would you care to go to the first night of Patience – Nov 7th?

Nancy McIntosh wrote to the Stokers (possibly around this time) giving instructions about how to care for the Gilberts' lemur, Job: 'Please slap him when he does wrong or he might get into bad habits. He likes best to sit in his little chair but will not sit in it unless it is somewhere near the fire … Mr Gilbert is feeling very stiff from the damp but is otherwise very much the same. We are glad to leave this weather.'[10] It appears from this that the Gilberts were lending Job to the Stokers while they went abroad. A story in the Stoker family relates that Gilbert once gave a monkey to Florence. The creature was not a popular hit in the household, and the final straw was the occasion when, swinging from a chandelier, it defecated into a bowl of fruit. It was immediately banished.[11] It seems likely that the 'monkey' was actually Job the lemur.

In spite of this distressing incident, the Gilberts remained on good terms with the Stokers through to the middle of 1901 at least:

3rd July 1901

My dear Mrs Bram,

Of course we expect you on the 15th July & you are a dear for proposing an early train. I heartily wish you could give us more than two days. I shall have to go to the Bench on Wednesday morning, the 17th – but I will get off, if you can remain until the afternoon. I am off, now, to administer what I am pleased to consider justice at Edgware.

We have been nicely freshened up by the rain, although we have not had nearly so much here as you have had in London. Alfred Austin, the poet laureate, was here yesterday – he has written a one-act play in blank verse & proposes that Mrs. Pat Campbell shall produce it & engage Forbes Robertson to play the lover! The piece is, of course, impossible – but it would never do to tell him so. He is a good little fellow but about as vain as they make them.

With best love from us both

Affectionately yours

WS Gilbert

But the relationship soured shortly thereafter, for an unknown reason. There was a serious falling-out, which Florence cunningly resolved at Christmas 1902 by sending a card for Job:

23rd Dec 1902

Dear Mrs Stoker

I am trying to cheat myself into the belief that the kindly message you sent to Job may have been meant to convey, indirectly, some kindly message to ourselves. Perhaps I am mistaken in this, but you will forgive a mistake that has its genesis in an earnest desire on my part that we may be, once more, on our old footing. I have never felt that I deserved the rebuke you administered to me a year ago – & more – & my wife & I have often spoken with real sorrow of the calamitous consequences of that rebuke. I have no friend whom I esteem & respect as I esteem & respect you – & it has been a source of great grief to me that you should have thought yourself justified in saying that which has had the effect of placing so wide a gulf between us.

I have long wished to say this, or something like this & your Christmas Card to Jobie has afforded me the necessary opening. I don't suppose you will be angry with me for having availed myself of it.

With every good wish for many new years

I am, always sincerely yours

WS Gilbert

This frank expression of feeling was kindly received by Florence, who immediately wrote a warm letter in response. Gilbert's reply to this is full of relief, and tentatively returns to his usual joking tone:

25th Dec 1902

My dear Mrs Bram,

Your kind letter has removed ten years from my shoulders – I've been worrying for a year & more over our estrangement, and – really there seems to be some virtue in Xmas time after all. It's delightful to think that it is 'As you were' with us. As my wife said when I showed her your letter 'She's much too charming a woman to quarrel with' – & so you are.

We come to London on 2nd Jany for three months so I hope we shall see a great deal of you & that I may be allowed to rival Willie Matthews in escorting you to public entertainments – though I bar concerts. Our address will be 4 Grosvenor Crescent –

between St George's Hospital & Belgrave Square – a really charming house & a fit casket for such a jewel as I.

Job is extremely fit & hasn't changed in the least. He is coming up to town with us – I bring him in order that we may be *quite sure* of a visit from you.

With all possible good wishes for this & many years to come.

I am

Your affectionate friend

WS Gilbert.

Thereafter, their relationship remained cordial, though Gilbert sometimes complained semi-humorously that she seemed to be avoiding them:

> I'm afraid there's not the remotest chance of seeing you here this year – we never seem to meet now – I'm afraid it is my motor that frightens you away. But if you *will* spare us a few days, I promise you that the motor shall be hidden away all the time & that no allusion will be made to it. [24 June 1904]

He kept her informed of their latest adventures and mishaps in the motorcar: 'We went to Aldershot yesterday in the motor &, coming back, a tyre burst near Frimley, so we had to leave the motor & return by train. The beauty of motoring is that it gives one so much healthy walking exercise' (16 May 1903). Sometimes his comments on being deprived of her company contained a tone of genuine hurt: 'I am sorry that the temptation of the Trowers' garden party prevents our seeing you on Saturday as well as Sunday. I have quite given up all hope of ever putting you up again. What we have done we don't know. It used not to be so' (22 July 1904). But they remained good friends until the end of his life.

By the beginning of the new century Gilbert had settled into retirement. Respected as a master librettist, he was plagued with offers of collaboration from young composers, but he refused them steadfastly:

16 Sept 1904

My dear Mrs Bram,

 I am sorry to disappoint Mr. Godfrey but I may say at once that no consideration would ever induce me to write another libretto. If Mozart rose from the dead & paid me the compliment of seeking me to write with him, I should make the same reply – a reply that I have given to a dozen composers during the last few years.

 I am sorry I did not see you at His Majesty's on Wednesday. Personally I think Tree renders a distinct service to dramatic literature by presenting Shakespeare's plays in such a fashion as to convince his audiences that they have been worshipping a false god. I was as bored by the Tempest as I was by Richard II & Julius Caesar – three ridiculously bad plays. I daresay Shakespeare was a great poet – I am not qualified to express a technical opinion on that point, but I consider myself an authority on dramatic work & I have no hesitation in expressing a professional opinion that all his works should be kept off the boards …

 With best love from us all

 Always affectionately from

 WS Gilbert

Even the most mundane of Gilbert's social letters take flight when he thinks of a phrase or an idea that amuses him. In 1887 he accepted an invitation to attend the wedding of one friend, a Miss Boughton – 'I hope you will always invite me to your marriages', he told her graciously[12] – but as it happened he was unable to do so because of a severe attack of gout in both his feet: 'if I presented myself in church it would have to be on my hands, with my feet in the air – which would attract attention.'[13] Though in considerable pain, he was humorist enough to turn it into a joke.

Mary Talbot was an American friend whom he always addressed as Cousin Mary despite the fact that they were not related. He often wrote to her for no reason except the whim of the moment:

A desire to write to you has come over me, and I always yield to temptations. Even Providence yields to them. If I do a rash thing, I'm told I'm tempting Providence; and if Providence can't resist my humble temptations, how can I be expected to resist His? So I don't; in I always go, head over heels.[14]

On a separate occasion he told her more seriously:

It is an infinite boon to possess, at the fag-end of a long life, a dear friend who can enter into and sympathize with one's pleasures, cares and troubles. Men of my age are like trees in late autumn – their friends have died away as the leaves have fallen from the trees; but it is enough for me to feel assured that there is at least one friend who will stick to me to the very end.[15]

Another favourite correspondent was Ellaline Terriss, the beautiful young star of plays and musicals in the 1890s, and wife of Seymour Hicks. She had portrayed Thora in *His Excellency* in 1894, and they became firm friends thereafter. When they first met, Gilbert joked that she should be called 'The Tuneful Nine' because 9=IX='Icks. In his early letters to her he addressed her formally as Mrs Seymour Hicks, but he soon became much more familiar. The following letter refers to a table cloth which Gilbert was supposed to sign with a quotation:

7 August 96

Dear Cousin Littleix,

Of course I will always do anything you want me to do. It will be pleasing to know that one line at least, of 'His Excellency' will be handed down to posterity.

When are you coming? And won't you bring it (the table cloth) yourself? Sunday week is going to be a very fine warm day – wont you both come then?

We haven't been to see the Gaiety piece. The notices frightened us – & I don't like to see you playing rubbish. You ought never to play even as low down as His Excellency.

My wife sends her love, & I send

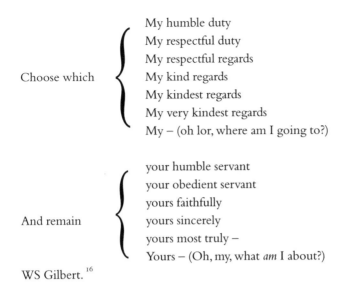

Choose which {
My humble duty
My respectful duty
My respectful regards
My kind regards
My kindest regards
My very kindest regards
My – (oh lor, where am I going to?)

And remain {
your humble servant
your obedient servant
yours faithfully
yours sincerely
yours most truly –
Yours – (Oh, my, what *am* I about?)

WS Gilbert.[16]

Unsurprisingly, Seymour Hicks disapproved of Gilbert. According to Hicks:

> [Gilbert] had a strange personality if ever there was one. His small piercing eyes, which looked as if they had been long robbed of sleep, were generally fixed, maliciously, it must be truly said, on big people and seldom directed towards the smaller fry … he seemed incapable of geniality, especially in the company of men, though being a great admirer of pretty women he took endless trouble to amuse them. But for the male species he seemed to trouble very little.[17]

Or, as Ellaline Terriss put it: 'Women liked him, men did not.'[18]

An entirely different side to Gilbert's personality emerges in these letters. Even the vocabulary is different: softer, more 'feminine', full of affection and consideration. He had, after all, grown up in a largely female household, with three younger sisters – this was the atmosphere he most understood and was most comfortable in. He was never happier than when surrounded by women, away from the usual male rivalry, allowed for once to be the Nice Kind Gentleman.

19

ON TRIAL (1897–98)

After *Brantinghame Hall*, Gilbert had let it be known that he would never write another play. But 'never' is a harsh word, and when the actor-manager Edward S. Willard commissioned him to write a serious drama, he accepted. Unfortunately, the play developed in a way that prevented Willard from playing in it, and it was returned on to Gilbert's hands. He offered it to George Alexander, but Alexander turned it down. It was finally accepted by May Fortescue, who had previously performed at the Savoy and now managed a touring company.

The Fortune Hunter is a rather stilted and melodramatic affair in three acts, concerning a dissolute French marquis who marries an English heiress, squanders her fortune, and then attempts to nullify this marriage according to the French *Code Civile* in order to free him to marry another rich woman and so pay his debts. In Act 3 he realises the infamy of his conduct and as the only way of atoning (and ensuring his son is not declared illegitimate) he provokes a duel and deliberately allows himself to be killed.

Its first performance took place at the Theatre Royal, Birmingham, on 27 September 1897, attended by a lively 'provincial' audience and a number of interested Londoners, including seventeen critics from the London journals. It was a most unusual occasion, tempting a good number of inveterate theatre-goers out of their usual metropolitan habitat. The reviewer for *The Daily News* (28 September) seemed rather shocked to find the stalls occupied by 'people in ordinary outdoor attire, the ladies wearing straw sailor hats or any other headgear they choose', but admitted that everyone was in the best of spirits and determined to be amused.

The play was received enthusiastically by the Birmingham audience, less so by the London critics. The critics agreed that the play was 'stagy' and unreal, the dialogue too verbose, the whole a disappointment. 'Its closest affinity in the stage at the present moment would have to be sought in the melodrama of the suburban theatres,' said *The Times* (28 September). The *Pall Mall Gazette* tried its best, but had to confess:

> [Gilbert's] dialogue ... is so wordy, of such inordinate length, and so unlike anything that people say in their everyday intercourse, that it fails altogether to carry conviction across the footlights. The fact is that Mr. Gilbert has resorted to stage methods of a byegone generation, which are no longer recognized as the best means for either the telling of a story, the teaching of a lesson, or the delineation of character. [28 September]

As for *The Era*, it declared on 2 October: 'People who like to be amused and interested will avoid *The Fortune Hunter* as they would their pet aversion.'

It must be admitted that *The Fortune Hunter* is not a good play. It was not merely old-fashioned, but clumsily written. Gilbert's literary style was not as flexible as it used to be. He had lost the knack of colloquialism that he had been able to command twenty or thirty years before. Still, there was something in the creaky script that held its audiences through to the end, and even managed to grip them as the action progressed. He was called before the first-night curtain and he was applauded; but all was not well.

The company went from Birmingham to Edinburgh, and Gilbert went with them, determined to pull the play together and make it a success. He arrived in a bad mood early on Monday 4 October, describing in a letter to Lucy his accommodation at the Windsor Hotel as having 'a fair sitting-room but a ghastly bedroom'.[1] Later that day he was visited by a Mr Isaac Donald, an interviewer from the *Edinburgh Evening Dispatch*. The results appeared in the paper the following day.[2]

The interview started innocuously enough. Gilbert was asked what kind of dramatic work he preferred. He replied: 'A blank verse play appeals most powerfully to me, because in every line I am doing all I know. In writing prose plays one is apt to let the pen be carried away by comedy scenes.' Asked about the modern style of 'problem' drama championed by Pinero, Henry Arthur Jones, Shaw and others, he said he did not admire it, adding tartly, 'In these so-called problem plays there is no problem whatever involved'.

It was later in the interview that Gilbert's views, as reported, became controversial. He afterwards insisted that he had been misquoted. Asked about the continuing prevalence of adaptations from the French on the British stage, Gilbert replied (according to the printed version):

> The fact is managers cannot judge a play when they see it in manuscript. If Pinero writes a play and sends it to Sir Henry Irving, it is accepted, not because it is a good play, but because it is Pinero. If a stranger who may be a clever dramatist sends Sir Henry, or Mr Tree, or anybody else a play, it is not accepted,

however good it may be, because they can't judge. Your manager nowadays crosses to France, sees a play that goes well, and how it can be slightly watered down to suit our censorious society, and immediately transplants it.

'Then you have no sympathy with translations?'

No! None! We ought to leave the French stage alone. They have good actors and atrociously bad plays … Their actors, of course, can so speak and deliver speeches as to claim the attention of the audience, while ours, why, we have no actors who can make a thirty-line speech interesting! Whoever heard in this country 'All the world's a stage' declaimed by a Jaques who did not in every line make it plain he had learned it off by heart? There is always the same dull monotony of delivery. Every living actor – Sir Henry Irving, Beerbohm Tree, Alexander, excellent though they may be otherwise, have that dull monotony of delivery. They keep to one note right through the sentence, and finish a semi-tone higher or a semi-tone lower as the case may be.

'In what direction would you say dramatic taste lies today?'

In the direction of musical comedy – bad musical comedy, in which half-a-dozen irresponsible comedians are turned loose upon the stage to do exactly as they please. These are our popular pieces.

Later on, Gilbert declared:

The press is largely responsible for the fact that there are so many adaptations on the English stage.

'How is that?'

Because they seem to draw no distinction between the production of an original play and the translation of a French one. When a boy I translated the works of the ancient Greek dramatists, but I have never considered myself the author of their works. I have always given Sophocles some credit for the writing of his own plays. It is the easiest thing in the world to call Monsieur Bertrand Mr Smith and Saint Cloud Richmond, and make your play into English. I myself twice translated French plays. On one occasion I sat up all night and did it, and I got about £3,000 for it, one way and another. But I only consider it a pot-boiler.

'And do you seriously mean that you blame the Press for the large number of adaptations on the British stage?'

I do. I do not blame the actors and actresses. I blame the Press for considering them seriously as original work. Why, I hear Sydney Grundy put on the same level as Arthur Pinero, while the fact is that Mr Grundy is only a translator. He is a creditable translator, but to put him on the same level as Mr Pinero is a monstrous injustice. Remember, I do not wish, in saying this, to decry Mr Grundy in any sense.

'Where do you think Mr Pinero is at his best?'

In 'The Magistrate' and 'Dandy Dick,' to which style I believe he will return. In wholly farcical plays he is at his best, and I like the quality of his work immensely. I think him a giant, but he finds his name bracketed with hacks.

'Have you any further work in progress?'

No! I will write no more plays. I mean to retire now. I am disheartened by the erroneous point of view from which criticisms are written in London. They never seem to dissociate the play from the author of the play. I am not complaining of bad criticisms. I have had plenty, and have learned much from them. But there is such a tendency to look upon the author of a bad or an unsuccessful play, not as a poor devil who has tried his best, but as a man who has committed an outrage against nature. The critics attack him as if he were a scoundrel of the worst type, and they go on at it week after week. I don't feel disposed to put myself forward as a cock-shy for these gentlemen. I think it better to refrain from writing as I am not obliged to write. I prefer to work in a different groove where anything I may do will stand upon its own merits.

Afterwards, upon reading the printed version of his encounter, Gilbert was horrified, and wrote to the actors and writers named in the interview, assuring them that he had not used the words ascribed to him, that he had been speaking generally and that the names of specific people had been suggested to him by the interviewer. He was particularly anxious to apologise to Sydney Grundy, whose work he admired. Grundy was a well-regarded playwright of the era, most of whose dramatic works were adaptations from foreign originals, but who had also written some successful original pieces, including the libretto of Sullivan's *Haddon Hall*. Grundy forgave Gilbert but others did not, and *The Era*, the theatrical world's weekly paper, got its own back with a long editorial on 16 October 1897:

The happy knack of non-endearing himself to his contemporaries which Mr W.S. GILBERT possesses in such a remarkable degree was once more employed by him the other day at Edinburgh …

According to Mr GILBERT, the author of a bad or unsuccessful play is treated by the critics as 'a man who has committed an outrage against nature,' and is 'attacked as a scoundrel of the worst type.' At first it is difficult to understand how so clever a man as Mr GILBERT could have made such nonsensical statements … We believe we possess the correct explanation. Mr GILBERT's abnormal self-esteem has, with advancing years, developed into a malady. In his own estimation, he is a kind of Grand Lama or Sacred Elephant of dramatic literature. The mildest criticism on his work, the most gentle disapproval of one of his plays, is a crime of *lèse majesté*, for which, if it were in his power, he would punish the culprit severely. It is evident that, did we live under a more despotic dispensation, he would commit all the London critics for contempt of

court. It is not so much a question of the honesty or reasonableness of the critics' objections to his plays as the fact that they – or, indeed, anybody – should
object to the work of GILBERT the Great at all. Such a view of life is obviously
unsuited to any condition except that of an Oriental potentate; and as a matter
of fact Mr GILBERT's career has been a succession of combats with the object
– alas! unattained – of vindicating the GILBERT Theory of the universe against
sceptics and rebels. It is a great mistake to consider Mr GILBERT as a cruel or
spiteful man. He has sometimes seemed so, but his real kindliness and good
nature have simply been obscured by the abnormal protuberance of his bump
of self-esteem ...

Mr GILBERT's absurd accusation against Mr GRUNDY is not, we contend, an
instance of spite, but simply an ebullition of the loud, puffy, colonel-of-a-regi-
ment kind – an expression, in short, of violent indignation with the erroneous
and imperfect arrangements of an injudicious Providence. It is the same with
the statement that 'we have no actor on the stage that can make a thirty-line
speech interesting.' It is as incorrect as Mr GILBERT's other accusations; but, again
we say, it is not to be regarded as a statement, but as an expletive. The actors and
the managers fight shy of Mr GILBERT's serious plays. Very well. It cannot be, he
argues, that there is anything the matter with the plays; something must be the
matter with the actors and the managers ...

We can understand Mr GILBERT liking to attack a rival like Mr SYDNEY
GRUNDY; but why he should insult wholesale the actors – some of whom have
rendered invaluable assistance to him in making his fortune by the stage – we
cannot understand. But this has always been the way with Mr GILBERT after
one of his failures. He has invariably attacked somebody or other; either a rival
author, the actors, or the critics. In this instance he has 'gone for' all three. The
fact is, when he is in one of his tempers there is no knowing what Mr GILBERT
will not say or do. At such times his friends should – if possible – keep interviewers from him and him from interviewers.[3]

Clearly, the editor of *The Era* was infuriated by Gilbert's quoted views quite as
much as Gilbert had been infuriated by the attitudes of the critics; and the article,
like the interview, would have been best taken as an expletive rather than an
attempt to state facts. But Gilbert was never inclined to take such things quietly,
and he sued Edward Ledger, the proprietor of *The Era*, for libel.

Gilbert was at a low ebb over the whole business as the new year arrived and
the court case still pended. He wrote to Maud Tree on New Year's Day:

I suppose I have been embittered by my recent experiences. There is more joy
in Lower Bohemia over one original play that fails than over ninety & nine
translations from the French that run their 300 nights. And it is not soothing to
be pointed at as a conspicuous failure at the end of a 30 year career.[4]

She responded with a letter full of sympathy and praise, received by Gilbert with a gratitude that he did not, at first, know how to express:

11 Jan. 98.

My dear N.K.L.

I gathered from what you said, last night, that you expected an answer to your last letter & were a little hurt that I hadn't written one. I didn't write because your letter was all about myself & I didn't want to bother you or take up your time with letters from me about myself. But I was so delighted with it that I learnt it by heart, & was even vain enough to try to believe that I deserved it all – but not vain enough to succeed in this. An awful idea came over me that it was 'only your fun' – but I dismissed that as you wouldn't cut a joke over a poor devil of a dead & gone play hack. (No flowers by request.)

I hope you have no head after your dissipation at Grossmiths. I find that that homuncule sent us an invitation – but I had forgotten the circumstance.

Yours affectionately

N.K.G.[5]

Finally, the case was heard in the Queen's Bench Division, before Mr Justice Day and a special jury, on Monday 28 and Tuesday 29 March 1898. The proceedings were attended by many members of the dramatic profession, including Sir Henry Irving, Herbert Beerbohm Tree, May Fortescue, Bram Stoker, Robert Buchanan and George Alexander. Long reports appeared in all the national papers, but by far the fullest appeared in *The Era* itself, on 2 April. With its keen eye for the theatrical, it took particular care to report the details of witness-box repartee.

Mr Lawson Walton, QC, stated the case for the plaintiff (Gilbert). He contended that the article in *The Era* was a personal attack on Gilbert's character and reputation, having no bearing on the actual quality of his work: it charged him with envy of his dramatic colleagues and with falsehood, conceit and ingratitude towards the actors he worked with. 'Mr. Gilbert felt that the picture was an untrue portrait, and one that he could not allow to go forth unchallenged.' Every one of the allegations in *The Era* article was dismissed as fundamentally untrue.

Gilbert was called to the witness stand and examined by Marshall Hall (Gilbert's counsel):

[Gilbert] admitted that he said the critics treated the author of an unsuccessful play as if he had committed an outrage against nature, but that was only a jocular expression. In fact, he was laughing when he said it to the interviewer.

[Marshall Hall said:] You have read what was said in the article about your bump of self-esteem. Do you regard that as written in joke or seriously? – [Gilbert replied:] I can hardly take it seriously, because I cannot suppose that anyone thinks I wish to reconstruct the universe. I am perfectly satisfied with the Cosmos as it is.

Is it true to say that you have had successive combats with anybody to vindicate your theory of the universe? – Oh, no; I have no theory of the universe, and I am not a combative man.

Gilbert then attempted to clarify his stated opinions on actors and blank verse:

what I objected to was the present fashion of delivering blank verse, which allowed the metrical – the iambic structure to dominate the sense, caused the audience to lose the thread of the discourse, and obliged them to give up the speech for a bad job, and wait for the next speech in the hope that they would find better luck with it.

You did not intend these remarks as an insult to Sir Henry Irving or Mr Alexander? – No, certainly not. It was merely my comment upon the state of the blank verse stage.

As a matter of fact, did you mention their names at all? – They were suggested to me by the interviewer, who said, 'Do your remarks apply to Irving and Tree and Alexander?' and I said, 'Yes; all living actors who deal with blank verse.'

Edward Carson, representing the defendant Edward Ledger, cross-examined Gilbert:

Hostile criticism of *The Fortune Hunter* appeared in most of the London morning papers? – I know nothing about that.

You don't like reading hostile criticism? – I have a horror of reading criticism at all, good or bad.

Do you know that hostile criticism appeared in *The Times*? – Yes.

In the *Morning Post*, the *Advertiser*, the *Daily Chronicle*, the *Morning*, the *Pall-Mall Gazette*, the *St. James's Gazette*, the *Daily Graphic*? – I don't know. I have not seen them.

But you would admit that that is a formidable list of hostile criticism? – Distinctly, I am quite prepared to admit that the play is a very bad play. A play that fails is for all practical purposes a bad play.

Carson then spoke of Sir Henry Irving's reaction to Gilbert's quoted comments in the interview. Irving had spoken at the Sheffield Press Club on Wednesday 20 October 1897, referring to Gilbert as a dramatist who 'laying aside his lyre ... has chosen again to dare the heights of serious drama, and with what success I fear is greatly shown by his very childish statements and his very jaundiced behaviour. He seems to me to be in the unfortunate position of the proverbial bull, but instead of going into a china shop has got into some ironmongery establishment, and has hurt nothing but himself ... '[6]

Did you observe from the public Press that a short time afterwards Sir Henry
Irving, at a dinner of the Sheffield Press Club, spoke good-humouredly but
warmly about the criticisms upon himself? – I do not admit that he spoke
good-humouredly but warmly. I noticed that he spoke most angrily and most
spitefully concerning me. He described me as a librettist who soared to write
original comedy … I have never had an angry word with him, and I cannot
conceive why he should be so spiteful.

Carson took Gilbert through the various opinions expressed in the interview and
got him to clarify what he had meant. Gilbert, warming to his theme, began to be
humorous on the subject; his counsel must have groaned in their seats:

[Gilbert] never said that no English actor could recite a thirty-line speech without making it plain he had learnt it off by heart. What he did say was that English
actors spoke blank verse in a monotone, raising or lowering the voice a semitone
at the end, according as the speech was a question or a statement. They spoke it
just as the boys at Harrow or Eton delivered blank verse on Speech Day …

[Carson asked:] Do you now mean to convey that these gentlemen [Irving,
Tree, and Alexander] have what you call a dull monotony of delivery? – I do
mean to convey that in dealing with blank verse they fall in with the prevailing
fashion. That is my opinion, and many others hold it.

Carson quoted back to Gilbert his reference in the interview to the public taste
leaning towards 'bad musical comedy, in which half-a-dozen irresponsible comedians are turned loose upon the stage to do exactly as they please'. Their exchange
became a sparring-match of wit:

What kind of pieces do you refer to? – Pieces in which low comedians are
allowed to do what they please.
    Will you mention one of them? – Oh, there are plenty of them.
    I wish you would mention one? – Well, take the pantomime at Drury-lane
Theatre, with the great Dan Leno.
    But that only goes on a short time in the year? – It goes on for a long time
in the evening.
    Is a pantomime a bad musical comedy? – It is not to be differentiated from it.
    Do you really describe a pantomime as a bad musical comedy? – No, but I
would describe a bad musical comedy as a pantomime.
    That is very clever, but I would like to know what you mean by bad musical
comedies; give us the name of one? – There are fifty of them.
    Give me one? – I would say such a piece as *The Circus Girl*.
    Would you call it a bad musical comedy? – I would call it bad. I believe the
manager calls it a musical comedy.

You give it as an instance of what you mean by a bad musical comedy? —Yes.

Have they half-a-dozen irresponsible low comedians turned loose in *The Circus Girl*? — I do not know how many there are.

Miss Ellaline Terriss, for instance? — She is an artist of the highest pretensions.

But she is in *The Circus Girl*? — She is the redeeming feature of it.

Carson still attempted to pin Gilbert down with a few names of irresponsible comedians. Eventually, Gilbert gave him the name of Arthur Roberts at the Lyric. 'He is an irresponsible comedian?' 'Certainly; most irresponsible and most amusing.'

Carson's intention was quite clear: to get Gilbert to repeat the disputed opinions from the interview. In this he was quite successful. He asserted in his final address to the jury that these opinions were so outrageous that they practically demanded the kind of response that *The Era* had provided; but the fact that Gilbert's statements caused loud and repeated bursts of laughter in court suggests some sneaking support for them.

After lunch, the cross-examination continued. Carson brought up the matter of Clement Scott and *Brantinghame Hall*:

Did you break off your friendship with Mr Scott? —Yes; because the criticism was unfair.

Then nine years ago you were of the same mind to give up writing that class of plays? —Yes.

You said, 'I am determined not to expose myself again to your insulting jibes?' —Yes; no doubt I wrote that.

You were cool and calm? —Yes, calm and deliberate. I don't know my temperature at the time.

Carson read out a passage from *Rosencrantz and Guildenstern*, in which King Claudius, mortified at the fact that the audience of a tragedy he had written had simply laughed at it, made their laughter an offence punishable by death. Gilbert had to break it to the barrister that 'I do not hold myself responsible for all the sentiments expressed by all my characters'. Carson continued:

There is a passage here [in *The Era* article] in which you are described as Gilbert the Great, to which you take exception? —Yes; I do not feel that I deserve that compliment.

Witness proceeded to explain that he did not read many criticisms, but he would rather read unfavourable criticism, because he knew how good he was, but did not know how bad he was …

Witness, in reply to further cross examination, said he had a dispute with Sir Arthur Sullivan, but he did not cease speaking to him. He had a law suit against Mr Horace Sedger, but he did not fall out with him.

Were you friendly with him afterwards? – I was not friendly with him before.

Did you fall out with Mr. John Hare at the Garrick? – I am not on terms with John Hare just now, because he chose to quarrel with me over the manner in which I referred to his action in transferring the lease of the Garrick Theatre, which belongs to me, to a syndicate formed to exhibit a music hall dwarf.

It was all his fault? – There was no fault on either side.

After this lengthy double-act, Mr Lawson Walton, acting for Gilbert, stood up and re-examined Gilbert, to clarify certain facts and perhaps to undo some of the damage done in cross-examination:

In speaking of the delivery of blank verse [Gilbert] only expressed a general view, and had no idea of reflecting upon the artistic eminence of any particular actors … He had never quarrelled with any dramatic authors, and with two exceptions he had never complained of criticism. These two cases were absolutely the only foundation for the allegation that he had been all his life quarrelling with those who criticised his plays.

The judge seemed in great confusion about the facts of the case he was trying:

Mr Justice Day said the action seemed to have been brought in a most crooked and roundabout manner. At first he could not make out how *The Era* had got into the matter at all. The action against *The Era* seemed to him to be very abnormal.

Mr Carson – They did not dare to take an action against the Edinburgh paper.

Mr Lawson Walton – The Edinburgh paper did not publish the article.

Isaac Donald, the Edinburgh interviewer, was called as a witness for the defence:

Did you take notes as the conversation proceeded? – Not at first; but afterwards, as the conversation went on, I thought it would be too bad to paraphrase the words of the librettist of the Savoy operas.

Mr Justice Day – Did you take notes in shorthand? – Yes …

Mr Walton – Did you understand that Mr Gilbert looked upon Mr Grundy as only a translator? – I did.

Did it not strike you as monstrously absurd? – It did; that is why I was particular to publish it.

Did you point out to Mr Gilbert that he had made a mistake? – I did not like to point out to a great playwright that some other writer might be as good as himself …

Is it the usual method in interviewing to try and get a startling statement, though it may be a mistake? – I did not try to get a startling statement. I did not want it. He sent for me to come and get it.

Closing speeches took place the following morning. Edward Carson's defence hinged upon the accuracy of the report of the Edinburgh interview. He said very little of the most libellous of the comments in *The Era* editorial, that 'Mr GILBERT's abnormal self-esteem has, with advancing years, developed into a malady' – and even stated, absurdly, that the piece had not contained any attack on 'the personal or private character of Mr Gilbert'. Carson concentrated on the outrageousness of Gilbert's own stated opinions. 'Mr Gilbert had made attack on leading actors, and accused them of being unable to make a thirty-line speech interesting. Was such a man to get damages?'

Gilbert rose from his seat in front of counsel and left the court while Carson was speaking.

Lawson Walton, giving his closing address in reply, emphasised that *The Era* article was indeed a personal attack, and added that it had been written while a letter Gilbert had written to the paper, describing the Edinburgh interview as inaccurate, was before them. 'Why had not the writer of the article gone into the witness-box and disclaimed any ill-feeling? Why had he not submitted to cross-examination?'

The judge's summing-up seemed designed to bewilder rather than to help the jurors:

> The defendant did not seem to be mixed up in any way with the dispute between the plaintiff and some other persons, or to have been in any way cognisant of the matter said to be the subject of the libel. He was a perfect stranger, as far as the libel was concerned, to either party.

The judge seemed not to realise that the libel in question was *The Era*'s long leader, and confusedly thought the point at issue was the Edinburgh interview. Unsurprisingly, the jury was unable to agree on a verdict (Gilbert reported that they were ten for him and two against); they were accordingly discharged. The discussion of Gilbert's character ended, as such discussions always do, inconclusively.

Almost immediately Gilbert shook the dust of London from his feet and travelled with Lucy to the Mediterranean. He wrote to Maud Tree from Sorrento on 12 April:

> We have had a perfectly ideal voyage, as smooth as a lake all the way from the Thames – a capital set of passengers (I am in love with most of the lady passengers) and everything admirable.
>
> I have not worried myself at all about the trial. I resolved not to look at a newspaper and, in short, I determined to clear my mind of it altogether. After all, I have done what I wanted to do … The case would have been mine but for the judge who was simply a monument of senile incapacity. To the very last he hadn't the faintest notion as to what the case was about. My case was comparatively trivial, but it is fearful to think that grave issues, in which a man's

fortune or a woman's honour may be involved, are at the mercy of an utterly incompetent old doll …

P.S. I am not at all surprised to find that the press strongly disapprove of actions for libel against newspapers.[7]

He had already written to Helen Carte on 28 March, telling her: 'The judge summed up like a drunken monkey.'[8] But the Mediterranean breezes cleared his brain. All these things were behind him now. He had said in the interview in Edinburgh that he would write no more for the stage, and he was resolved to keep his word. He had said it before, but this time he meant it.

A new edition of *The Bab Ballads* had been published at Christmas 1897 with many new 'Bab' drawings, interspersed with the lyrics from his most successful operas, which he called his 'Songs of a Savoyard'. Gilbert took great care in arranging this new collection and there was a deliberate point in his choice of the last item in the book: a lyric from *His Excellency*, here given the title 'The Played-Out Humorist':

Quixotic is his enterprise, and hopeless his adventure is,
    Who seeks for jocularities that haven't yet been said.
The world has joked incessantly for over fifty centuries,
    And every joke that's possible has long ago been made.
I started as a humorist with lots of mental fizziness,
    But humour is a drug which it's the fashion to abuse;
For my stock-in-trade, my fixtures, and the goodwill of the business
    No reasonable offer I am likely to refuse.
        And if anybody choose
        He may circulate the news
    That no reasonable offer I'm likely to refuse.

For his final refrain he subtly altered the last line from the version performed in *His Excellency*, changing the word 'the' to 'my':

        Though the notion you may scout,
        I can prove beyond a doubt
    That my mine of jocularity is utterly worked out.

And he followed it with a little drawing of a candle – extinguished.[9]

20

THE MENAGERIE (1898–1906)

The decision to retire must have been a great wrench to Gilbert. Possibly Lucy had something to do with it. He had been a professional writer for over thirty-five years, no sooner finishing one piece than starting on the next, striving to improve and attempting to keep ahead of his competitors in the foot-race. But now, it seemed, he had to concede the race was over for him. Others had joined the competition after him and were taking the lead: Pinero, Bernard Shaw, Granville Barker and others. But the metaphor did not hold, really. There was no overall winner, and there never could be. Still, Gilbert had earned his prize: wealth and prestige and, now, the time to enjoy these things. He did not fully retire from life in the theatre. He continued to stage-manage revivals at the Savoy, even when, crippled with gout, he had to be carried to the stage in order to do so. But as for the rest of his time, it was his to spend as he chose, going on cruises, travelling to Egypt, Italy and spa resorts, or merely staying home and enjoying his little grand duchy at Grim's Dyke, happy in the company of Lucy, Nancy and his true friends.

Life at Grim's Dyke was played by Gilbert's rules. He sat at dinner with a pretty woman on either side of him, and when the ladies rose at the end of the meal, he did not stay with the men to talk over the brandy and cigars, but rose to join them. A room was dedicated to the coaching of actresses and was jocularly called the Flirtorium. It is unlikely that anything untoward took place in that room; it was no secret, even being mentioned as an item of interest during an interview with Gilbert in 1900.[1]

Once, surrounded by young women at dinner and greatly enjoying himself, Gilbert was challenged as to why he showed such inconstancy to his wife. 'Because,' he explained, 'I am too good to be true.'[2]

Sometimes these harmless flirtations became serious enough to cause him exquisite pain. 'What ought a married man of sixty-five to do who passionately loves a young widow whom he took down to dinner last night?' he asked Ethel Tweedie in a letter. 'God help him – as his peace of mind is shattered.'[3]

Nancy, now a permanent member of the household, took special care of the many animals resident, but particularly of Job the lemur. She recalled that he 'never seemed to care very much for anyone else, and, while he liked others to pet him, he would always leave them to come to me'.[4] Job was a much-loved pet, allowed his own way in many things, but sugar basins were banished from the dining room table after he was seen burying his muzzle into one and licking up the sugar. He died in the autumn of 1904, apparently pining for the Gilberts while they were on holiday in Biarritz. He was replaced by two Madagascan lemurs called Adam and Eve, who in September 1905 gave birth to a baby lemur that Gilbert called Paul – the first ring-tailed lemur ever born and bred in England. Paul proved mischievous and wilful, but was a great favourite; he would sit on Gilbert's shoulders while Gilbert changed for dinner, shifting position when necessary – a feat which greatly amused him.

The house and grounds were filled with animals of all sorts: the monkeys in the monkey house; a fawn that was a great friend of the Grim's Dyke donkey, Adelina; parrots and bullfinches; pigeons, chickens and turkeys (a number of which once invaded Gilbert's library and roosted round the desk and chairs, seemingly in order to examine the manuscript he was working on); dogs and cats (which dined with the family, each having a separate tablecloth on the floor). Gilbert tamed a garden robin one year, until it fed from his hand. In the same year (1910) Nancy eccentrically made a pet of a bee, feeding it with moistened sugar and putting it to bed in a box.[5]

In the 1890s, they cycled; later, they owned motorcars. Gilbert, characteristically, treated with special severity those who came before him in his capacity as a magistrate with motoring offences. In 1899 he had a large artificial lake constructed in the grounds.

L. V. Fildes, the son of the painter Luke Fildes, had a happy memory of visiting Grim's Dyke: 'After dinner one evening we listened to Gilbert, seated on a sofa, his pet lemur balanced on his shoulder, and Nancy McIntosh – who was the adopted daughter of the Gilberts – seated by his side. She with the voice of a Savoyard and he with a one-note croak, sang Sea Shanties together, whilst Mrs. Gilbert smiled approvingly.'[6] It was a Gilbertian ideal of domestic bliss.

One of their friends, Ethel Tweedie, wrote several accounts of the Gilberts' years at Grim's Dyke. '[Gilbert] farms the land himself, and talks of crops and live stock with a glib tongue, although the real enthusiast is his wife, who loves her prize chickens and her roses.'[7] Ethel Tweedie viewed Gilbert with great affection, but she knew his faults. 'Gilbert was a most excellent host,' she wrote after his death, 'and his wife, who happily survives him, a delightful hostess. She is a woman of unruffled temper and extraordinary tact, for with all his good points he must certainly have been a difficult man to live with, and she managed him superbly.'[8] Ethel

Tweedie disliked his touchy temper but understood that some of his other seeming faults, like his apparent arrogance, were born of his taste for straight-faced humour:

> Many people called him conceited, and no doubt he was; but most of the conceit was uttered in a spirit of fun. He would tell you unblushingly that he was the most beautiful person in the world, that his forty-eight inch waist was exactly correct for a man of sixty, that his weight was that of the Apollo (not in marble), that his life had been faultless like a clean and beautiful crystal; and he never ceased to impress upon you the talent and genius of W.S. Gilbert, and the incompetence of everyone else; but it was all done with a grave face and hidden laughter.[9]

As the old century closed and the new one began, there was a sudden and shocking depletion amongst his old colleagues. Sullivan, ill for many years with kidney problems, died of bronchitis and heart failure on 22 November 1900. He was buried with great pomp and state at St Paul's Cathedral on 27 November. Gilbert was out of the country, in Egypt, so he was represented at the ceremony by his sisters Florence and Maude. Richard D'Oyly Carte was another non-attendee, desperately ill at home; he died of dropsy within a matter of months, on 3 April 1901. As for Gilbert, he was crippled with gout and arthritis. For some time he was convinced he would never walk again.

There had been a brief and trivial falling-out with Sullivan in 1899, but it had been patched up by the time of the composer's death. Gilbert remembered Sullivan with nothing but affection, forgetting their disputes.

He did not look back upon their operas which much pride, however: 'it was when I was tired of [writing plays] that I tried my hand at a libretto,' he wrote to Ethel Tweedie on 3 December 1901, 'and I was so successful that I had to go on writing them. If d—d nonsense is wanted, I can write it as well as anybody.'[10] Sometimes, she remembered, he even disparaged his entire body of work for the theatre. 'I have been scribbling twaddle for thirty-five years to suit the public taste,' he said:

> Light flippery and amusing nonsense is what I have endeavoured to write. But I can tell you, that after thirty-five years of that sort of thing, which I am glad to say has brought grist to the mill, I am about sick of it, and I shouldn't mind if I never wrote another word.[11]

On another occasion, probably around the time of *The Era* trial, he said, 'I shall never work any more; I am sixty, my days are numbered, and the few years or months that are left to me I hope to enjoy with the aid of my friends.'[12] So he entertained guests, played croquet in summer, petted fawns and robins, surrounded himself with women and generally did as he wished. In the opening years of the twentieth century the gout and the rheumatism receded when he changed his diet to one of fish, vegetables and fruit, and he became a fit, active man once more. His doctor warned that his heart was weak and that he should not bathe in the lake when the water was too cold. But Gilbert took no notice of this advice.

About this time Gilbert's attitude to Clement Scott thawed. He wrote to his old friend on 1 December 1897 in affable terms, addressing him as 'My dear Scott' and telling him: 'I am very glad indeed to learn that you are still gaining strength.'[13] But in fact Scott's health was deteriorating. Like Gilbert, he was afflicted with gout. In 1902 he suffered an accident from which he never fully recovered. When in 1903 Scott was confined to his bed and his life was despaired of, Gilbert would pass by the Scotts' house, slip a card into the letterbox with a message of inquiry written on it, and steal away before Scott's wife saw him. But one day she met him on the doorstep. She remembered: 'Utterly confused, he turned to go away, but I stopped him, and when I told him of Clement's dangerous condition he was genuinely overcome.'[14] From that moment, Gilbert called almost daily to enquire after Scott and helped as much as he could. He contributed at least one article to Scott's journal *The Free Lance* at this time, his fragment of autobiography 'My Last Client' appearing in the issue dated 10 October 1903.

'When I hear others sneering at Gilbert's heartlessness,' Mrs Scott wrote:

I recall those generous acts of his to Clement Scott. Those journeys that he made so frequently, just to get a stray bit of news of his old comrade, his almost affectionate attitude directly he heard the truth, and I smile to myself, as I've smiled so many times when I've jostled against those queer people who live in such a tiny world of their own, a world that is full of nothing beyond 'I know,' 'I am sure,' 'I am certain'.[15]

Scott died on 25 June 1904, and Gilbert attended the funeral, grief-stricken.

One of Gilbert's longest friendships, with Frank Burnand (now Sir Frank), somehow survived despite the spirit of rivalry that existed between them. For many years Burnand had used his position as editor of *Punch* to denigrate the Gilbert and Sullivan operas. When, in 1884, Burnand had suggested to Gilbert that he write an article for *Punch*, Gilbert replied, 'I am simply lost in astonishment that you who have for so many years, systematically decried my work, should think it deserving of insertion in the columns of your paper'.[16] But even so they continued to see each other socially, and Gilbert greatly admired Burnand's humorous gifts. In 1905 he attended a dress rehearsal of Burnand's Drury Lane pantomime *Cinderella*, and wrote to him afterwards: 'I went in the faint hope that you would have succeeded in reducing the blatant comedians to something like order – but they were clearly too many for you. It's a pity, for such a book as *you* could write ... ought to restore Pantomime to its proper rank as an entertainment.'[17]

Gilbert did not fully retire from writing. In 1899 the American actor Nat Goodwin commissioned him to write a play; but nothing came of it.[18] In 1900 he wrote a short story for *The Graphic* Christmas number, 'The Fairy's Dilemma', which he later turned into a two-act play, performed at the Garrick under the management of Arthur Bourchier. *Harlequin and the Fairy's Dilemma*, as it was advertised for the first night on 5 March 1904 and printed in the programmes (it lost the 'Harlequin' very early in the run), was a good last shot at a 'Gilbertian' comedy, and returned to an idea he had been toying with all his professional life: uniting a consistent modern drama with an old-fashioned pantomime. The involved plot of a modern society drama becomes mixed up with the naive attempts of a good fairy to create a happy ending, resulting in chaos and, finally, the transformation of the cast into the harlequinade characters – a cavalry officer becomes Clown; a judge becomes Pantaloon; a clergyman becomes Harlequin. It was not his best work, and his dialogue was ever more verbose as he grew older, but its sense of mischief was infectious and it was kindly received by audiences and critics. 'Mr. W.S. Gilbert has scored a success with his "original domestic pantomime"', *The Graphic* announced (7 May 1904). 'The *Message from Mars* was commonplace in comparison.' The *Illustrated London News* called it 'a tissue of joyous nonsense' (7 May), and *The Times* told its readers: 'Here was the fantastic Gilbert that we knew at something very near his best … we find *The Fairy's Dilemma* most excellent fooling, and so, we fancy, did the whole house' (4 May). Audiences dwindled, but it lasted ninety performances, almost to the end of the theatrical 'season': a solid though not showy run.

On 19 July it was performed in a charity matinee at the Garrick for Bushey Heath Cottage Hospital (one of the many charities Gilbert supported.) The play was part of a double-bill, the other piece being a special performance of *Rosencrantz and Guildenstern*, with a cast entirely composed of dramatic authors. Gilbert himself was King Claudius (*The Times* stating on 20 July that he played the role 'admirably'), Lady Colin Campbell was the Queen, and Captain Robert Marshall and Sir Francis Burnand were among the other participants.

By now, Gilbert seemed like a relic of a former age, as, of course, he was: Victoria was dead, and her son Edward was king; Elgar was the new hero of English music; pomp and circumstance were in the air; the bumptious self-confidence of empire was at its height. England, shouldering the 'White Man's Burden' round the world, could do no wrong.

The Savoy had seen revivals of some of the old Gilbert and Sullivan operas in the closing years of the Victorian age, ending with *Patience* in 1900 and *Iolanthe* in 1901, but since then the D'Oyly Carte Company had been touring, and by 1906 the operas had not been seen in London for nearly five years. Helen Carte proposed a repertory season at the Savoy of some of the most popular operas, with new casts and Gilbert stage-managing as usual. Unfortunately, she proved less than tactful in dealing with Gilbert. She hired the casts for the operas without consulting him. Not unnaturally, he was furious. It was a shocking departure from the method that had helped to create his reputation. He had always insisted upon absolute control over the productions of his pieces, including the casting, because he felt he was responsible for creating on stage a perfect realisation of the piece he had written. Some of the cast Helen Carte had chosen were, he believed, utterly inadequate. He agreed to rehearse the operas and to make the best of a bad job, but he never forgave her for what he described hyperbolically as 'the deepest – I may say the only – indignity ever offered to me during my 40 years connection with the stage'.[19]

The repertory season opened at the Savoy in December 1906 with *The Yeomen of the Guard*. On 30 December 1906 Gilbert, now 70 years old, was the guest of honour at a 'Savoyard Celebration Dinner' held by the O.P. Club at the Hotel Cecil to mark the new season. Many of the familiar faces, old and new, were there: Jessie Bond, Leonora Braham, Rutland Barrington, George Grossmith, Durward Lely, Richard Temple, Frank Cellier, Nancy McIntosh, Henry Lytton and many others. Gilbert, responding to the toast 'The Savoy Opera' was in reminiscent and sentimental mood:

> during the twenty years that I had the absolute control of the stage-management of the Savoy operas, I never had a seriously angry word with any member of the company, principal or chorus. Death has sadly thinned their ranks – Alfred Cellier, their esteemed conductor; Miss Everard, the original Little Buttercup; George Bentham, the original Alexis in *The Sorcerer*; Alice Barnett, the stately Lady Jane of *Patience*, and the Fairy Queen of *Iolanthe*; poor little Emmie Owen; D'Oyly Carte, our enterprising manager; our three stage managers, Richard Barker, Charles Harris, and William Seymour; and lastly, my old friend and invaluable co-worker, Arthur Sullivan, whose untimely death, in the fullness of his powers, extinguished the class of opera with which his name was so honourably identified – a composer of the rarest genius, and who, because he was a composer of the rarest genius, was as modest and as unassuming as a neophyte should be but seldom is.[20]

He looked back with pride upon their achievement in the creation of English comic opera. He praised the old days and he praised the cast of the new production at the Savoy.[21] He mentioned by name most of the major Savoyards. But he made no allusion to Helen Carte.

21

THE HOOLIGAN (1907–11)

On 15 July 1907, Gilbert went to Buckingham Palace, was tapped with a sword on both shoulders by King Edward VII, and became Sir William Gilbert.

In a sense, the honour was many years overdue. When, in May 1883, it had been announced that Sullivan was to be knighted, *The Penny Illustrated Paper and Illustrated Times* had suggested that 'Mr. W.S. Gilbert should also be knighted now'.[1] Gilbert and his friends agreed, it seems. But for such an honour to be given to such a man was without precedent: no knighthood had ever been conferred for dramatic authorship alone. And Gilbert had never courted the favour of royals or politicians. He did not make it easy for the honour to be bestowed upon him.

However, the king's private secretary had written to him at the beginning of 1907 asking him if he would accept a knighthood were it to be offered, and Gilbert had responded positively. Someone in a position to make such judgements had decided that the time was ripe for Gilbert. 'It is a tin-pot, twopenny-half-penny sort of distinction,' he wrote to Mary Talbot, 'but ... I felt I ought not to refuse it. I suppose it is to be given to me as a sort of impalpable old-age pension in consideration of my being a broken-down old ruin'.[2]

He received many messages of congratulation from his friends and admirers. He wrote back to one of them: 'The good will evinced by old friends is, to my thinking, the pleasantest feature of the transaction.'[3] He made no great effort to show that he was pleased by the honour itself. Indeed, he seemed determined to be as ungracious about it as possible. 'In the recent "Honour Lists",' he told Bram Stoker in an interview published by the *Daily Chronicle* on 2 January 1908:

I found myself politely described by some Court flunkey as 'Mr. Gilbert, playwright.' ... The term 'wright' is properly applied to one who follows a mechanical calling, such as a wheelwright, a millwright, a cartwright or a shipwright. We never hear of novel-wrights, or poem-wrights, or essay-wrights; why, then, of play-wrights? There is a convenient word, 'dramatist'.

It was a complaint he had already rehearsed in letters to his friends. He seemed uncomfortable with being presented with a reward for his achievement and almost happy to be able to pick holes in it.

Elsewhere in the interview he was more generous in his attitudes, even suggesting that the new generation of dramatists was not as bad as he sometimes grumbled. When Stoker asked him what the tendency of the modern stage was, he replied: 'Forward! Distinctly forward.'

He had been brought forcibly up against the rising generation's views of drama the previous year when the young journalist Edith A. Browne wrote his biography. She interviewed him a couple of times and sent the proofs to him to check over. Gilbert was furious to read her opinion of his non-musical plays and on 10 March 1907 wrote back:

> You are good enough to chastise me, *ex cathedra*, as though you were an acknowledged and indisputable authority on the subject of dramatic composition and I an inexperienced neophyte … I say nothing about the lukewarm opinion you seem to entertain as to the literary quality of these plays (especially those in verse) except to express a wonder that the author of such a series of banalities should have been thought to deserve a biographer. I can hardly believe that I owe the compliment to the easy trivialities of the Savoy *libretti*.[4]

She replied in terms that soothed Gilbert wonderfully, and when he wrote to her again on 21 March he was in a mood of good humour and contrition:

> Your very kind letter heaps coals of fire on my head … Rightly or wrongly, in the pre-Savoy days I held the foremost position among dramatic authors (there were not many of them then) and it hurt me not a little to find that work which was so well esteemed when it was produced, appealed so feebly to so keen an intelligence as your own.[5]

Even in the published version of the book, Edith Browne was far from complimentary about the bulk of his work, saying of his farcical comedies that 'when reading these plays I hear the crackling of thorns under a pot', and of his beloved blank-verse plays that 'the sum total of his efforts is a splendid failure'.[6] She knew, like most of her contemporaries, that Gilbert's achievement did indeed lie in the easy trivialities that he so despised; but he found it a shocking and unwelcome fact to find in what was intended as a sympathetic account of his life.

Nancy was not at Grim's Dyke for Christmas 1907: her aunt had died and she went out to the United States in November to see her uncle. Gilbert feared she would not come back, and wrote to her on 3 January 1908: 'My wife sends her best love & all wishes for a happy new year *which we hope & trust you will spend with us*, but we seem to see difficulties ahead. I only hope you are not going to chuck us after so many years.'[7] But she returned at the end of January, and all was well.

The revivals at the Savoy continued, and they continued to be cast without reference to Gilbert. He continued to be dissatisfied, but there was nothing to be done.

In the meantime, he was also working in another direction. For some years he had nursed the idea of turning his old fairy comedy, *The Wicked World*, into an opera. He had previously tried to interest Sullivan in the idea, and several other composers, but they declined it one and all, put off perhaps by the fact that the chorus had to be all-female and perhaps also by Gilbert's double-edged reputation. It was only at the end of 1908, when Gilbert wrote to Edward German with the idea and German approved, that the project finally began to take shape. He set to work on the libretto in January 1909 and had completed a draft by the end of February.

They had some difficulty securing financial backing. Gilbert had approached Helen Carte, but he had been insulting the character of her revivals of the operas again, and she was not disposed to interest herself in the new piece. C.H. Workman, who had been playing the patter roles in the revivals and had earned Gilbert's approval, formed a syndicate to take a lease on the Savoy and produce several pieces, including the new opera.

Gilbert recommended Nancy McIntosh for the central role of the Fairy Queen Selene. There was a dispute with Workman over this, who had become committed to engaging another soprano, Elsie Spain, in the leading role of his first three productions at the Savoy; but Gilbert was inflexible, and eventually Workman agreed to accept Nancy. Gilbert and German worked well together. The music was completed and rehearsals commenced. Gilbert argued with Joseph Harker, the set designer, over the set as it had been constructed. These preliminaries over, the opera was ready for performance.

The first night of *Fallen Fairies; or, The Wicked World* took place on 15 December 1909. *The Graphic* recorded that the audience greeted the opera with 'enormous enthusiasm, not to say hysteria' (25 December), but added that the new lyrics were better than the old dialogue. The enthusiasm seems to have been of the nostalgic sort, whipped up by the mere fact of seeing a new Gilbert opera at the Savoy rather than by the piece's actual quality. The authors were cheered at the curtain, and Gilbert happily told the audience, 'There is life in the old dog yet'; but *Fallen Fairies* was not a lasting hit with the public. It was too old-fashioned; it did not engage people's fancy. Nancy McIntosh's voice was not strong enough for her part and she was replaced in the role by Amy Evans at the beginning of January 1910. A song which had been previously cut was restored without Gilbert's consent, and he even attempted to apply for an injunction preventing its being sung. But it was scarcely worth the effort; the opera closed at the end of January after just fifty performances.

If *Fallen Fairies* had been Gilbert's last work for the theatre, it would be universally agreed that he had written himself out. *The Fortune Hunter* had been a drama of a very old-fashioned type, *The Fairy's Dilemma* had harked back to the pantomimes of his youth, and now *Fallen Fairies* was merely a warmed up version of his 36-year-old museum piece *The Wicked World*. But as it happened his creative juices were not quite dry yet; it only took special circumstances to get them to flow.

The playwright Sydney Blow was convinced that new theatre-going audiences could be created if writers of the highest class could be persuaded to write short plays for the music halls. He suggested the idea to Oswald Stoll of the Coliseum music hall, and Stoll encouraged him. Stoll suggested that Blow might try to get Bernard Shaw to write a play less than thirty minutes long for the Coliseum. Blow went to see Shaw and got nothing but a blast of rhetoric for his trouble: 'My dear Blow, it is impossible. It's like going to a tailor and ordering from him only a waistcoat.'[8] Gilbert was next on his list. Blow went to see him at Grim's Dyke, catching him just as he was about to attend a session at the magistrates' court. Gilbert said he would think it over and asked whether Jimmy Welch would be available if he had something for him. Blow had caught his interest. Gilbert had previously seen Welch performing in a comedy, and his immediate thought had been, 'There is the man to play tragedy'.[9]

All this took place towards the end of 1910. By January 1911 Gilbert had his idea: a convict in the condemned cell, awaiting his execution. He went to Pentonville Prison, looked over the condemned cell, and was told of the routine. The set painter also paid a visit and afterwards described the cell to Welch, mentioning that the only adornment was a picture of the Crucifixion. 'I see,' Welch said. 'They show the poor wretch how they used to do it.'[10]

Rehearsals began. All was going well until Welch, not realising Gilbert was in the house, began improvising round the script. Gilbert immediately stormed out and wrote a letter to Welch: 'It is not my practice to let actors gag in my plays … It is my practice, if an agreement is not adhered to, to stop the production of the play.' It was a tough moment, but Welch found exactly the right response. He wrote a rather cheekily worded letter of apology to Gilbert: 'I know, Sir William, that you are a great dramatist, a great producer of plays, and also a Justice of the Peace, but now I have received your letter I see that you are evidently a lawyer as well.'[11] Gilbert read the letter, laughed, and forgave him.

The Hooligan is an extraordinary little play. About fifteen minutes in length, its plot is simple: Nat Solly, a young man condemned to death for killing his girlfriend, is terror-stricken at the prospect of his execution on this, his last morning. He pleads, he makes excuses and he insists that he does not deserve the punishment. He describes a hallucinatory dream he has had of a courtroom and a judge who reaches out to strangle him. His excuses become more desperate and acquire a tinge of ironic self-revelation: 'I never cut a gal before – not in the 'ole course of my bloomin' life I didn't … and my 'and slipped on account of youth and inexperience. Now I arst you fair, is a bloke to be 'ung becos 'e never cut a gal afore?'[12] The Governor enters as his terrors are at their height and announces that his sentence has been commuted to penal servitude for life. Nat Solly is seized with a heart attack and dies.

Performed on 27 February 1911 at the Coliseum as part of a long bill of music hall variety, it held the audience breathless. Welch's performance was magnificent and harrowing. He took one curtain call after another, the audience shouting and applauding. The *Illustrated London News* (March 11) was shocked and impressed: '[The play] is absolutely sincere, unflinchingly realistic, and makes no concessions in the way of fine writing or sentiment … If playgoers are not moved by the almost bald simplicity of the episode and by the superb acting of Mr. James Welch as the criminal, then nothing will move them.' *The Observer* (5 March) gave the play the kind of bad review that any dramatist would be delighted to receive:

> Those who are in search of a 'mauvais quart d'heure' had better hie forthwith to the Coliseum, where, with 'The Hooligan' in his condemned cell, they may be assured of finding what they want … How far such a subject as this is suited for illustration on the stage may be open to doubt. But there can be no question about the relentless art with which Sir William has elaborated his gruesome study of character, or about the remorseless sincerity with which Mr. Welch has made the grim picture a living one in its terrible fidelity to human nature. If the thing was to be done at all it could not have been done better, and there criticism must leave it.

The Penny Illustrated Paper expressed unqualified admiration (11 March):

> It disturbed everyone. Most to applause; a few to resentment … A play that can wing a ruddy, ample gentleman [in the audience]; leave him puzzled, gasping, unsettled; stir up vague doubtings about killing folk and giving them 'no chanst' – a play like that is a play which you ought to pop in and see at once.

It grappled with the times in a way that no work of Gilbert's had done for a very long while, and audiences responded with a new emotional immediacy.

Winter became spring. The Gilberts, who had as usual taken a house in London for the winter months, returned to Grim's Dyke in April. The trees blossomed. Gilbert swam in the lake almost daily.

Monday 29 May 1911 was Oak Apple Day, a celebration of the restoration of the monarchy in 1660. In the morning Gilbert visited the Royal Hospital at Chelsea, where his old friend Sir Charles Crutchley was lieutenant-governor, to see the annual parade and inspection. He refused Lady Crutchley's offer of lunch, because he had to hurry back to Grim's Dyke: he had an appointment to bathe in the lake with two girls.

He took luncheon at the Junior Carlton Club, and there bumped into his old friend and enemy, William Kendal. Gilbert came to his table and they lunched together, burying their old differences and chatting of old times.

His last appointment in London that day was to see May Fortescue, who was confined to a darkened room after a riding accident. Her mother said apologetically to him afterwards, 'I won't ask what you think of her appearance, for you can scarcely see her'. Gilbert replied, 'Her appearance matters nothing. It is her disappearance we could not stand.'[13]

He returned on the 3.20 Great Central train, arriving at Harrow-on-the-Hill at 3.38, and at the station he met up with the two young women he had promised to teach to swim in his lake. These were Winifred Emery, known as Isabel, who was a drama teacher, and Ruby Preece, a young pupil of hers. Gilbert gave them a lift up to Grim's Dyke in his motorcar.

On arrival, they immediately went down to the lake. The two women entered the water first, while Gilbert changed into his blue-and-white-striped bathing costume. Ruby Preece, who was the better swimmer of the two, swam further out. It was deeper than she thought, and, finding she was unable to touch the bottom, she panicked. She cried out that she was drowning. Gilbert, now changed into his bathing costume, called out to her that she was not to be frightened and that he was coming. He dived into the lake and swam out to Ruby Preece. 'It is not very deep,' he said. 'Don't splash, you'll be all right.' He told her to put her hands on his shoulders. As soon as she did so, he sank. Ruby Preece sank as well, but when she came up again she felt the mud under her and struggled to shore. Gilbert, however, did not surface. The two women cried out for help and two gardeners came running up. They rowed out into the lake, found Gilbert's body and brought it to the bank. Lucy was alerted and doctors called. The body was laid on a rug, pillows put under the shoulders and hot water bottles were applied. Two doctors arrived, including Gilbert's usual medical attendant, Dr Shackleton. The other, Dr Wilson, attempted artificial respiration, but there was no sign of life. The exertion of the moment had been too much for Gilbert. He had died of a heart attack.

The next day's papers were full of the news. There was shock and there was sorrow, and there were long reflections on his productive life. *The Times* obituary (30 May), which had been compiled with the aid of an interview with Gilbert himself, paid due attention to his earlier works as well as the operas for which he was by then mainly known:

> The satire in these [earlier] plays bites sharper than that of the Savoy operas; the author was younger and less inclined to be merciful … With regard to the literary quality of his work, he may be compared to his own Strephon; he was a fairy down to the waist, but his legs were mortal – and too often he wrote his

prose with his legs ... He was the first of his day to restore [to comic drama] its literary self-respect.

A leader in the same issue suggested (employing a metaphor that was very badly chosen in the circumstances) that 'if originality, humour, and wide outlook, and the gift of happy expression count for anything, the name of W.S. GILBERT ought long to remain, unsubmerged by the waters of oblivion'.

An inquest was held on 31 May in the billiard room at Grim's Dyke. Ruby Preece was greatly upset, and the foreman of the jury asked if her name could not be suppressed, but the coroner said, 'I cannot interfere with the Press at all'.[14] The coroner told the jury that it was 'quite clear that Sir William died in endeavouring to save a young lady in distress. It was a very honourable end to a great and distinguished career.'[15]

Lucy was inundated with letters of condolence from all quarters, friends, old colleagues, strangers. Even in death Gilbert caused dispute. He had expressed a wish to be buried in the churchyard of St John the Evangelist in Stanmore. However, the rector, the Rev. S.F.L. Bernays, objected that Gilbert did not belong to the parish and that the parishioners would not like their churchyard to be taken up with strangers. Bernays suggested a solution: if Gilbert were cremated, he would not take up so much valuable space and accommodation might be found for him. Lucy agreed to this. The funeral took place on 2 June, attended by Rutland Barrington, Richard Temple, Jessie Bond, Lady Tree, Sir John Hare, Sir Arthur Pinero, Rupert D'Oyly Carte, Arthur Bourchier, the Bancrofts and many others.

Ruby Preece left the neighbourhood, seeking to escape the publicity associated with Gilbert's death. She changed her name to Patricia, and in later years became the muse and wife of the artist Stanley Spencer.[16]

Gilbert left over £110,000 in his will, most of which went to Lucy: his money, his stocks and shares, his copyrights, Grim's Dyke, and the Garrick Theatre. There were, of course, numerous other bequests to family, friends and employees. Lucy lived twenty-five more years at Grim's Dyke, protecting her husband's reputation quietly and with dignity. Nancy McIntosh continued to live with her. No one bathed in the lake ever again.

22

VERDICTS

Ethel Tweedie

Gilbert was the most brilliant companion I ever met. He could be dull: who cannot? But when in good vein, happy, contented and well, his conversation was as sparkling as, and even more spontaneous, than his books. It was impossible to catch the glint of his thoughts on paper; they rattled from one subject to another. But one's remembrance of him is that of a genial friend – friendship personified – a brilliant conversationalist, and a delightful English gentleman.[1]

Seymour Hicks (1910)

I had been brought up to believe that he was a very terrible person, who snapped off your nose with an epigram if you ventured an opinion, and who wanted no better pretext for a quarrel than if you asked him to pass the salt politely. Greater nonsense as to the difficulty of getting on with Mr. Gilbert has never been thought of. I have had the great pleasure of knowing him for many years, and a kinder host or more helpful and encouraging gentleman never stepped in shoe leather.[2]

Seymour Hicks (1930)

He always gave me the impression that he got up in the morning to see with whom he could have a quarrel.[3]

Sullivan (1880)

The libretto [for *The Pirates of Penzance*] is ingenious, clever, wonderfully funny in parts, and sometimes brilliant in dialogue – beautifully written for music, as is all Gilbert does, and all the action and business perfect.[4]

Sullivan (1885)
Speaking of Gilbert's work, have you noticed what an extraordinary polish there is to his versification? There is never a weak syllable or a halting foot. It is marvellous.[5]

Sullivan (1890)
How I have stood him so long!! I can't understand.[6]

Gilbert (on being asked why he never witnessed a performance of his own works)
I know what rubbish these comic operas are, and I should feel ashamed to sit and hear them and know they were mine.[7]

Obituary in The Times
It has been well said that for lyrical facility he can only be compared with Shelley. He was absolutely at home in song-writing, and only then. It is as well to claim for him definitely and at once the title of poet ... If his poetry is nearly all humorous, it is none the less exquisitely musical, easy, and perfect in form ... he not only did in his patter-songs what no one had done since Aristophanes and his *parodoi*, but he attained to a classical perfection of form that few English poets have ever equalled.[8]

Richard D'Oyly Carte to Sullivan (1882)
We often hear people say and I have heard you say that it is difficult to get on with Gilbert and it really is. He takes views of things so totally unlike what any one else would ... If a discussion arises he will look at matters solely from his point of view, he will not see them from any other, will be very disagreeable about it ... And at other times you know how nice and agreeable he can be. Well – I suppose his exceptional ways are part of his exceptional genius and that he could not write as he does if he were different.[9]

The Era (1897)
Mr GILBERT's abnormal self-esteem has, with advancing years, developed into a malady. In his own estimation, he is a kind of Grand Lama or Sacred Elephant of dramatic literature.[10]

Gilbert to Maud Tree (1893)
I don't think I am a vain man or I shouldn't have so poor an opinion of what I do.[11]

Seymour Hicks (1910)
He knows every turn and twist of the stage and more about its technique than 95 per cent. of all the actors alive to-day put together.[12]

Gilbert (on a signed photograph)
To Seymour Hicks, from W.S. Gilbert, born 1836; died —; deeply regretted by all who didn't know him.[13]

Gilbert's niece, Mary Carter (1956)
When I was a little girl Uncle Schwenck … always sent us a box for the Drury Lane pantomime. Another treat was the wonderful children's party he and his wife gave annually at their lovely house in Harrington Gardens … As I let my mind wander among these memories I wonder if the W.S. Gilbert as portrayed in film and on radio as a brusque, unlikeable autocrat can have anything in common with the kindest and most human of uncles.[14]

Mary Anderson
He was a very kind-hearted man, but he did not want anybody to know it. For the most part, he was very kind in our dealings at the theatre, but he took offence very easily, and the result was that he used his great wit like a two-edged sword – often with sharp words. I am sure he was always sorry if he had hurt one. I could not help liking Gilbert, even though one was uncertain of him.[15]

On the W.S. Gilbert Memorial, Thames Embankment (unveiled 1915)
His foe was folly & his weapon wit.

NOTES

Abbreviations:
PML   Pierpont Morgan Library
BL   British Library
OP1–4 W.S. Gilbert, *Original Plays*, Series 1–4. The editions used are described in the Bibliography.

Prologue: 1891

1 Harry How, 'Illustrated Interviews, no. IV: Mr W.S. Gilbert', *The Strand Magazine*, Vol. 2 (October 1891), p. 339.

2 Letter to Edith Browne, dated 10 March 1907, quoted in Hesketh Pearson, *Gilbert: His Life and Strife* (London: Methuen & Co. Ltd), p. 247.

3 'Interview with Mr W.S. Gilbert', *Edinburgh Evening Dispatch* (5 October 1897), p. 2.

4 How, 'Mr W.S. Gilbert', pp. 337–8.

5 Ibid., p. 337.

6 Ibid.

7 Ibid., p. 340.

8 Ibid., pp. 332–3.

1 The Gilbert Family (1836–53)

1 David Eden, *W.S. Gilbert: Appearance and Reality: Essays in Clarification* (Saffron Walden: Sir Arthur Sullivan Society, 2003), p. 3.

2 Many of the standard 'facts' of William Gilbert's early life are unreliable. One major source of information used by the author of the entry on

William Gilbert in the old *Dictionary of National Biography* was William Gilbert's novel *The Memoirs of a Cynic*, which was, of course, never intended as anything other than fiction. David Eden, who has done an astonishing job in attempting to tease out fact from fiction concerning William Gilbert's life, comes closer to finding the truth than any predecessor. For instance, an examination of the records of the East India Company shows that William Gilbert was never employed by them, despite previous claims to the contrary. See Eden, *Gilbert: Appearance and Reality*, pp. 8, 22, footnote 41.

3 Eden, *Gilbert: Appearance and Reality*, pp. 7–8.

4 For details, see ibid., pp. 8–9.

5 Ibid., p. 11.

6 Edith A. Browne, *W.S. Gilbert* (London: John Lane, The Bodley Head, 1907), p. 10.

7 See David Eden, *A Tale of Two Kidnaps* (Sir Arthur Sullivan Society, 1988); also Dr Leon E.A. Berman, 'The Kidnapping of W.S. Gilbert', *Journal of the American Psychoanalytic Association* (May 1985), pp. 133–48.

8 For the 1841 census, see Eden, *Gilbert: Appearance and Reality*, p. 45; for the codicil witnesses, see Eden, *A Tale of Two Kidnaps*, p. 5.

9 'Little Mim', W.S. Gilbert, *Foggerty's Fairy and other Tales* (London: George Routledge and Sons, 1890), p. 120. 'Little Mim' first appeared in *The Graphic Christmas Number*, 1876.

10 Gilbert, *The Story of The Mikado* (London: Daniel O'Connor, 1921), p. 14. This book, published posthumously, was written in 1908.

11 W.S. Gilbert, 'Men We Meet, by the Comic Physiognomist: The C.P. In Love', *Fun* (2 March 1867), p. 256.

12 Most of the information about this episode is taken from Eden, *A Tale of Two Kidnaps*.

13 Letter to John Samuel Schwenck, dated 10 January 1845, quoted in Eden, *A Tale of Two Kidnaps*, p. 10.

14 Eden, *Gilbert: Appearance and Reality*, p. 49.

15 *Morning Post* (20 January 1843); *Sunday Times* (22 January 1843): both quoted in Eden, *Gilbert: Appearance and Reality*, p. 49.

16 Browne, *W.S. Gilbert*, p. 9. This passage is written as if by Browne, but it is so like Gilbert that one can only assume it was written by him or taken down directly from his words in interview.

17 W.S. Gilbert, 'Getting Up a Pantomime', *London Society* (January 1868), pp. 50–1.

18 Sir Francis C. Burnand, *Records and Reminiscences, Personal and General*, (London: Methuen, 1904), Vol. 1, pp. 98–9.

19 Gilbert, 'Getting Up a Pantomime', p. 51.

20 Catherine Gilbert testified, in an affidavit made between November 1845 and March 1846, that 'Wm Gilbert has for nearly three years past resided in the Kingdom of France', as quoted in Eden, *A Tale of Two Kidnaps*, p. 13. The date of the affidavit can be deduced from information on p. 19 of the same pamphlet. Therefore she dated William Gilbert's move to France to the beginning of 1843.

21 Quoted in Eden, *A Tale of Two Kidnaps*, p. 8.

22 Gilbert, 'An Autobiography', *The Theatre*, 2 April 1883, p. 221.

23 Quoted in Eden, *A Tale of Two Kidnaps*, p. 11.

24 Browne, *W.S. Gilbert*, p. 11.

25 W.S. Gilbert, 'Foreword' to *Rutland Barrington by Himself* (London: Grant Richards, 1908), p. 8.

26 Browne, *W.S. Gilbert*, pp. 10–1.

27 *Scribner's Magazine*, Vol. 18 (September 1879), p. 752.

28 Sidney Dark & Rowland Grey, *W.S. Gilbert: His Life and Letters* (London: Methuen & Co. Ltd, 1923), p. 5.

29 Browne, *W.S. Gilbert*, p. 12.

30 'Men We Meet', *Fun* (9 February 1867), p. 226.

31 'Men We Meet', *Fun* (2 February 1867), p. 216.

32 'Men We Meet', *Fun* (9 February 1867), pp. 226–7.

33 'Men We Meet', *Fun* (2 February 1867), p. 216.

34 Ibid., p. 217.

35 Ibid., pp. 216–7.

36 Ibid., p. 216.

37 See Michael Ainger, *Gilbert and Sullivan: A Dual Biography* (Oxford: Oxford University Press, 2002), p. 21.

38 Leslie Baily, *The Gilbert & Sullivan Book* (London: Cassell & Company Ltd, 1952), pp. 12–3. I have ignored the rather eccentric indentation which Baily created for the poem.

2 Drifting (1853–61)

1 *The Calendar of King's College, London for 1855–56* (London: King's College, 1855), p. 17.

2 King's College Archives, Department of General Literature and Science Attendance List, KA/SRB/1.

3 'The Physiognomist Among the Scum', *Fun* (15 October 1864), p. 41.

4 'The C.P. in Love', *Fun* (3 March 1867), p. 256.

5 Ibid.

6 This portrait is reproduced in black and white in Leslie Baily, *The Gilbert and Sullivan Book*, p. 12. I have been unable to find where the original is held.

7 'The C.P. in Love', *Fun* (3 March 1867), p. 256.

8 Browne, *W.S. Gilbert*, p. 17.

9 King's College Archives, King's College Engineering Society Minute Book, KSE/M2.

10 King's College Archives, King's College Engineering Society list of books loaned out, KSE/SB10. The list gives the date but not the year in which Gilbert took the book out, but it can only have been 1854.

11 King's College Archives, King's College Engineering Society Minute Book, KSE/M2.

12 King's College Archives, Department of General Literature and Science: Register of Attendance, KA/RAT/GS, and Attendance List, KA/SRB/1.

13 King's College Archives, Department of General Literature and Science, Register of Attendance, KA/RAT/GS.

14 King's College Archives, King's College Engineering Society Minute Book, KSE/M2. W.O. Skeat, in his *King's College London Engineering Society 1847–1957* (privately printed for the King's College London Engineers Association, 1957), says this meeting took place on 31 October 1854, but the actual date was 31 October 1855. The minutes of the King's College Shakespearian and Dramatic Reading Society do not survive.

15 Gilbert, 'Autobiography', p. 217.

16 'What I Wanted to Be: Some Boyish Aspirations of Famous Men', *The Captain*, Vol. 1 No 1 (April 1899), p. 30. I am grateful to Arthur Robinson for drawing my attention to this piece.

17 This account of Gilbert's attempts to become a commissioned officer is my best guess at what happened, bearing in mind that many of the details given by Gilbert himself are simply impossible. For instance, in his 1883 'Autobiography' he speaks of the Crimean War as coming to an end in the autumn of 1856, whereas in fact the peace treaty had been signed in March 1856 and the war had effectively ended with the fall of Sebastopol in September 1855. I am grateful to David Eden and Michael Ainger for their attempts to make sense of this episode, details of which I have used in this account.

18 *The Times* (12 October 1855), p. 6.

19 *The Captain*, Vol. 1 No 1 (April 1899), p. 30.

20 I am indebted to Vincent Daniels and David Jacobs for this information. The original record is held in the archives of the British Museum.

21 National Archives, Office of the Committee of Council on Education Pay Ledger, ED 270/1.

22 Gilbert, 'Autobiography', p. 217.

23 National Archives, Office of the Committee of Council on Education Pay Ledger, ED 270/1.

24 W.S. Gilbert, 'The Key of the Strong Room', in Tom Hood (ed.), *A Bunch of Keys* (London: Groombridge & Sons, 1965), pp. 109–10.

25 'The Comic Physiognomist in a Government Office', *Fun* (6 February 1864), p. 205.

26 Ibid.

27 Reproduced in Hesketh Pearson, *W.S. Gilbert: His Life and Strife*, facing p. 64.

28 *The Times* (23 January 1860), p. 10.

29 Eden, *Gilbert: Appearance and Reality*, p. 89.

30 *The Times* (19 January 1860), p. 11.

31 Ibid.

32 Ibid.

33 *The Times* (7 February 1860), p. 11.

34 Ainger, *A Dual Biography*, p. 45, from Edward Merrick, *A History of the Civil Service Rifle Volunteers* (London: Sheppard and St John, 1891), p. 25.

35 Gilbert, 'Autobiography', p. 217.

36 See Eden, *Gilbert: Appearance and Reality*, p. 90.

37 William Archer, *Real Conversations* (London: William Heinemann, 1904), pp. 122–3.

38 Jane W. Stedman, *W.S. Gilbert: A Classic Victorian and his Theatre* (Oxford: Oxford University Press, 1996), p. 31; the letter is held by the Harry Ransom Humanities Research Center, University of Texas, Austin.

39 Browne, *W.S. Gilbert*, p. 18.

3 Bohemian Nights (1861–64)

1 F.C. Burnand, *Records and Reminiscences*, Vol. 1, p. 405.

2 Byron asked Blanchard to contribute to the first issue, and on 11 October 1861 Blanchard attended *Fun*'s inauguration dinner, along with Maclean and his son, Burnand, Brough, Byron, Ince (an artist) and Urquhart (commercial director). See Clement Scott & Cecil Howard, *The Life and Reminiscences of E.L. Blanchard* (London: Hutchinson, 1891), Vol. 1, pp. 260 & 262.

3 Gilbert, 'Autobiography', p. 218.

4 Clement Scott, *The Drama of Yesterday and To-Day* (London: Macmillan & Co. Ltd, 1899), Vol. 2, p. 254.

5 See, for instance, a letter from Tom Hood to the Dalziel brothers (engravers) requesting a meeting to discuss some of his illustrations because 'as I am not a professional artist, but an amateur, I fancy I may give you more trouble to understand me at times'. Quoted in George & Edward Dalziel, *The Brothers Dalziel: A Record of Work, 1840–1890* (London: Batsford Ltd, 1978), pp. 276–8.

6 Browne, *W.S. Gilbert*, p. 20.

7 National Archives, Office of the Committee of Council on Education Pay Ledger, ED 270/1.

8   Ibid.

9   Gilbert, 'Autobiography', p. 217.

10 See Richard L. Abel, *The Legal Profession in England and Wales* (Oxford: Basil Blackwell, 1988), p. 41.

11 See the *Dictionary of National Biography's* original entry on Gilbert, first published in 1912. In previous Gilbert biographies, Williams' name is erroneously given as Sir Watkin Wilkins. Williams became a QC in 1873, was a Liberal MP between 1868 and 1880, became a judge in 1880, was knighted in 1884, and died in the same year in what the new DNB intriguingly calls 'disreputable circumstances'.

12 Clement Scott, *The Wheel of Life* (London: Lawrence Greening & Co., 1898), p. 104.

13 Scott, *The Drama of Yesterday and To-Day*, Vol. 1, p. 482.

14 Ibid., Vol. 2, pp. 251–2.

15 John Coleman, *Players and Playwrights I Have Known: A Review of the English stage from 1840 to 1880*, Vol. 2 (Philadelphia: Gebbie & Co., 1890), pp. 153–5.

16 See Charles E. Lauterbach, 'Taking Gilbert's Measure', in John Bush Jones (ed.), *W.S. Gilbert: A Century of Scholarship and Commentary* (New York: New York University Press, 1970), p. 210.

17 'A Digression', *Fun* (30 January 1864), p. 202.

18 Ibid.

19 'The Physiognomist Among the Players', *Fun* (13 February 1864), p. 215.

20 '… the absurd verses [of "The Lie of a Lifetime"] were not written by me': letter from Gilbert to E. Bruce Hindle (29 January 1885), quoted in James Ellis (ed.), W.S. Gilbert, *The Bab Ballads*, (Cambridge, Mass.: Belknap Press of Harvard University Press, 1980), p. 7.

4 The Road to Recognition (1865–66)

1   The list of Gilbert's contributions to *Punch*, taken from the *Punch* ledgers, is published in John Bush Jones, '"Bab" and *Punch*: Gilbert Contributions Identified', in James Helyar (ed.) *Gilbert and Sullivan: Papers Presented at the International Conference held at the University of Kansas in May 1970* (University of Kansas Libraries, 1971), pp. 85–90.

2   George and Edward Dalziel, *The Brothers Dalziel: A Record of Work*, p. 272.

3   Gilbert's contributions, as identified from the proprietor's copy of *Fun*, are listed in John Bush Jones, 'W.S. Gilbert's Contributions to *Fun*, 1865–1874', *Bulletin of the New York Public Library* 73 (April 1969), pp. 253–66.

4   Gilbert, 'Autobiography', p. 219.

5 Terence Crolley, 'W.S. Gilbert: A Newly Discovered Letter', *W.S. Gilbert Society Journal*, Vol. 2, Issue 17 (Summer 2005), pp. 526–8.

6 'Our Library Table', *Fun* (30 December 1865), p. 158.

7 Quoted in Spielmann, *The History of 'Punch'*, p. 528.

8 From a speech delivered by W.S. Gilbert on 2 February 1908, quoted in the *Daily Telegraph* (3 February 1908), p. 12.

9 Ibid.

10 W.S. Gilbert, Preface to *Fifty 'Bab' Ballads* (London: George Routledge & Sons, 1878), p. vii.

11 This is the wording in Gilbert's original poem, as published in *Fun*. He altered some of the phrases in later republications.

12 Squire Bancroft & Marie Bancroft, *Mr. And Mrs. Bancroft On and Off the Stage* (London: Richard Bentley & Son, 1888), Vol. 1, pp. 207–8.

13 Ibid., pp. 208–9.

14 William Tinsley, *Random Recollections of an Old Publisher* (London: Simpkin, Marshall, Hamilton, Kent & Co. Ltd, 1890), Vol. 2, p. 248.

15 Ibid., pp. 249–50.

16 Annie Thomas, *Played Out* (London: Chapman & Hall, 1866), Vol. 1, pp. 3–4.

17 Ibid., pp. 14–5.

18 Ibid., pp. 10–1.

19 Ibid., pp. 157–9.

20 Ibid., p. 64.

21 Ibid., p. 190.

22 Ibid., pp. 30–1.

23 Ibid., Vol. 3, pp. 298–9.

24 This sketch, which is held in PML, is reproduced in Stedman, *W.S. Gilbert*, p. 46.

25 Gilbert, 'Autobiography', p. 219.

26 See Laurence Irving, *Henry Irving: The Actor and his World* (New York: Macmillan, 1952), p. 132.

27 W.S. Gilbert, *New and Original Extravaganzas*, ed. Isaac Goldberg (Boston: John W. Luce & Co., 1931), p. 17.

5 Enfant Terrible

1 Horace G. Hutchinson, *Portraits of the Eighties* (London: T. Fisher Unwin, 1920), pp. 256–7.

2 P.G. Wodehouse, *Over Seventy: An Autobiography with Digressions* (London: Herbert Jenkins, 1957), p. 57.

3 Seymour Hicks, *Between Ourselves* (London: Cassell, 1930), p. 49.

4   Hutchinson, *Portraits of the Eighties*, p. 259.
5   'Men We Meet: Concerning Some Bald People', *Fun* (9 March 1867), p. 261.
6   Quoted in Percy M.Young, *George Grove* (London: Macmillan, 1980), p. 228.
7   Hutchinson, *Portraits of the Eighties*, p. 260.
8   Ibid., p. 260.
9   Tinsley, *Random Recollections of an Old Publisher*,Vol. 2, p. 314.
10 Dark & Grey, *W.S. Gilbert: His Life and Letters*, p. 3.
11 'The C.P. in Love', *Fun* (3 March 1867), p. 256.
12 Annie Thomas, *Played Out*,Vol. 1, p. 207.

6 Marriage (1867)

1   See Harley Granville-Barker, 'Exit Planché – Enter Gilbert', in John
    Drinkwater (ed.), *The Eighteen-Sixties: Essays by fellows of the Royal Society
    of Literature* (Cambridge: Cambridge University Press, 1932), p. 105.
2   The letter is quoted in full in Eden, *Gilbert: Appearance and Reality*, p. 98.
    The original is held in PML.
3   'Britons at Boulogne', *London Society* (November 1868), pp. 476–7.
4   See Stedman, *W.S. Gilbert*, p. 51. A footnote alludes to conversations
    between Stedman and people who knew Lucy Gilbert in later life: 'they
    all found Lady Gilbert dominating.'
5   W.S. Gilbert, *OP2*, p. 58.
6   Dark & Grey, *Gilbert*, p. 26. Gilbert erroneously identified the ballad as
    'Prince Il Baleine', which he wrote two years later in 1869.

7 Bab, Ballads and Burlesques (1867–69)

1   Harry How, 'Mr W.S. Gilbert', *Strand*,Vol. 2 (October 1891), p. 339.
2   Browne, *W.S. Gilbert*, pp. 35–6.
3   By 1876, Gilbert had earned £2,200 from his play *The Palace of Truth*: see
    Stedman, *W.S. Gilbert*, p. 84.
4   W.S. Gilbert, 'My Pantomime', *The Era Almanack 1884* (London), p. 77.
5   Ibid., pp. 77–8.
6   Ibid., p. 78.
7   Ibid., pp. 78–9.
8   W.S. Gilbert, 'A Stage Play', *Tom Hood's Comic Annual for 1873* (London:
    The Fun Office), p. 102.
9   William Archer, *Real Conversations* (London: William Heinemann, 1904), p. 114.
10 W.S. Gilbert, 'The Triumph of Vice', *The Savage-Club Papers* (London:
    Tinsley Brothers, 1867), p. 195.

11 'The Frozen Deep', *Fun* (17 November 1866), p. 101.

12 *Fun* (5 June 1869), p. 135.

13 Clement Scott, *The Drama of Yesterday and To-Day* (London: Macmillan & Co. Ltd, 1899), Vol. 2, pp. 254–5.

14 See James Ellis (ed.), *The Bab Ballads* (Cambridge, Mass.: Belknap Press of Harvard University Press, 1980), p. 25.

15 W.S. Gilbert, *The 'Bab' Ballads* (London: John Camden Hotten, 1869), pp. v–vi.

16 Quoted in John Bush Jones (ed.), *W.S. Gilbert: A Century of Scholarship and Commentary* (New York University Press, 1970), p. 4.

17 Gilbert, *New and Original Extravaganzas*, p. 180.

8 In Demand (1869–72)

1 John Hollingshead, *Gaiety Chronicles* (London: Archibald Constable & Co., 1898), p. 94.

2 John Hollingshead, *My Lifetime* (London: Sampson Low, Marston, 1895), p. 20.

3 A convincing argument for this date is given in David Eden, *Gilbert and Sullivan: The Creative Conflict* (Cranbury, NJ: Associated University Presses, 1986), pp. 19–20.

4 Harry How, 'Illustrated Interviews: Mr W.S. Gilbert', p. 340.

5 Ibid., p. 340. Gilbert had taken the phrases from an old encyclopaedia called *Pantologia* (1808–13). See Andrew Crowther, 'The Tetrachord of Mercury', *W.S. Gilbert Society Journal*, Vol. 4, part 1, issue 27 (Summer 2010), pp. 46–7.

6 Ibid., p. 341.

7 'Paris Preparing for the Siege (From Our Special Correspondent)', *Observer* (11 September 1870), p. 5. These dispatches are quoted extensively in Andrew Crowther, 'Paris, 1870: Gilbert's War Correspondence', *W.S. Gilbert Society Journal*, Vol. 4, part 1, issue 27 (Summer 2010), pp. 31–41.

8 *Observer* (11 September 1870), p. 5.

9 Ibid.

10 Ibid.

11 William Archer, *English Dramatists of To-Day* (London: Sampson Low, Marston, Searle & Rivington, 1882), p. 164.

12 W.S. Gilbert, 'A Stage Play', *Tom Hood's Comic Annual for 1873* (London: The Fun Office, 1872), p. 98.

13 Ibid., p. 100.

14 Ibid., p. 101.

15 Ibid.

16 Ibid., p. 102.

17 Ibid., p. 103.

18 Jane W. Stedman (ed.), *Gilbert Before Sullivan: Six Comic Plays by W. S. Gilbert* (London: Routledge & Kegan Paul, 1969), p. 145.

19 W.S. Gilbert, 'My Last Client', *The Free Lance* (10 October 1903), p. 35.

20 Ibid.

21 Gilbert, *OP1*, p. 53.

22 Madge Kendal, *Dame Madge Kendal by Herself* (London: John Murray, 1933), p. 169.

23 Quoted in Arthur Jacobs, *Arthur Sullivan: A Victorian Musician* (Oxford: Oxford University Press, 1984), p. 31.

24 Selwyn Tillett and Roderic Spencer, 'Forty Years of *Thespis* Scholarship', a talk given at the Sullivan Society Festival Weekend in Cirencester, 21 September 2002.

25 Arthur Lawrence, *Sir Arthur Sullivan: Life Story, Letters and Reminiscences* (Chicago and New York: Herbert S. Stone & Co., 1900), p. 85.

26 Ibid.

27 See Terence Rees, *Thespis: A Gilbert & Sullivan Enigma* (Terence Rees, 2003), pp. 74–7.

9 The Lord High Disinfectant (1873)

1   There are indications (especially in the Bab illustrations) to show that 'The Wicked World' was written about the same time as the Bab ballad 'The Fairy Curate', which appeared in the issue of *Fun* dated 23 July 1870.

2   W.S. Gilbert, 'The Wicked World: An Allegory', *Tom Hood's Comic Annual for 1871* (London: The Fun Office, 1870), p. 82.

3   Ibid., p. 89.

4   Gilbert, *OP1*, p. 9.

5   Ibid., p. 43.

6   Gilbert to Planché (4 January 1873), PML.

7   T. Edgar Pemberton, *The Kendals: A Biography* (London: C. Arthur Pearson Ltd, 1900), p. 72.

8   Gilbert, *OP1*, pp. 3–4.

9   Quoted in Wyndham Albery (ed.), *The Dramatic Works of James Albery*, Vol. 2 (London: Peter Davies, 1939), p. 800.

10 Ibid., pp. 800–1.

11 Gilbert, *OP1*, p. 42.

12 Kendal, *Dame Madge Kendal by Herself*, p. 168.

13 Dark & Grey, *Gilbert*, p. 153.

14 Kendal, *Dame Madge Kendal by Herself*, p. 168.

15 Gilbert, 'Autobiography', p. 222.

16 'Great Britain and Ireland', BL Add. MS 49306.

17 Gilbert, 'Autobiography', p. 222.

18 Ibid.

19 Edward Righton, 'A Suppressed Burlesque – *The Happy Land*', *The Theatre* (1 August 1896), pp. 63–4.

20 Arthur William à Beckett, *Green-Room Recollections* (Bristol: J.W. Arrowsmith, n.d. [1896]), p. 195.

21 F. Tomline & Gilbert à Beckett, *The Happy Land: A Burlesque Verson of 'The Wicked World'* (London: J.W. Last & Co., 1873), p. 10.

22 Righton, 'A Suppressed Burlesque', p. 64.

23 Tomline & à Beckett, *The Happy Land*, p. 18.

24 Ibid., p. 28.

25 National Archive, LC1/275.

26 Quoted in Terence Rees, '*The Happy Land*: Its True and Remarkable History', *W.S. Gilbert Society Journal*, Vol. 1, No 8 (1994), p. 232.

27 *The Times* (8 March 1873).

28 Quoted in John Russell Stephens, *The Censorship of English Drama 1824–1901* (Cambridge: Cambridge University Press, 1980), p. 121.

29 *The Times* (10 March 1873).

30 BL Add. MS 49330.

31 Ibid.

32 Ibid.

33 There is some confusion about the title of this play. Reviews and advertisements variously call it *The Realm of Joy* and *The Realms of Joy*. The former, however, is now usually accepted as the 'official' version, and this is the title printed in a first-night programme owned by Terence Rees.

34 W.S. Gilbert (ed. Terence Rees), *The Realm of Joy* (London: Terence Rees, 1969), p. 11.

35 National Archives, LC1/276. Also quoted in Stephens, *The Censorship of English Drama*, p. 122.

36 All quotations are taken from 'The Action for Libel Against the "Pall Mall Gazette"', *Pall Mall Gazette* (28 November 1873), pp. 6–7.

10 The End of the Beginning (1874–75)

1 BL Add. MS 49330.

2 Ibid.

3 Gilbert, *OP1*, p. 99.

4 Ibid., p. 106.

5 Henrietta Hodson, *A Letter from Miss Henrietta Hodson, an Actress, to Members of the Dramatic Profession, being a Relation of the Persecutions which she has Suffered from Mr. William Schwenck Gilbert, a Dramatic Author* (London, 1877), pp. 3–4.

6 Ibid., p. 5.

7 BL Add. MS 49930.

8 Henrietta Hodson, *A Letter from Miss Henrietta Hodson*, p. 7.

9 'Trial by Jury', *Fun* (11 April 1868), p. 54. It is possible that the piece's origins go back further even than this. At the start of 1867 several papers (such as the *Penny Illustrated Paper*, 2 February 1867) announced that Gilbert was writing a 'comic cantata' for the Oxford Music Hall on Oxford Street. Nothing more is known of this fugitive piece; it was probably never performed at the Oxford.

10 This is the spelling used in the original advertisements and programme. Many other variations have been imposed upon it since then.

11 W.S. Gilbert, *Topsyturvydom* (Oxford: Oxford University Press, 1931), p. 8.

12 T. Edgar Pemberton, *The Criterion Theatre* (London, Eyre & Spottiswoode, 1903), p. 9.

13 Letter dated 31 May 1931, held at the British Library with a copy of *Topsyturvydom* and other letters relating to the play.

14 Squire Bancroft and Marie Bancroft, *Mr. And Mrs. Bancroft On and Off the Stage*, Vol. 2, p. 12.

15 Letter to Miss Bessle dated 4 June 1891, BL Add. MS 49332.

16 'Rosencrantz and Guildenstern', *Fun* (12 December 1874), p. 239.

17 Peyton Wrey, 'Notes on Popular Dramatists: III. – Mr. W.S. Gilbert', *London Society* (January 1875), pp. 13–14.

11 Trial and Tribulation (1875–77)

1 Kendal, *Dame Madge Kendal by Herself*, p. 181.

2 William Archer, *Real Conversations*, p. 126.

3 See George C. McElroy, 'Whose *Zoo*; or, When Did the *Trial* Begin?' *Nineteenth Century Theatre Research* (1984), pp. 48–9.

4 Quoted in Lawrence, *Sir Arthur Sullivan*, p. 105.

5 *The Times* (29 March 1875).

6 W.S. Gilbert, 'My Last Client', *The Free Lance* (10 October 1903), p. 35.

7 Ibid.

8 Kendal, *Dame Madge Kendal by Herself*, pp. 174–5.

9 Ibid., p. 174.

10 Quoted in Mrs Clement Scott, *Old Days in Bohemian London* (New York: Frederick A. Stokes Company, n.d.), pp. 70–1.

11 Letter to Gilbert (16 June 1875), BL Add. MS 49331.

12 Gilbert to Fred Sullivan (14 May 1876), BL Add. MS 49331.

13 Gilbert Murray, *An Unfinished Autobiography* (London: George Allen & Unwin Ltd, 1960), p. 78.

14 Quoted in a letter from Gilbert to Anne Gilbert (4 June 1876), BL Add. MS 49304. This entire correspondence between Gilbert and his parents is quoted in full in Pearson, *Gilbert*, pp. 79–82.

15 Gilbert to Anne Gilbert (29 May 1876), ibid.

16 Gilbert Murray, *An Unfinished Autobiography*, p. 79.

17 Ibid., p. 78.

18 W.S. Gilbert, 'W.S. Gilbert and Henrietta Hodson: A Letter addressed to the Members of the Dramatic Profession in Reply to Miss Henrietta Hodson's Pamphlet', *The Era* (27 May 1877), p. 9.

19 Ibid.

20 Henry Howe to Henrietta Hodson, quoted in 'W.S. Gilbert and Henrietta Hodson', *The Era* (13 May 1877), p. 12. This letter as reprinted in *The Era* is dated 'Tuesday, September 21st', but 'September' is probably a misprint for 'November'. Negotiations about the revival of *Pygmalion and Galatea* took place in November and not, it seems, before. Moreover, 21 September 1876 was a Thursday.

21 Quoted in Hodson, *A Letter from Miss Henrietta Hodson*, p. 11.

22 Ibid., pp. 13–4.

23 Ibid., p. 16.

24 Gilbert to Marion Terry (21 January 1877), PML.

25 Quoted in Hesketh Pearson, *Labby: The Life and Character of Henry Labouchere* (London: Hamish Hamilton, 1936), p. 57.

26 Ibid., p. 7.

27 Quoted in Pearson, *Gilbert*, p. 71.

28 Hodson, *A Letter from Miss Henrietta Hodson*, p. 22.

29 'W.S. Gilbert and Henrietta Hodson', *The Era* (27 May 1877), p. 10.

30 Harriett Jay, *Robert Buchanan: Some Account of his Life, his Life's Work and his Literary Friendships* (London: T. Fisher Unwin, 1903), pp. 231–3.

31 Letter to Gilbert (23 January 1873), quoted in Stedman, *W.S. Gilbert*, p. 123.

32 'W.S. Gilbert and Henrietta Hodson', *The Era* (27 May 1877), p. 9.

12 A Very English Opera (1877)

1 Letter written in 1877 by Carte to 'My Lord', quoted in Isaac Goldberg, *The Story of Gilbert and Sullivan* (London: John Murray, 1929), p. 185.

2 Letter (8 April 1880), quoted in Baily, *The Gilbert and Sullivan Book*, p. 97.

3 Interview with Arthur Sullivan, *San Francisco Daily Chronicle* (22 July 1885), quoted in Jacobs, *Arthur Sullivan*, p. 218.

4 Speech by Gilbert to the O.P. Club (30 December 1906), quoted Dark & Grey, *Gilbert*, p. 194.

5 Gilbert, *OP2*, p. 42.

6 Ibid., p. 66.

7 Ibid., p. 62.

8 Quotations from the original reviews are taken from 'Criticism of *Engaged*', in M.R. Booth (ed.), *English Plays of the Nineteenth Century, Vol. III: Comedies* (Oxford: Clarendon Press, 1973), pp. 385–94.

9 W.S. Gilbert, *Engaged* (London: Samuel French, n.d.), p. 4.

10 Gilbert to Sothern (16 December 1877), BL Add. MS 49338.

11 George Grossmith, *A Society Clown* (Bristol: J.W. Arrowsmith, 1888), p. 95.

12 Ibid., p. 96.

13 Rutland Barrington, *Rutland Barrington: A Record of Thirty-five Years' Experience on the English Stage* (London: Grant Richards, 1908), p. 28.

14 Ibid., pp. 27–8.

15 Gilbert to Sullivan (27 December 1877), PML.

13 Harlequinade (1878)

1 All quotations from the diary refer to BL Add. MS 49322.

2 W. Yardley, 'The Amateur Pantomime of 1878 and the Amateur Burlesque of 1881', in W.G. Elliot (ed.), *Amateur Clubs & Actors* (London: Edward Arnold, 1898), p. 117.

3 Quoted in Thomas Head, 'Gilbert, Sothern and *The Ne'er-do-Weel*', *Nineteenth Century Theatre Research*, 4:2 (Autumn 1976), p. 65.

4 Sothern to Gilbert (25 August 1876), quoted in ibid., p. 67.

5 Sothern to Gilbert (12 January 1877), quoted in ibid.

6 Gilbert to Sothern (30 January 1877), quoted in ibid., pp. 67–8.

7 Ainger, *A Dual Biography*, pp. 164–5.

8 In the 1881 census Marion Terry is recorded as living with her parents and other relatives at 30 Cambridge Gardens, very close to Notting Hill underground station, now called Ladbroke Grove. Her sister Kate lived with her husband and children at Moray Lodge on Campden Hill, which was not far from the Uxbridge Road station, now closed, and the High Street Kensington station. The Gloucester Road, Latimer Road, Westbourne Park and Bayswater Road stations were also in the vicinity.

9 'Drury Lane' does not appear to be a reference to the nearby Olympic Theatre, where Marion was performing; Gilbert more than once refers to the Olympic and Drury Lane in the same entry as if he was referring to different locations.

10 Simon Moss, the dealer in Gilbert and Sullivan memorabilia
    (www.stagememories.com), kindly allows me to quote the following
    verse written and signed by Gilbert on the back of a shopping list,
    presumably at one of his clubs. It is headed 'A Fact':

There was a young fellow named 'Georgie'
Who thought he'd go in for an orgie–
   But when he got there
   The cupboard was bare,
And so the poor dog had none.

It is rumoured that Gilbert wrote more ribald material than this, but
reliable evidence has not come to light.
11 Yardley, 'The Amateur Pantomime of 1878 and the Amateur Burlesque of
    1881', pp. 121 & 123.
12 'The Amateur Pantomime at the Gaiety', *Mirth: A Miscellany of Wit and
    Humour* (March 1878), p. 169.

14 All Ablaze (1878–81)

1 Gilbert to Sullivan (27 December 1877), PML.
2 Letter from Sullivan to his mother (19 April 1878), ibid.
3 George Grossmith, *A Society Clown*, p. 102.
4 Jessie Bond, *The Life and Reminiscences of Jessie Bond, The Old Savoyard, as told
   to Ethel MacGeorge* (London: John Lane, The Bodley Head Ltd, 1930), p. 56.
5 Grossmith, *A Society Clown*, pp. 102–3, p. 106.
6 See, for instance, 'Theatres', *The Graphic* (18 July 1874): 'The migrations
   of the theatrical managers during the heats of July afford some curious
   tokens of the habits of the people ... At the West End of London no
   maxim is better established than the difficulty of attracting audiences
   when the thermometer ranges at any point above seventy in the shade. In
   the suburbs, however, and in provincial towns, summer appears to be the
   chief season for theatrical entertainments. Thus it is that whole companies,
   who have been compelled to close their doors in the Haymarket or the
   Strand, re-appear in Shoreditch or Hoxton, or move in their predestined
   orbit round the United Kingdom.'
7 Quoted in Tony Joseph, *The D'Oyly Carte Opera Company 1875–1982: an
   Unofficial History* (Bristol: Bunthorne Books, 1994), p. 17.
8 W.S. Gilbert, 'A Hornpipe in Fetters', *The Era Almanack, 1879* (London), p. 91.
9 Ibid.
10 Ibid., pp. 91–2.

11   Gilbert's 1878 diary, BL Add. MS 49322, also contains some entries relating to 1879.

12   Gilbert to Sullivan (2 August 1879), PML.

13   For research and detail about the evolution of *The Pirates of Penzance*, see Kevin Wachs, 'Let's Vary Piracee/With a Little Burglaree!', *Gasbag*, No 227 (Winter 2005), pp. 6–11, 20–2; and No 228 (Spring 2005), pp. 6–11, 23–8.

14   *New York Herald* (6 November 1879), p. 5.

15   *New York Times* (9 November 1879).

16   Letter to Percy de Strzelecki (14 August 1902), PML.

17   See Selwyn Tillett and Roderic Spencer, 'Forty Years of *Thespis* Scholarship', a talk given at the Sullivan Society Festival Weekend in Cirencester, 21 September 2002.

18   See Andrew Goodman, *Gilbert and Sullivan at Law* (London: Associated University Presses, 1983), pp. 205–6.

19   George R. Sims, *My Life: Sixty Years' Recollections of Bohemian London* (London: Eveleigh Nash Co. Ltd, 1917), p. 218.

20   Letter from Sullivan to his mother (2 January 1880), quoted in Arthur Jacobs, *Arthur Sullivan: A Victorian Musician* (Oxford: Oxford University Press, 1984), p. 133.

21   From an interview with Gilbert published in *The World*, reprinted in the *Cincinnati Daily Gazette*, 28 June 1880. My thanks are due to Arthur Robinson for drawing my attention to this.

22   Ibid.

23   W.S. Gilbert, *Introduction to* Patience (New York: Doubleday, 1902).

24   *Pall Mall Gazette* (3 December 1889).

25   Gilbert to Sullivan (1 November 1880), BL Add. MS 49338.

15 The Making of *Iolanthe* (1881–82)

1   'Workers and their Work: Mr. W.S. Gilbert', *The Daily News* (21 January 1885), p. 3.

2   Quoted in Percy Fitzgerald, *The Savoy Opera and the Savoyards* (London: Chatto & Windus, 1894), p. 113.

3   'A Chat with Mr. W.S. Gilbert', *Cassell's Saturday Journal* (21 March 1894).

4   Ibid.

5   'How They Write Their Plays: Mr. W.S. Gilbert', *St. James's Gazette* (23 June 1893), p. 5.

6   Ibid.

7   Quoted in Ainger, *A Dual Biography*, p. 204.

8   Ibid., p. 207.

9   Jacobs, *Arthur Sullivan*, p. 176.

10 Rutland Barrington, *Rutland Barrington*, p. 46.

11 Reginald Allen (ed.), *The First Night Gilbert and Sullivan* (London: Chappell & Co. Ltd, 1958), p. 199.

12 Jacobs, *Arthur Sullivan*, p. 179.

16 A National Institution (1884–89)

1 Sometime in the 1880s Gilbert was introduced to L.V. Fildes, the son of the artist Luke Fildes, as '*the* Mr. Gilbert', and Gilbert replied: 'One of the *many* Mr. Gilberts, I'm afraid.' Fildes' mother explained the comment afterwards: 'Mr. Gilbert feels it very much that he was not made a knight when Sir Arthur Sullivan was, and all his friends feel the same.' See L.V. Fildes, *Luke Fildes, R.A.: A Victorian Painter* (London: Michael Joseph, 1968), p. 171.

2 'The House of a Successful Dramatist', *Pall Mall Gazette* (6 November 1883).

3 L.V. Fildes, *Luke Fildes, R.A.: A Victorian Painter*, pp. 91–2.

4 Gilbert to Burnand (16 May 1886), PML.

5 Quoted in Jacobs, *Arthur Sullivan*, p. 189.

6 Ibid.

7 Ibid., pp. 189–90.

8 Ibid., p. 190.

9 Ibid., pp. 190–1.

10 Quoted in Herbert Sullivan and Newman Flower, *Sir Arthur Sullivan: His Life, Letters and Diaries* (London: Cassell & Company Ltd, 1950), pp. 141–2.

11 Ibid., p. 144.

12 Quoted in Ainger, *A Dual Biography*, p. 233.

13 Sullivan to Gilbert (8 May 1884), quoted in Jacobs, *Arthur Sullivan* p. 194.

14 W.S. Gilbert, 'The Story of a Stage Play', *New York Daily Tribune* (9 Aug 1885).

15 Ibid.

16 Ibid.

17 Ibid.

18 George Grossmith, *A Society Clown*, p. 125.

19 Gilbert, 'The Story of a Stage Play'.

20 'Workers and their Work: Mr. W.S. Gilbert', *The Daily News* (21 Jan 1885).

21 'The Dramatic and Musical Sick Fund', *The Era* (21 February 1885).

22 Gilbert to Sullivan (2 June 1885), quoted in Stedman, *W.S. Gilbert*, p. 232.

23 James Pope-Hennessy (ed.), *Baron Ferdinand de Rothschild's Livre d'or* (Cambridge: Cambridge University Press, 1957), pp. 120–1. My thanks to David Stone for drawing this to my attention.

24 '"Ruddy-gore" and Savoy Operas: An Interview with Mr. W.S. Gilbert', *Pall Mall Gazette* (21 January 1887).

25 This version of the story is told in *The Ipswich Journal* (24 February 1887), but with 'bloody' delicately replaced with the word 'sanguinary'.

26 Sullivan's diary (4 September 1887), quoted in Jacobs, *Arthur Sullivan* p. 261.

27 Quoted in Ibid., p. 265.

28 Ibid.

29 Gilbert to Jessie Bond (17 June 1887), PML. The P.S. is written round the edge of the letter.

30 See Ainger, *A Dual Biography*, p. 274.

31 *Glasgow Herald* (26 March 1888).

32 Letter to William Archer (5 October 1904), BL Add. MS 45291.

33 'The Newest Theatre in London: An Interview with Mr. W.S. Gilbert', *Pall Mall Gazette* (22 March 1888), p. 2.

34 Sir John Martin-Harvey, *The Autobiography of Sir John Martin-Harvey* (London: Sampson Low, Marston & Co. Ltd, 1933), pp. 43–4.

35 Gilbert to Clement Scott (10 December 1883), PML.

36 Gilbert to Mary Anderson (27 February 1888), quoted in Dark & Grey, *Gilbert*, pp. 156–7.

37 'The Newest Theatre in London', *Pall Mall Gazette* (22 March 1888), p. 2.

38 Gilbert to Edward Lawson, quoted in 'W.S. Gilbert and Clement Scott', *The Era* (29 December 1888). The italics appear to have been added by *The Era*.

39 Gilbert to Clement Scott (10 December 1888), PML.

40 'Mr. Gilbert and Mr. Clement Scott', *Pall Mall Gazette* (15 December 1888).

41 'The Newest Theatre in London', *Pall Mall Gazette* (22 March 1888).

42 Sullivan's diary, quoted in Jacobs, *Arthur Sullivan*, p. 282.

43 Gilbert to Sullivan (20 February 1889), quoted in ibid., p. 282.

44 Ibid.

45 Draft letter from Sullivan to Gilbert (12 March 1889), quoted in ibid., p. 283.

46 Gilbert to Sullivan (19 March 1889), quoted in ibid., p. 284.

47 Draft letter from Sullivan to Gilbert (8 May 1889), quoted in ibid., p. 288.

48 Gilbert to Sullivan, reproduced in Reginald Allen and Gale R. D'Luhy (eds), *Sir Arthur Sullivan: Composer & Personage* (New York: The Pierpont Morgan Library, 1975), p. 156.

49 Quoted in a letter from Gilbert to Sullivan (8 May 1890), quoted in Ainger, *A Dual Biography*, p. 304.

17 The Bitter End (1890–96)

1 Carte to Gilbert (26 April 1890), quoted in Jacobs, *Arthur Sullivan*, p. 313.

2 Helen Carte to Gilbert (7/8 May 1890), quoted in Baily, *The Gilbert & Sullivan Book*, p. 328.

3 This description of the meeting is taken from accounts made by Gilbert in a letter to Sullivan (22 April 1890), quoted in Pearson, *Gilbert*, p. 137; and by Helen Carte in a letter to Gilbert (7/8 May 1890), quoted in Baily, *The Gilbert and Sullivan Book*, pp. 328–9.

4 Quoted in Pearson, *Gilbert*, p. 137.

5 Gilbert to Sullivan (5 May 1890), quoted in Pearson, *Gilbert*, p. 140.

6 Sullivan's diary (6 May 1890), quoted in Ainger, *A Dual Biography*, p. 310.

7 Quoted in a letter from Sullivan to Gilbert (6 May 1890), which is quoted in Jacobs, *Arthur Sullivan*, p. 312.

8 Sullivan to Gilbert (6 May 1890), quoted in ibid., p. 313.

9 Gilbert to Salaman (15 May 1890), PML.

10 Sullivan to Gilbert (16 May 1890), quoted in Jacobs, *Arthur Sullivan*, p. 316.

11 Gilbert to Salaman (16 May 1890), PML.

12 Gilbert had written to Sedger proposing the new opera on 7 May 1890: see Stedman, *W.S. Gilbert*, p. 273.

13 *The Daily News* (4 September 1890), quoted in David Eden, *The Carpet Quarrel: A Documentary Narrative* (Sir Arthur Sullivan Society, 2010), p. 30.

14 See Eden, *The Carpet Quarrel*, pp. 1 & 15.

15 Quoted in Eden, *The Carpet Quarrel*, p. 23.

16 Gilbert to Helen Carte (6 September 1890), quoted in Baily, *The Gilbert & Sullivan Book*, p. 330.

17 Gilbert to Sullivan, (6 September 1890), quoted in Ainger, *A Dual Biography*, p. 317.

18 Sullivan to Gilbert (8 September 1890), quoted in Pearson, *Gilbert*, pp. 141–2.

19 Gilbert to Sullivan (9 September 1890), quoted in Pearson, *Gilbert*, p. 143.

20 See Ainger, *A Dual Biography*, p. 318.

21 See Eden, *The Carpet Quarrel*, pp. 36–7.

22 'Theatrical Gossip', *The Era* (28 November 1891).

23 Nancy McIntosh, 'The Late Sir W.S. Gilbert's Pets', *Country Life* (3 June 1911), reprinted in *The W.S. Gilbert Society Journal* (Vol. 2, Issue 18, Winter 2005), p. 554.

24 'Mr. W.S. Gilbert as a Magistrate', *The Era* (25 June 1892). Many thanks to Arthur Robinson for drawing this to my attention.

25 Quoted in Baily, p. 333.

26 Gilbert to Cellier (25 September 1891), quoted in Pearson, *Gilbert*, p. 154.

27 'The Mountebanks: A Christmas Day Interview with Mr. W.S. Gilbert', *Pall Mall Gazette* (26 December 1891).

28 Sullivan to Frank Cellier (29 December 1891), quoted in Stedman, *W.S. Gilbert*, p. 283.

29 Gilbert to Sullivan (15 November 1892), quoted in Pearson, *Gilbert*, pp. 167–8.

30 Quoted in Pearson, *Gilbert*, p. 171.

31 '"Utopia (Limited)" at the Savoy', *Pall Mall Gazette* (9 October 1893).

32 Gilbert to Sullivan (7 April 1894), quoted in Pearson, *Gilbert*, p. 185.

33 Sullivan to Gilbert (11 August 1895), quoted in Pearson, *Gilbert*, p. 185.

34 '"The Grand Duke" at the Savoy', *Pall Mall Gazette* (9 March 1896).

35 Sullivan to Burnand (12 March 1896), quoted in Jacobs, *Arthur Sullivan*, p. 367.

36 Gilbert to Florence Stoker (9 March 1896), PML.

18 The Nice Kind Gentleman

1 Quoted in Hesketh Pearson, *Beerbohm Tree: His Life and Laughter*, p. 77.

2 Ibid.

3 Letter in the Tree Family Archive, Theatre Collection, University of Bristol.

4 Quoted in Pearson, *Beerbohm Tree*, pp. 74–5.

5 Letter in the Tree Family Archive, Theatre Collection, University of Bristol.

6 Gilbert to Mary Talbot ('Cousin Mary') (19 November 1902), quoted in Dark & Grey, *Gilbert*, pp. 169–70.

7 Quoted in Pearson, *Gilbert*, p. 34. It is undated but appears to have been written in autumn 1867.

8 Letter dated 19th [November 1910], quoted in Pearson, *Gilbert: His Life and Strife*, pp. 262–3.

9 All letters from Gilbert to Florence Stoker here quoted are in the PML.

10 Undated letter, quoted in Daniel Farson, *The Man Who Wrote 'Dracula': A Biography of Bram Stoker* (London: Michael Joseph, 1975), pp. 65–6.

11 Paul Murray, *From the Shadow of 'Dracula': A Life of Bram Stoker* (London: Jonathan Cape, 2004), p. 131. Ann Stoker, granddaughter of Bram and Florence, told the story to Paul Murray in 1997 (personal email from Paul Murray, 10 July 2010).

12 Letter to Miss Boughton (19 November 1887), PML.

13 Letter to Miss Boughton (5 December 1887), PML.

14 Letter to Mary Talbot (7 February 1907), quoted in Dark & Grey, *Gilbert*, p. 179.

15 Letter to Mary Talbot (3 December 1908), quoted in ibid., p. 178.

16 Letter to Ellaline Terriss (7 August 1896), PML.

17 Seymour Hicks, *Between Ourselves* (London: Cassell & Co., 1930), p. 49.

18 Ellaline Terriss, *Just a Little Bit of String* (London: Hutchinson & Co., 1955), p. 114.

19 On Trial (1897–98)

1 Letter from Gilbert ('your devoted Old Boy') to Lucy Gilbert (4 October 1897), quoted in Pearson, *Gilbert*, p. 192.

2 'Interview with Mr W.S. Gilbert: The Press, the Play and the Players', *Edinburgh Evening Dispatch* (5 October 1897). I have adjusted one or two details of spelling and punctuation. Many thanks to Arthur Robinson for sending me a copy of this.

3 'Mr. Gilbert and Mr. Grundy', *The Era* (16 October 1897). Previous biographers, in quoting this leader, have usually taken *The Era's* reference to the 'Grand Lama' and 'corrected' the second word to 'Llama'!

4 Letter to Maud Tree (1 January 1898), Tree Family Archive.

5 Letter to Maud Tree (11 January 1898), Tree Family Archive.

6 'Henry Irving on W.S. Gilbert', *The Era* (23 October 1897).

7 Gilbert to Maud Tree, quoted in Pearson, *Beerbohm Tree*, pp. 122–3.

8 Gilbert to Helen Carte (28 March 1898), quoted in Ainger, *A Dual Biography*, p. 372.

9 W.S. Gilbert, *The Bab Ballads, With which are Included Songs of a Savoyard* (London: George Routledge & Sons, 1898), pp. 553–4.

20 The Menagerie (1898–1906)

1 Malcolm C. Salaman, 'William Schwenck Gilbert: the Man, the Humourist, the Artist', *Cassell's Magazine* (March 1900), p. 421.

2 Dark & Grey, *Gilbert*, p. 209.

3 Gilbert to Ethel Tweedie (November 1901), quoted in Mrs Alec-Tweedie, *My Table-Cloths: A Few Reminiscences* (New York: George H. Doran Co., 1916), p. 43.

4 Nancy McIntosh, 'Sir William Gilbert's Lemurs', *Strand*, Vol. 38 (November 1909), p. 604.

5 See Nancy McIntosh, 'The Late Sir W.S. Gilbert's Pets', pp. 548–56. Nancy McIntosh refers to herself and the Gilberts as 'the family' throughout.

6 L.V. Fildes, *Luke Fildes, R.A.: A Victorian Painter* (London: Michael Joseph, 1968), p. 171.

7 Mrs Alec-Tweedie, *Behind the Footlights* (New York: Dodd Mead & Co., 1904), p. 190.

8 Alec-Tweedie, *My Table-Cloths*, p. 34.

9 Ibid., pp. 32–3.

10 Gilbert to Mrs Alec-Tweedie (3 December 1901), quoted in Mrs Alec-Tweedie, *Thirteen Years of a Busy Woman's Life* (London: John Lane, The Bodley Head, 1912), p. 151.

11 Alec-Tweedie, *My Table-Cloths*, p. 46.

12 Ibid., p. 33.

13 Gilbert to Scott (1 December 1897), PML.

14 Mrs Clement Scott, *Old Days in Bohemian London*, p. 71.

15 Ibid., p. 72.

16 Gilbert to Burnand (27 May 1884), PML.

17 Gilbert to Burnand (24 December 1905), PML.

18 See Alec-Tweedie, *My Table-Cloths*, pp. 38–41.

19 Gilbert to Helen Carte, quoted in Pearson, *Gilbert*, p. 230.

20 Quoted in Dark & Grey, *Gilbert*, pp. 193–4.

21 'Savoyard Celebration Dinner', *The Times* (31 December 1906): this report includes parts of the speech not included in Dark & Grey, *Gilbert*.

21 The Hooligan (1907–11)

1   'The College of Music Knights', *The Penny Illustrated Paper and Illustrated Times* (12 May 1883).

2   Gilbert to Mary Talbot, quoted in Dark & Grey, *Gilbert*, p. 196.

3   Gilbert to Mrs Terry (30 June 1907), in the collection of Dr J. Donald Smith.

4   Gilbert to Edith Browne (10 March 1907), quoted in Pearson, *Gilbert*, p. 247.

5   Gilbert to Edith Browne (21 March 1907), quoted in ibid.

6   Browne, *W.S. Gilbert*, pp. 38 & 54.

7   Gilbert to Nancy McIntosh (3 January 1908), BL Add. MS 49345.

8   Sydney Blow, *Through Stage Doors, or, Memories of Two in the Theatre* (Edinburgh: W & R Chambers Ltd, 1958), p. 204.

9   Alec-Tweedie, *My Table-Cloths*, p. 45.

10 Sydney Blow, *Through Stage Doors*, p. 206.

11 Ibid., p. 207.

12 Gilbert, *OP4*, p. 484.

13 Dark & Grey, *Gilbert*, p. 222.

14 *Nottingham Guardian* (1 June 1911), quoted in Stedman, *W.S. Gilbert*, p. 347.

15 'The Death of Sir W.S. Gilbert: Evidence at the Inquest', *The Times* (1 June 1911).

16 Ken Pople, 'Who Was Patricia Preece?' *Bristol University Alumni Magazine* (Autumn 1994), pp. 45–7. Many thanks to John Cannon for drawing this to my attention.

22 Verdicts

1   Alec-Tweedie, *My Table-Cloths*, p. 48.
2   Seymour Hicks, *Seymour Hicks*, p. 144.
3   Seymour Hicks, *Between Ourselves*, p. 49.
4   Letter from Sullivan to his mother (2 January 1880), quoted in Jacobs, *Arthur Sullivan*, p. 133.
5   'Sir Arthur Sullivan Unbosoms Himself', *New York Mirror* (3 October 1885).
6   Sullivan's diary (6 May 1890), quoted in Ainger, *A Dual Biography*, p. 310.
7   Quoted in Mrs Alec-Tweedie, *Behind the Footlights*, p. 198.
8   *The Times* (30 May 1911).
9   Quoted in Ainger, *A Dual Biography*, p. 207.
10 'Mr. Gilbert and Mr. Grundy', *The Era*, 16 October 1897.
11 Gilbert to Maud Tree (16 June 1893), quoted in Pearson, *Beerbohm Tree*, pp. 74–5.
12 Hicks, *Seymour Hicks*, p. 145.
13 Ibid., p. 147.
14 Letter in the *Daily Telegraph* (6 January 1956).
15 Quoted in Dark & Grey, *Gilbert*, p. 157.

SELECT BIBLIOGRAPHY

Selected Works by Gilbert:

'An Autobiography', *Theatre* (2 April 1883), pp. 217–24.

The Bab Ballads, James Ellis (ed.) (Cambridge, Mass.: Belknap Press of Harvard University Press, 1980).

Foggerty's Fairy and other Tales (London: George Routledge & Sons, 1890).

'Getting Up a Pantomime', *London Society* (January 1868), pp. 50–7.

'A Hornpipe in Fetters', *Era Almanack 1879* (London), pp. 91–2.

'My Last Client', *The Free Lance* (10 October 1903), p. 35.

'My Pantomime', *The Era Almanack 1884* (London), pp. 77–9.

New and Original Extravaganzas, Isaac Goldberg (ed.) (Boston: John W. Luce & Co., 1931).

Original Plays: First Series (London: Chatto & Windus, 1925).

Original Plays: Second Series (London: Chatto & Windus, 1925).

Original Plays: Third Series (London: Chatto & Windus, 1924).

Original Plays: Fourth Series (London: Chatto & Windus, 1922).

The Realm of Joy, ed. Terence Rees (London: Terence Rees, 1969).

The Story of The Mikado (London: Daniel O'Connor, 1921).

Topsyturvydom (Oxford: Oxford University Press, 1931).

Many contributions to *Fun*, 1861–74. For a list of contributions after 1865, see John Bush Jones, 'W.S. Gilbert's Contributions to *Fun*, 1865–1874', *Bulletin of the New York Public Library* (April 1969), pp. 253–66.

Gilbert Before Sullivan: Six Comic Plays by W. S. Gilbert, ed. Jane W. Stedman (London: Routledge & Kegan Paul, 1969).

Tomline, F. & à Beckett, Gilbert, *The Happy Land: A Burlesque Verson of 'The Wicked World'* (London: J.W. Last & Co., 1873).

Other Works Consulted:

à Beckett, Arthur William, *Green-Room Recollections* (Bristol: J.W. Arrowsmith, n.d. [1896]).

Abel, Richard L., *The Legal Profession in England and Wales* (Oxford: Basil Blackwell, 1988).

Ainger, Michael, *Gilbert and Sullivan: A Dual Biography* (Oxford: Oxford University Press, 2002).

Albery, Wyndham (ed.), *The Dramatic Works of James Albery* (London: Peter Davies, 1939), 2 Vols.

Alec-Tweedie, Mrs, *Behind the Footlights* (New York: Dodd Mead & Co., 1904).

———, Mrs, *My Table-Cloths: A Few Reminiscences* (New York: George H. Doran Co., 1916).

———, *Thirteen Years of a Busy Woman's Life* (London: John Lane, The Bodley Head, 1912).

Allen, Reginald (ed.), *The First Night Gilbert and Sullivan* (London: Chappell & Co. Ltd, 1958).

Allen, Reginald & D'Luhy, Gale R. (eds), *Sir Arthur Sullivan: Composer & Personage* (New York: The Pierpont Morgan Library, 1975).

Archer, William, *English Dramatists of To-Day* (London: Sampson Low, Marston, Searle & Rivington, 1882).

———, *Real Conversations* (London: William Heinemann, 1904).

Baily, Leslie, *The Gilbert & Sullivan Book* (London: Cassell & Co. Ltd, 1952).

Bancroft, Squire & Bancroft, Marie, *Mr. and Mrs. Bancroft On and Off the Stage* (London: Richard Bentley & Son, 1888), 2 Vols.

Barrington, Rutland, *Rutland Barrington: A Record of Thirty-five Years' Experience on the English Stage* (London: Grant Richards, 1908).

Blow, Sydney, *Through Stage Doors, or, Memories of Two in the Theatre* (Edinburgh: W & R Chambers Ltd, 1958).

Bond, Jessie, *The Life and Reminiscences of Jessie Bond, The Old Savoyard, as told to Ethel MacGeorge* (London: John Lane, The Bodley Head, 1930).

Browne, Edith A., *W.S. Gilbert*, (London: John Lane, The Bodley Head, 1907).

Burnand, Sir Francis C., *Records and Reminiscences, Personal and General* (London: Methuen, 1904), 2 Vols.

Cellier, Francois & Bridgeman, Cunningham, *Gilbert, Sullivan and D'Oyly Carte: Reminiscences of the Savoy and the Savoyards* (London: Sir Isaac Pitman & Sons, Ltd, 1914).

Coleman, John, *Players and Playwrights I Have Known: A Review of the English stage from 1840 to 1880* (Philadelphia: Gebbie & Co., 1890), 2 Vols.

Crowther, Andrew, *Contradiction Contradicted: The Plays of W.S. Gilbert* (Cranbury, NJ: Associated University Presses, 2000).

Dalziel, George & Edward, *The Brothers Dalziel: A Record of Work, 1840–1890* (London: Batsford Ltd, 1978).

Dark, Sidney & Grey, Rowland, *W.S. Gilbert: His Life and Letters* (London: Methuen & Co. Ltd, 1923).

Eden, David, *The Carpet Quarrel: A Documentary Narrative* (Sir Arthur Sullivan Society, 2010).

———, *Gilbert and Sullivan: The Creative Conflict* (Cranbury, NJ: Associated University Presses, 1986).

———, *A Tale of Two Kidnaps* (Sir Arthur Sullivan Society, 1988).

———, *W.S. Gilbert: Appearance and Reality: Essays in Clarification* (Saffron Walden: Sir Arthur Sullivan Society, 2003).

Elliot, W.G. (ed.), *Amateur Clubs & Actors* (London: Edward Arnold, 1898).

Farson, Daniel, *The Man Who Wrote 'Dracula': A Biography of Bram Stoker* (London: Michael Joseph, 1975).

Fildes, L.V., *Luke Fildes, R.A.: A Victorian Painter* (London: Michael Joseph, 1968).

Fitzgerald, Percy, *The Savoy Opera and the Savoyards* (London: Chatto & Windus, 1894).

Goldberg, Isaac, *The Story of Gilbert and Sullivan* (London: John Murray, 1929).

Grossmith, George, *A Society Clown* (Bristol: J.W. Arrowsmith, 1888).

Halliday, Andrew (ed.), *The Savage-Club Papers* (London: Tinsley Brothers, 1867).

Helyar, James (ed.), *Gilbert and Sullivan: Papers Presented at the International Conference held at the University of Kansas in May 1970* (University of Kansas Libraries, 1971).

Hicks, Seymour, *Between Ourselves* (London: Cassell & Co., 1930).

———, *Seymour Hicks: Twenty-Four Years of an Actor's Life* (London: Alston Rivers, Ltd, 1910).

Hodson, Henrietta, *A Letter from Miss Henrietta Hodson, an Actress, to Members of the Dramatic Profession, being a Relation of the Persecutions which she has Suffered from Mr. William Schwenck Gilbert, a Dramatic Author* (London, [1877]).

Hollingshead, John, *Gaiety Chronicles* (London: Archibald Constable & Co., 1898).

———, *My Lifetime* (London: Sampson Low, Marston, 1895).

Hood, Tom (ed.), *A Bunch of Keys* (London: Groombridge & Sons, 1965).

Hutchinson, Horace G., *Portraits of the Eighties* (London: T. Fisher Unwin, 1920).

Irving, Laurence, *Henry Irving: The Actor and his World* (New York: Macmillan, 1952).

Jacobs, Arthur, *Arthur Sullivan: A Victorian Musician* (Oxford: Oxford University Press, 1984).

Jones, John Bush (ed.), *W.S. Gilbert: A Century of Scholarship and Commentary* (New York: New York University Press, 1970).

Joseph, Tony, *The D'Oyly Carte Opera Company 1875–1982: an Unofficial History* (Bristol: Bunthorne Books, 1994).

Kendal, Madge, *Dame Madge Kendal by Herself* (London: John Murray, 1933).

Lawrence, Arthur, *Sir Arthur Sullivan: Life Story, Letters and Reminiscences* (Chicago and New York: Herbert S. Stone & Co., 1900).

Martin-Harvey, Sir John, *The Autobiography of Sir John Martin-Harvey* (London: Sampson Low, Marston & Co., Ltd, [1933]).

Murray, Gilbert, *An Unfinished Autobiography* (London: George Allen & Unwin Ltd, 1960).

Murray, Paul, *From the Shadow of 'Dracula': A Life of Bram Stoker* (London: Jonathan Cape, 2004).

Pearson, Hesketh, *Gilbert: His Life and Strife* (London: Methuen & Co. Ltd, 1957).

———, *Labby: The Life and Character of Henry Labouchere* (London: Hamish Hamilton, 1936).

Pemberton, T. Edgar, *The Criterion Theatre* (London, Eyre & Spottiswoode, [1903]).

———, *The Kendals: A Biography* (London: C. Arthur Pearson Ltd, 1900).

Rees, Terence, *Thespis: A Gilbert & Sullivan Enigma* (Terence Rees, 2003).

Scott, Clement, *The Drama of Yesterday and To-Day* (London: Macmillan & Co., Ltd, 1899), 2 Vols.

———, *The Wheel of Life* (London: Lawrence Greening & Co., 1898)

Scott, Clement & Howard, Cecil, *The Life and Reminiscences of E.L. Blanchard* (London: Hutchinson, 1891), 2 Vols.

Scott, Mrs Clement, *Old Days in Bohemian London* (New York: Frederick A. Stokes Co., n.d.).

Sims, George R., *My Life: Sixty Years' Recollections of Bohemian London* (London: Eveleigh Nash Co. Ltd, 1917).

Skeat, W.O., *King's College London Engineering Society 1847–1957* (Privately printed for the King's College London Engineers Association, 1957).

Spielmann, M.H., *The History of Punch* (London: Cassell & Co., Ltd, 1895).

Stedman, Jane W., *W.S. Gilbert: A Classic Victorian and his Theatre* (Oxford: Oxford University Press, 1996).

Stephens, John Russell, *The Censorship of English Drama 1824–1901* (Cambridge: Cambridge University Press, 1980).

Sullivan, Herbert & Flower, Newman, *Sir Arthur Sullivan: His Life, Letters and Diaries* (London: Cassell & Co., Ltd., 1950).

Sutton, Max Keith, *W.S. Gilbert* (Boston: Twayne Publishers, 1975).

Terriss, Ellaline, *Just a Little Bit of String* (London: Hutchinson & Co., 1955).

Thomas, Annie, *Played Out* (London: Chapman and Hall, 1866), 3 Vols.

Tinsley, William, *Random Recollections of an Old Publisher* (London: Simpkin, Marshall, Hamilton, Kent & Co., Ltd, 1890), 2 Vols.

White, Jerry, *London in the Nineteenth Century: A Human Awful Wonder of God* (London: Vintage Books, 2008).

INDEX